Arise to God's Truth

Restore and Keep America's Freedom

Divine Messages

By

Lisa Lucia Arden, MDIV

If My people who bear My name humble themselves, and pray and seek My presence and turn from their evil ways, then I will listen from heaven and forgive their sins and restore their country.

2 Chronicles 7:14

Title Page Love does not delight in evil but rejoices with the truth. It always protects, always trusts, ever hope, always perseveres.

Cor. 13:4

Nicene Creed

We believe in one God,
the Father, the Almighty,
Maker of all that is, seen and unseen.
We believe in one Lord, Jesus Christ,
the only Son of God,
eternally begotten of the Father,
God from God, Light from Light,
true God from true God,
begotten, not made, consubstantial
of one Being with the Father.
Through Him all things were made.
For us men and for our salvation
He came down from heaven,
and by the Holy Spirit was incarnate of the Virgin Mary,
and became man.
For our sake He was crucified under Pontius Pilate;
He suffered death and was buried.
On the third day he rose again
in accordance with the Scriptures;
He ascended into heaven
and is seated at the right hand of the Father.
He will come again in glory to judge the living and the dead,
and His kingdom will have no end.
We believe in the Holy Spirit, the Lord, the giver of life,
who proceeds from the Father and the Son.
With the Father and the Son He is worshipped and glorified.
He has spoken through the Prophets.
We believe in one holy catholic and apostolic Church.
We acknowledge one baptism for the forgiveness of sins.
We look for the resurrection of the dead,
and the life of the world to come. Amen.

Urgent

Together as a nation, we have to obsolete the treacherous plans of the left, Communist: MARK OF THE BEAST

1. The American People, President Trump, and the American Freedom Warriors have had a severe conspiracy against them from the leftist, Democratic and silent Communistic and Socialist and technological powerful deceptive individuals.
2. We also know that there are conspiracies to kill off many of the people; they want to de-populate the peoples and have fewer people that is why they build all those coffins at the FEMA compound.
3. Furthermore, today December 10, 2020; they want to give the people a vaccine for the Covid-Virus that the syringe has a tracker in them, the tracker can be considered, "the mark of the Beast." Each microchip has a unique I.D. code. This would enable them to control the Americans and peoples of the world.
4. "Cashless society. Using cards they can, track, and identify the persons in the technological systems. Even controlling their amounts of income and economic position."
5. "They the people in power, to create the world that they want."
   "The people in power, they want on the digital program."
   "They the people in power, want to use these technologies to take back control of humans (the Communist, Socialist, and Technological persons in power)."
6. Under President Trump and the Team and the American Freedom Warriors: Continue to Control our Economic Systems America First, and Safety and working to putting the American people first.

   (See under President Trump we put God first and the American First.)

   ARISE TO GOD'S TRUTH AMERICA AND THE WORLD.

Dedication

The Trinity: The God of Abraham, Jesus Christ, Holy Spirit
Blessed Queen Virgin Mary the Mother of God
All the Saints
All the Arch Angels and the Angels of God
My Mother and Father, Alvera and Frank
My Children
My Grandchildren
My Sisters and Brothers
All My Professors
All the Priests and Ministers and Rabbis
All My Friends

*The leaders then made an offering for the **dedication** of the altar, on the day it was anointed. They brought their offering before the altar, [11] and Yahweh said to Moses, 'Each day one of the leaders must bring his offering for the **dedication** of the altar.'*

Numbers 7:10

No, God chose those who by human standards are fools to shame the wise; He chose those who by human standards are weak to shame the strong.

1Corinthians 1:27

It is as scripture says: What no eye has seen and no ear has heard, what the mind of man cannot visualize; all that God has prepared for those who love Him; to us, though, God has given revelation through the Spirit, for the Spirit explores the depths of everything, even the depths of God.

1 Corinthians 2:9-10

Who does the truth comes out into the light, so that what he is doing may plainly appear as done in God.

Copyright@2020 Lisa Lucia Arden, MDIV
This is a work in progress
Arise to God's Truth America
Restore and Keep America's Freedom
Author Lisa Lucia Arden, MDIV
Printed in the United States of America

For God so loved the world that He gave His only Son, so that everyone who believes in him might not perish but might have eternal life. [17] For God did not send his Son into the world to condemn the world, but that the world might be saved through him.

John 3:16-17

The Rosary is a powerful weapon to put the demons to flight(disappear) and to keep oneself from sin…If you desire peace in your hearts, in your homes, and in your country, assemble each evening to recite the Rosary. Let not even one day pass without saying it, no matter how burdened you may be with many cares and labors.

Pope Pius XI

In the course of its history, Israel was able to discover that God had only one reason to reveal Himself to them, a single motive for choosing them from among all peoples as His special possession: His sheer gratuitous love.[38] And thanks to the prophets, Israel understood that it was again out of love that God never stopped saving them and pardoning their unfaithfulness and sins.[39]

Catholic Catechism 218:38,39

America's Authority in God, America's Miracle

I Saw the Light Upon You

I saw the Light Upon you
I saw the light upon your forehead of all the dreams
And truths and beauties that have been
Entrusted with you to bring to others:

> The smile that meets the sad heart
> The voice that speaks of all is well
> The vision that opens up the path of new life
> The embrace that soothes the sorrows to refreshment
> The walking beside the one who is in confusion
> To the path of all is well, all is well, with thy soul

I saw the light upon your hands of all the dreams
The truths and the beauties that have been entrusted with you to bring to others:

> The compassion to give to the homeless heart
> The guidance to give to the grieving soul
> The works to bring about miracles
> The tenderness that touches the deepest crevice within the hidden sufferings
> The healings that change hopelessness into a heavenly realm on earth to miracles of God.

I saw the light upon you to have grace to bring God's miracles.

Table of Contents

Nicene Creed 2
Introduction 9
Chapter One 12
Chapter Two 75
Chapter Three 153
Chapter Four 246
Chapter Five 315
Chapter Eight 443
Chapter Nine 455
Chapter Ten 458
Chapter Eleven 468
Chapter Twelve 471
Chapter Fourteen 498
Chapter Sixteen 512
Chapter Seventeen 515
Chapter Eighteen 517
Bibliography 523

Introduction

"In [God's] hand is the life of every living thing and the breath of all mankind."

Job 12:10

When once men recognize, both in private and in public life, that Christ is King, society will, at last, receive the great blessings of real liberty, well-ordered discipline, peace, and harmony.

Pope Pius XI

In truth, I tell you once again, if two of you on earth agree to ask anything at all, it will be granted to you by my Father in heaven. For where two or three meet in My name, I am there among them. (God's will is the answer)

Matt. 18:19

On the onset to introduce you, this is not a sophisticated exegetical book to remind you. I am called to bring God's Spirit of Truth to the people. Much of the information is in messages to bring awareness of truth, encouragement, hope, and God's truth for the Protection and Freedom of America presently and in the future. יֹעֵץ, **yoʻēṣ,** n.m. *or* v.ptcp. [3619]. counselor, adviser, one who gives advice and direction, with the implication that the advice given is wise and valuable. [3135] יוֹאָשׁ, **yoʻāš,** n.pr.m. [3378 + 6429]. Joash, *"Yahweh has bestowed.*[i]

America is in God's love in the people.

"I have no private purpose of accomplishing, no party project to build up, no enemies to punish, nothing to serve but my country (in God's truth)."

(God will punish those who deceive, kill, and destroy God's work.)
President Zachary Taylor April 22, 1848

I am a prayer warrior for the protection, freedom of America and the messenger that Jesus Christ is our Lord and Savior; I am a messenger of the Trinity and in Queen Virgin Mary and the Arch Angels and Saints of the God of Abraham. I am a Freedom Warrior of Peace in the Armor of God. Believers wear God's Armor. Armor is truth, of life of God's intention to live toward God's truth is the protection of His promises. However, if those who do not believe in Jesus Christ as their Savior and believe in Jesus Christ's works, Jesus will profess them to the Father. However, Jesus Christ does not accept cheap grace. Remember, God is a Sovereign God He uses all humanity as He desires. The armor is vast. We will not discuss it in this book. Later in another writing, I will discuss the Armor of God. It is mystical and powerful yet tender and soft as the soothing breeze on an evening after mission accomplished. I know it may seem different to you for me to state these proclamations, yet these are in the promises of God to His people that are given in the Holy Scriptures.

Furthermore, I have been working prayerfully to show President Trump's delivery of the faithfulness to follow God's Divine Messages and Commands, to restore America and keep her great in the justice and the truth, and for the life of the American people and her legacy. **Moreover, in doing this, I have been called to help the people awake and arise to God's truth that God calls President Trump to be President of the United States of America in 2020.** *Our Need to Give to the World, Heal America, Love in God*, are Divine Messages and Commands for America to vote in Trump and Divine Messages and strategies for the restoration and healing of America, 2016.[ii] In this book, I have proven documented facts by the specialist that President Trump has brought our country in a position again more excellent and vital and just in God's intention. Hear, believe people;

God is at peace when His people are doing justice and loving Him first with their first fruits and loving their neighbor in truth.

Listen, He, God uncovers and brings to anything that needs to be exposed to bring true justice, **peace, and love in God.** Hence, with living waters of life in God that the American people have awakened and realized President Trump's love and peace and wisdom in God to restore and keep America great. I have been giving the people the Divine Messages and Commands I have received in prayer. The Divine Messages and Commands bring warnings for protection, guidance, and strategy to help America. I continue in God's direction and, pray, and work to love America and the world with God's purpose and wisdom.

Make love your aim, but be eager, too, for spiritual gifts, and especially for prophesying.

1Cor. 14:1

Even in my humanness, He God, trusts me, teaches me, and is patent with me, strengthens me, and even forgives me because He knows my first intention is to love Him.

Communism teaches and us two objectives: unrelenting class warfare and the complete eradication of private ownership.

Pope Pius XI

Together, We will make America strong again. We will make America wealthy again. We will make America proud again. We will make America safe again. And yes, together, we will make America great again. Thank you. God bless you. And God bless America.

President Donald Trump

Chapter One

4 FOUNDATIONAL TRUTHS   FIRST PEACE

May the Lord of peace Himself give you peace at all times and in every way. The Lord be with you all.

2Th. 3:16

"Her glory is not dominion, but liberty. Her march is the march of mind. She has a spear and a shield, but the motto upon her shield is Freedom, Independence, Peace."

President John Quincy Adams

Earthly peace is the image and fruit of the *peace of Christ*, the messianic "Prince of Peace." By the blood of His Cross, "in His own person, He killed the hostility," He reconciled men with God and made his Church the sacrament of the unity of the human race and of its union with God. "He is our peace." He has declared: "Blessed are the peacemakers."[iii]

Safeguarding Peace

Peace is the essence of the life of happiness and wellbeing to the people in being human. PEACE IS THE PROTECTION OF PEOPLE FIRST. I will never forget this vision. I saw women and men running through the streets. Their faces were shocked with fear and the environment filled with a thick chemical poison, and the children were screaming at the top of their lungs. And the unforgettable scream of the children that know God's truth echoed in my heart. The children understand God's truth can only save us.

When there was almost incessant fighting in the country, Simon, son of Mattathias, a priest of the line of Joab, and his brothers courted danger and withstood their nation's enemies to **safeguard** *the integrity of their sanctuary and of the Law, and so brought their nation great glory.*

1Mac. 14:29

*Since your obedience to the **truth**, you have purified yourselves so that you can experience the genuine love of brothers, love each other intensely from the heart.*

1Pet. 1:22

Belligerence continues to rise... we should not only condemn aggression. We must force the dictates of our charger. And resume for the struggle of peace . . . a peace of justice.

President Ronald Reagan[iv]

I am trusting in God forever.

"You shall not kill," our Lord asked for peace of heart and denounced murderous anger and hatred as immoral. *Anger* is a desire for revenge. ". . . but it is praiseworthy to impose restitution "to correct vices and maintain justice."* [v] The action of "killing," the authentic being of the person, is the taking away freedom or not empowering liberty of the individual to be living a life toward God's creation of humanity. Taking away freedom is a root that needs to be pulled out of the soul of the soil of communities. Suppression and oppression are a form of violent actions of a Socialistic and Communistic regime. We will not acquiesce to these regimes. We stand in God's right arm of His power and truth of God's Spirit and overcome; we will have a continuous victory for freedom.

He safeguards the steps of His faithful, but the wicked vanish in darkness (for human strength can win no victories).

1Sam. 2:9

The first essence of God's Peace is the First commandment. *Thou shalt love the Lord thy God with all thy heart and with all thy soul, and with all thy mind.*

Mat. 22:35-40

Yes, God is with us. *For a son has been born for us, a son has been given to us, and dominion has been laid on His shoulders, and this is the name He has been provided, 'Wonder-Counsellor, Mighty-God, Eternal-Father*, **Prince-of-Peace'** [6] **to extend His dominion in eternal peace**, over the throne of David and over His kingdom to make it secure and sustain it in fair judgment and integrity. From this time onwards and forever, the jealous love of Yahweh Sabaoth will do this. [vi] *Isaiah 9:5-6*

Thou should not have any other gods before Me. When we love God, we have faith beyond human expectancy, and it is not human timing; it is God's timing. **Come as little children in faithfulness and love yet speak and sing and proclaiming boldly.** Come as little children in devotion and love yet speak and sing and proclaiming boldly. *Then He said, 'In truth, I tell you unless you change and become like little children you will never enter the kingdom of Heaven. ⁴ And so, the one who makes himself as little as this little (humble and pure is God's most incredible wisdom) child is the greatest in the kingdom of Heaven. Matthew 18:3* When we face God as a faithful child, we will know all necessary for His intention and will have deliverance and victory, His victory. He is a sovereign God.

Peace is not just the absence of war. We do not want a phony peace or a frail peace we did not pursue in some type of illusionary detente. We cannot be satisfied with cosmetic improvements that will not stand the test of time. We want to will peace.

There can be no greater good than the quest for peace and no more acceptable purpose than preserving freedom.

President Ronald Reagan

Blessed are the peacemakers, for they will be called children of God.

Mat. 5:19

Note: look below the footnotes for various words of peace; choose a word that resonates with you to use as a peace catalyst. How can you bring peace? And how can you bring peace to your country? The rebirth of the restoration of America and the world is in God's love in the people. The revival of America is in God's love for the people.

Peace. [vii] 8017. שְׁלֻמִיאֵל **Shlumiy'el,** *shel-oo-mee-ale';* from 7965 and 410; **peace** of God; Shelumiel, an Israelite:—Shelumiel. Peace is in God's Wisdom. The Wisdom of God is only for God's intention, not humanity; however, God lovingly allows us to create with Him in His choice, and He even accommodates us. Especially when we love Him, all things will flourish in His purpose, that is the most beautiful of the living truth of life.

I, LISA LUCIA ARDEN, have been given an honorable gift to proclaim in truth song, deed, and proclamation the love God has for His people. In the mercy of God with all my heart and soul with God's grace, He guides me to proclaim the Divine Messages and Commands. I answered God's call. **AMERICA ARISE TO GOD'S TRUTH ANSWER GOD'S.** I continually pray without ceasing for America and the world to provide the Divine Messages and Divine Commands, to guide, to direct, to warn, and to bring mustard seeds of faith of miracles.

When there was almost incessant fighting in the country Simon, son of Mattathias, a priest of the line of Joab, and his brothers courted danger and withstood their nation's enemies to safeguard the integrity of their sanctuary and of the Law, and so brought their nation great glory.

1Mac. 14:29

Have no fear either of sudden terror or of attack mounted by wicked men, [26] since Yahweh will be your guarantor; he will keep your steps from the snare.

Now America we need to do more than kindness we need to see how we can be that redeeming love of justice that brings peace in the Spirit of God's Truth. And God will have the victory over "wicked men."

Refuse no kindness to those who have a right to it if it is in your power to perform it.

Prov. 3:25-27

The American people should be first in the USA's standing. The American people have the right to justice and peace.

We ask how can we bring justice and freedom to our America?
The power of prayer is the working hands of the Spirit of God.

My mother knew the power of prayer. And at the Grotto, in Saint Elizabeth Catholic Church in Altadena, California, we prayed for the entire city and state and the world. At the feet of the powerful Queen Virgin Mary, we prayed the Bible and the Rosary. My Mother Alvera, the resilient American woman, and my Father Frank, the resilient American man, both sought all the Bible principles of the Judeo-Christian belief in the Trinity. I climbed up on the side stairs in faithfulness and peace, on the side of Queen Virgin Mary soothed by the living freshwater fountain. The moonlight shimmered and danced upon my Mother's face while she prayed. In my prayer, in the healing of the mystery of the promise of God's love in Queen Virgin Mary's glowing light of peace guiding us to Him, God.

In prayer, when we receive the covering of the holy anointing of the Holy Spirit of a miracle, we present ourselves and our faith and the first fruits of our love. God is with us and will guide us.

In truth, I tell you once again, if two of you on earth agree to ask anything at all, it will be granted to you by my Father in heaven. [20] *For where two or three meet in My name, I am there among them. (God's will to answer prayer.)*

Matt. 18:19

That night God appeared to Solomon and said, 'Ask what you would like me to give you.' 8 *Solomon replied to God, 'You showed most faithful love to David, my Father, and you have made me king in succession to him.* 9-*Yahweh God, the promise you made to David my Father is fulfilled since you have made me king over people as numerous as the dust of the earth.* 10 *Therefore, give me wisdom and knowledge to act as leader of this people, for how otherwise could such great people as yours be governed?*

2 Chronicles
1:7-10

I have proof God is with us; God answers our prayers; The answers are in the relationship with God and His people. God has given me Divine Messages and Commands; the evidence is in America's actions, and the Freedom Warriors of America and President Trump have faithfully forced through and accomplished all the successes for America. Please, my first book, *Our Need to Give to the World, America Love in God, Heal America. Lisa Lucia Arden, MDIV.*[viii]

Wisdom of Solomon is Peace that President Trump and the American Freedom Warriors, have and are continuing to GIVE

We have given our heart and soul and mind to the Lord thy God for us to be in the position we are in under the Freedom Warriors of America and President Trump. Even in our failures, when we seek forgiveness and seek righteousness, God forgives us. However, God knows the minds of men. The United States of America is now put first to take care of her land and her people. NEVER BEFORE IN AMERICA'S HISTORY HAS A PRESIDENT DONE MORE TO HEAL AMERICA'S FREEDOM AND PROTECTION AND LEGACY THAN PRESIDENT TRUMP AND THE AMERICAN FREEDOM WARRIORS. **Protection of the seed of life**, Employment flourishing, Tariffs of fair business, war on drug protection, Redeeming America of the Virus, Development of the infrastructure, Protection of the Borders, Military development, Keeping America safe. The list is vast and endless of the fruits of God's love.

"The only Maxim of a free Government, ought to be to trust no Man living, with power to endanger the public liberty."

President John Adams

President Trump and the American Freedom Warriors and those who love America to keep their freedom and legacy have brought God's peace to the nation. It is proven and documented that America is in a better position than she has ever.[ix] We are regaining, rapidly; Even with the fight to overcome and now toward the victory of the Chinese Virus, our America is in the hands of God is being redeemed in God's peace, שְׁלֻמִיאֵל Shlumiy'el, *shel-oo-mee-ale*[x], *God's peace*. In God's peace שְׁלֻמִיאֵל Shlumiy'el, *shel-oo-mee-ale'* *and God is knowing*. אֱלְיָדָע 'Elyada', *el-yaw-daw*, And the God of His love אֱלְיָדָע 'Elyada', *el-yaw-daw is with us*. Yes, we know God; God is love; God is peace, America, and the world. The Prince of Peace is God in America. **We America are Freedom Warriors of Peace. We work together, yet we have individual works for the mission.**

"*Freedom warriors of Peace,*"
> Peace is when all are working toward that inner intuitive Godly soul within the person to bring a life that demonstrates and lives by peace.

"*Freedom warriors of Peace,*"
> It is a brave resolution to build forward to bring life. It is an illuminating truth of recognition, revelation, illumination, awareness, and sometimes heartfelt anger with the reality that there is not peace. It is a must to bring peace.

"*Freedom warriors of Peace,*"
> Whether it is a powerful indirect pure catalyst of revelation or noise to those who do not know peace to speak, create, act upon, and show peace is needed. NO VIOLENCE-

"*Freedom warriors of Peace,*"
> Peace warriors heal when there is a wound in the soul of the land.

"*Freedom warriors of Peace,*"
> Peace warriors heal, there will be the individual, the families, the people, the businesses, the culture, and the life peace essential for life's existence

> During the Civil War, President Lincoln sought peace and never gave up.

Listen America, Abraham Lincoln "A House divided

> "*A House Divided against itself cannot stand. I this government cannot endure permanently half slave and half free.*"[xi]

> `   Abraham Lincoln 1858

Divine Message: God wants freedom and peace and truth and justice, not an ideology of thieves of human life and the country. A country cannot stand in division. When we do not bring peace, we enslave ourselves and others. We are "half slave and half free." Our ideological differences and selfish ignorance cause hatred that brings slavery of even self and others to be the citizen or community member to be respected and peace. When we bring peace, we have the freedom flowing exchange of each human in truth. Hence, Americans respect the police and military and guards; they need your "friendship of agreement" St**שָׁלֹ׳ם shalom,** *shaw-lome* of justice. And in return, treat the citizen and immigrants, and community members with the utmost respect and without violence. I want you to know when safety is compromised then other more extensive and severe safety can be at risk. Awake Americans. Security needs to be first in communities. Do not you know that the enemy, the larger enemy, uses the disagreements between the country's citizens as a tool to give us a diversion so that they, the treacherous enemy, could stealthily plan a conspiracy and even severe causalities to our country. This has been explicit in the voting fraudulent conspiracy and conspiracy against President Trump. We need to protect and seek peace with our policemen and military, and guards. Otherwise, eventually, your communities will have severe causalities; this is the strategy of war America. Most of all we need to reconcile past abuses against citizens.

Now let us have the Emancipation Proclamation of "The Beginning of Freedom for All." [xii] *Thenceforward, and forever free. So said President Abraham Lincoln's Emancipation Proclamation on January 1, 1863.* The proclamation referred only to slaves in the rebellious states over which Lincoln had no control, so the mandate had little actual force. However, it did convert the Civil War into a crusade against slavery, thus making European intervention impossible. It also allowed the Union to recruit black soldiers, nearly 180,000 of whom enlisted during the war.[xiii] *I pray, we today have peace and liberty, and love between the peoples in America. Thenceforward, and forever free. So said President Abraham Lincoln's Emancipation Proclamation on January 1, 1863.* **All American police,**

military, guards, and peoples of each community and American Peace warriors let us be "forever free in peace and justice."

Definitions as a "*Freedom Fighter of Peace,*" righteousness, we have no choice than to take up the truth of love to protect our children's legacy so that WE, AMERICA, will have peace. Otherwise, our children could be enslaved into a conspiracy and a hidden strategy they would not even know. There is a plan of the remote control of the technological powers. We have to be careful.

Let us be "forever free" in God's Truth, then we have a happy life even in trials.

God's chosen ones, are His humanity He creates pure and beautiful, and that is why He wants to redeem us to the authentic being He created us for; holy and beloved, heartfelt compassion, kindness, humility, gentleness, and patience, bearing with one another and forgiving one another He gives us in our heart; if one has a grievance against another we need to forgive; as the Lord has forgiven you, so must you also forgive. Though we do not have to accept abuse. And over all this put-on love, that is, the bond of perfection. And let the peace of Christ control your hearts, the peace into which you (are called) in one body. And be thankful. ⁱ⁶ Let the word of Christ dwell in you richly, as in all wisdom you teach and admonish one another, singing psalms, hymns, and spiritual songs with gratitude in your hearts to God. ⁱ⁷

Colossians 3:14-17

Peace has definite truth accepted individually; yet agreed together what is truth; that is why they demand or seek peace because they know what God commands and allows the Peace Warrior to choose in free-will. The Peace Warrior lives in the choice of God's truth of free will, that is, freedom a gift of peace, justice, restoration, and forward building in God's genuine intention for humanity. God's heart flows in the body of society and the nation; He wants His sovereignty to flow because it is the most peaceful, and it is organic. Hence, the government needs proper nutrition and a righteous hand of God; we can ask what has changed concerning the?[xiv] Innately, humans know what is wrong from right... And God tells us to be good so that He can continue to bring us good. We have a heavenly garden of the land of American encompassing the most extraordinary natural beauties and supplications. However, God tells us to love Him and turn away from violence and love our neighbor. And bring justice to our land. As people, we are given America's dominion and need to protect her land and her people.

For example, we as Americans need to keep the dominion a land of liberty and truth in the justice of fair-business and protection and empowerment for the future

PRODUCTION OF CHINA OVER 25 YEARS HAS MADE BILLIONS AND BILLIONS FROM USA; NOW FOR THE FIRST TIME UNDER PRESIDENT TRUMP, WE TOOK IN BILLIONS FROM CHINA in 2019 FROM FAIR-BUSINESS TARIFFS; THE INK WAS NOT DRYED BEFORE THE CORONA VIRUS WAS KNOWN.[xv]

President Trump

Note: this was a Divine Command.

    We do not want to be turned away by God. God has given us a gift to take care of America; taking care of America is the "pearl of great price," giving all to take care of America and even the world in the reflection of God's truth, Arise! Adam and Eve were told not to eat from the Tree of good and evil, and they did, and they were turned away by God in the Garden of Eden. Our America is a Garden of a Gift of God; we cannot accept evil and injustices and "eating" from and with a tree of injustice. We had to put on tariff restrictions—an excellent job from President Trump and the American Freedom Warriors. Today we have a merciful God in our Savior, Jesus Christ. He has forgiven us; we can prove in the excellent work President Trump and the Americans and the America Freedom Warriors of Peace have delivered, making America great again.

    This very moment we need to strive to continue to restore America in our difference.

Jesus Christ, the Prince of Peace, we have AUTHORITY AMERICA IN GOD'S HANDS

America, we are "*Freedom Warriors of Peace," with* righteousness, we will take up peace.
America, we are "*Freedom Warriors of Peace*," with justice, we will take up peace.

America, we are "*Freedom Warriors of Peace*," with love, we will take up peace.
Remember, peace also has realized justice and treating humanity with righteousness.

Divine Message 2020

St. Bede's, La Canada, California

Arise and answer to the call, each person God wants you to receive the letter of His love. From the Holy Scriptures, He has a message for each one of us. He wants us to go to Him in prayer for a love letter of a message from Him in particular for each one of us. I saw a white and blue room that did not have walls. It has the light of a banner of white light and blue. I saw folded notes that we are supposed to open up, first to receive and open and then act upon. *Let the one who has M*y Word follow and receive My precepts. Remember, peace also has the characteristic of delivering protection. Here are a few life-saving God's Divine Commands that President Trump strategically achieved to bring peace. In harmony, there is safety.

PRESIDENT TRUMP SPENT 2.5 TRILLION DOLLARS ON THE MILITARY WAS BADLY DEPLETED
OBLITERATED ISIS AND KILLED ITS FOUNDER AND ABU BACAR ALBAGDADI SEPARATED OPERATION ELIMINATE THE MOST TREACHEROUS TERRORIST KASIM SOLAMINI

Definitions of Peace God's Wisdom is God in our peace.

We are Freedom Warriors of Peace In Hebrews 7:2, "King of Peace" (*shalom*); Peace is bringing truth even proclaiming aloud in the passion of God's purpose. Yes, cannot you see, nature every morning wakes up, from the heart of the sun, the light of God's promise, He gives to nature, for the people giving them life. True life for justice must be and the fact in the working of motion continuously toward peace. In the peace of God, the conscious is always evolving; it is infinite, and peace is toward perfection. The Peace Warrior can heal and restore the others that are not in harmony because peace is the result of justice and truth and love as life, God's purpose of life. God created the people because of His love, and He wants us to live in His intention and even commands us to bring peace when there is injustice. God created a world that has armistice in life that all of the truth of life has a working order and toward peacemaking, transforming, healing, and creating beauty on beauty. The jewels of justice and polish with their compassion to bring light to life. America knows when there needs to be peace when those jewels of justice need to be found and given.

President Reagan brings to light the truth: Eisenhower states, "We are peace, first, last and always for every simple reason, we know in a peaceful atmosphere a peace with justice one in that we can be confident ~~can~~ America will prosper as we have to know prosperity

. Those who seek peace are looking for honor proposals and genuine progress. After World War II, we were the only industrial power that was not damaged globally; our Military supremacy was unquestioned. We had harnessed the atom. We could unleash its destructive course anywhere in the world. We could have achieved world dominations though that was contrary to the character of our people. Instead, we wrote a new chapter in the history of humanity. We used our power and wealth to rebuild the world's war-ravaged economy, both East and West, including those nations who have been our enemies. We took the initiative of creating other international institutions, as the United Nations. **We are leaders of goodwill to come together to build bridges of peace and prosperity.** America has no territorial ambitions. We occupy no countries. OUR COMMITMENT OF FREEDOM AND PEACE IS THE SOUL OF AMERICA THAT COMMITMENT IS AS STRONG TODAY AS IT EVER WAS. In each war of the United States, we struggle to defend freedom and democracy. We were never the aggressors. America's strength and, yes, her military power is a force for peace.[xvi]

AMERICA'S MILITARY POWER IS FOR PEACE, NOT CONQUEST.

America is the Light of God. The furthest scientists have found to the edge of the known universe, they find "light." GOD IS ALPHA AND OMEGA. HE IS THE LIGHT OF THE UNIVERSE AND BEFORE THE LIGHT. God's steadfast love's purpose is peace, justice, transformational healing(restoration), and forward building in love. The ancient philosopher *Hesiod* even proclaims *Pre-eminence is love.*

St. Paul tells us love is the greatest thing. Love is peace of God's zenith of the light everlasting.

Definitions of Peace.[xvii]

In Arabic, the root SLM is common to *salam*, **peace**, *Islam*, **submission**, and *Muslim*, one who **submits.** Moreover, the consonantal script in which Hebrew is written also calls attention to a word's root. An eighteenth-century philologist, A. Schultens, suggested that the Hebrew word *hôšîa'* (יְשַׁע save, help) is derived from an Arabic word meaning *"give room to."* He then moved, mistakenly, from Barr's point of view, from word to concept by arguing that **salvation** consequently carries with it some connotation of spaciousness. [xviii] "Spaciousness," is the movement in life and place and even measurement, hence, God wants to bring Salvation not only to our hearts but to our life and even our land.

Peace in Islam is *salam* **submission** and Muslim one who **submits**. In Hebrew *hôšîa'* (יְשַׁע save, help) and even salvation. The "Black life Matters," yes, many are Muslim, and all other religions realize that peace is "submission" to each other to bring peace in tranquility. Submitting is likened to a son or a daughter submits to his or her parents to bring peace to receive help, and save, and then have salvation *hôšîa'* (יְשַׁע save, help) My professor at the Angelicum, Pontifical University Saint Thomas Aquinas Bishop Mored reminded us, we realize the holy language of Hebrew is God's Words to His humanity. We recognize and live in the relationship of God, as proven in that the Church still exists. Even Spiritual Divine Godly experiences are happening and given, is the pure fact of the living Church amongst the people of God. Even those who know that God is alive and sovereign and have not accepted Him, He is still waiting for their knock at the door of His love.

Mandatory Safety for Peace

1. SAFTEY: "safety," בֶּטַח

Without safety, life cannot continue. As stated in the book, "*Our Need to Give to the World," America Loves in God, Heal America*. America's safety is paramount because our country has become weak from past political powers, a secret plan to take down the people's freedom and make a Socialistic, Communistic Regime, controlled by hierarchies of political elites and technological traitorous mastermind's forerunners to control all parts of life. Listen to what these political elites of Socialist, Communistic Regimes do not realize is that the "traitorous masterminds of technological" would also take them over, eventually. Hear when there is a door of evil, sometimes men chose that, and terrible treacherous doors form in humanity's evolution. The analogy of the protestors of violence in our country; Hence, just like any other time in history, we need to trust God to give us strength and wisdom to overcome these human wounds.

Divine Message

Our Lady of Mount Carmel February 9, 18, 2020[xix]

The technology lines that are [build] from the community to state to global aspects of life whatever has a business transaction for forming bills or transactions of every type of business regarding money and agreements and even communication… If the invoice and transactions and all information delivered are pure in a righteous way on both sides then its transmission and transaction will be clean and clear to the "light of God!" [See there has not been a justice of sharing, especially among those that have pure gifts of God, and those who planned the path of righteousness for America; she has wounds even in the physical body; because there is injustice even among the believers, they think of their ideas not God's and use the gifted for their purpose and even do not share life. Hence, the gifted gives all the life of God. See this is reflective of when Jesus gave and they did not have faith to return the love. Hence, He had to leave.]

Suppose the transaction in technology carries God's gain of natural organic substance connected to the human soul {entire being}. And also, there can be tension between opposing forces. Though God always overcomes all things either way. The person involved will send what the motive or[the attitude] that is applied. However, we know that there are many variables with the human connection and the technological apparatus used; hence sometimes, there will not be the total or delivery desired.

Moreover, we need to seek peace injustice, not to allow technology to control human life. Technology, when used correctly, is a tool for compassion and accommodation, and life. Otherwise, when understanding is, and accommodation is not delivered, there will be less of life on both sides. Moreover, each needs the other in making a life.

    "Good to more Good than before."
     "Good to better." "Good or Bad"
    "Evil or Saintly"
    "Loss or Gain"
    "Stealing or Given"
    "Cheating or Honesty"
    "Stagnation or Production"
    "Unjust or just."

These substances of the transaction that are being transmitted of the purpose's organic attitude will come across the technological lines. It will be apart of the human makeup and society itself. Consequently, if we do not take these transactions and transmissions in God's intended way for pureness (justice), our communities can become so dark- death and only by Jesus Christ's cross can be redeemed. God cannot sustain evil, He redeems evil [and all humanity]. However, He accommodates society in His time though we never know when He will strike. Hence, all monetary transactions have to be just and righteous.

    . Hence, all monetary transactions have to be just and righteous. Accordingly, all financial transactions transmitted in person and technology has to be a flow of truth not like before...[in all forms of life from the state to the community, to global,] Now these transactions have to flow of truth of God's intended justice and love for humanity. Not necessarily to make the most money for the onset, FIRST JUSTICE, AND SAFETY FOR THE PRESENT AND THE FUTURE.
    Safety is the command that has to be carried out in all aspects of the nation, from communities to families to individuals.

WHEN PRESIDENT TRUMP TOOK OFFICE MIDDLE EAST WAS IN CHAOS

ISIS WAS RAMPAGING- PRESIDENT TRUMP A HERO SUCCESSFULLY SEPARATED OPERATION ELIMINATED THE MOST TREACHEROUS

TERRORIST KASIM SOLAMINI; ALSO, HE OBLIBERATED THE ISIS AND KILLED ITS FOUNDER AND ABU ALBAGDAD; PRESIDENT TRUMP WITHDREW FROM IRAN NUCLEAR DEAL ONE SIGHTED IRAN; PRESIDENT TRUMP WITHDREW 4K TROOPS - KEEPING AMERICA OUT OF WARS; TROOPS ARE COMING HOME; THE MILITARY WAS BADLY DEPLETED PRESIDENT TRUMP URGENT NOW STRATEGICALLY PROTECTING USA AND HER PEOPLE FOR SAFETY FIRST OF AMERICANS SPENT 2.5 TRILLION DOLLARS.[xx]

My first book, "*Our Need to Give to the World,*" *America Love God, Heal America,*[xxi] I was given the Divine Commands and Messages that I heard in prayer that President

Trump needed to be President 2016 to protect and restore America and be a reflection of God's justice to the world with the direction of the Spirit of God with American Freedom Warriors. Also, I was given Divine Commands and Messages to tell President Trump and the team to proceed and it was followed;

The first is to be a reflection of God's justice in the world... God trusts the American
Freedom Warriors and those who love America.
He is giving us a merciful chance to save America. He gave us the most magnificent country as our dominion, and God demands righteousness to flow.

<u>Today in 2020, this is also a Divine Message, and Command President Trump needs to be President 2020 with the Freedom Warriors of America to protect and restore America and reflect God's justice to the world. America is called to be a reflection of God's justice in America and the world; we America need to be the reflection of God's face, that effervescent light of peace that is from heaven. Pray, God will enter into our lives and be a reflection of His face of life.</u>

    Moreover, I have listed all the restoration Divine Commands and Messages that God requires us to follow. I was given these lists of DIVINE

Commands and Messages of urgencies before President Trump's Presidency. Miraculously and faithfully, President Trump and the American Freedom Fighters have worked and are working on these Divine Commands and Messages for restoring America. We are succeeding in God's victory. These Divine Commands and Messages are from Jesus Christ of the Trinity and Queen Virgin Mary. Awake and Arise to God's Truth, He listens to our prayers: many of the Divine Commands and Messages have come to the Divine fruition for peace and justice for America and even the world. These Divine Commands and Messages are all biblically sound. It is the answer to wholehearted pray in hearing the Words of God from the Holy Scriptures. Continually I give Divine Messages and Commands to guide and warn and pray and provide mustard seeds of miracles for God's land. No matter where I am in the world, I am for America first, and she is at my heart. The people have awakened and have realized that America needs to be protected and restored. America's gift is from God. He has given the country and the people His love and promises. Awake America, **γρηγορέω** be or keep **awake**; watch, be alert; be alive (1Th 5:6) put that where watch the cities. **διεγείρω** (aor. διήγειρα; aor. pass. ptc. διεγερθείς) **awake**, wake up; rise, grow rough (of the sea) people have to awaken **G605 | S G572 ἁπλότης haplotēs** 8x

*Simplicity, sincerity, purity of mind, Rom. 12:8; 11:3; Eph. 6:5; Col. 3:22; liberality, as **arising** from simplicity and frankness of character.[xxii] 2Cor. 9:13*

Because when you have proved your quality by this help, they will give glory to God for the obedience which you show in professing the gospel of Christ, as well as for the generosity of your fellowship towards them and towards all.

Cor. 9:13

We should not go on sleeping, as everyone else does, but stay wide awake and sober. [7] but we belong to the day, and we should be sober; let us put on faith and love for a breastplate and the hope of salvation for a helmet. [9] God destined us not for His retribution, but to win salvation through our Lord Jesus Christ, [10] who died for us so that, awake or asleep, we should still live united to him. [11] So encourage each other, and keep strengthening one another, as you do already.

1 Thessalonians 5:9-12

      Yes, America is awakening and is waking up and rising and growing in the heart of God. The people voted in President Trump; this reflects the agreement that the people want PEACE. The agreement to bring love, SAFETY, AND PROTECTION OF AMERICA, KEEPING AMERICA GREAT, because that is what President Trump AND THE AMERICAN FREEDOM WARRIORS ARE DOING, NOW. Today, I also heard and in wholehearted prayer that President Trump and the American Freedom Warriors have to continue restoring America and to protect America's legacy and America's people and future. **Please, Millennials, God's intentions are for freedom. I am not presenting my ideology. I am showing you facts and logic and the history of America and the world that is proven. Also, I am showing you God's purpose and His living redemption in history in the world is again verified and logical. These writings are not is not a partial truth; this is not a half-truth; this is not a truth of me; this is not a truth of man; <u>this is the truth of God</u>.** These words, Divine Messages, and Divine Commands are truths of God's factual history and essential facts. Hear, Millennials, you are the future you for our America. You are the essence of the Tree of Life that the forefathers and your legacy have worked blood, sweat, and tears.

      When you vote Democratic, you vote death to freedom because the Socialistic has become dangerously more sided Communist, and the powerful have become more secretive about using technology in the future to control America and even in the world, for "One World Government."

DIVINE MESSAGE, NOVEMBER 2020

<u>**CERTAIN DEMOCRATS SECRETLY USED TECHNOLOGY AND OTHER CRIMES TO CHANGE THE VOTE COUNT.**</u>

<u>**THE LEFT AND CERTAIN DEMOCRATS ARE DOING CONSPIRACIES AGAINST THE AMERICAN PEOPLE**</u>

<u>**FOR YEARS THE DEMOCRATIC, LEFT HAS CONSPIRED AGAINST PRESIDENT TRUMP.**</u>

<u>**PRESIDENT TRUMP WON THE 2020 PRESIDENTIAL ELECTION**</u>

<u>**GOD IS COMMANDING OPEN UP BUSINESSES PROTECT THE PEOPLE'S LIVELIHOOD CALIFORNIA AND MANY OTHER STATES NEED OPENING.**</u>

WE WILL RESTORE OUR COUNTRY IN THE POWER AND WISDOM AND HUMBLENESS OF THE AUTHORITY OF GOD. GOD DOES NOT WANT US TO BE VIOLENT OF WAR EVEN IF there are injustices.
VIOLENCE WILL BRING DEATH TO THAT WHO ACT UPON VIOLENCE.
SAFETY BRINGS PEACE AND PEACE to BRING JUSTICE.
THE SPIRIT OF THE LORD OF THE SACRED HEART AND MARY TELL US EVERY CITY NEEDS TO seek PEACE AND JUSTICE AND TO BE WATCHED.

Children need to be protected with the harvest of clean from pesticides, pharmaceuticals are uncontaminated and sterile. The infrastructure's rebuilding is yet appropriately done and reviewed before the foundation is poured and or finished. Because the worker is trustworthy, dedicated, and reliable; however, always check the work. The economy needs to be protected in fair business.

DR. KING PROCLAMATION IS, I have a DREAM, AND WE WILL WORK IN PEACE.
GOD IS THE DELIVERY OF PEACE.
Protestors and Police

1. We need to respect one another and swiftly forgive each other. We need to forgive the wounds on both sides, protestors, victims, innocent, police, and all those involved and all those who have experienced violence.
2. Today in our communities, never before in history have we had the various types of crimes and multiple types of illegal drugs and even abused pharmaceuticals.
3. Furthermore, in the age of the rapid tool of technology and life-threatening intensity and treacherous crimes involving technology singularly and simultaneously used with other crimes, our community's crimes are enormously complicated.
4. Both sides, criminals, protestors, and police, are in fear that is unusual, and there are more variables to consider the current effects of crimes than any time in history. THIS IS WHY POLICE ARE NEEDED MORE THAN EVER. MOREOVER, THIS IS WHY THE LEADERS OF GREAT MONETARILY WEALTH BILLIONAIRE'S NEED TO HELP RESTORE THE POVERTY OF THE HOMELESS AND THE HUMAN TRAFFICKING AND HUMAN HEALTH.
5. Moreover, there is globalization representing different cultural

beliefs and acceptance of communication. Therefore, reflecting specific ways of ethics and life that are considered in favor of humanity's wellbeing truly is death to society's wellbeing.

1. Moreover, another aspect that causes the breakdown of humanity's wellbeing is the communities that have assimilated to a multicultural belief system that has become confusingly heterogeneous; there is no specific ethical standard. Hence, it is happenstance and opposing directions of ethical standards and conflicts that will have detriments upon the communities.
6. Simultaneously, with the new millenniums affected by the technology and the multicultural society of globalization that has never been the highest is today in the United States of America.
2. When my grandparents came to America, they only could speak English, and it was the only acceptable protocol in most daily life experiences. Today we as a nation are given the freedom to allow the people to express their cultural roots. However, we have not put America first and its traditions.
7. We need to identify in an agreement what our country represents. We need certainty and acceptance, even under differences.
8. We need to keep the foundation of America for her to deliver the life of the American Dream.
9. We should be respectful of all the legacy that was and is to be; they all have and will pave the roads and the lands and protect our country and her people.
10. Now, we are being restored, giving us and the best economy and life, and being empowered to be a human being of the greatest well-being in God's love, the United States of America.

GOD WANTS FORGIVENESS; GOD WANTS RIGHTEOUSNESS.

So stand your ground, with truth a belt round your waist, and uprightness a breastplate, [15] wearing for shoes on your feet the eagerness to spread the gospel of peace [16] and always carrying the shield of faith so that you can use it to quench the burning arrows of the Evil One. [17] And then you must take salvation as your helmet and the sword of the Spirit, that is, the word of God.

Eph. 6:14

Peace of is found in retribution

2. **RETRIBUTION:** שְׁלֻמָה, repayment, retribution.

Where there are injustices, retribution is a requirement of the natural law of God. In incidences of compassion toward justice, one will regain what was lost. One needs tools to recover to make and develop and build. America needs to continue to be in retribution. Peace is a process toward perfection. Again, I state peace is justice. First, it is forgiveness, in both parties and by the action in delivering what injustice was, and in the retribution; this is an act of God's redemption characteristics. Human nature does not forget what they have achieved or worked for. Perhaps it may have been obstructed or taken by fraud or trespassing or kidnapping in the individual's life in the sense of control through political and monetarily means communities constrictions, and even hidden power elite groups common.

Please, below the footnotes that peace represents. Ask yourself, what peace is to you?

We know when all happenings are toward peace:
γρηγορέω *be* or *keep* **awake**; *watch, be alert; be alive* (1Th 5:6)[xxiii]
America should not go on sleeping, as everyone else does, but stay wide awake and sober. 1Th 5:6

> *Awake, let there be life pristine penetrating peace*
> *Awake, let there be life in flowing safety*
> > *Keep watch Anointed with the protectors that watch and deliver safety*
> *Awake, let there be transformation healing in the jovial friendliness.*
> > *Keep watching Anointed in friendliness in joy the protectors should be. There needs to be respect and law in reciprocating and making peace, rendering injustice to restore.*
> *Awake, let there be forward building in God's love*
> *Awake, let there be forgiveness in the people*
> > *Keep watch Anointed with the complete requital and recompense in bring peace.*
> *Awake, let there be life in flowing justice*
> > *Keep watching, Anointed in making the restoration of truth for peace.*

Awake, let there be transformation healing
    Keep watch, Anointed and receive and give that peace offering
Awake, let there be forward building in God's love
Awake, let there be forgiveness in the people
    Keep watch, Anointed make complete a requital
Yes, I God's truth in the people
Yes, I God's peace in the people
Yes, I God' love in the people
Yes, I God's miracle in the people

The watcher is awake to bring peace is that police and security and military. <u>The first is safety.</u>

There is a Divine Message that all police and the military have the Rosary and Michael Arch Angel card or medal with them. Furthermore, they should recite the Rosary before work. Prayer unceasingly is the hand of God's strength, especially praying in righteousness. The watcher is awake to bring peace is that American Freedom Warrior. *Peace is found in the Agreement of Truth.*

שׁלוֹם shalowm, *shaw-lome* 7965. '; or **שָׁלֹם shalom**, *shaw-lome';* from 7999; safe, i.e. (figuratively) well, happy, friendly; also (abstractly) welfare, i.e. health, prosperity, **peace**:—x do, familiar, x fare, favour, + friend, x great, (good) health, (x perfect, such as be at) peace(-able, -ably), prosper(-ity, -ous), rest, safe(-ty), salute, welfare, (x all is, be) well, x wholly.

    *My heart, be at **peace** once again, for Yahweh has treated you generously.*

Psa. 116:7

NATIONAL ANTHEM THE LAND OF THE FREE AND THE HOME OF THE BRAVE AMERICA WE ARE.

3. AGREEMENT, שָׁלַם

PROOF NOW SHOWN WE HAVE AN AGREEMENT: Each one of us needs to have an open mind of our actions of decisiveness, never to control or abuse; there needs to be an agreement, though the agreement has to be in truth as individuals, yet in one accord in mind(the mission) the heart of the mind and each body is an authentic being not used for man's ideas only for God's ideas individually. The nature of the mind needs to be God's intention. In the humanity of life, we know there are endless variables of consequences of agreements. However, sometimes agreements are broken. For all sorts of reasons, contracts between humans have unexpected happenings. When we progress toward justice and peace toward forgiveness, we work together, redeeming that agreement. A political party cannot use the people, the victim, the immigrant, the poor, for violence and bring about their bias in an inhuman purpose. God's wisdom He gives to humans is life under the Trinity.; God's gifts to humans have are intended for forwarding building in love. When the brilliant individual's God's skills give rare gifts to humans ideas of control and abuse, there can be death and even destruction on a community o0r nation. These gifts are to be used to help all humanity at specific timing and purpose that cannot be accommodated or given mercy. We all have to be careful. God is tender and can take one millisecond look and see the entire world's heart of each person. When the person with the gift works to do the best and maybe impeded temporarily. Even God is happier because those who have temporary roadblocks do God's will, are being polished with a more jeweled faith. And He is a sovereign God. Remember, Moses continued to warn the Pharaoh to let the Israelites go. Interestingly remember the Pharoah was Moses' brother. We, as people, need to give each other freedom and truth, and justice. Those in power politically and silent instigators to bring violence in our country are being watched by the eyes of God and His watchers. God has given you these worldly gifts, and He created good skills, and we all need to seek righteousness, and even if we are impeded, He knows our heart. He puts His hand to rule.

The plagues God inflicted on Egypt resulted from Pharaoh's refusal to listen to God's word through Moses and let them go.

That you may know that I am the Lord. Exodus 10:2

<u>God will redeem us when we respect and live in Him first.</u>
<u>First Commandment is the foundation of life precepts.</u>
<u>Respecting Him is respecting His precepts.</u>
<u>Precepts we will discuss later in the other work.</u>

<u>Even with the development of vocational and economic hierarchies, we can form a peaceful agreement with compassion and truth.</u> I pray without ceasing for America, my sisters, and brothers to have peace and justice and freedom and restore the USA. I pray without stopping for China, my sisters, and brothers to be released by Communistic abuse and control.

Prayer is the greatest miracle; it is the hand of God when one is seeking to live in righteousness. Unity of peace is all working together yet allowing each human to be individuals; the agreement is working for the common goal of peace adorned with the truth. **A society of God's purpose nurtures freedom without any chains of control and replicated technological actions and restrictions of the delivery of funds and even the development of vocational and economic hierarchies. There will soon be a time for those who enslave others or treat others with injustice, as the ancient Egyptian King Pharaoh will be destroyed. The present reality is the COVID-19 Virus.** *Question: think about the development of the virus and the life-changing catastrophe from every world's level of life.*

"The intellect is, he says, a "spiritual automaton" that operates according to its own laws, independent of external stimuli and inputs (Paragraph 85-86). By this metaphor, Spinoza suggests that the intellect is a kind of "computing system" that generates by its own rules the primary sources of its cognitive capital…. The intellect forms and assents to on its own."[xxiv] Hence, we need peace for freedom of the development of each intellect in a human. Life is to have the peace of independence to live to express an individual's intelligence.

Whether any created intellect can the essence of God? Now God is not something existing, but He is super-existent, as Dionysius says (Div. Nom. iv). Therefore, God is not intelligible; but above all intellect. *It is written: "We shall Him as He is" (1 Jn. 2:2).* **He is the sacrifice to expiate our sins, and not only ours, but also those of the whole world.** Hence, it must be granted that the blessed the essence of God. **[I.17.3] Whether falsity is in the intellect?** There is, however, this difference, as before mentioned regarding truth (Question [16], Article [2]), that falsity can exist in the intellect not only because the intelligence is conscious of that knowledge, as it is conscious of truth; whereas in sense falsity does not live as known, as stated above (Article [2]).[xxv] Hence, this is why we need to seek God first in our life. God directs us toward all truth. He will guide you into the truth. Truth is God's intellect. Whoever shall hear, He shall speak to. He will also show you the things to come. John 16:13

Arise, and awake and open your heart, America and the world we can overcome all things in Jesus Christ, He even "expiates the whole world's sins," therefore, we can have peace when we seek peace and restoration and life abundant.

Divine Message

St. Bedes, La Canada March 1, 2020

Divine Message that we are to give love notes to each other from the Holy Scriptures regularly once a week and or daily and ask God to help us. I know this may seem like a simple task of inconsequence to you, though I have to remind you that it is the Word of God, the Word became flesh amongst us. Just as you have any type of manual or book with information, God also has a manual for His directions, yet it is infinite, and He is Alpha and Omega. When the Trinity were all present, creating the universe, the Word of God, the Voice of God, has the power to create and reflects the Holy Scriptures and prayer. It is the Word of God, and you receive the Voice of God.

The word of God is something alive and active: it cuts more incisively than any two-edged sword: it can seek out the place where the soul is divided from the spirit, or joints from marrow; it can pass judgment on secret emotions and thoughts. No created thing is hidden from Him; everything is uncovered and stretched fully open to the eyes of the one to whom we must give an account of ourselves.

Heb. 4:12-13

4. PROSPERITY

שָׁלוֹם **shalowm,** *shaw-lome*

7965. '; or שָׁלֹם **shalom,** *shaw-lome'*; from 7999; safe, i.e. (figuratively) well, happy, friendly; also (abstractly) welfare, i.e. health, **peace**:—x do, familiar, x fare, favour, + friend, x great, (good) health, (x perfect, such as be at) peace(-able, -ably), prosper(-ity, -ous), rest, safe(-ty), salute, welfare, (x all is, be) well, x wholly. God desires to take care of His humanity, and when the peace is delivered in righteousness, then prosperity is delivered, and the favor of God is upon the people, and the nation is in good welfare. And the government is happy.

President Trump Successes of Peace, please see a few of the successes. Here are few paramount life savings works for the American People.

1. TAX CUTS IN 3 YEARS STRONGEST ECONOMY
2. MANUFACTURING MORE THAN 500,000 JOBS
3. JOBS CREATING 7 MILLION PAYING JOBS

Covenant of Peace is with God and His people. The covenant is an agreement to follow God's given agreement of respect and wisdom given to His people. In America, we seek to have a **Covenant of Peace** when we work in unity of truth. When treating each humankind and fair and compassionately, the Covenant of Peace is directed from the heavens שָׁמַיִם

8065. שָׁמַיִן shamayin, *shaw-mah'-yin*; (Aramaic) corresponding to 8064:—heaven.

Contemplate we my friends that living peace lean up on the שְׂמִיכָה smiykah, *sem-ee-kaw'* **mantle, rest, stand fast, and sustain in the favorable way; on the mantle of God's heart to pray in the** שָׁמַיִם shamayim, *shaw-mah'-yim-roo'*; from the same as 5105; illumination, i.e. (figuratively) **wisdom**:—light. And we will receive the wisdom of intelligence; knowledge, reason, understanding מַנְדַּע manda', *man-dah*. 4486. מַנְדַּע manda', *man-dah'*; (Aramaic) corresponding to 4093; **wisdom** or intelligence:—knowledge, reason, understanding.[xxvi]

"The mantle of Mary "like a loving child, run to your spiritual Mother and hide under her mantle for comfort and protection. 'While Jesus was (crucified) on the cross, He said to John the Apostle, "Behold your mother" (John 19.27). Open your heart, here this is not a merely a sweet way of Jesus caring for Mother, but a bold declaration that all of us are called to share Mary as our true spiritual Mother."[xxvii]

The Priesthood of the Old Covenant

God constituted the chosen people as "a kingdom of priests and a holy nation." But within the people of Israel, God chose one of the twelve tribes, that of Levi, and set it apart for liturgical service; God himself is its inheritance. A special rite consecrated the beginnings of the priesthood of the Old Covenant. The priests are "appointed to act on behalf of men concerning God, to offer gifts and sacrifices for sins. **The peace was given by God when the gifts were sacrificed for their sins. The New Covenant one priesthood of Christ**: Everything that the priesthood of the Old Covenant prefigured finds its fulfillment in Christ Jesus, the "one mediator between God and men."[1] The Christian tradition considers Melchizedek, "priest of God Most High," as a prefiguration of the priesthood of Christ, the unique "high priest after the order of Melchizedek;" "holy, blameless, unstained," "by a single offering he has perfected for all time those who are sanctified," that is, by the unique sacrifice of the cross."[xxviii]

Covenant of Peace in Jesus Christ is a gift to us that He is our Lord and we are His people by a single offering he has perfected for all time those who are sanctified," that is, by the unique sacrifice of the cross."[xxix]

He pours peace upon us when we accept Him as our Savior. America has always been a reflection of God's love to the world for all. Esther was a Freedom Warrior for her people of God and her country. Though remember, her foundation was in the covenant of faith in God overcoming all seemingly powerful obstacles such as a King. Esther 6

It for the USA now a time of happiness and joy, gladness, and honor.

Esther 8:16

[שָׁלֵם] vb. denom. be in the covenant of peace —[xxx]

In the *Covenant of Peace,* we are "being" at peace. We are "making peace." We are "causing peace." We are "living in peace.". *In Christ Jesus, the New Living Covenant as the Lord and Savior, we are delivered. When we humble ourselves and seek him with all our heart and soul, we have peace in our soul even in trials. Of course, there are some aspects that all do not* agree with or even disagreements; we are Americans, and we can forgive and make the *Covenant of Peace* live in truth. Yet, it takes faith, and love can overcome all things.

What is proven is that -causes peace, and what is **justice in the foundation of forgiveness** to keep the peace in a rapidly changing world that moves at the speed of light? When we forgive, we have peace with each other; then, we even work toward what is proven to bring justice in unity, and then we have peace.

WE ARE A PEOPLE OF PEACE AND FORGIVENESS AND LOVE AMERICA. We Americans can deliver the pace, bringing *Covenantal Peace*. We Americans can provide **what is proven** and justice in the foundation of forgiveness because we have the "Authority in God" when we seek righteousness. Bishop Jakes reflects this in God's wisdom. We, humanity, no matter religion, need to be in the love of God.

Human beings are psychosomatic unities, simultaneously spiritual and material beings, and thus they live in space and time. Moreover, they are not isolated individuals, but social beings born, grow, and become themselves in mutual interdependence and interaction. In other words, human beings live in history and are affected and evolve by historical events speaking to the whole person, rather than to his soul alone.[xxxi]

I will never forget a man of great justice; you could see in his bright eyes and almost too brilliant that you can see things beyond the unexplainable and an attorney in Italy. He has a deep seriousness and brilliance, yet he has deep compassion. Hence, he would be aware of what people need. I happened to be sitting next to him at the time. He asked me, "Lucia, what do you think is needed to help the people, to be able to exist."

First, I did say, of course, "first to love God and then your neighbor." We were talking in a social, political, humanistic way, of what is needed. I said, "Jobs, jobs, that is what they need." He said, "correct." My Italian friend's English favorite phrase is "do you agree, do you agree." I love it when he says that we will work on life toward the goal and the mission because we have an agreement that is known together. He is also present and believes in having a plan and then carrying it through to discourage litigation.

Discourage litigation. Persuade your neighbors to compromise whenever you can. As a peacemaker, the lawyer has a superior opportunity of being a good man. There will still be business enough.

Abraham Lincoln

Please, the USA government does not waste the tax dollars on not agreeing on a bill to protect the people during this time of crisis or other times. For example, when we are peacemakers, we can bring life redeemed and get a door finding the best, so all things shall be more beautiful and more living and just. In some cases, we know some individuals have more tools to win an issue than others, whether they are guilty or not. First, being peacemakers in all of life brings an agreement even when there are different views, there can be a flowing river meeting of one flow. When each side takes the truth of what they have to offer, there is a hope to bring peace and compassion to life. We need to ask whether it brings wellbeing for humanity and the environment, peace, justice, restoration, and forward building of understanding.

Most importantly, the First Commandment to Love God is the great peace offering giving oneself to peace for the offer of what God chooses and then accepting the delivery to provide for God's glory. "The deeply religious, peaceful Muslims, (Buddhist, Hindus, etc.) may be a providential warning and a powerful witness in God's hands for contemporary Christians who have forgotten the majesty of God. Only a genuine rediscovery of God's infinite greatness, power, and holiness can bring us to appreciate his infinite humility in becoming one of us in Jesus Christ." [xxxii] To have peace in America, we have to offer our first fruits, our gifts, our life we sow, to bring it to God's purpose and heart. Offer in a way that God chooses working first for God, and then He will deliver it. Our gifts cannot be maimed or distorted or made in the hands of men's desires. Then the blessings of humanity become the distortions of men's ideas. In the love of God, first, our gifts flourish and live to the highest.

> **RECONCILE ...** *Turn away from youth's passions concentrate on uprightness, faith, love, and peace, in union with all those who call on the Lord with a pure heart.*

2 Tim. 2:22

διαλλάσσομαι (aor. impv. διαλλάγηθι) *be reconciled to, make **peace** with* **εἰρήνη, ης** f ***peace**, harmony;* often used in invocations and greetings; *order* (opposite *disorder*) **εἰρηνικός, ή, όν** *peaceful; peace-loving.*

Reconciliation takes restitution *and compassion, opening many windows and even main doors so that truth can walk through giving to life.* **εἰρηνοποιέω** *make **peace*** **εἰρηνοποιός, οῦ** m *peacemaker.* Reconciliation for some will be a definition of giving something to someone that perhaps that they may might not even know; yet, they are God's offering of a peacemaker. **ἱκανός, ή, όν** *worthy, fit; sufficient, able* (ἱκανόν ἐστιν *it is enough!* (Lk 22:38); τὸ ἱ. ποιῶ *satisfy* (Mk 15:15); τὸ ἱ. *security, **peace** bond* Ac 17:9); *large, great, much,* pl. *Many* or *some* (ἐν λόγοις ἱ. *at some length* (Lk 23:9); ἀπὸ ἱ. ἐτῶν *for many years* Ro 15:23); *long, considerable* (ἐφ' ἱ. *for a long while* Ac 20:11) UBS Lexicon. Peace is to give willingly without force abuse and there is an exchange of life, whether, honor, friendship, identification, material, spiritual, compensation, restitution, reconciliation, restoration, offering, and agreement to submit to peace and be salvation for peace. The credence of the peace that can restore justice and forward building love will bring truth for each individual's wellbeing.

Peace is to pour God's love upon the people
Peace is to sow
Peace is to reconcile

For many, it is an innate desire to have everyday work and life to seek justice and truth. If you notice when someone is not following the truth, they eventually have to deal with the Divine Nature of life. Though remember seeking Divine Nature in the world there are dangers, and that makes the seeker a target for mistakes, yet God redeems. Therefore, we, as people, reach into our heart to God to protect. We also need to understand that it is evil in the world. We need to teach our children the righteousness of God and tell them there is wrong and always turn away from evil.

The Imitation of Christ Thomas à Kempis notes:

1. Voice of Christ Jesus in God
   Peace and True Liberty- do the will of God serve others.
2. Serve others as a disciple of Christ
3. Prayer for those you know that have deep sadness or discord or hatred for all sorts of reasons, politically, the hierarchical economic delusion of human worth, gossip of untruth, the judgment of misunderstanding, and even false defamation. Did you ask the question? If America has become 3 -5 in production though now reaching back up. How did America get there?
4. Since the USA birth in 1776 under President George Washington, countless have benefited from those that have worked the legacy of America, need to respect America; and various monetary benefits were also monopolized in multiple ways at all different levels.
5. Sometimes, there needs to be mercy for what has happened in people's lives; the people are being controlled by the circumstances of human tragedy or injustices.

"A just man [should] never seek his advantage in another man's disadvantage."

Pope Ambrose

Remember, this is just not the powerful taking advantage of the poor. It is the poor also not respecting the given justice and laws. Also, the visibility of truth is paramount for the future life of all nations Actions that have motives other than toward justice will plant inside the soil of the spirit of a country. Most are secretive in regarding a group of "cultural masonry and masonry and even witchcraft." Because I have given much of my life to humble prayer, I have been given a responsibility to speak about this subject, "politically incorrect," in a warning. Since I have been working on this book, many have tried to change the document. If there are mistakes, please understand.

When people are aware and realize what has happened to a community or a state or a nation, they need to ponder the prerequisite of the present history and follow the changes. However, when one forgives and brings to light what has happened, injustice, upon a nation, or in general not protecting the people, and only focusing on the economic power for the very few, and masonry practices of destroying the human individual, God's Divine Nature shall eventually bring justice and life flowing as a fresh continuous clean river. Human choices of life are poured upon the trials of life's treacherous terrain that cannot be stopped; only in the power and presence of God's ability to heal the people and the land can they be stopped.

If My people who bear my name humble themselves, and pray and seek my presence and turn from their wicked ways, then I will listen from heaven and forgive their sins and restore their country. 15 Now and for the future, my eyes are open and my ears attentive to the prayer offered in this place, 16, for now, I have chosen and consecrated this Temple, for my name to be there forever; my eyes and my heart will constantly be there 17And if, for your part, you walk before me as your Father David did, and do everything that I have commanded you to do, and keep my laws and my ordinances.

2 Chronicle 7:14--18

Many, the American people, had realized that we had to make a change when they voted in President Trump and the Team of Freedom Warriors for the American legacy. Again, in 2020 we are command by a Divine Command to vote in President Trump. Finally, many Americans have addressed the emergencies to save our land, our legacy, our people, and our future of America's life.

"In the field of epistemology, however, and in philosophy generally, the subjective experience offers an indisputable superiority over the objective. In the first place, because of subjective experiences, the awareness I have of myself is an intimate experience of my conscious activities grasped as they are products of self, their driving principle. In the second place, because the object of this activity in part transcends matter and shows me a way of existing superior to the world of bodies. Therefore, the subjective experiences have taken me further, in certain respects, than objective experience, the more complex, the more wearisome."[lxxxiii]

Consequently, we have to live in the greatest truth, and that is in God and His precepts, the Ten Commandments. Although they remember, God has made humans have the freedom to think and pursue peace and love first.

If My people who bear My name humble themselves, and pray and seek my presence and turn from their wicked ways, I will listen from heaven and forgive their sins and restore their country.

2 Chronicle 7:14

You can the documented success that has been accomplished to save and restore America to have free land and free people. Please, President Trump's victories AND PEACE WILL FLOW IN EACH PART OF THE LAND AND HEARTS OF EACH AMERICAN.

Forgiveness and love will bring peace, then bring justice. We need continuously have forgiveness yet the wisdom of God's truth to bring healing to America. There have been severe injuries to America. Let us be true!

    a.   *Forgiveness occurs when one realizes there has been "not peace, not justice, not the truth, not healing, not love."*

    b.   *When one forgives and works toward justice, healing, forward building in love toward humanity, there is peace.*

America forgives now: now peace, now justice, now the truth, healing, love. Now is the patience of patience in God's time; that is, God's love is patient with us.

Love is patient; love is kind. It does not envy; it does not boast; it is not proud. It is not rude; it is not self-king, it is not easily angered; it keeps no record of wrongs. Love does not delight in evil but rejoices with the truth. It always protects, always trusts, ever hope, always perseveres.

1Cor. 13:4

Message to heal, Message of Love, April 18, 2017

a. We cannot divide America, we need to heal, and we need to grow stronger in love for America to be alive for our children, our legacy!
b. We need to recognize our division and heal and forgive and love and treat others with love and equality.
c. There are injustices in our cities and the disrespect of peoples. There are many evils, and we need to speak up and pray:

As a Catholic: I only know the God of Abraham, I only know Jesus Christ, I only know the Holy Spirit, and I only know Queen Mother Mary, and I only know the Saints. Yes, there is only one God for all humanity.

"The very existence of a believing Jewish remnant confirms our Christian faith in God's fidelity and our hope in the eschatological fulfillment of Salvation History. We are gradually discovering what it means that we Gentile Christians are like wild branches grafted into the cultivated olive tree, historical Israel. "We do not support the root (the sacred beginning of Israel), but the root supports us." Unless we share in the rich sap of the root, we will wither away (Rm 11:11-24)."[lxxxiv]

America, Mother of all Nations,

Though we America love all peoples of all nations, *"America the Mother of all Nations,"* and all beliefs, they are my brothers and sisters. Though we love all peoples and respect and love each one; They are in the creation of God's purpose to treat others with love. America, God, is your goodness: Though even in our humanness, we seek to Love God first, with all our being, and love our neighbor as ourselves. Our neighbors are all peoples from all nations and all beliefs.

The Lord allowed me to present the information this way in two meetings **to pause and seek to be aware of the division and forgive each other.** ***When you pray, ask where do we need to forgive?*** We have the information to recollect and encourage us to come together and love one another, no matter what religion and or belief system are what we have done or what injustices have been against us. We can forgive in God's love, and then we will have peace. *Forgiveness is an urgent moment by moment, endeavor toward fulfilling peace, justice, healing, and forward building of love toward humanity. Forgiveness is essential. Though, truth is vital. The position is also merited to understand and achieve proven directions of accomplishments; some workers have guided the powerful and leaders because they have the answers to God's truth. Just because someone has had made money and has a rhetorical plan does not mean they can run a country, especially the United States of America is God's land. He has specific intentions for the land and her people; the United States is responsible in the covenant to reflect the truth of what God's will is.*

PRESIDENT TRUMP HAS ANOTHER HISTORICAL BREAKTHROUGH TODAY; OUR TWO GREAT FRIENDS ISRAEL AND THE KINGDOM BAHRAIN, AGREE TO A PEACE DEAL, *the second Arab country to make peace with Israel in 30 days.*

a. God has no favorites, and He loves all His human creatures and creation. However, each has a place and a mission that He gives. And one should not abuse the other because God has provided individual gifts to certain people. All donations, talents of each person need to be appropriately used for God. Otherwise, God will strike eventually. He is asking for each human to come to His heart and to love our neighbor as ourselves. God is asking us to help heal each other in love.
b. The Spirit the Lord tells us there is more than a division of religious belief; there is a division on how we treat our neighbor, rich and poor, powerful and weak, black or white, or yellow. We need to love each other equally and give each other love. God is asking us to love one another, **now to make peace.**
c. **DIVINE MESSAGE November 25, 2020: The LEFT IS FRADULENT AND MADE CONSPIRACY AGAINST THE AMERICAN PEOPLE, THE**

VOTERS, AND PRESIDENT TRUMP.
d. PRESIDENT TRUMP WON THE 2020 ELECTION
e. GOD WILL STRIKE IF WE DO NOT BRING JUSTICE TO THE AMERICAN PEOPLE AND
ACCEPT THAT PRESIDENT TRUMP WON 2020.
f. He is asking us to come to Him in our way that we feel comfortable toward righteousness; then He will guide us toward unto all truth to become to know Him, and receive His love, and ask God.
g. ASK: 'What is Your desire of me, God?' Learn from Him, love like Him, God, He loves you.
h. He tells us all of us we need to turn back and give our love to each other. *America is the Mother of all Nations* that has been shown to us by God for our home. He is a King of love. YET, HE IS A KING OF VINDICATION! He, the Lord God, loves all His created humanity and creation. **Did you ever contemplate and realize, awake, arise to the truth, that God gave America to those who needed a home all over the world? Do you think God will give up His America for the Democratic Socialistic, Communistic, the direction in power against the people's freedom?**

President Reagan tells us: *'Extreme taxation, excessive controls, oppressive government competition with business, frustrated minorities and forgotten American [middle class] are not the products of free enterprise. They are the residue of centralized bureaucracy, of government by a self-anointed elite.'*

Speech, "The New Republican Party," Fourth annual CPAC, Washington D.C. February 6, Inaugural address, Washington, D.C. January 20, 1981

These virtues that America is built on **PEACE OFFERINGS** *He is the sacrifice to expiate our sins, not only ours, but also those of the whole world.*

1 John 2:2

CHRIST OFFERED HIMSELF TO HIS FATHER FOR OUR SINS
Christ's whole life is an offering to the Father

The Son of God, who came down "from heaven, not to do [his] own will, but the will of him who sent [him]," [413] said on coming into the world, "Lo, I have come to do your will, O God." "And by that will we have been sanctified through the offering of the body of Jesus Christ once for all." From the first moment of His Incarnation, the Son embraces the Father's plan of divine salvation in his redemptive mission: "My food is to do the will of Him who sent me and to accomplish his work." [415] The sacrifice of Jesus "for the sins of the whole world" [416] expresses His loving communion with the Father. "The Father loves me because I lay down my life," said the Lord, "[for] I do as the Father has commanded me, so that the world may know that I love the Father."[xxxv]

But Jesus said: My food is to do the will of the One who sent Me and completes His work.

John 4:34

     Our country American has the most remarkable leadership under President Trump "does the will of God" is the first President that has taken the big dipper of bravery and the most incredible justice of the zenith of the stars. To restore our country, the UNITED STATES OF AMERICA UNDER GOD, it, in a sense, shocked the Socialist and Communist and even some the Democrats. They felt like they lost their power. (Is this why the Democrats are trying to get Trump out of office? And they are also treacherously conspiring against American Freedom Warrior, the severe protestors of Black life Matter?) In a globalized world and receiving America with a multiplicity of complexities and badly need restoration, President Trump has served the people and has made America safe, flourishing in the most outstanding economy and most excellent working to restore the USA. Even when the facts and patterns of the mainstream media and Democrats go against President Trump, he and the Americans are brave. He continues to serve and protect the Americans first and most faithful wisdom to bring America to restoration and safety.

For the Son of the man himself came not to be served but to serve.

Mark 10:45

     We as Americans need to serve in truth and justice to put **America First.** We Americans need to continue to take up the right arm of strength in God that has been given to us in the leadership of President Trump and the American Freedom Warriors.

**Let us work in peaceful joy of and for justice and speak in truth.
In the Eucharistic gift of God, we have Peace; Yet, I would have to say we become brave and talk about the fact when there is abuse:
Eucharistic, thanksgiving offerings, expressive of gratitude for blessings received**

a. God's Eucharistic peace is in those who receive the eternal miracle of Jesus Christ's from heaven on earth; and even in trials, God brings redemption and mercy and healing and justice forward into life in His Eucharistic body, taking on the sin of the believer and nonbeliever.
b. Peace is due to life itself. Peace is the intention that is without saying present in God. God wants His humanity and all creation to be at peace. When life is not at God's peace, there will be a battle to bring peace; God never gives up on His promises; He does accommodate; yet, He has timing that He will strike if life is not at peace, the Father is the sovereign God. I have already received multitudinous blessings to be in America and live in a country that allows all to have new life in justice toward peace.

God, I Alpha and Omega, He states the first direction, and He says the last order in all life processes.

a. The "Sacred power" of God's people that God bestows on to the people who receive will bring God's peace and what is Most Highest for God. When we are in Jesus Christ's intimate relationship with Him, we have many enlightenments for His life existing living Spirit in and through and with us.

Blameless: "The Eucharistic offering and accepting it and receiving it is accepting that Jesus Christ is the redeemer of all human sin. He took up the cross for all human sin. He has made man blameless when they repent and seek forgiveness, and seek to live in righteousness. In His love, the King of peace gives us the essence of true peacemaking of forgiveness; and the act of sin that is done upon the man has to be redeemed. It can only truly be saved by a perfect offering and only redeemed by God; when there is sin, there is a change in the original intention of the substance and being of the creation; hence, it can truly and fully only be redeemed by the Creator, God who knows how it was created and what needs to be saved.

God can only look into the human heart thoroughly and beyond; God can only make the soul, and God is the only one with a life of the soul. When peace is not present, through God's redeeming Son Jesus Christ, He makes humanity blameless."[xxxvi] If a person does not believe in the Savior, that seek righteousness God still loves righteousness.

In virtues, present in the Holy Scriptures, and are permeated in us from the Holy Spirit when we seek God, we find peace. Virtues are the roots of the Tree of Peace. Virtues are the ethereal tapestry of the eternal God on earth as it is in heaven. Virtues are the food of the spiritual cell of the human. We need an intimate Eucharistic relationship so that we can overcome the worldly life. The Holy Spirit is present at the Eucharist meal. The Trinity is at the Eucharistic meal. Since the Trinity was present at the creation, so is the Trinity present at the Eucharist.

VIRTUE[xxxvii]

- (From the Latin "vir," manliness)
- Power (R. V.) (Luke 6:19; 8:46)
- Excellence (Philippians 4:8; 2 Peter 1:5)
- CHASTITY
- CONTINENCE (self-control)

COURAGE

In fulfillment of a vow, but expressive also of thanks for benefits received; Deuteronomy 5:9- You shall not bow down to them or worship them; for I, the LORD your God, am a jealous God, punishing the children for the sin of the fathers to the third and fourth generation of those who hate me, **free-will offerings, something spontaneously devoted to God.**
Thus the LXX can identify the *basileia* with the four cardinal virtues (4 Macc. 2:23), and in Wis. 6:20, we read, "The desire for wisdom leads to a kingdom of God."[xxxviii]

Catechism-E (Title) PART THREE: LIFE IN CHRIST "Christian, recognize your dignity and, now that you share in God's own nature, do not return to your former base condition by sinning. Remember who is your head and of whose body you are a member. Never forget that you have been rescued from the power of darkness and brought into the light of the Kingdom of God."[xxxix]

שָׁלַם shalam, *shaw-lam´;* a primitive root; to be safe (in mind, body or estate); figuratively, to be (causatively, make) completed; by implication, to be friendly; by extension, to reciprocate (in various applications):—make amends, (make an) end, finish, full, give again, make good, (re-)pay (also), (make) (to) (be at) peace(-able), that is perfect, perform, (make) prosper(-ous), recompense, render, requite, make restitution, restore, reward, indeed.

Political Psalms 21: The first part of this royal psalm is a thanksgiving (2-8), and the second is a promise that the king will triumph over his enemies (9-14). The king's confident prayer (3. 5) and trust in God (8) enable him to receive the divine gifts of vitality, peace, and military success. V 14 reprises 1. When kings ceased in Israel after the sixth century B.C., the Psalmist sang of a future Davidic king.

Let us sing and worship the Lord God.

Yahweh, the **(Leaders) rejoices in your power;** How your **saving help fills him with joy! You have granted him his heart's desire**, not denied him the prayer of his lips. For you, **come to meet him with blessings of prosperity,** put **a crown of pure gold** on **his head. (of righteousness, yet humbleness to God.)** He has **asked for life; you have given it to him**, length of days forever and ever. Great his glory through your saving help; you invest him with splendor and majesty. You **confer on him everlasting blessings; you gladden him with the joy of your presence. For the Lord, thy Savior Jesus Christ and Queen Virgin Mary put their trust in Yahweh, the faithful love of the Highest will keep all from falling.**

Your **hand will reach all your enemies, your right hand, all who hate you.** You will hurl them into a blazing furnace on the day when you appear; Yahweh will engulf them in His anger, and fire will devour them. You will purge the earth of their descendants, the human race of their posterity. They have **devised evil against you but, the plot as they may, they will not succeed** since you will make them turn tail by shooting your arrows in their face. **Rise, Yahweh, in your power! We will sing and make music in honor** of your strength. <u>God has many great gifts for those who love Him, gifts of eternal treasures.</u> [xl]

Individual Presence Salvation:

I shall make a covenant of peace with them, an eternal covenant with them. I shall resettle them and make them grow; I shall set my sanctuary among them for ever. ²⁷ I shall make my home above them; I shall be their God, and they will be my people. ²⁸ And the nations will know that I am Yahweh the sanctifier of Israel, when my sanctuary is with them for ever."'

Ezek. 37:26

When I thought of nothing but to end my days in these troubles (which did not at all diminish the trust I had in GOD, and which served only to increase my faith), I found myself changed all at once; and my soul, which till that time was in trouble, felt a profound inward peace as if she were in her center and place of rest.[xli]

Serving God with confidence in Him (25f) requires helping one's neighbor through kindness (27f), peace with the good (29ff), no envy of the wicked (31) because the Lord's friendship and heart are with the just; His curse is with the wicked. Proverbs 3:25-34

Sometimes the wickedness becomes thick and abusive that one has to speak the truth and reveal to protect others and themselves. Otherwise, the child or innocent and tender can be their next victim. I sing and proclaim aloud in concern and love for my neighbor.

If you love genuinely, you speak and believe in reconciliation. You do not allow the abuse and injustices to be accepted.

The Twenty-Fifth Chapter: Continued notes from the Catholic Catechism.

THE BASIS OF FIRM PEACE OF HEART AND TRUE PROGRESS
THE VOICE OF CHRIST

MY CHILD, I have said: *"Peace I leave with you, My peace I give unto you: not as the world giveth, do I give unto you."*

John 14:27

All men desire peace, but all do not care for the things that go to make trustworthy peace. My peace is with the humble and meek of heart: your peace will be in much patience. If you hear Me and follow My voice, you will be able to enjoy much peace. I have to proclaim in my neighborhood, I have professed the unrest of abuse and even trickery and need to protect our nation and our children.

Peace: the Hebrew word includes the idea of "prosperity, happiness. And Jehovah spake unto Moses, saying, Speak unto Aaron and unto his sons, saying, On this wise ye shall bless the children of Israel: ye shall say unto them. **Nation Numbers 6:26**

Num. 6:24 *Jehovah bless thee, and keep thee:*

Num. 6:25 *Jehovah make His face to shine upon thee, and be gracious unto thee:*

Num. 6:26 *Jehovah lift His countenance upon thee and give thee peace.*

Today in America, many have arisen and realized God's Truth to bring restoration and freedom keeping in our blessings in God. Integrated into the solution toward peace for each person is evident and can be a catalyst to manifest in truth; we have always been a multicultural and incredibly diverse culture we can force through in the power of truth. Arise to God's truth that is what most of our families came to America for, was for freedom. God allowed the passageway for all new people to migrate to the USA. God will allow the USA's protection, freedom, and life for the people and the land when we wholeheartedly seek God's truth and love God with all our heart and soul and love our neighbor to work and live for peace and liberty. However, God is a merciful God.

The truth shall not be suppressed; The truth of God shall be revealed. Of course, this connivance of God, this the holding of His peace; St. Paul has himself just before declared that the wrath of God was revealed from heaven against the unrighteousness of humanity. Romans 1:18-32

BOOK ONE: THOUGHTS HELPFUL IN THE LIFE OF THE SOUL The Eleventh Chapter:
ACQUIRING PEACE AND ZEAL FOR PERFECTION

If you consider what peace a good life will bring to yourself and what joy it will give to others, I think you will be more concerned about your spiritual progress.[xlii]

"But I say to you, Love your enemies and pray for those who persecute you, so that you may be sons of your Father who is in heaven." Luke 6:27-36

The greatest love is to love others even when there are differences. I pray for all of us.

Common unity

The next day, when he came across some of them fighting, he tried to reconcile them and said, "Friends, you are brothers; why are you hurting each other? But the man who was attacking his kinsman pushed him aside, saying, "And who appointed you to be prince over judge and us?

Acts 7:28-27

GOODNESS AND PEACE IN MAN

FIRST, for me, keep peace with myself in God; then, you will bring peace to others. We know maintaining stability is one of the most extraordinary characteristics a human can have, especially today in the world. The strength of the Lord God in the power of the Holy Spirit is the most incredible living peace, even when trials come deep in your way. You know the hands of the Lord God hold you.

ON THE PEOPLE OF GOD

Finally, Christian spouses, in **virtue** of the sacrament of Matrimony, whereby they signify and partake of the mystery of that unity and fruitful love which exists between Christ and His Church, help each other to attain holiness in their married life and the rearing and education of their children While faithfully adhering to the Gospel and fulfilling her mission to the world, the Church, whose duty is to foster and elevate all that is found to be right, good, and beautiful in the human community, strengthens peace among men for the glory of God.[xliii] Many profess to be for peace who will do nothing towards it: not so Abram. When God condescends for us to be reconciled, we prayerfully will be reconciled to one another. Though God had promised Abram to give this land to his descendants, he offered an equal or better share to Lot, who had not an equal right; and he will not, under the protection of God's promise, act hardly to his kinsman. It is noble to be willing to yield for peace's sake. The first and the best evidence of the pardon of sin, and peace with God, is the writing of the law in the heart.[xliv]

Peace with God makes men thunder-proof. Pharaoh was frightened by the tremendous judgment, but his fair promises were forgotten when that was over.

God has told us He watches over us. He watches with His eyes and will teach us the thing we need to know. He also tells us He will not give us more than we can handle. Even God sends Angels to help us.

Angels "Summa Theologica (Content) 277

Objection 1: Angels grieve for the ills of those whom they guard. For it is written (Is. 33:7): "The angels of peace shall weep bitterly." But weeping is a sign of grief and sorrow. Therefore, angels grieve for the ills of those whom they guard."[xlv] God's Angels are sent to guard; hence, they know some of the past, present, and future that God allows. They are sent here to guide, warn, teach, and even bring miracles from heaven to earth that is God's truth that brings peace. The peace is for God indeed first because when His creation is in danger, death, and betrayal, He, God, is tears pour from His heart. God is a God of love. I cry out and feel Angel's sorrows and the Trinity. When I enter into new places and even places, business to business, where I go from home to home; I weep; I think it is from the people and their sorrow that they carry and have not been soothed and not been healed and have not sometimes forgiven others or have forgiven themselves. Lingering in the memory of their heart, they are tender as a flower petal or a child. Only a specific few may only realize some of their sufferings, not knowing all the specifics just that they have carried much weight of human suffering upon their life. Also, there needs to be healing for the other side, yes, healing: First, if they need to stop any actions that they put upon the person because of their pain or brutality. Second, they need to seek God in meditation and their Priest or minister to heal and forgive. Of course, these are not a full direction on healing sorrow though it is a start. When we fulfill or need to be soothed, we ask God in His love to heal us. You know the tree and the flowers, and the soil is waiting to be taken care of and cultivated and trust life. Subsequently, we also need to trust God. I write this because the more I seek God, the more I realize I need Him and have to be patient. Patience, however, is waiting in peace, an active working peace, movement toward His truth. These are simple elementary words, yet the most difficult to live by.

I cry out for immigrants and human trafficking and the little children, lost, abused, abandoned, and I have felt deep sorrow for them. I cry out for the protection of our freedom of America and countless other human conditions. "According to the allegorical sense, the "angels of peace" are the apostles and preachers who weep for men's sins." Enemies will be at peace with those who please the Lord. Oh Lord, I seek to please You. We have delighted the Lord we believe and follow Your precepts.

Yours is a strong arm, mighty Your hand; Your right hand raised high; Saving Justice and Fair Judgement the foundations of Your throne, Faithful Love and Constancy march before You.

Psa. 89:13-15

"Prince of Peace, but He also makes it a promise that justice and righteousness will accompany His might. Consequently, as it points out the authentic and noble meaning of peace and condemns the frightfulness of war, the Council wishes passionately to summon Christians to cooperate, under the help of Christ the author of peace, with all men in securing among themselves a peace based on justice and love and in setting up the instruments of peace. . . Since peace must be born of mutual trust between nations and not be imposed on them through fear of the available weapons, everyone must labor to put an end at last to the arms race, and to make a true beginning of disarmament, not unilaterally indeed, but proceeding at an equal pace according to the agreement, and backed up by true and workable safeguards."[xlvi] Consequently, as it points out the authentic and noble meaning of peace and condemns the frightfulness of war, the Council wishes passionately to summon Christians to cooperate, under the help of Christ the author of peace, with all men in securing among themselves a peace based on justice and love and in setting up the instruments of peace.[xlvii]

Person of Peace

I will never forget my father and Mother, who are leaders of their family. They have taken a generation of a business from one year to the next and has developed the AMERICAN DREAM! My father, I remember, I was fearfully respectful of him, likened to the definition in Hebrew fear is respect. He always made me feel peaceful yet confident in loved when times were in chaos or seemingly hopeless. We have 16 siblings! Within my heart, I had(have) a quietness with the beauty of shimmering light that I felt when both my mother and father were at their best. Especially during the Christmas holidays, our house would Spiritually illuminate with intricate beauties. Recollecting clear in my heart's yearning eyes that I saw in my parents to continue to live the truth, I saw the alluring red Christmas bulbs reflecting the joyous time of love and gifts of the Messiah Jesus Christ's birth! My parents made handmade Christmas celebrations to a velveteen green Christmas tree stitched with God's colors of lovely heavenly blue, miracle green, royal gold, and infinite silver- platinum from various nations together embroidery sewn by my Mother's hands. My father built another Christmas tree of different larger shelves of reddish, orange, painted flowers upon the perfect wooden tree and bringing to each frame the life of truth, the nativity and fruit and holly of "blooming blessing from the American Land and Holy Land of God." And then the Christmas Tree from our beauty of our American mountaineer's fragrance of the living freshest pine trees, danced in the light of ethereal blue and holy white Christmas, never been forsaken light of God's birth of His Son, Jesus. The Christmas bulbs were heavenly blue, and from one bulb to the next, they carried the light of the Holy Spirit within our home and glistened and lived in the hearts of our family and my parents, Frank and Vera. I know I mentioned Christmas, and some may not understand. It is just that it is my living experience and living toward the truth of God with me and in me and through me. I am saying I could only exist with God, physically, spiritually, mentally, and aspects of life. Though I believe we evolve, we need a continuous intimate spiritual relationship, especially in these times. Just as the eco-systems need to be redeemed from the human conditions upon them, humanity needs to be saved by the human's abuse and injustices upon each other.

Divine Message in Pasadena California 2020

There is a natural carved tree of Joseph holding baby Jesus, in Pasadena California. It is amazing! Here is a mysterious message from God. There is no bottom part of the legs from the knees down. This may symbolize that we believe to follow the footsteps of Jesus Christ.

The Word is the light unto our path. The arms are branches and vines. God is the vine. We are the branches. *John 15:4 Remain in me, as I in you. As a branch cannot bear fruit all by itself, unless it remains part of the **vine**, neither can you unless you remain in Me. I am the **vine**, you are the branches. Whoever remains in Me, with Me in him, bears fruit in plenty; for cut off from me you can do nothing.* **Yes, God is with us.** *For a son has been born for us, a son has been given to us, and dominion has been laid on His shoulders, and this is the name He has been provided, 'Wonder-Counsellor, Mighty-God, Eternal-Father, Prince-of-Peace'-to extend His dominion in eternal peace, over the throne of David and over His kingdom to make it secure and sustain it in fair judgment and integrity. From this time onwards and for ever, the jealous love of Yahweh Sabaoth will do this.* [xlviii]

Isaiah 9:5-6

Divine Message Pasadena, California October 14, 2020

Queen Virgin Mary also told me to look up the center of a tree what it means.

In other Divine Messages, Mary told me before the tree's trunk symbolizes the exchange of the heavenly and the world. "The trunk consists of five main parts: **the bark, inner bark, cambium, sapwood, and heartwood.**[2] From the outside of the tree working in, **1. the first layer is the bark**; this is the **trunk's protective outermost layer.** Under this is the **2. inner bark** which is made of **the phloem. The phloem is how the tree transports nutrients from the roots to the shoots and vice versa.** The next layer is **3. the cambium, a very thin layer** of **undifferentiated cells that divide to replenish the phloem cells** on the outside and the **xylem cells to the inside.** The **cambium contains the growth meristem of the**

trunk. [3] Directly to the inside of this is **4. the sapwood** or the living xylem cells. These **cells transport the water through the tree. The xylem also stores starch inside the tree**. Finally, at the center of the tree is **5. the heartwood**. The **heartwood** is made up of old xylem cells(Holy Spirit, in with and through the Trunk) that **have been filled with resins and minerals that keep other organisms from growing and infecting the center of the tree."** [xlix]

1. **The bark:** this is the protective outermost layer of the trunk.
2. **The Inner bark:** tree transports nutrients from the roots to the shoots
3. **The cambium**: replenish the cell's inner bark on the outside and the cells to the inside the sap.
4. **The sapwood:** cells transport the water through the tree. The xylem also stores starch inside the tree. Finally
5. **The heartwood:** has been filled with resins and minerals that keep other organisms from growing and infecting the tree's center.[l]

Protection, ---→ transport nutrients -----→ replenish -----→, transport water through the tree stores starch ----→ filled resins and minerals keep other organisms growing and infecting the center of the tree.

God and Humanity the Center of the Tree

We need to protect humanity and God's creation in God's omniscient love in the mystery of the Holy Spirit, bringing nutrients in the Salvation of Jesus Christ and the reflection of God's Holy Scripture; The precepts of protection are nutrients, getting replenishment in God through the Trinity in the Holy Spirit transporting. The Eucharistic life of living waters intimate relationship with God and growing in the love and truth to protect His humanity is the center of our Tree in God.

God and the Country is the center of the tree of American life. Expressions of the center of the Tree of Life of America in God.

1. Protection and safety of a human and the wellbeing of a human is
   Protected by God's center first purpose His love His Sacred Heart.

2. Feeding life and having nutrients for life to exist of the livelihood and jobs and doing them so all the country can benefit is essential for the Tree of life the country. When the pros and cons are listed and contemplative justly and compared in truth, incorrect information about the feeding of life will be known.
3. The continued life of empowerment to bring jobs and protection, and life needs to be given now, for future, and in the distant future healthiness of America and humanity.
4. Delivering into the people not holding back empowering in a balanced way for existence and storing strength in a country will bring the healthiest Tree of Life.
5. The continuous growth of the country by putting America first, using the prayerful direction in God's precepts, protection, for the people, in the land, in the business, in the jobs, in the days of life, is the Tree of Life of God on earth.

Father, Jesus Christ, Your Great Tree of Life, Poem

Father, God, Your tree of life is a home that stands firm in love that we can always go to. Father, God, the trunk of Your tree upholds us in strength and stability
Father, God, the great branches of Your tree guard us and give us shade to grow.
Father, Your tree roots are planted in God's soil, given us all we need to succeed.
Father, the fruits of Your tree feed us with the empowerment of wisdom to love in truth.

Father, Your tree of life, gives us all we need to be who we are, a significant branch from you.
Your are the greatest Father.
Lucia

And live to Your children's children! Psa. 128:6
God is Alpha and Omega, He has no end.

Peace to Israel, peace to the world, peace to America.
Though we have to admit most enjoy Christmas.

Love in gifts
Love in relationship
Love in Family
Love in Business

These Christmas Holidays that America has is built on just as the Jewish Holidays, the Muslim, the Buddhist Holidays, and all other religions and cultural beliefs, let us enter into a love peace relationship in the spirit of reconciliation.

I have experienced afterlife experiences and present life experiences, and I know God lives. For me, it is in the Trinity in Jesus Christ in the mystery of the Holy Spirit is the Father of Abraham. I have accepted Jesus

We need to keep our freedom and love. We are all God's created human beings.

Let us as Americans continue to bring our freedom of the Spirit of God in our hearts to bring justice and love to our family, friends, and all those around us.

The **Holy Land**. Holy.] *(Bot.)* A species of Althæa (*A. rosea*), **bearing flowers of various colors**; — called also *rose mallow*. (Webster's Dictionary.)

The **Holly-leaved oak** *(Bot.)*, the black scrub oak. Scrub oak.

The **Holly rose** *(Bot.)*, a **West Indian shrub, with showy, yellow flowers** (*Turnera ulmifolia*).

The **Sea holly** *(Bot.)*, a species of Eryngium. Eryngium.

The **Holly** (hŏl'lў), *n.* O.E.E *holi, holin*, AS. *holen, holegn*; akin to D. & G. *hulst*, OHG. *huls hulis*, W. *celyn*, Armor. *kelen*, Gael. *cuilionn*, Ir. *cuileann*. Cf. 1st Holm, Hulver.] **1.** *(Bot.)* A tree **or shrub of the genus *Ilex*. The European species (*Ilex Aquifolium*) is best known, with glossy green leaves, a spiny, waved edge, and berries that turn red or yellow about Michaelmas.** The *holly* **is much used to adorn churches and houses** at **Christmas time**, and hence is associated with scenes of **goodwill and rejoicing.** It is an evergreen tree and has a fine-grained, heavy, white wood. Its bark is used as a febrifuge, and the berries are flourishing purgative and emetic. **The American holly is the *Ilex opaca* and is found along the United States coast, from Maine southward.** *Gray. (Webster' Dictionary)*

   Choose what Holly best inspires you this Christmas and every day to be God's people of peace. There might be different holly and different cultural traditions in America, though we can be a tree of holly next to each other and sharing the beauties of each holly.

God's Love is the Holly of His love giving His Son; the Savior was Born for on the first Christmas
God's goodwill
God's rejoicing
God's evergreen tree
God's fine-grained, wood
God's bark
God's flowers
God's rose mallow
God's fruit of berries

We America let us live in that peace of each
O taste and that the Lord is good;
How blessed is a man who takes up God's love and justice.

I will continue to take up "the golden scepter," that my God has given me the God of Abraham in the Trinity, as He did to Esther.

Esther 8:4

March 12, 2019, St Bede's Church La Canada, California
Divine Message for the people of America

God has a gift for the people this is a gift is that He stated for each to plant a "fruit tree," because" this is a symbolism of the fruit that we now are being blessed with because under the leadership of President Trump and his team; we have had much fruit. We are an instrument to save America, in following the commands that God has ordered President Trump, and the team and the American Freedom lovers; we have brought fruit to our county and states our communities, our people, our children, and each one that believes in the goodness of what it is to be American and respect America and its justice system.

God told us also to put food on our shelves. The shelves should be filled with food, knowing that the fruit will bring harvest and restoration to America because of the justice and work and brilliance and strategic dedication to upholding America. Because of those whom the gifts of justice and righteousness have been worked for wholeheartedly in the government and the people. **America's face should follow God's precepts**

of the Ten Commandments, and the children being held by the parent, the children being guided by the adult by hand. Children could then be sat down and given a book of our great country's history and children being allowed to live, grow, nurturer creative aesthetically and scientific development, and had a vision where I saw the children carrying a small book.

For Religious Schools, The children must have a book that they carry that is biblical prayers and bible verses. This book could be the Bible and used in schools that teach the bible.

Public Schools should have it with them when they go to school, and it is a reference in different classes. If they cannot use biblical prayers, they need to have ethics, and they need to teach the history of our USA.

The phone is a personal item that most kids have today that they use for their daily communication, which does not generally promote ethics precepts.

The truth book they carry has rules and regulations and **ethics with Catholic teachings** and Christian teaching in Religious Schools. Each course should be the cornerstone of each learning. The Ten Commandments should be the precepts. (For the public schools, there is the Judeo-Christian ethics that are universal to most cultures that would bring reconciliation and brotherhood.)

And the Four Foundational Truths, Peace, justice, restoration (reconciliation, restitution), and Forward Building in Love, should be the foundation of these teachings.

There is a foundation for God's precepts in this small, brilliant truth book. Then they should be addressed in each subject matter that can be referred to answering questions of truth since our country and communities have become globalized with different aspects of all nations and all cultures and ideologies. The children do then not know what is correct just for small questions and answers. For public schools, this can support children in realizing a foundation of ethics on treating each other.

There is a division in the country because different belief systems are not in unity. We will continue to find the beauty in each tradition and share it. Although, we know there are hidden peoples and elites that want division. We can overcome this has been going on for years, and they the hidden Socialists and Communist never won.

Also, America's history should be required and discussed, and all the beautiful and extraordinary achievements that our country has achieved. It should be remembered and used to inspire the students regularly each year. Whether it is a Christian Catholic School or a Public School, the people in history should be recognized, understood, and developed on their pure ideas, uplifting them and creating them. Because when they are pure ideas to bring the four foundational truths of peace, justice, restoration, and forward building, the people can be that authentic person God wants them to be. And the land is living freshwater. (Note: again, another Divine Command has been listened to and followed. I wrote this and put it on social media, and the team attended. I believe in the restoration and miracle of our USA and the world in God's purpose.)

Note: To recollect your memory, this writing was written before the installation into America's laws were used for that purpose.

"If a woman makes a vow to the Lord, and binds herself by an obligation .. all her vows shall stand, and every obligation by which she has bound herself shall stand."

Numbers 30:4

I will continue to work toward the freedom of peace.
I will continue to work toward the justice of truth.
I will continue to work toward a life of love.

Joseph answered Pharaoh, saying, "It isn't in me. God will give Pharaoh an answer of peace." Gen. 41:16 We never vindicate or decide God's choice He does, even if He uses us to bring about peace. The "Pharaoh" is that is what are injustices in each life. There cannot be a division. Unity of agreement of basic ethics and well-being is God's life in America. Unity of understanding and peace and respect and love now will only bring peace and life.

Fear of Yahweh in Hebrew means to care. When you respect someone, you will not do anything against them; otherwise, you know there will be contraindications. There cannot be violence or death; it will fill and problematic to the homes, hearts, and communities. For the generation to come and all will have to have retribution. We, even now, there, have to be retribution. [li] Now we will continue to bring America and the world back to freedom and God's love. We, as God's people, never stop loving and loving and loving.

When you offer a sacrifice of **peace** *offerings to Yahweh, you shall offer it so that you may be accepted.*

Lev. 19:5

For He is our God, and we the people of His sheepfold, the flock of His hand.
If only you would listen to Him today!

Psalm 95:7

NEW COVENANT IN JESUS CHRIST

Jesus Christ, His Covenant is the New Covenant through the power of the Cross His life to redeem us through the power of the His Cross forgiving all our sins and giving us a new resurrected life.

So for anyone who is in Christ, there is a new creation: the old order is gone and a new being is there to . It is all God's work; he reconciled us to himself through Christ, and he gave us the ministry of reconciliation[9] I mean, God was in Christ reconciling the world to himself, not holding anyone's faults against them, but entrusting to us the message of reconciliation.

2 Cor. 5:17

There can be neither Jew nor Greek; there can be neither slave nor freeman, there can be neither male nor female—for you are all one in

Christ Jesus. ²⁹ And by merely being Christ's, you are that progeny of Abraham, the heirs named in the promise.

Gal. 3:28

God's love is for all peoples, not just the chosen Jewish people of the God of Abraham. Jesus Christ reconciles the entire humanity through his redeeming Cross as the perfect sacrificial lamb. He resurrected to a new life in heaven so that we may have a unique experience. Christ is our Lord and Savior, and when we bring our sins, fears, trials, and all of life, He resurrects all that is not of God, and redeems us when we humble ourselves.

Waiting in hope for the blessing which will come with the appearing of the glory of our great God and Savior Christ Jesus.

- Titus 2:13

"In [God's] hand is the life of every living thing and the breath of all mankind."

Job 12:10

When we have our lives in God's hand, we live and have the breath that God gave humans. God is a God of peace, justice, restoration, and love. Therefore, we will have a life to the fullest living.

First, we have to make a **peace** offering.
Peace offering
Will bring **justice**
Justice brings **restoration**
Restoration brings forward the building of the **Love** of Humanity.

"And it shall come about if you listen obediently to My commandments which I am commanding you today, "to love the Lord your God and to serve Him with all your heart and all your soul, that I will give the rain for your land in its season, the early and late rain, that you may gather in your grain and your new wine and your oil."

Deut. 11:13-14

As we express our gratitude, we must never forget that the highest appreciation is not to utter words but to live by them.

President John F. Kennedy

All Americans need to live in the gratitude of our America, that has given us land to live, to be, to be protected, to be sustained, to work, to grow, to have happiness and a future for our children. We know it is the most difficult to live by all these commands and messages. I know for myself; I begin to seek to do my best, pray and work in the Trinity, and Arch Angels, God's Angels and Virgin Mary, and pray that God does good work in me. There is a mystery in all of life, the personage of God, that directs the entirety, and when we share experiences in all the senses, it brings life. It may not seem relevant to the making of life, yet it is mandatory. Life in its fullness lives in a mystery because life in its fulness in God's life is in its fullness. And we cannot measure all God's reasons and life plans.

We have to remember this is an urgency to open the eyes of your hearts. God created men and women separately; we are not a collective body without individuality. We are individuals. *We are the body of Christ and members individually.*   *1Cor.12:27*

When an individual cannot be an individual and based and controlled by other individuals, life will decrease. Even the individual who seeks to be in control will reduce because they are cutting off life that they are a part of life. There have been detrimental contraindications on the way individuals seek and plan to work strategically.

George Washington One of the most of 1796 one of the influential Republicans with the help with Hamilton

Advice Necessity of national union, the value of the constitution, government party evils are prohibitive, and the proper virtues for the republican people.

St. Aquinas enlightens us of peace in St. Thomas Summa Theologica:

We must now consider Peace, under which head there are four points of inquiry:
Studying at the Pontifical University Saint Thomas Aquinas Rome, in all the courses has taught me and introduced me to these Wisdom of God, under St. Thomas Aquinas:

(1) Whether peace is the same as a concert (agreement)?

"There can be concord in evil between wicked men. **But "there is no peace to the wicked" (Is. 48:22). There is no peace to the wicked,** between one man and another. The latter alone is opposed to concord. Augustine is speaking there of that peace between one man and another. He says that this peace is concord, not indeed any kind of harmony, but that which is well ordered, through one man agreeing with another regarding something befitting to both of them. For if one-person consensus with another, not of his own accord, but through being forced, as it were, by the fear of some evil that besets him, such concord is not peace, because the order of each concordant is not observed, but is disturbed by some fear-inspiring cause. For this reason, he premises that "peace is the tranquility of order," which tranquility consists of all the appetitive movements in one man being set at rest together.

If one-person consents to the same thing together with another man, his approval is nevertheless not perfectly united to himself, unless at the same time all his appetitive movements are in agreement:".[lii]

> *The desires of self-indulgence are always in opposition to the Spirit. The desires of the Spirit are in opposition to self-indulgence: they are opposites, one against the other.*
>
> Gal. 5:17

Hence, in agreements of peace, we need to be in the same appetite

(2) Whether all things desire peace?

Augustine says (De Civ. Dei xix, 12, 14) that "all things desire peace,": and Dionysius says the same (Div. Nom. xi). Hence it follows of necessity that whoever desires anything desires peace, in so far as he who wants anything, wants to attain, with tranquility and without hindrance, to that which he wants: and this is what is meant by the peace which Augustine defines (De Civ. Dei xix, 13) "the tranquility of order." True peace is only about good things, as the real good is possessed in two ways, perfectly and imperfectly, so there is a two-fold true peace. One is perfect peace. It consists in the perfect enjoyment of the sovereign good and unites all one's desires by giving them rest in one object. Psalm, 147:3: "Who hath placed peace in thy borders." The other is imperfect peace, which may be had in this world, for though the soul's chief movement finds rest in God, there are certain things within, and without which disturb the peace.

Today, the Peace of God wants to flow in the people's lives in their gift God has given them. Peace is life, life is love, and love is living as a created human God has for each person.

Divine Message April 5th, 2019

Jesus Christ said these are the gifts the missions for each person I have given them and have ordained at their birth. These missions are gifts of honor (From God) that are given to My people. These gifts will, and I will direct them, and this will restore America. These gifts are from heaven above. They are In the Light of God; they are being brought down to the earth into the darkness to bring life and sustain life in God in the light of God. [All that is healed and in the morning is good; yet, still needs to be maintained in God's light through His love and power and peace and truth through the people to deliver His purpose then what they do and offer is in His light.] I then saw the sunlight, bright yellow rays magnificent yet powerful full of fullest life yet with a permeation of reflection of great glory to give of itself to renew and redeem and bring life. This light was behind the shelves. God is behind and at all sides us in all we do for and in and with Him. God is at all sides and in front of already what He has made for each individual. The light on the shelves of your life He created is the foundation behind your purpose of who you are. . God is waiting for us all to ask Him:

What is my purpose for Your glory God?

He maintains the peace of your frontiers, gives you your fill of most refined wheat.

Psa. 147:14

Comment: In peace, we have the utmost life because the soul finds life in God. And we know in trials He overcomes all things. **Remember, in peace, there is not trickery, abuse, deceiving, and using the person. We are responsible to bring these things to light; this is an analogy to the voting fraudulence and the masonry.**

(3) Whether peace is an effect of charity?

It is written (Ps. 118:165): "Much peace has they that love Thy Law."

"Peace implies a twofold union, as stated above (Article [1]). The first is the result of one's appetites being directed to one object; while the other results from one's appetite being united with the appetite of another: and each of these unions are affected by the charity—the first, in so far as a man loves God with his whole heart, by referring all things to Him, so that all his desires tend to one object—the second, in so far as we love our neighbor as ourselves, the result being that we wish to fulfill our neighbor's will as though it were ours: hence it is reckoned a sign of friendship if people "make choice of the same things" (Ethic. ix, 4), and Tully says (*De Amicitia*) that friends "like and dislike the same things" (*Sallust, Catilin.*)

Peace is the "work of justice" indirectly, in so far as justice removes the obstacles to peace: but it is the work of charity directly, since charity, according to its very nature, causes peace. For love is "a unitive force," as Dionysius says (Div. Nom. iv): and peace is the union of the appetite's inclinations."

Comment: Perfect yes, without justice, we cannot have peace; The Four Foundational Truths God has given me is Peace, Justice, Restoration (healing, reconciliation, retribution), Forward Building in love (Transformation). Let our appetites be your purpose in your plan to have a mustard d of faith, to bring a miracle. Remember, "appetites," will be different and God gives us the grace to go through the trials of GOD'S victory.

(4) Whether peace is a virtue?

Since then, charity causes peace precisely because it is the love of God and our neighbor; as shown above (Article [3]), there is no other virtue except charity whose good act is peace, as we have also said about joy (Question [28], Article [4]).[liii]

The *Catechism of the Catholic Church* defines virtue as "a habitual and firm disposition to do the good."[1] Traditionally, the **seven Christian virtues** or **heavenly virtues** combine the four classical cardinal virtues of prudence, justice, temperance, and courage with the three theological virtues of faith, hope, and charity. The Church Fathers adopted these by as the seven virtues.[liv]

There needs to be other virtues besides charity to have peace, justice, temperance, courage, and faith and hope there will be an agreement.

Vatican II Notes on Nuclear War

Since peace must be born of mutual trust between nations and not be imposed on them through fear of the available weapons, everyone must labor to put an end at last to the arms race, and to make a right beginning of disarmament, not unilaterally indeed, but proceeding at an equal pace according to an agreement, and backed up by real and workable safeguards.[lv]

Speak about the Iranian Nuclear Position

Iran has violated the 2015 nuclear deal by tripling its stockpile of low enriched uranium over three months and now probably has enough to make a single bomb. The regime has been stonewalling International Atomic Energy Agency inspectors from site to that they were guaranteed access under the deal. They suspect nuclear-related actives took place in the mid-2000s.[lvi]

President Trump has boldly sought to negotiate the nuclear position of Iran.
Peace in Islam is *salam* submission one who submits.
Let us pray and seek reconciliation to form a coalition *salam* submission, of brotherhood between the Iranian, Islam people and leaders and the world leaders.

At Pontificial University Saint Thomas Aquinas Rome my professor taught me endless wisdom of God; here is a few truths:
My Political Science Professor Stéphane Bauzon, author of *Le Devenir Humain, Réflexions éthiques sure les fins de la nature.* He taught in his

courses and dynamically made it alive when you have faith and follow Godly justice, you will prevail. **He would not acquiesce; he was as sure as we know the sun rises up in the morning and the moon brings excellent light of God to all the earth.**

My Professor, Father Walter, a world-renowned specialist on Thomistic Philosophy and prolific writer in the course Epistemology, reminded me of this and expressed it in his teaching. When Father Walter spoke, it was as if he is the Trinity and all the Arch Angels and Virgin Mary. The sound of his voice is the musical instrument in the music of heaven. Each word had a sound as if it was connected to the Holy Spirit with wings of cherubs and light of refreshment of eternal waters, to water upon the learning Father Senner was teaching us. https://thomistica.net/news/2020/7/6/rip-walter-senner-op

Love Jesus Christ; he is the truth. Trust Him.
Each professor has taught me God's love.

All my professors, Father Lamoreux, O.P. Lamoureux, Françoise TAVUZZI, O.P   Michael E, O.P. Albert, GLADE, O.P. Albert, **CAMP, Isobel BAUZON, Stephane,** Rev.Dominic Holtz, Father Holtser, glows with mercy and light in their being and spoke of the following: *The greater the miracle of Jesus Christ, the greater chance for offending and needing to harken the present situation having a mustard d of faith, forgiving, and love. However, there are times when one has to speak in zeal and truth, even if we may offend. The most and the least holy, brilliant, strong, patient, compassionate, and faithful all need to keep evolving. God desires your love to help Him.*

> *Let the one among you who is guiltless be the first to throw a stone at her.*
>
> *John 8:7*

Today there are some racial discrepancies and hatred of racial discrimination that have turned to a demonic division of unforgiveness. Today there is the secrecy of conspiracy to seek to bring Socialistic and Communistic rule to our USA that has turned into massive violence and death of criminals and innocent victims between the people. There has been fear and destruction in our streets and even homes and between family members and friends. *We, the people of the United States of America, have the warning to be a perfect union.* God will not allow continued violence, unrest of the young children and their adult friends, family, and community members to bring power upon our states. This is more than a revolution of opposing political parties and racial discrimination and the silent elite and the technological controllers.

It is a battle between
evil and good
darkness and light
violence and peace
hatred and love
death and life
We, the people, a perfect union of the same mission to have freedom and life as individuals, can bring
Right to the people of safety
Light to the people of victory
Peace to the people of empowerment
Love to the people of the life of living waters

New York, our Beloved State

New York, our great state where many immigrants are embraced by the arms of America love, the liberty of life. Has had violence, now redeemed; by those same people, America gave a home and sustenance them from a pillow to rest their head, food, to sustain their bodies, and education and a future.

Let us reconcile, and do not provoke these protestors. Yet, let us treat the police with respect and our country and never do violence upon our beautiful land America.

Now, priests and ministers, and prayer people need to walk through the streets and pray over all the people, businesses, homes, and communities.

In the faith and forgiveness in peace, we can overcome.

Hence, we as a people need to look at the peace, that was, that is, and that will **be uplifting America first in God** in protecting her people and land for peace, and restoring her people and her land to justice and life and forward building in transformation in God's love.

Peace is the absence of conflict; it is the ability to handle conflict by peaceful actions.

Ronald Reagan

He offered himself for us in order to ransom us from all our faults and to purify a people to be His very own and eager to do good.

Titus 2:1

Chapter Two

Justice   Foundational Truth

Simon Peter, servant, and apostle of Jesus Christ, to those who have received a faith as precious as our own, given through the saving justice of our God and Savior Jesus Christ. ² *Grace and peace be yours in abundance through the knowledge of our Lord.*

2
Peter1:1

Observe good faith and justice towards all Nations; cultivate peace and harmony with all."

President George Washington

I desired to give you the most genuine taste of the quintessential meaning of justice to be a catalyst so that you can set in motion a Pure Justice that is God's in His gifts He has given you. *This book is not a sophisticated exegetical book to remind you. God has called be God's Spirit of Truth to the people.* It is in the process. Remember, as a nation, we need to restore our country, and each one of us needs to be involved. Even if our Freedom Warriors of America may be smaller in number, we have the Divine Grace and the Divine Power and the Divine Nature of God to have all we need to have **victory.**

It is by Him that you exist in Christ Jesus, who for us was made Wisdom from God, and saving justice and holiness and redemption.

1Cor. 1:30

(God's) Peace with justice is only when America can prosper.

President   Ronald

Reagan

Note: The circumference eternal controlling every electron His omniscience of God that is Pure Wisdom; God demands in certain times of history, without accommodation; when there is God's believer to bring God's Pure Justice to the world, there is a great danger when the believer enters into impure injustice because the molecules are opposite. When there is a purpose to bring God's love, the believer will need to be tested and grow to learn to carry the heavenly love and power of God the Pure Justice to heal the impure justices. Divine Grace God gives us.

Qohelet states that **everything has been immutably foreordained by God**; therefore, it is useless for a person to complain about what God has done (Eccl 6:10–11). Because God is more powerful than humans**, the more they argue against God**, the less they accomplish: ", The more the words, the more the futility (הֶבֶל)" (6:11).[lvii] Eccl. 6:11 **However, we are responsible to bring justice even in acts of injustices of life occur**.

<u>Immutable: unchanging over time and unable to change.</u> [lviii]
<u>Arise this is why there are trials and dysfunction and even happy times, because, God has already pre-planned everything and foreordained and they cannot be changed. And if it seems to be changed and the human life and life itself is "incomplete," to God's will there is the Cross that God in Jesus Christ gives us for the redemption of all that was not suppose to be, that is sin. However, God uses His people and humanity to help Him to awake us, arise us, to see the truth of life that is immutable and foreordained in Him at creation.</u>

However, we still have to plead with God when we know that people need mercy.

Just be good, mama, just be good daddy, just be a good child, just be a good friend, how simple the sentence is this above has **nothing attached**; it is just pure "good." Just as a child is genuine; when we seek pure goodness, we can then have justice. Because purity is toward virtue, and virtue, are the hinges of the pure ethereal light of the Creator's *"Door of Justice."*

Numerous examples have convinced me that God ultimately saves him, whose motive is pure.

Gandhi

Authority there be given that respect and obedience which is its due; that the laws which are made shall be in wise conformity with the common good; and that, as a matter of conscience, all men shall render obedience to these laws.

Pope Pius XI

When we have God's justice, there will then be an authority to heal impure injustices because of righteousness, the Divine nature of life, and the Divine law of the Sovereignty of God's intentions. What do you want, and need do you think for Divine life and law or precepts of God? Justice's soothing peace is the gift of restitution, and first, toward God's perfect truth. Similarly, when you keep the water and the ocean clean, protecting it with justice smells good, looks gorgeous, (BEAUTY IS TRUTH AND LOVE) feels fantastic, and you can feed and keep the animals and the people healthy. When you support the community toward justice, the scents are fresh and good with the Spirit of God; they look like the sunshine of God, feels likes the living waters of God, and gives the eternal living of the life of the beauty in the Trinity. Beauty is life, living, fairness, merit, and honor, all in God's truth.

The people of God, we have all the things we need for life justice, grace, and peace in God's Divine Power and Divine Nature. We also have God's Divine Power to escape the corruption in the world of disordered passion.

2 Peter 1:1,2,3,4

Basic Definition of Justice: is rendering to everyone that which is his due. It has been distinguished from equity in this respect that while justice means merely doing what positive law demands, equity means doing what is fair and right in every separate case.[lix]

The moral arc of the universe is long, but it bends toward Justice.

Martin Luther King

God's Divine Nature, Grace, and Power.

Because of the world's uncontrollable happenings, it is irrational to accept that you can measure the strategy for justice in the same process to deliver it. There is a "Divine Grace" of God that has the power to bring justice; God has shown the His promise to save humanity and His people throughout history; under the most shocking happening of human in tragedies, of COVID Virus, dis-unity of the people, poverty, economic crisis, environmental crisis, the immorality of humans, breakdown of the wholesomeness of the culture and a list of other atrocities and severe tragedies, Divine Grace is the power and strength of God's Right Arm.

However, because of the deception of the dark hidden veil of COVID-19, a holocaust to treacherously destroy American and the world's freedom, most people have become in need and devastated. There is a Divine Command to help the American people. We need to put the American people first. President Trump has put the American people first; it is evident in his work and accomplishments; we have shown them in this book. He has followed the Divine Commands and Messages given shown in the Our Need to Give to the World, Heal America, Love in God, 2016, 2019 author Lisa Lucia Arden, MDIV. Note these Divine Messages have been written also before 2016.

*Yahweh brought us out of Egypt (Devastation) with a mighty hand and outstretched **arm**, with great terror, and with signs and wonders. Deut. 26:8*

The Administration of Justice is the firmest Pillar of Government.

President George Washington

Never in the history of America have we have had treacherous variables (there are more I am just listing a few) simultaneously; **first variable** China used a humanmade virus as an attempt for warfare and even a Holocaust; **a second variable** was the economic imbalance of tariffs of America with China (AFTER TRUMP SIGNED THE AGREEMENT WITH CHINA THEN THE VIRUS WAS EXPOSED "Prominently."); **a third variable** never in the history of America have we had a treacherous conspiracy of the division between Americans at this level in the disrespect of the Police and citizens (Promoted by the silent powerful, to attempt to destroy peace and our freedom, this is an art of war that is trickery to get the people against each other); **a fourth variable**, is the third party silent Elite that is connected to the technological powers that also funded the Socialistic and Communistic ties with Democrats. Wake up, America, there is a severe danger of the technical elite control, https://youtu.be/cWaiSxr1QkE. [ix] The Socialist, with the silent Elite, of the Communist, and Technological powers are in evil anger; because they are not IN POWER WITH THE Democrats RUNNING THE COUNTRY. Many crimes unintentionally and intentionally have been done upon her America, under the hidden leaders that control Democratic rule. Our jobs, safety, manufacturing, the development of life, and even our future existence under freedom of the individual have become in grave danger (approximately 3,700,000 WOMEN BECAME IN

POVERTY, and we did not have the CHINESE VIRUS) under the Democratic before President Trump. The facts have been shown.; Now the eyes have been open; many Americans have awakened, arisen, to the truth when voting in President Trump. Did it take a plague of the China Virus to the fact?

Divine Message 2020

China knew of the danger of the virus. China could have stopped the spread of the virus. China was warned to stop the work in the laboratory while developing the virus. They did not; they allowed evil to overtake them, the Communist Regime. The Chinese government knew the catastrophic contraindications of the Virus. The Chinese Virus of the Communistic Regime caused the deformity of a human-made demonic evil throughout the world. We can forgive and investigate the Chinese Communistic Regime of the virus, with what tools are allowed. Most important prayer for the redemption of the people, of China. Remember, God does not allow abuse in His justice!

"Divine Nature" in the "Divine Grace" that God gives to us individually in God's virtues that can bring His "Divine Purpose and healing" to reconcile and forward building. It is individually we have this Divine Nature, Grace, and Power of God. An individual is responsible for his or her own life in choosing God or worldly ideas. Hence, the Divine Nature, Grace, and Power of God will carry in God's sovereign will. God continues to sanctify us when we accept His Grace seek to love Him with all our heart and soul and life. Then our life is more in the Divine Nature of God and is even more in the Divine Power of God. It is not by might but by the Spirit of God.

*The Spirit of the Lord says, "**My Grace** is sufficient for you."*

2 Corinthians 12:9

*The Spirit of the Lord says," **The Divine** Nature I give you."*

2 Peter 1:1-4

*The Spirit of the Lord promises, "**My Power** of My mighty hand and outstretched right arm is with you."*

Jeremiah 27:3

Although there is sometimes tension and even betrayal, God wants us to understand the hidden and even exposed evil. We are individuals and have a myriad different God-given gift to bring justice; nevertheless, when we can reconcile; we can agree; we do have God's love in us; God will in His sovereign choice let us receive the Divine, Grace, Nature, and Power; individually though in Christ Jesus in the God of Abraham in the Trinity God works through all humanity.

<u>In the past,</u> the Americans did not put America first. Now in <u>the present, Americans finally awoke,</u> realizing we need to put America and her people toward God's justice. Yes, America first at our heart.

We know that justice has not been "render where it is due," from individuals to families, to communities, to states, and the nation.

Consequently, we need to receive all back what America lost and even more beautiful milk and honey of God's gifts for humanity and His land. *We know each one of us what we have gained or lost. Ask God to heal America. God loves America. The restitution may not always come back as what you think it should be; it is God's will to be a restitution of His will.*

For God created man to be immortal and made him be an image of His eternity. The righteous, because they are made in the image of God, can rest in the full hope of eternal life.

Wisdom of Solomon 2:23

Who being the brightness of HIS GLORY, AND THE EXPRESS IMAGE OF THIS PERSON, AND UPHOLDING OF ALL THINGS BY THE WORD OF HIS POWER, WHEN HE HAD BY HIMSELF PURGE OUR SINS, SITS DOWN ON THE RIGHT HAND OF THE MAJESTY ON HIGH.

Hebrew 1:3

By His divine power, He has lavished on us all the things we need for life and for true devotion, through the knowledge of Him who has called us by His glory and goodness · . . . understanding with self-control, self-control with perseverance, perseverance with devotion, devotion with kindness to the brothers, and heart to the brothers with love for in this way you will be given the generous gift of entry to the eternal kingdom of our Lord and Savior Christ.

2 Pet. 1:3

God's precepts and love is the Wisdom to bring Justice is to reconcile and be forgiven and then enter more into God's love.

The leaders in the power of the global financial markets and political and social most influential will have to bring justice in delivering gifts for the peoples, not only monetarily but also to exist. Otherwise, there will be a <u>breakdown of those that do not follow God's Heart</u> their authentic being and creation and development of what a nation needs to exist; in these technological times and evolving patterns that have uncontrollable speed and therefore have a multiplicity effects more than any time of history that **may not coexist properly with humans essential elements for development.**

Let us Americans love God; we can do nothing only with God.
When we do something, and if it is not good enough to create, it brings not life. Hence, if we adore and respect God first, we can know and make justice; and He will give us the grace to bring justice.

For You alone are holy, and all nations will come and adore You for the many acts of saving justice You have shown.

Revelations 15:4

My child, keep My words, and treasure My precepts, keep My precepts, and you will live, keep My teaching as the apple of your eye. Bind these to your fingers, write them on the tablet of your heart. [4] Say to Wisdom, 'You are my sister!' Call understanding your relation,

Prov.
7:1-5

Queen Virgin Mary is with us; ask her to protect you; she has overcome the devil and his demons. We need to be aware of what we need to pray for, and she will guide us to the truth in Jesus Christ. The omnipotent sword of the Spirit, with one extra throng of our faith, the Holy Spirit brings authority and protection.[lxi] *God himself confirmed their witness with signs and marvels and miracles of all kinds, and by distributing the gifts of the Holy Spirit in the various ways he wills.* Heb. 2:4

God and the Angels of God and Queen Virgin Mary are the protectors. praetorianus -a -um **belonging to the imperial authority, praetorian, the chief guide, the bodyguard with the Angels of God, Michael, Gabriel, Raphael Arch Angel. *Mary is our Shield. She guards our faith and protects us from evil; She has the victory. She is a leader, chief, a magistrate,* esp. one who helped(s) the *consuls by administering justice, commanding armies, general commander, and the general's bodyguard.*[lxii]**

Authority there be given that respect and obedience which is its due; that the laws are made shall be in wise conformity with the common good; and that, as a matter of conscience, all men shall render obedience to these laws.

Pope Pius XI

We discussed this concept in the book elsewhere; however, due to the vast infidelities and uncontrollable trials of life upon the people, there has to be unconditional love and unconditional justice for the people to exist.

Americans are responsible for working toward justice.
God has given us virtues as the tools of in, through, and with Him in
DIVINE NATURE
DIVINE GRACE
DIVINE POWER
Again, this is a proclamation to have a living justice; our God is a God of justice. God guides us to justice, and even in a right relationship with God, we will have trials, some more dangerous than others, and need to be sanctified and transformed into His virtues.

Virtues

Justice is the connection working toward virtues; we can have justice tools when seeking God's Divine, Grace, Nature, and Power. Virtues are the many hinges to hold the platinum door that shimmers of purity of the "Door of Justice." That light of the eternal God of Abraham is illuminating on that "Door of Justice," in the eternal heaven. The "Door of Justice" is the resurrection of sin to be redeemed into Justice. For me, Jesus Christ saves sinners. Yet, He uses His humanity for humanity's redemption to have justice flow.

What happened that caused justice to deteriorate in the living? There is the sin of the person and crime upon the person. Sometimes it is even disagreement and misunderstanding; even it may be the difference of beliefs. Moreover, it could even be "survival of the fetus," which causes crime because those individuals seek to exist? Our communities are wounded; These wounds will be healed; we always have faith, and God will heal the wounds of our souls and life. Listen let us have compassion: The child's tears of fear and deep sorrow drip down his pure face when the parents argue about how they will pay their bills and their mortgage and rents; Since COVID-19, many Americans have also had to deal with their generational hardships and even diseases and with the shocking realities of their financial uncertainties. Open our cities and schools. The Democrats, without any further ado, accept the Republican's negotiations to make a support system for the country speedily.

America can be healed by the miracles of peace, justice, compassion, in reconciliation in the foundation of virtues. Pray is the tool to open these doors of the foundational truth. We ask, how can we heal our country to healthy humanity and a healthy land? How can we get justice? We need tools of virtues because virtues are the nearest to the Pure Justice of God. Tools of virtues are in the Holy Scriptures.

Prayer and intimacy with God ask Him, "God, I want to love you with all my heart and soul. I want to be forgiven of any sin I have done intentionally or nonintentional. I want to change to be that human you created me to be. I accept you as my Savior giving your life to Me, redeeming me through the cross. I want you to be first in my life in all that I do."

After Pope Gregory I released his **seven** deadly sins in 590 AD, the **seven virtues** became identified: chastity, temperance, charity, diligence, patience, kindness, and humility. Practicing them is said to protect one against temptation from the **seven** deadly sins. Lust, gluttony, greed, sloth, wrath, envy, and pride are the seven deadly sins.[lxiii]

Each one of us needs to work on one or many of these virtues at all different levels. As my Philosophy Professor in Ethics class told me in Rome, the more responsibility or difficulty you have to seek justice, the more you have a problem to deliver virtues in a large and vast position—, because you have surrendered to God and are working to enlighten and awake yourself and others to God's truth and intentions that they need, it will take a mustard d of miracles. *There is nothing I cannot do in the One who strengthens me. Phil. 4:13 Do you know how He balances the clouds— a* ***miracle*** *of consummate skill?* ***Job 37:16*** *Then He took the* ***five loaves and the two fish****, raised His eyes to heaven, and said the blessing; then He broke the loaves and began handing them to His disciples to distribute among the people. He also shared out the two fish among them all.* ***Mark***

***6:41* He** fed thousands of people. Today we can do this in God's love in the hearts of the people.

We have to be careful; those who help to bring justice may appear to "prideful." We cannot mix pride up with confidence and faith in delivering. Forgiveness is essential, and the King's peace because we do not always know all the problems' variables. Though we know only God can judge His people that seek His purpose. We know who we are in God's justice, even if someone misjudges us.

There are disastrous happenings in the world that are uncontrollable; it is irrational to accept that you can measure the strategy for justice in the same process to deliver it.

February 20, 2020

Virgin Mary

Mary said, "TRUTH a path is living in God's will; Though to help one has to take a detour into the darkness to bring the light of God; because [God's light of redemption] the light needs to be in the darkness child." ( )= explanation Remember, those who have gifts of God others cannot judge them.

"How will you be able to help people if you do not go into the dark, my child. They need to experience the light; however, you cannot be abused; you need to use the protection tools to go into the darkness. Ephesians 6. This is why you have them. They need to wake up that there is darkness, and when they are shocked in God's overwhelming light, they are then awakened and arise. It takes a change in the mind, child, and the heart; to the truth, there needs to be a catalyst. **From time to time, force, and even natural disasters and evil are exposed to wake up and arise.** This is why you need to protect yourself; and all those in the light toward in and sanctify God's truth when those attempts to place and promote and instigate and even put into law those things that are not of the wholesomeness for humanity.

February 20 and 21, 2019
Our Lady of Mount Carmel
Eucharist of the Sacred Heart of Jesus Christ.
"There is a truth, a daughter, and the truth is only My truth."

This truth is a truth of redemption. Because those have not followed My truth, there has not been My truth. It is reflective in the country's production funds distribution child. A small number of people have all the funds, and most are left with a small portion, with little to seek to live day by day to get their produce. "

We know the law is to give those to those who want to know and live toward truth. However, many people live day by day, as have been victims, of this long-term cycle of the untruth of injustices. This is why when one is in need, one cannot say they get what they deserve.

"Hence, to get My truth in balance, the more those have need to bring truth. Even if they are not believers of God or even the Trinity or Mary; they, need to rectify and restore the reality of *America then, they will know more of the truth of God, and the truth of God will be in America.*"

There have been those who go "straight on the path," what does that mean? "I know Mary, that means to be with you." "Those have been straight in the path in the soul of My love to bring about truth. However, there is only a remnant, and the remnant is keeping My truth together, child. The rest has held My truth in the communities and the world. It is powerful and full of wisdom and justice."

America's history of keeping truth and protecting the people:

In Congress, July 4, 1776

The unanimous Declaration of the thirteen United States of America, *When in the Course of human events, it becomes necessary for one people to dissolve the political bands which have connected them with another, and to assume among the powers of the earth, the separate and equal station to which the Laws of Nature and of Nature's God entitle them, a decent respect to the opinions of humankind requires that they should declare the causes which impel them to the separation.*

We hold these truths to be self-evident that all men are created equal, that their Creator endows them with certain unalienable Rights, that among these are Life, Liberty and the pursuit of Happiness.--That to secure these rights, Governments are instituted among Men, deriving their just powers from the consent of the governed, --That whenever any Form of Government becomes destructive of these ends, it is the Right of the People to alter or to abolish it, and to institute new Government, laying its foundation on such principles and organizing its powers in such form, as to them shall m most likely to affect their Safety and Happiness.[lxiv]

The system has abused countless people. And those who want to help these people have had conspiracies upon them. Even politicians such as President Trump, the Democrats blatantly attempted to remove him from office and stop production. The Democrats were not able to succeed. President Trump has justice and pursues justice and put America first, in full force to make America great again.

Hand in hand, God works with nations and peoples and His Divinity for the justice of the people:

Only in the sovereignty of the Divine Intervention of God's Divine Grace will there be "Divine Grace" for humanity that has the power to bring justice. To be exposed under the most shocking happening of human trials, COVID Virus, dis-unity of the people, poverty, economic crisis, environmental crisis, the immorality of humans, and breakdown of the culture's wholesomeness. The Divine Grace of God is given to us when we ask forgiveness for our sins and humble ourselves to His purpose. (First, Commandment). Loving the Lord with all our heart and soul and leaning not on our understanding but acknowledging all we do. **God trusts us that we will seek to live in His righteousness; that is why He gave us these virtues.**

Seven Virtues and Deadly Sins Listed

After Pope Gregory I released his seven deadly sins in 590 AD, the seven virtues became identified as chastity, temperance, charity, diligence, patience, kindness, and humility. Practicing them is said to protect one against temptation from the seven deadly sins.

Virtue	Latin	Gloss	Sin	Latin
Chastity	Castitas	Purity, abstinence	Lust	Luxuria
Temperance	Temperantia	Humanity, equanimity	Gluttony	Gula
Charity	Caritas	Will, benevolence, generosity, sacrifice	Greed	Avaritia
Diligence	Industria	Persistence, effortfulness, ethics	Sloth	Acedia
Patience	Patientia	Forgiveness, mercy	Wrath	Ira
Kindness	Humanitas	Satisfaction, compassion	Envy	Invidia
Humility	Humilitas	Bravery, modesty, reverence	Pride	Superbia

We can just take one of these VIRTUES each one of us that we need to work on! THEN WE CAN WORK TOWARD HEALING IN OUR COMMUNITIES. WE CANNOT ABUSE THE PEOPLE.

The Catechism of the Catholic Church defines virtue as "a habitual and firm disposition to do the good."[1] Traditionally, the **seven Christian virtues** or **heavenly virtues** combine the four classical cardinal virtues of prudence, justice, temperance, and courage with the three theological virtues of faith, hope, and charity. The Church Fathers adopted the seven virtues.[lxv]

For our children to develop honest communication in a globalized, multicultural world, it is essential to agree with a proper standard protocol. There is hidden treachery of masonry and culture witchcraft that even President George Washington speaks of these demonic evils that cannot control a government or a community; otherwise, destruction will come upon the city as did it the Israelites worshiping pagan gods. The miracle to restore America is hope and the decisive prerequisite to reconcile and give restitution in the redeeming virtues of the purest intentions toward God's love. Please, America.

For instance, a scar in privation to the ointment of the Holy Spirits' love upon it is: Putting the immigrant children in the facilities made by the prior President was an action that caused much emotion and injustice to all. Let us forgive each other. And all pray unceasingly for this atrocity for children. Remember, children need a home, food, education, proper ethical parenting, and well-being. They were brought into the world, thousands of these children, **without sufficient tools to live.** Perhaps, the children being in cages symbolized that if America did not help these immigrants (most of us remember are immigrants), they would be human beings in their country's cage. The analogy is cold deep in the heart yet thought-provoking. The question, what do you think? Why would they build a structure as cages to hold people and were not dangerous criminals? Not unless that defined them as dangerous criminals.

"Family reunification and protection of appropriate measures to ensure the protection of the unity of the family." Article 44 Migrant Rights are Human Rights. Protection Across the Border

Even though America is a *Mother of All Nations*, we have forgotten that we can take care of both immigrants and citizens in moral law and justice.

The tree grew taller and stronger, until its top reached the sky, and it could be n from the very ends of the earth. ⁹ Its foliage was beautiful, its fruit abundant, in it was food for all. The wild animals provided shade, the birds of heaven nested in its branches, and all living creatures found their food on it.

Daniel
4:8-9

We are responsible for human beings when they seek to enter the country to bring justice and just law; Let us forgive the 2019 count homelessness found 58,936 homeless people living in Los Angeles County and 36,3000 residing in Los Angeles. There was an increase of 12 percent and 16 percent, respectively, over 2018. The 2018 count found that Los Angeles County had 52,765 homeless people, a slight dip from the year before." [lxvi]. Let us forgive all the injustices we have put on our American people and her land**. I believe we can bring a miracle in God's Right Arm of strength and love of His Sacred Heart.**

Awake, America, Awake America. Arise America

I want to reiterate; these are daily endeavors that I need to deliver justice, so I understand it diligently. In prayer, I have received a command to address these endeavors. We have a multicultural community with evident differences and traditional beliefs that are sometimes conflicting. Therefore, it is mandatory to form a **standard based on *international and Judeo-Christian* ethics that America's foundation is built on.**

God's blessings are in God's commands to take care of our people, our creatures, our land, and hold on to our precious pearls of His Sacred Heart that pours upon us the sanctifying power of Grace, Mercy, and Nature.

In President Ronald Reagan, Speech on the Evil Empire, he discusses America as God's foundation in the Judeo-Christian Ethics.[lxvii]

Freedom prospers only when the blessings of God are avidly sought and humbly accepted.

President Ronald Reagan

America, we are command to "avidly" seek God's precepts and humbly accept Him.

*I have been driven many times **to my knees** by the overwhelming conviction that I had nowhere else to go.*

Abraham Lincoln

If God does not govern us, we will be governed by tyrants.

William Penn

The God that gave us life gave us liberty.

Thomas Jefferson

The Blood of Jesus brings redemption to all liberty and life of all that exists. Believe in the Savior. He loves you.

'Be on your guard for yourselves and for all the flock of which the Holy Spirit has made you the guardians, to feed the Church of God which he bought with the blood of his own Son.

Acts 20:28

And through him to reconcile everything to him, everything in heaven and everything on earth, by making peace through his death on the cross.

Col 1:20

I am not just telling you my belief in the Virgin Mary. She is known throughout the world. Many leaders keep quiet about her for various reasons. These leaders are politicians; President John F. Kennedy and President Reagan were Catholic. The apparitions and the experience individuals have with Mary to bring God's justice₇, and purpose are a reality, and they have countless witnesses.

First, Queen Virgin Mother Mary, the Mother of God, is the *Mother of All Nations.* America a country of the *Mother of All Nations*, because she is under the protected veil of Queen Virgin Mary with the Trinity and Michael, Raphael, Gabriel, and the Angels of the God of Abraham. **praetorianus**

Consequently, with the change of modernity and contemporary beliefs of what it means to be human in a globalized, multicultural, technological society, we have had a breakdown of the truth of ideologies that bring impure injustice at every corner of life. Today if President Reagan were here, he would prohibit Marijuana smoking in public and not agreed places, and only to have for medicinal purposes; it has contraindications that are dangerous, damaging for many people. Breathing in the drug is a severe contraindication to many.[lxviii] And it is rampant in Los Angeles. Marijuana is just one assimilation into a culture evident for the dysfunction of people's well-being as an entire community. Babies and young children are vulnerable to breathe in the smoke of marijuana. A question to ask, marijuana is a business that has increased since its legalization in California; simultaneously, homelessness has increased dangerously with contraindications morally and well-being of human dignity for the homeless and the citizen. Have we put the people first in need, or did we put first an ideological bias and business? When the children or people breathe in marijuana, THERE ARE SERIOUS DETRIMENTAL BRAIN DAMAGES.[lxix] I understand marijuana is a medicine for many and helps their disease; I disagree with the legalization. However, it can be in a pill or agreed not to smoke in a vicinity where there are children or someone in the allergic area or does not agree with the smoke in their environment.[lxx]

Furthermore, there are many complicated urgent concepts and happenings in the community that need to be addressed for peace, justice, healing, and forward building in love. The Presidents of the United States of America George Washington, Lincoln, Teddy Roosevelt, John F. Kennedy, and Jesus Christ, Martin Luther King, Billy Graham, Gandhi, Pope Francis,

Benedicto, Pius X, ect, and many more would prohibit hidden deceptions of evil witchcraft and masonry. I know Billy Graham and Pope Francis and Pope Benedicto and Pope Pius X would fight back at the pulpit and their proclamation.

President Ronald Reagan used the term "Evil" in 1983; hence, if we used the word "demons," is that politically incorrect in 2020? Ethics will help define and reveal the opposite beliefs to bring justice for a more peaceful and just society—we, as the Freedom Warriors of Justice and peace and love in God's truth, win.

In bringing a Divine foundation in clarity that is the basis of human ethics that is, in most cases, innately understood, then we can and will have a more flourishing nation in God's Divine Justice. We need to teach virtues and speak about the seven deadly sins in public and private schools.

We need to tell the children there is a difference between good and evil. Just as there is a subject for an answer to a question or a science working, there are absolute answers. Right and wrong, especially in the Judeo-Christian context, are presenting the cornerstone of our thesis.

Humans do not want to breathe in gas or sewage from leaky pipes; it causes cancer and other unhealthy dangers to our bodies and well-being. I spoke up and have advocated new infrastructure, and our brilliant leaders in America are fixing the infrastructure. FIRST WATER NEEDS RESTORATION. In my first Book, *Need to Give to the World,* Lisa Lucia Arden. And the water system needs cutting edge *Our* updates. **News Releases from Headquarters 'Water (OW) President Trump Signs Executive Order on Modernizing America's Water Resource Management and Water Infrastructure 10/13/2020** [lxxi] **This is a Divine Command President Trump has carried through.**

Divine Message answered Governor Gavin Newsom of California for Answering the Prayer to Help the Homelessness. WE STILL NEED HELP

PLEASE ALLOW YOUR BROTHER AND SISTER OF HUMANITY TO WORSHIP. WORSHIPPING TO GOD AND PRAY WILL HELP BRING YOUR ANSWERS TO CALIFORNIA TO RESTORATION MY BROTHER GOVERNOR GAVIN NEWSOM.

WE NEED A MIRACLE NOW DIVINE COMMAND FOR BILLIONAIRE WOMAN THE MOTHERS OF THE NATION MERITED TO TAKE CARE OF OTHERS TO HELP

We today need to address homelessness in America, especially in Los Angeles, since COVID 19. Homelessness in 2019 count found 58,936 homeless people living in Los Angeles County and 36,3000 residing in Los Angeles. Those were an increase of 12 percent and 16 percent, respectively, over 2018. The 2018 count found that Los Angeles County had 52,765 homeless people, a slight dip from the year before." [lxxii] There has been a kind miracle to begin to help the homeless, California "Laser Focused" on Homelessness, Mental Health Reform in February 2020. However, the count has increased substantially since the Covid virus.[lxxiii] "Almost half (47 percent) of all unsheltered homeless people are found in California, about four times as high as California's share of the overall U.S. population."[lxxiv]

We should have put the money into the homeless. If the financed and powerful silent protesters cared about the USA injustices, honestly, they would have taken care of the homelessness first. **DIVINE WARNING: There can be a bacteria or virus that can spread in homelessness of that magnitude. It is essential to b*ring a healthy environment for each homeless person.***

The righteous care about justice for the poor, but the wicked have no such concern.

Proverbs 29:7

It is difficult for most surviving everyday life. When we all work together, we can make a miracle to help the homeless.

"CBS News' Norah O'Donnell says mostly peaceful protests caused $1Billion to $2Billion in damage from looting and arson." Foxnews.com[lxxv]

Divine Message California Technology Pasadena, California September 17, 2020

1. Listen while they are creating the curriculum for the History of America. Moreover, history America shows a country of four foundational truths, Peace, Justice, Restoration, and Forward Building in Love (Compassion). Make sure they also make that small book based on Judeo- Christian ethics. They have to memorize in understanding that is the foundation of America. They have to learn to understand the Constitution and the Declaration of Independence.
2. Make sure all other curricula in the Public and Private School Systems are correct. Some of the curricula are incorrect and (communistic, socialistic, and false documentation and information Norah O'Donnell on that is missing)
3. Also, I told you before that they did not begin it. Each child has to study the eco-system of choice.

    They studied choices, such as the ocean, forest, water, soil, atmosphere, oil, natural gas, coal, gas, etc. Electricity even and also the choice of a Science related, however, first eco-systems. Every year they have to have a written notebook report, and each should be for every year of education. They can do raw studies and also go on field trips.

4. The children also have to have the entrepreneurial skill and learn basic survival, living, and accounting. . spending.. They can have stores at their schools where they trade goods.

5. They have not begun the homeless redemption project forward in compassion with great speed and power. I saw the way they put up building in places fast. Can we do that for the homeless together? We can. We can. In Los Angeles, over 30,000 are homeless. Let us restore impure injustices on the people's full force. America first, we need to put America first. If they start now, I will bless them a triple, and when there is an earthquake, there will be causalities. All leaders with finances and ingenious AND INNOVATIVE strategic planning could do this. I pray.

6. The water needs to be corrected and the filter systems and basins now so no bacteria and virus can be detrimental.

7. All water fountains in the schools need to be filtered.

8. In Universities and all schools, all studies and projects need to be in the welfare of the people and protecting the seed of life. The research and delivery need to be the four foundational truths, Peace, Justice, Restoration, and Forward building in love. For example, I met a student at the California Technology School of Sciences while I was writing the book. He is tall physically and in stature to find answers to help God's science deliver to help America and the world. He is a pillar to learn of the scintillating light of God chosen as each one of us is to give what

God has provided us in return to do God's will; he a Tree of Life given rooted to do God's will and the light of truth is upon His heart. And he said, " he wants to be careful of the secrets of findings in science only to help humanity's well-being."

Present Multicultural Society

Multicultural communities are the beauty of each tradition of God's hand of human creation; we want to agree with ethics in communication and actions. As you know, practices and cultural beliefs cause individuals to respond and react in particular ways that may be incongruent with another individual cultural idea. Especially in adult circumstances, these differences could be detrimental in all areas of life, integrating into the public's communication at large.

In working to understand virtues and the deadly sins, we "hopefully" become more compassionate and respond accurately. In communities, to understand neighbors and the streets and their traditions, we respond with more accurate and peace forming communication even when there are differences. And when we do not react FOR justice, in virtues, The Divine law and Divine Nature of God's sovereign power will shock us and awake us. No, not one is infallible. **Though is God is infallible, and He can make His warriors infallible at the time He wants to use us. However, the infallibility is from the Pure Holy Spirit.**

When working toward perfect virtue, then reason becomes truth, and truth becomes the tools to justice. Hence, we can resolve and build and live toward justice for each person's gifts to give and to keep America and the world. **Each person has a beauty in their tradition that is a gift God has given. We can share all our differences, find the proper boundaries and**

understanding, and find reconciliation—being the most compassionate first. We can build on our strengthens and weaknesses. And when we realize the opposite, or vague, and differences, the truth becomes identified more clearly, in the fact whether it is in the

God's truth in the virtues will be toward **reconciliation, restitution, redemption that brings justice.**

Humble belief in God as Redeemer and Lord –Respect each other Justice → Reconciliation of self and others →Love---→Virtues -→God's Truth--Reason-→ Justice→ Faith→ Righteousness.

Moreover, most important is the different serious generational deficiencies and *genograms* of a family and life issues the people carry with them, no matter what traditional or cultural background or socio-economic level. America has received all types of people. America is the *"Mother of All Nations."*[lxxvi]

America has different genogram deficiencies and conditions, God-given traditions and beliefs, and different vast socio-economical positions that cause a plethora of acceptance or non-acceptance of reality. Hence, we, the people, need to begin now to find a commonality of truth. **The** foundation of the principles of the virtues that are in God's precepts many may not believe. Although when the virtues are revealed and discussed I know the people's hearts will be open because the VIRTUES are the Word of God, that is the characteristic personality of the Son of God. And we know most virtues are the basis of successes.

Protestors and Police God's Love will redeem AMERICA IS GOD'S LAND

We need to respect one another and swiftly forgive each other. We need to forgive the wounds on both sides, protestors, victims, innocent, Police, and all those involved and those who have experienced violence. Today in our communities, never before in history have, we had the various types of crimes and multiple kinds of illegal drugs and even abused pharmaceuticals and masonry. Furthermore, with the age of the rapid tool of technology and life-threatening intensity and treacherous crimes that involve technology that is used singularly and simultaneously with other crimes, make the criminal protection of our communities complicated. Both sides, criminals, protestors, and Police, are in fear and unclarity because of the complex criminal variables and political discourse of division in our country and globally, and even there are countless other corruptive variables to consider of the current effects of crimes than any time in history.

Moreover, there is globalization and different cultural beliefs and acceptance of the communication and way of ethics and life that is considered acceptance of humanity's well-being that genuinely is death to society's well-being. Even though police officers understand many cultural groups, the communities' police still have to assimilate in understanding the multicultural belief systems that have become heterogeneous with contraindications and complexities. This is making it more dangerous and complex for the Police; simultaneously, with the new millennials being affected by the vast crimes of criminals and technology crimes; Furthermore, the position of the multicultural society of globalization has never been at the highest level as it is today in the United States of America, is causing a vast diversity of belief and what is identified as the truth of protocol for social understanding living in the community. When my parents came to

America, they only could speak English, and it was the only acceptable protocol in most daily life experiences. Today we as a nation are given the freedom to allow the people to express their cultural roots across the entire compass**. First the First Commandment; In return, we should first put the truth and justice of God in the American legacy first and respecting her history.**

Malcolm X became convinced that Islam embraced all colors. (Malcolm X sought to bring justice in the way he knew how). Martin Luther King's nonviolence completely integrated, beloved community" toward freedom and justice, also received a miracle into America's society and justice. [lxxvii]

Man must evolve for all human conflict a method that rejects revenge, aggression, and retaliation. The foundation of such an approach is love. Martin Luther King, Jr.

EVIL WE CANNOT ACCEPT **to expose evil it is a prerequisite to deliver truth**, and pray for protection in God. I know that Martin Luther King would not tolerate the masonry and witchcraft rampant in some states against those who want a free country in America OF GOD.

It is evident that our country America is a multicultural society that needs to reassess and reconcile the truths in respecting people's traditions, and even socio-economic positions, and the well-being of justice in a community that has other controlling variables of technology and globalization, making justice more complex than before ever in the history of humanity. Otherwise, human nature strikes violently, and even sometimes with cause, and then hatred is formed and hopelessness to make things change, then brings conspiracies that seek to rectify justice. Yet, it is death to the multicultural understanding of justice.

Resurrect America, let us live in the justice of Martin Luther King's "nonviolence,"[lxxviii] proclamation, and action to bring our dream of freedom and civil rights and bring unity with no divisions between all cultures and peoples and races."

We are America Freedom Warriors toward God's freedom of justice. And yes, and yes, America is being redeemed. Yet, the heavenly robe is omniscient, saving light with no rips or torn or stained in the Trinity. The rips and thorns and tears of sin are at the Cross of Christ, that God has mended in the Resurrection of His life-giving and redeeming all life anew. At the Church of Mount Carmel in Montecito, in front of the Holy Statue of Virgin Mary, I was prompted to look at her hands; she is holding the world in her hands; they are muddy. Then I thought we have to stick our hands sometimes in mud to clean up the mess. Look, we are responsible for us to do our best. Best is finding and knowing what needs to be given and nurtured and redeemed and unveiled so life can live.

Yes, life will live in the person, yes life will live in the believer of life, yes life will live in the land, yes life will live in the soil, yes life will live in the heart of the people, yes life will live in the animals, yes, life will live in nature. Yes, life will live. Yes, life is God.

St. Jerome, Author of the first Latin edition of the Bible (The Vulgate, the official version of the Church of Rome.) Much respected for his enormous intellect. He attracted a bevy of widows and instructed and accompanied the women.[lxxix] The Vulgate is a Bible, and the Bible has all the Seven Virtues, and each delivers the Divine Nature, Divine, Grace, and Divine Power of God. He protected them and guided them, the women. Let America continue to be the St. Jerome all that needs justice and bring guidance to love toward equality. The Second Commandment to love your neighbor as yourself.

America, we now have to nurture America, love her, and adorn her with the Tree of Life of the Seven Virtues in the Biblical Judeo-Christian ethics that America is birthed on. America's fruit is waiting to be again delivered. There is enough food of **God's love in His Seven Virtues of God's Divine Nature, Divine Grace, and Divine Power. Daniel 4**

We cannot deny there have been miracles of God's love for all peoples from all nations and situations here in America, God's Land, God's Truth, and God's Love.

Let us be as St. Jerome and help bring God's Pure Justice in the truth of the Seven Virtues that we uphold to obtain righteousness.

There is nothing so powerful as truth and often nothing so strange.

Daniel Webster

Listen, America's Divine Power of God is the powerful truth, and the strange part is the miracle of God's Omniscient Spirit in the heart of the people. Look, America, in you is the blessings of God's Seven Virtues. Traditionally, the **seven Christian virtues** or **heavenly virtues** combine the four classical cardinal virtues of prudence, justice, temperance, and courage with the three theological virtues of faith, hope, and charity. These were adopted by the Church Fathers as the seven virtues.[lxxx]

Someone may ask, 'How is justice greater than all the other virtues?'

The other virtues gratify the one who possesses them; justice does not give pleasure to the one keeping it but instead pleases others.

St. Jerome^{lxxxi}

(We know women and children and men are those that need most justice. Those who have worldly power are those who have to deliver justice. Those who do not have control have to reflect fairness and pray for those who need to provide justice.)

The Purity of Justice Queen Mother Mary story Divine Message

Please, let me be a friend of light to you open your eyes. I cannot find anyone else as pure in history that has brought a d of life upon the earth, Jesus Christ. This is my experience. This is my life experience that is living and understanding.

Queen Mother Mary has been tested, tried, and lived in the living of God's purpose. She prepared Jesus' life for a man perfect to be a Savior yet transcendent as the Son of God.

Many that were Gentiles and even Jews believed in Jesus Christ's miracles. Josephus, the Jewish historian, documented Jesus Christ's miracles.

Justice is an action of life of the living in God's intention, and Queen Virgin Mary, the Mother of God, nurtured God's Pure Justice in Jesus as a child.

Queen Virgin Mary is the human that lived in this justice of righteousness in her "purity."[lxxxii] Queen Lady, Virgin Mary Pure Justice, and Wisdom of God. The "perfect virtue" gives her the most significant reason and the purest woman with the most physically, mentally, and spiritually perfect; Mary has the greatest of God's purity than any person has ever had, after Jesus Christ. She is the Mother of God and guides humanity when they ask. Virgin Mary, since she has the highest Wisdom, after the Trinity has hindsight, and she wants to warn us of those things that are not God's Pure Justice. God's purity God is the purity of Himself, absolutely no mixture, only pure.

Protecting ourselves *Ephesians 6*

So stand your ground, with truth a belt round your waist, and uprightness a breastplate, wearing for shoes on your feet the eagerness to spread the gospel of peace and always carrying the shield of faith so that you can use it to quench the burning arrows of the Evil One. And then you must take salvation as your helmet and the sword of the Spirit, that is, the word of God.

Eph. 6:14

Charity of Justice

Charity is also a form of justice; just as St. Jerome, states "justice" is in the virtues that we uphold to bring that righteousness of God in freedom.

Statue of Liberty Queen Virgin Mary

May I say, the "Statue of Liberty" is the Queen Virgin Mary symbolizing the freedom of America toward the Godly justice in God's intention in the highest Wisdom and living in righteousness.

Queen Virgin Mary "is the mirror of justice." [lxxxiii]

Working for justice are the actions one has to have of great faith in that their efforts will bring God's life to the people and the land.

Remember, God will protect those that are working and living toward His righteousness and justice.

Justice is pursuing faith to reach and obtain the purpose of voiding out what is deteriorating the minds and hearts and lives of the people AND bringing PEACE AND JUSTICE, RESTORATION, AND FORWARD BUILDING IN LOVE.

Justice is pursuing faith to reach and obtain the purpose of bringing what is deteriorating the land, creatures, and the earth's gifts to bring peace, restoration, and forward building of love.

Spinoza proclaims:

"Faith consists of a knowledge of God, without which obedience to Him would be impossible, and which the mere fact of obedience to Him."

I). Faith is not wholesome in itself, but only in respect to the obedience, it implies, or as James puts it, compliance is granted, confidence must also be granted.
II). He who is truly obedient necessarily possess true and saving faith.
Ep. lv. 7:
    "Everyone that loveth is born of God, and knoweth God: he that loveth not knoweth not God; for God is love."[lxxxiv]

Remember, again I will say as a Divine Command given: love is protecting oneself against abuse because love is being human with freedom and beauty and love; Love is protecting others from this abuse from the deceiver. I have to proclaim because of my belief in God, protecting the American people, and believing in President Trump's God given call as President, I have had much abuse, violence, deception, and trickery on me; however, I have the victory in God's power, I have been redeemed.

Spinoza proclaims faith and obedience, and the love of God. God is peace, and peace is justice.

PLEASE, MY AMERICA, WE HAVE TO REALIZE WE HAVE TO CHOSE TO WORK TOWARD **JESUS CHRIST'S VIRTUES** THE SCEPTER OF AUTHORITY FOR JUSTICE The Scepter is the Holy Scriptures of Truth in the power and love and tenderness of the Trinity, Virgin Mary, the Saints, and God's Angels Community
Justice begins with those who are the parent of the children.
Justice begins with the individual.
Justice also begins in the community. Some are excommunicated from the city because of the blatant truth they speak. They have evolved IN GOD'S TRUTH and need to tell those of the community the revelations of good and evil. I fear the Lord, not men; consequently, we are speaking and proclaiming in community God's truth.
Justice is the virtue of the life of the people.

Justice begins in the community when one makes evident that there is no justice.

If we wait too long and do not proclaim the urgency of America's severe deterioration of justice, we will have the wounds in the people's hearts of the non-believers that do not believe in the Holy Spirit and the redemption of the Cross.

America's life is in the heart of God, in the heart of the people.

I have to say I need forgiveness from my neighbors and the community, I have proclaimed in a loud voice. Sometimes singing, sometimes proclaiming like a warrior for America, the many injustices. I was speaking of the Seven Virtues and the deadly sins indirectly. If we do not state these injustices, then these injustices can and will deteriorate our community over some time. Because we are individuals that live in a city and influence each other, the good and good revelations to work in hindsight for protection will bring justice.

Laws, regulations, and the protection of the people of the community are paramount to keep justice. Some people need to be taught obedience in society because justice is in the treacherous hands of those who may not even know what truth is, and perhaps be forced to do acts of criminal injustices, to evil crimes.

Against justice, there are many urgencies around the world. I am just mentioning a few.

CHINA THREAT

Divine Message agreed by Physician in China the Virus was made as a Weapon to kill humanity Coronavirus whistleblower speaks out about possible COVID origin on 'Tuc... https://youtu.be/qFlqXPI_hZQ via @YouTube.[lxxxv]

PRESIDENT TRUMP IN 2020 AND THE AMERICAN FREEDOM WARRIORS HAVE WON OVER CHINA'S THREAT OF THE FOLLOWING

1. China's real attempt of a <u>holocaust in the Corona Virus Conspiracy to destroy humanity</u>, in America and other parts of world AMERICA &THE WORLD ARE HEALING
2. <u>CHINA LOST</u> THEY wanted to take over the geopolitical power. A country is in global geopolitical power when they take the SEAPOWER AND LAND POWER.
<u>AMERICA WON President Trump and the American Freedom Warriors</u> bring to the justice system of fair business of tariffs and protecting our USA WITH military power AND THE ECONOMY.
Proven facts we will discuss later in the book.
3. China Using Fentanyl as Chemical Weapon Against U.S.
Fentanyl, a synthetic opioid 50 times more potent than heroin, is killing tens of thousands of Americans each year.

4. And other deceitful crimes against their people and the world.
5. There has been a Divine Message, that China has other crimes and plans to destroy and gain power. I pray they are revealed and stopped. Most of all I pray China is redeemed to love like God loves, her people and the world.

<u>Forgiveness and reconciliation is the answer to the catastrophic destruction of humanity. However, today we cannot accept crime and even the secrecy of evil even if it seems hopeless and we know it takes a miracle. Usually, something that is being used for evil is not exposed and many do not recognize it; evil remember, is the greatest deception; Hence, when evil is exposed, some do not believe because they have been deceived. And the one who exposed it seemingly for a while is considered delirious or even mentally incorrect. Yet, we know in all sciences of life, many things known by one may not be known by others, and it then does not exist in their understanding until they wake up or are threatened by life's existence.</u>

Behind the deadly opioid epidemic ravaging communities across the United States lies a carefully planned strategy by a hostile foreign power that experts describe as a "form of chemical warfare."

It involves the production and trafficking of fentanyl, a synthetic opioid that caused the deaths of more **than 32,000 Americans in 2018-19 alone, and fentanyl-related substances.**[lxxxvi] Recently, in 2020 September, fentanyl was found in Delaware's pharmaceuticals, which could have brought death to 75% of the people in Delaware. Epoch News September 22, 2020

6. **CHINA CONSPIRED TO MAKE GOVENERMENTAL LOANS FROM AMERICAN TO MAKE MILITARY TOOLS a**

7. **China in Focus September 22, 2020, NYPD Officer's Hidden Ties to the CCP** China in Focus (September 22): NYPD Officer's Hidden Ties to the CCP[lxxxvii]

8. **America's freedom fighters protect the people of the Communistic leaders of China. God will bless us for this.** Divine Message **agreed by Physician in China** made the Virus as a Weapon to kill humanity Coronavirus whistleblower speaks out about possible COVID origin on 'Tuc... https://youtu.be/qFlqXPI_hZQ I repeat this youtube documentation because I want you not to forget and to contemplate on the evidence of the plan of China to control and have "One-World Government." and its attempt and failure to destroy American. Also, contemplate on the training that China is getting from Canada. This has also been a Divine Message that China wanted to use military force to attempt to destroy the USA.

9. **China's Geopolitical strategy of destroying the USA failed:**
Economically-
Silent War on Drugs-
Poison of the Virus as to create a Hollucasut of **human**ity **AND** USA Inside crimes of PP Loans given to China from the USA government to produce warplanes and war machinery
INSIDE CRIMES - BIDEN'S governmental officials and USA companies

10. China In Focus (August 17): Chinese River Tainted, Turned Blood Red https://link.theepochtimes.com/mkt_app/china-in-focus-chinese-river-tainted-turned-blood-red_3465009.html This depicts when the Pharaoh of Egypt did not let the Israelites go the Nile River became red of the blood of one of the plagues. , the Communist or the reflection of the pagan power as the Pharaoh, holding in captivity their people, the Chinese; moreover, they attempted to control the world by using the Chinese Virus to destroy humanity. Exodus 7:14-24

> *For we know him who said, "it is Mine to avenge; I will repay, " and again, "The Lord will judge His people."*
>
> *Hebrews 10:30*

ALL AMERICANS ARISE TO GOD'S TRUTH, ASK YOURSELF:

WHY WOULD YOU VOTE IN A PRESIDENT THAT SUPPORTS A COMMUNISTIC IDEOLOGY AND "ONE WORLD GOVERNMENT."

When we live in the community, many work to strive and live and succeed without thinking about justice. The survival of the fetus is necessary to have to pour into life. However, abuse and betrayal, and impure injustices are not allowed in God's intentions for humanity. Hence, we may address justice as an agreement of laws and ethical understanding to <u>not abuse and treat humanity with injustices.</u> Therefore, it is evident and clear we need the purest justice available, and that is the Judeo-Christian ethics with virtues. God's truth is the most pristine; serenity will be of justice in the people. The quorum of the Wisdom of truth is in the most progressive ideas without any motives just for pure life living toward God's purest compassion, oneself to find yourself in God's purpose, and flowing that purest love to others.

<u>NOW WE HAVE PROTECTED THE COMMONWEALTH to help all those entering into America to enjoy and flourish to have the American dream and even begin a new life of necessary existence.</u>

Protection for justice is first.[lxxxviii] Spinoza addresses the urgency of the commonwealth to protect society. The "commonwealth" of America, we have saved her in God's strength in all ways with laws and respect. I have this passion deep in my soul, and this fantastic drive that is even knowing what has already happened to attempt to stop me, I keep going to listen to the call and succeed. It is not my justice; it is God's justice; I seek to deliver. Think, awake, when you want justice and even speaking of the term, what is this saying? Consequently, something needs to be rectified and corrected and brought to the truth because you are mentioning the concept.

Those are aware of it and realize that injustice has been against them. However, there are differences and different belief systems. As people, we need to have a common understanding; We can have a miracle of the foundation of the virtues of treating a human with peace and God's Pure Justice.

Let's do it! America. Let us enter the integrity in the individuals, families, communities, schools, businesses, and America NOW.

WHAT VIRTUE DO YOU CHOOSE TO UNITE AMERICA?
GOD KNOWS YOUR NAME, ASK HIM
You know that you can bring living OF THE GREATEST HAPPINESS toward PURE JUSTICE.
Justice is protecting the innocent unborn.
Justice is protecting the legacy of the men and women that made America the great land she is for all peoples.
Justice is protecting each citizen and human with respect and nonviolence.

Justice is respecting the Police Officers that protect our communities and country.
Justice is protecting American respect toward one another.

Justice is not accepting any practices that seek to deceive or harm the human mind, the human body, and social life.

Justice is protecting the children minds, hearts, souls, energy and teach them the salvation of God for those who

Justice is rebuilding the inner cities.
Justice is protecting and restoring our America to continue to be free and empowering others to live as humans and well-being.
Justice is the awareness of what is truth will bring justice.
Justice is protecting the elderly and compassion for all human needs.

Justice is the intention to bring a nation to uphold IN GODS PURE JUSTICE.

Justice is taking care of the water first in the eco-systems. [lxxxix]
Justice is taking care of the ocean and succeeding in correcting the present and future needs are the characteristics and precepts of justice.
Justice now is to build an infrastructure to take care of recycling that urgency beyond recall and all the cities and states and nations this will give work.

In 2007 I began studying and promoting recycling and addressing the environmental resolutions and world poverty.[xc] Today, now we do not have an infrastructure to process recyclables. Also, our environment eco-systems are in danger of existence.

In our being and life, we know that we are doing the best we can to restore and sustain and find (ASK GOD) to bring peace that is justice. NO "Sell out," of America, we cannot and will not have giving America away. We will stand TOGETHER IN GOD'S truth and restore America's.

Here are just a few gifts American has given to all peoples of all nations

Safety and Military: we need to realize our freedom is valuable. We need to be grateful that all the men and women in the Military and Police

Officers have kept our country safe. We now have to forgive and work together and treat each on each side with respect.

Legacy of our country in American, all the nations would not want to be here and develop their home life, education, work, and vocation.

Education: America is one of the most significant countries for education. America is at the top of higher education. People come all over the world to be educated.

Economy: has sustained Americans and allowed them to flourish.

The economy has allowed many from all nations to build revenue and wealth.

And we will restore and renew and regain and we will bring a healthy nation to greater life God will redeem us from the Chinese Virus when we seek His righteousness.

The economy has supported and imported immigrants since her birth. Presently, she takes the immigrant under her wing of God and empowers the immigrant to exist and be self-sufficient. And she also supports the immigrant.

Businesses are allowed vast enterprises to be successful and to develop innovative ideas to be completed and growing.

Infrastructure: has been the greatest in the industrial revolution with Britain. Now today, we are restoring our America so that the next legacy and generations in the future will have a working infrastructure.

St. Thomas Aquinas defines justice:

"Justice "in a philosophical sense, justice is understood as fairness, correct treatment, or equitable distribution of resources, but biblical justice is more than a mathematical delivery of goods. The Bible speaks of justice as a chief attribute of God, with biblical justice inextricably tied to God's mercy and grounded in the relationship between God and humankind." (**221**)[xci]

From the time of the wilderness wanderings, when the Hebrew people have been given ethical instructions about the treatment of widows, orphans, and strangers, there was justice.

Justice! Justice! Justice!

We need to have justice to continue to have a country that will uphold and allow its people to survive and live in a flourishing and healthy community.

Whether particular justice has an individual matter?

Augustine says (Questions. lxxxiii, qu. 61) that "the soul has four virtues whereby, in this life, it lives spiritually, viz.

1. **Temperance,** temperance with desire, the fortitude with fear and daring, summa theological (Content) 24
   Her people have planned and worked in action rocket ship spiritual delivery, in and toward justice with desire, the fortitude without fear and daring.
   Desire to work in unity to live and express their cultural heritage, yet respecting America's legacy, and all its forefathers paved the roads for them.
   Fortitude, to work diligently in overcoming the trials and tribulations in unexpected life situations and realizing and understanding simple strategies to respect society's laws and regulations.
2. **Prudence**, meaning between moral and intellectual virtue since it is reckoned among the intellectual virtues (Ethic. vi, 3, 5) Summa Theologica (Content)
   The moral and intellectual virtue America has reflected beauty upon her land and upon the world. Yet, throughout America's history and today, she remembers the protection of morals and intellectual integrity.
3. **Fortitude** America work's with great optimistic force and truth to accomplishing justice. Each member of society should respect her. She has given each one of us a home to be an individual. They allow each culture and traditional practices to live and work in accommodation to America's legacy and her foundational heritage.
4. **Justice** and he says that "the fourth is justice, which pervades all the virtues." Therefore, particular justice, which is one of the four cardinal virtues, has no specific matter.

[II–II.58] OF JUSTICE (TWELVE ARTICLES)[xcii]

Sacrifice and justice, justice is more important.
Justice: not merely the cardinal virtue of that name (cf 8:7), but the universal moral quality, which is the application of Wisdom to ethical conduct. (English Content)

Here, justice is a cardinal virtue and the universal moral quality, which is the application of Wisdom to ethical conduct. Because of the global moral quality of Wisdom, we can understand unity in the world today of the agreement and well-being in the technological world.[xciii]

First, Justice of giving and receiving

Justice is the love of someone's heart to bring justice to deliver what the truth is to redeem:

The sanctity of life and breath, is God the deliver of life
The well-being of the individuals, communities
When giving our heart, the heart of God of our Gifts we bring, His truth so that those who need receive they will receive His justice
Because we are His right arm of His strength, we are in the fullness of His heart.
We are the Wisdom of His purpose
We are Americans. We bring a life of healing in the supernatural power of God to heal all to all tragedies: IN THE MIGHT OF THE HOLY SPIRIT AND VIRGIN MARY AND THE ARCHANGELS AND THE ANGELS OF THE GOD OF ABRAHAM.
We never give up. We are justice. We seek to understand how to bring justice to the individual and find to bring justice to Americans.
America is justice wrapped in the heart of God's love. In the red robe of righteousness in Christ Jesus and the guidance of the Queen Virgin Mary, we will bring justice.
Let us continue to heal America and bring God's love giving justice, so those who need to receive will have the truth.

Justice, what is it defined in your understanding?
Justice, how can you bring more to you and others with peaceful actions?

Justice takes truth, and it takes the tools of virtues; what truth and tools of virtues do you need to work on?

Virtues, remember:			**Deadly Sins**	
Virtue	Latin	Gloss	Sin	Latin
Chastity	Castitas	Purity, abstinence	Lust	Luxuria
Temperance	Temperantia	Humanity, equanimity	Gluttony	Gula
Charity	Caritas	Will, benevolence, generosity, sacrifice	Greed	Avaritia
Diligence	Industria	Persistence, effortfulness, ethics	Sloth	Acedia
Patience	Patientia	Forgiveness, mercy	Wrath	Ira
Kindness	Humanitas	Satisfaction, compassion	Envy	Invidia
Humility	Humilitas	Bravery, modesty, reverence	Pride	Superbia

America The Brilliant Kissed By God Always New Fresh

You are the blossom of a new fresh flower of the first blossoming of the season.

Your smile glistens so brilliantly with distinct brilliance kissed by God.

You are unique beauty, a breed of flower-like no other that stands and shines even in the storms and always comes to life and becomes even more beautiful and never turns back to the old.

Yes, new refreshment, and illuminating shimmering life of your rare fragrant blossom speaking:

"I know the Wisdom of the way."
    "I know the loving light."
    " I know the Precious Peace."
    "I know the tender truth."
    "I know the luring love."

Yes, the beauty of your smile receives the enlightenment of the living truth of God:

    I will love,
    I will receive,
    I will ask,
    I will seek,
    I will listen,

> I will embrace,
> I will hear,
> And I know I am the child of the King of Kings.

Yes, I will take up the living waters of God's love gift to keep my blossoms always shimmering in the serene peace and love of God's Justice in my heart.

Lucia

Write on a piece of paper or journal, who you have to forgive, and what you have to forgive. What do you want to do in applying these virtues in your life?

First of Justice is Giving and Receiving

1. "The one consists in mutual giving and receiving, as in buying and selling, and other kinds of business intercourse and exchange."

2. This the Philosopher (Ethic. v, 4) calls commutative justice that directs exchange and intercourse of business.

3. In the first definition of justice of ethics v. 4, this is giving and receiving, requiring communication. Communication has to be in a peaceful place and not abusive. If contact is offensive, it needs to be corrected. Otherwise, it impedes the authentic flow of justice and knowledge and even Wisdom that humans exchange in the transaction.

Including the volatile expression of communication or abusive is allowed could become the norm if it is not corrected justly. As humans have unexpected happenings for various reasons, whether the action is negative or positive, actions cannot always be controlled. Hence, we need to begin at the onset of business communication with a protocol to seek our best, disclosing what we know relevant to the subject.

Furthermore, in exchange for business, there is sometimes information beneficial and detrimental. This information needs to be revealed. The more interaction with contemplation, the more aspects will be a complete eye and glorious light of the face of God's revelation. When I pray and need to grow and be reminded and even healed, my eyes and eyebrows lift up wide-eyed and lifted eyebrows of the revelation of God.

4. Communication sometimes is not used in words but in actions.

Let us make our actions love creating AUTHENTIC justice, correcting our virtues.

AMERICA, YOU ARE THE TOOLS GOD HAS to GIVE YOU
WHAT VIRTUES DO YOU HAVE?

When distributing justice, it needs to be fair in all different levels from the individual, community, states, national, and international. We know this and speak of this concept. However, we need to begin from the bottom-up individuals.

LET US work together to CONTINUE to be able to heal America.
Each person can work to its highest and original purpose, AMERICA.
Peace, Justice, Transformational Healing, Forward Building

   a. Honesty is essential in entrusting a transaction to be completed where both parties are in agreement.
   b. We need to disclose all relevant entities and complexities that could potentially change the transaction toward detrimental contraindications, and even augmentation and development for further expansion is necessary to reveal.
   c. Furthermore, what you are paying for, the products given and received, do they have value, and how long? What you invest in is the future of the item. ARE YOU WORKING WITH VIRTUES OF THE PURPOSE FOR JUSTICE? The products are developed and produced to protect human wholesomeness and environmental contingencies that are best for the longterm.

   d. Is the supplier and recipient bringing one or the other in danger in exchanging business, such as chemical or nuclear, or monetarily or even endangering another human life and animal life and environmental depletion or eradication? What are the foods we eat? What about the water? The pharmaceuticals, what are the contraindications? And as we have n recently, the dangers of fertilizers in Beirut can bring great tragedy and the uncontrollable catastrophe of death and destruction.

I have had various concerns regarding chemical fertilizers. I have warned America about the fertilizers we use that could be detrimental to human life. Especially those who work close to the crops and harvest them. Also, transportation or hold vessels of foods are essential to keep clean and safe. As I stated, I will also publish the Divine Messages and Commands in another volume.

Second, Justice of Distributive

"The other consists in distribution and is called distributive justice, whereby a ruler or a steward gives to each what his rank deserves."

The proper order displayed in ruling a family or any multitude demonstrates the justice of this kind in the ruler.

Hence, the universe's request is both in the effects of nature and in the results of the will, showing forth the justice of God. In Daniel 4 Nebuchadnezzar realized that all His kingdom is from God. And because he humbled himself to God and was righteous to all, His kingdom became more glorious for God's purpose and even more magnificent. God's love is justice.

I have given countless Divine Messages to bring that Distributive Justice that I have been given. For example, the development of the evil Chinese Virus and all their ability to make reconciliation to stop its deathly spread of humans; however, they covered their hearts of life and caused deaths across the world.

Dionysius says (Div. Nom. viii, 4): "We just need (to HAVE A REVELATION IN OUR HEARTS) that God is truly just; in how He gives to all existing things what is proper to the condition of each; and preserves the nature of each in the order and with the powers that properly belong to it."[xciv]

Dionysius, you, "God is truly just . . . He gives to all existing things what is proper."[xcv] When I was writing the corrections on this sentence, I was prompted to go in prayer. Listen, God is there to help us America and the world bring and work toward pure justice. He gave me encouragement and tools to compete and succeed in the writing of this book.

Many talk about "wishful thinking," and ignore the things that are really true that you want to be true. Tesla.
I agree though we can have miracles:

God, Himself confirmed their witness with signs and marvels and miracles of all kinds, and by distributing the gifts of the Holy Spirit in the various ways He wills.

Heb. 2:4

As stated in the Book Our Need to Give to the World, America love in God, Heal America, PLEASE GOD'S INTENTIONS.[xcvi]

God has all omniscient intentions for each aspect of creation and life to exist in its fullness, all can be redeemed.

1466 [[1472]. Righteousness, what is right, justice, the act of doing what is in agreement with God's standards, the state of being in proper relationship with God.[xcvii]

Question: How do we determine what is righteousness? We need a universal constant. God is a universal constant. VIRTUES ARE UNIVERSAL CONSTANCE.

NOW PROVING WHY WE NEED TO HAVE THE JUDEO-CHRISTIAN ETHICS IN AMERICA .. NOW FLOWING IN THE INDIVIDUAL HUMAN PSYCHE, FAMILIES, COMMUNITIES, BUSINESS, STATES, NATION, AND THE WORLD.

Live on America, the Judeo-Christian Ethics, and ethics of cultures of moral beauty OF THE CREATOR IN THE TRINITY what America is built on.

Do we give what is deserved? Do we hide what may be a catalyst to HELP? Do we have a motive for actions because we want power or rectify our purpose because we think we deserve it through non-merited work? Of course, one wants to make profitable transactions to the highest outcome, whether short or long. It needs to be under justice between both parties is the foundation of the virtues.

Do we take and use other valuable information without including or giving nothing in return to the person who worked blood, sweat, and tears and even much of their purse? This is the field workers across America in the cotton fields and in the vegetable fields and the dairy and meat and poultry farms, that have given their backs for the "Fed's [a man told me to write that I cannot mention his name.] and all American workers.

The great virtue is the Veteran that has given their life for the freedom of America.
The great virtue is the advocate that speaks out in truth of God and freedom for all Americans to be human.
The great virtue is those who work for years for a company.
The great virtue is those who seek virtues and fashioning justice and having a life of righteousness.
righteousness, what is right, justice, the act of doing what is in

Mother Nature does not give the tree oil to water it, Mother Nature gives

ist

I have to tell you I heard in a Divine Prayer and Divine Command to be sweet as a dove. I have been tested and was not. However, my Spirit in God in my heart has a deep peace, yet my heart for America and the world has unrest; because I know something is just not right, the rivers of justice upon the land of America and in the souls of the people.

I know there is a conspiracy to seek to take America to the gutters of Socialism.
I know we will conquer God's strength to keep her freedom.
I seek to listen day and night to what God wants from me to give the Divine Messages and Commands and to be that person to help Him, God, for America and the world. Lift your eyelids of your heart truly. He wants us to contribute to the redemption because we have to live with those things

<u>and peoples that need to be redeemed. And those things and peoples that need to be saved will have a miracle when we reflect God's love is a mystery of His blessing.</u>

The day voting is the day of November 3rd, 2020. President Donald Trump will be voted in President 2020; we need to pray that all goes smoothly and there are no casualties. We all need to pray triple what we usually pray. For protection, a victory for the American people and the world.

<u>When we ask America, God will give us His purpose:</u>

Remember, I desire to be sweet as a dove, and all America should be, that truly means the overflowing of the love of one's heart in the VIRTUES in God to be life for the people and justice.

I am reminded of the sweetness because we need to love and not react and forgive fast. Otherwise, all justice is stopped and blocked. We also need to be wise as King Solomon remembering we cannot allow the deception, deceiving, and stealing of America's legacy. We pray for victory, God's success.

WE ARE AWAKE, AMERICA

THE LIGHT IS SHINING ON AMERICA OUR EYES ARE OPEN

**GOD HAS GIVEN A CALL FOR AMERICA TO KEEP AMERICA FREE-
We are awake! AMERICA
TO WAKE THE PEOPLE UP OF AMERICA:**

I pray unceasingly and wholeheartedly with my entire being, and I study and plead for answers in prayer. I fight in faith, and I live in victory and in God's purpose to be a catalyst for God's promises that give His people when they seek His intention.

We are awake! AMERICA

" I was frank when I had said that Britain was asking no more than its due, and my anger when such a proposition was regarded with cynical indifference was equally genuine." [xcviii]   We as Americans in America and only ask in return what is due for us to be in restoration **to save our freedom of America, our God-given legacy.**

Let us come unto the virtues of the truth and correct America's body in the fullness of justice.

LET US STOP THIS: the nation has entered an age of post-constitutional soft tyranny. As French thinker and philosopher, Alexis de Tocqueville explained.

"It covers the surface of society with a network of small, complicated rules, minute and uniform, through which the most original minds and the most energetic characters cannot penetrate, to rise above the crowd."[xcix]

I have risen, we have risen, above the crowd, and we are the most original minds, and the most energetic characters that cannot be penetrated; We will work with Americans for justice to allow the truth of the individual to express their authentic being. Queen Mother Mary has told me that they will seek to try to impede the minds of humanity. ***Even with all the Divine Messages and Commands and years of work to Consult and guide America Our Need to Give to the World and Writings, Lisa Lucia Arden***, I had to see that it is God's Divine Blessings of eternal treasures, that they are true. And the success is in the acceptance of the people of the message and taking truth in action. We are not to be abused or allow our country to be abuse. God wants us to have freedom; we are connected by an umbilical cord of control; we are released and are nurtured as an individual at birth and sustained by God's gifts to the people.

Humanity has a command to treat humanity as if it is God's Church of love.

DEVELOP IN EDUCATION AND INDIVIDUAL SUCCESS

My God, My God, help me! My God, My God, help us. My God, My God, My God, help America!

Let not the children be separated from the parents in the immigration policy. There should be no excuse; these are the people who have given their backs and life for America's growth. IN AMERICA, the most significant wealth, the greatest minds, the most fabulous hearts of America, and we can work together to bring justice. Furthermore, "American Warriors of God's light" is at times considered and improperly "politically correct" when they address the issues of the dark and light forces. There is a battle out there; we will win even under persecutions; because we have a heavenly home, *"On earth as it is in heaven," God brings is Holy Spirit to protect and guide us*. We need to recognize and respect justice and the restoration measurements under the present leadership to the "Keeping America Great," we cannot have division. America has God's love of humanity and our *Mother of all Nations;* our country is a gift from God;

"We must support our rights or lose our character, and with it, perhaps, our liberties. A people who fail to do it can scarcely be said to hold a place among independent nations."

President James Monroe

When there are confusion and division, it needs to be exposed, and the current chaos and division needs fresh light upon it.

We need to ask ourselves **why, how, when, and what?** **Why** is there confusion and division? What would God want?

"If not us, who? If not, now, when?"

President John F. Kennedy

It is now; this is why when God calls, we lift the eyelids of our hearts and see we need to restore our America and be that reflection of God's love in America and the world's justice for freedom.

When there are division and confusion, it identifies injustice; especially when we as a people live in the land in the world in the Hands of God, America.

First, we ask: What was the past? What is the present? What will be the future?

We America as the godliest heart and generous country for humanity in her land that God has given to all nations.

What was the past? Even if the people's intentions were good, and there was a treacherously hidden purpose of making her Socialistic/Communistic, void of a humanitarian, ethical truth for the future. Each day I am reminded by the Spirit of the Lord, for America's freedom and her protection.

America was not put first in her Military and her business and her legacy and her land. In the past, it depicts her position across all areas of her life were in danger. Please, the information on America, Our Need to Give to the World, Heal America love in God.^{c} I mention this to prove a point, and it is essential and paramount for your life and America's life and legacy. If we stayed in the past paradigm, we would be in severe detriment as a country.

I mention the past because we have to be grateful for the present and continue to restore America; hence, we need to continue the strategic plan to restore her; as we do now. I ask you, then who would you vote in to take care of America?

DIVINE MESSAGE PRIOR TO THE 2020 ELECTION IN NOVEMBER.

For me, it is President Trump, to vote for, in deep prayer, the Spirit of the Lord and Virgin Mary told me PRESIDENT TRUMP WILL BE PRESIDENT 2020; HOWEVER, WE NEED TO BE CAREFUL OF THE PROCESS FOR THE AMERICAN PEOPLE. When we vote, we also vote for ourselves. We are in America. We are the driving force to bring her to that flowing river of the most incredible beauty and truth God has for her.

America, we are America when we are together in the purpose of God's most generous justice, and that is His truth, to bring freedom, life to the fullest for each individual, and safety for America and her legacy now and in the future.

What is the present? Under President Trump, the enlightened Americans and the Team

Finally, evident and with clarity, we have taken up the Authority of God's nature of His intentions of America and the world. We are **to put America first in truth, tradition, and justice** they saw, and we prayed, underpinning with the platinum promises of God's promises to continue to certain aspects of America's life in general that need urgent restoration. Also, in the leaders' growth, because the Divine Commands and my prayers are answered, they would the urgency to restore and save our legacy.

I began studying and praying for America with my Mother. After all, the children were fed and settled calmly; I think about 12 were living in the house then, and the babies in the nursery and my Noble father were home.

My noble faithful, enduring mother and I would go to the Grotto a Saint Elizabeth, Altadena, California. She had this sparkling light purple Corvair car, a two-door sports car. I loved it. My father bought it for her. It as if we were flying downhill on Lake Street to the Church on Michael Arch Angels Wings inside the Shekinah and Raphael and Gabriel on the front and back and sides. I never felt so serene and excited and peaceful. We would pray for many, our family members and my mother, she counseled at the school as a volunteer, or those she met at her classes at Pasadena City College, and those whom my brother's friends that were on drugs. I am now more aware of America's truth that we never give up to protect our America. Remember, God gives us the sick to help and we even sometimes have to take on their pain to help them through until God says, it is time, for them to decide. I have lived different homes, and I have taken on much of the pain and life conditions of the people. The Spirit of the Lord told me, it to shall pass, " I am praying for the daughter they will accept Me as their Lord and Savior, you have given them in My love in you an expression of eternal love."

We pray again for President Trump and all Americans to work to restore America in 2020 Their soul works and speaks and works for justice; we can bring a catalyst of truth and justice to those aspects of our country that need severe improvement: What will be the future? Of course, only God knows, He is imminent; however, He accommodates us**.** **When we do** what is justice for America, we can help restore America. Jesus Christ IS SHOWING us the future; He came to the world, showed us miracles, and gave His life. Remember, we were given America for our liberty and justice for all, by the bowing humble knees in prayer to God in the most astounding faithfulness; the leaders: President George Washington and the people to have freedom from Britain and President Lincoln, and the great leader Martin Luther King, and President Reagan, and now President Trump and all of Americans, that believe in her freedom, bow in humble prayer.

Denis Feeney, in his Book *Literature and Religion at Rome, cultures, contexts, and beliefs*, brings a picturesque authentic brilliance to this period in history. Mr. Feeney's Book is a dynamic and captivating presentation; my mere words cannot explain his writing of the Roman empire's history. Here in this brief discussion on justice, we will only be able to mention it briefly. We are not "crossing the line" of America. We are **not representatives of a god or a goddess.** We are not a 'divinized human;" [ci] God in us the breath of God and the Holy Spirit is the "Divine, "in us, and as humans, we are directed by the "God in the Trinity."

Today in America, this gives us the power of the Right Arm of God, not in our strength, in Jesus Christ's strength in the God of Abraham.

As the "The traditional Roman links between religion and exercise of people, the supreme ruler of the world was redefined not only as a religious agent but as a religious personality," with "patronage of deities such as Jupiter, or Venus.[cii]

AMERICA: We do not put our trust in men. **We put our faith in God. I need to tell you America there are Masonite and they seek to torture the body and abuse it;** God said "do not allow them to abuse you, here are the tools to destroy them. I am using you child in that they will come to My heart. This shall pass."

Do not put your trust in princes, Nor in a son of man, in whom there is no help .I will praise the LORD all my life; I will sing praises to my

God while I have my being. 3 Put no more trust in man, who has only the breath in his nostrils. I am a singer and have many songs.

Psalm 146:3

Feeney's "aim in his book has been a limited one, to argue that we should adopt a less patronizing attitude towards, the great body of religious knowledge that does, fortuitously, survive, in the form of Roman literature. . . After reading Cicero, I then realized, we know very little about the Romans."[ciii] *We, have been given a covenant in God through our relationship with Jesus Christ. We America are NOT intended to have a "pantheon" of gods.*

We are under one Monotheistic God, The God of Abraham IN THE POWER OF THE TRINITY. Yes, America's truth and tradition and supernatural experience in the "Divine."

Luke 1:46-55

Canticle of Blessed Virgin Mary[civ]

We tell God we love Him. God asks us to "feed His sheep." Each one of us has a particular gift we are given by God and can participate in God's sovereign plan to restore and redeem America.

John 12:15-17

Individual

You do not need "only," the intellectual equations of human-made ideas. You need FIRST, the virtue in the foundation of pure equations of the intentions the way nature works, imputing the Divine Promises God and life itself has given us. Although the plan has to be toward purity, remember, you put the purest food in the body; otherwise, it deteriorates.

Let us America, prepare the most genuine food of God's Virtues in the relationship with God and His people, body, mind, and the in the Holy Spirit.

Litany of The Sacred Heart of Jesus[cv]

Lord Jesus, healer of our souls and bodies,
During your life on earth, you went about doing good,
Healing every manner of sickness and disease, strengthening, curing, comforting, and consoling. Healer of our broken souls and bodies
and enemy of death and illness, lay your healing hand on …….and by Your grace, restore to good health that he and she may praise You without casing and serve you among your holy people for many years to come. Blessed, be Jesus, a friend of the human race! May God the Father bless us and keep us, God the Son lay his healing hands upon us, God, the Holy Spirit, strengthen and console us. May the Holy and Undivided Trinity guard our body, save our soul, and bring us in safety to our heavenly home. Amen
We are lifting our eyes to God's truth of what God's nature has intended; in prayer and supplication in the promises that God has given to humanity proven throughout history with humankind His never forsaking justice.

What is your form of justice for America to bring healing?
I will not "remit[cvi]," I will not give up my calling from the Lord God and Virgin Queen Mary to carry out their commands to bring their love of justice.
I WILL ARISE:
WE WILL ARISE;

352. ἀνακύπτω **anakupto,** *an-ak-oop´-to;* from 303 (in the sense of reversal) and 2955; to unbend, i.e. **rise**; figuratively, be elated: — lift up, look up.
Psalm 98 The Lord Does Marvelous Things Antiphon Break forth in Joyous song to the Lord.

Hymn

I bind unto myself today IN mystery of the almighty power and love in the name of the Trinity)
The (mystery of the almighty power and love in the name of the Trinity)
By invocation of the same,
The Three in One, and One in Three.
I bind this day to me forever,
By the power of the Spirit, Christ's incarnation

His baptism in the Jordan River.
His death on the cross for my salvation.
His bursting from the spiced tomb.
His riding up the heavenly way.
His coming at the day of doom.
I bind unto myself today.

Remember, when we bind in Christ is taking on missions He wants. **I Bind unto Myself Today Author: Saint Patrick, Translator: Cecil Frances Alexander Charles Villiers StanfordSections:** https://hymnary.org/text/i_bind_unto_myself_today
https://my.hymnary.org/song/dynamic/542/i-bind-unto-myself-today?toolkit=veroviostatic&width=1600

Divine Message Justification September 19, 2019

(We are justified in our intimate relationship with God. Just as you are justified in a solution or redemption between individuals or groups, it is the same with God, yet Holy and filled with Wisdom and Love of God.)

In prayer, there is a room: You will go into the space of justification.

"I will justify you, daughter because the sin that has been done upon you will be justified." What is justification? This is for everyone, so we do not feel guilt for our mistakes and other mistakes.

The Spirit of the Lord said, "justification is love." Sing the Lord a new song, for the Lord has done marvelous things. God's right hand and holy arm have gotten the victory.

A Novena to Good Pope John XXIII[cvii]

Community: people know and have a message from God and even a basic gift, whether business or for justice of their community, we know many times they are not accepted in their community. Yet, we as faithful believers and even nonbelievers(do also in their way many do not speak of it.) take God's gifts first to Him for continuous direction and then to those He sends to us and those whom He sends us toward. I am grateful that the American people heard the call to protect our freedom and our legacy.

They listened to the call when they voted for President Trump. There is a from God for us to protect our freedom and our land for our children God's' truth." There is a command from God for us to protect America. **We have to be careful with America of infiltrating ideas of a Socialistic, Communistic Rule.**

The inherent vice of capitalism is the unequal sharing of blessings. The inherent virtue of socialism is the equal sharing of miseries.

Speech, Demobilization," The House of Commons London, English October 22, 2020, President Winston Churchill

You cannot build character and courage by destroying men's initiative and independence.
Rev. William J. H. Boetcker

The worship of the golden calf of old has found a new and heartless image in the cult of money and the dictatorship of an economy that is faceless and lacking any truly human goal.
Pope Francis

This social order requires constant improvement. It must be (integrated always) on truth, built on justice, and (polished) by love; in the freedom, it should grow every day toward a more humane balance. An improvement in attitudes and abundant changes in society will have to take place if these objectives are to be gained.[cviii] In being repetitive, I want to say attitudes are molecules(electrons also) and can affect the environment, the people, and all of creation. God does bring a balance, and those obedient to His call are allowed to experience injustices to bring His Pure Justice. *In His hand is the soul of every living thing and the breath of every human being! Job 12:10* God has given us an authentic being; each one of us is beautifully created. Hence, we are His breath *"ruah"* that has infinite possibilities.

Consequently, we as a person never should be suppressed. Because God is a God of life and infinite possibilities, of potentiality and actuality bringing life.

Integration into the Solution for Each Person political Unity Justice

"Justified in the name of the Lord Jesus Christ and the Spirit of our God," "sanctified . . . [and] called to be saints,"14 Christians have become the temple of the *Holy Spirit*.15 This "Spirit of the Son" teaches them to pray to the Father16 and, having become their life, prompts them to act to bear "the fruit of the Spirit"17 by the charity in action. Healing the wounds of sin, the Holy Spirit renews us interiorly through a spiritual transformation.18 He enlightens and strengthens us to live as "children of light" through "all that is good and right and true."

III. *The Babylonian Crisis (40:1-66:24), For the mouth of Yahweh has spoken.'* [17] *Learn to do good, search for justice, discipline the violent, be just to the orphan, plead for the widow.* [cix]

The word of Yahweh came to me, saying before I formed you in the womb I knew you; you came to birth I consecrated you; I appointed you as a prophet to the nations.

Jeremiah. 1:4

God has consecrated America to His heart call upon Him for justice.

The Covenant of Peace **Colossians** 54:1-17) *For me, it will be as in the days of Noah when I swore that Noah's waters should never flood the world again. So now I promise never to be angry with you and never to rebuke you also. For the mountains may go away and the hills may totter, but my faithful love will never leave you; my covenant of peace will never totter, says Yahweh who takes pity on you.*

God asks for your love in that we are be fully blessed by His covenant in peace for justice. However, some will have to have recompense for the past.

V. Raised with Christ (3:1-4:6)] You have stripped off your old behavior with your old self, and you have put on a new self which will progress towards true knowledge the more it is renewed in the image of its Creator; and in that image, there is no room for distinction between Greek and Jew, between the circumcised and uncircumcised, or between barbarian and Scythian, slave and free. There is only Christ: He is everything and He is in everything.

> *The chosen of God, then, the holy people whom He loves, you are to be clothed in heartfelt compassion, in generosity and humility, gentleness and patience. ¹³ Bear with one another; forgive each other if one of you has a complaint against another. The Lord has forgiven you; now, you must do the same. ¹⁴ Over all these clothes, put on love, the perfect bond. ¹⁵ And may the peace of Christ reign in your hearts, because it is for this that you were called together in one body. Always be thankful.*
>
> Col. 3:12 -15

God knows and s the compassion Americans have given each other in this time of the Covid-19 virus. He knows that we seek to do our best. We are thankful. Thankful is respect and respecting America and her people and her land.

> *Let the Word of Christ, in all its richness, find a home with you. Teach each other and advise each other in all wisdom. With gratitude in your hearts, sing psalms and hymns and inspired songs to God;—¹⁷ and whatever you say or do, let it be in the name of the Lord Jesus, in thanksgiving to God the Father through Him.*
>
> Col. 3:16

America has always been a country to build one's dreams. They are sharing the goals and knowledge. For example, people come all over the *world to study at California Technology in Pasadena, California. The scientist advises each other of wisdom and knowledge.*

Moreover, we, as people have to have justice to continue to sing psalms and hymns to God in thanksgiving.

This is God's land

"Pastors arrested. Criminal charges and threats for worship, including parishioners. County requests armed police to block church entrances. Daily fines of $1,000 per day fines for the faithful. Home Bible studies were banned. Churches under threat of losing parking, power, and water.

For the first time in our history, the Body of Christ is under widespread assault here in America. California officials are going to insane lengths to try to silence the Word of God.

Today, I will present an oral argument before a panel of three judges on our emergency motion. Pray for victory. – Mat

In California, Liberty Counsel represents Pastor Ché Ahn, Harvest Rock Church, and Harvest International Ministry, and 162 other California-based churches.

<u>On June 6, Gov. Newsom banned singing and chanting. On July 13, he banned ALL worship for about 80 percent of the state, including Bible studies and fellowship in private homes or apartments</u>. Under orders, a person cannot visit a neighbor in the same apartment complex for Bible study or worship. The criminal penalty for doing so carries up to one year in prison and daily fines of $1,000. On August 11, Pasadena city officials sent a **"Cease and Desisted"** letter demanding that churches comply with Gov. Newsom's illegal "no worship" orders. If they continued to meet for worship, they would face **"misdemeanors under California and Pasadena law punishable by a fine and imprisonment."** Another Pasadena prayer ministry received a similar letter for having five people gathered for prayer in a 7,000 square foot facility – and this is in a country that is *supposed* to have religious freedom!"[cx]

Be persevering in your prayers and be thankful as you stay awake to pray. ³ Pray for us, especially, asking God to throw open a door for us

to announce the message and proclaim the mystery of Christ, for the sake of which I am in chains; ^{4} *pray that I may proclaim it as clearly as I ought.*

Col. 4:2

We as Americans will persevere. Pray to ask and seek and knock; that God wants righteousness in our country America, and to be a reflection of God's justice

Divine Message March 2, 2020, Pasadena Spirit of Queen Virgin Mary

Those who vote need to take care of and have the most moral decision that would be the decision God will make. (God wants us to vote for our country to be safe, to have freedom, to have life, to protect the **development** of life, to be that person God created us to be, to enjoy all God created.)

Act wisely with outsiders, making the best of the present time. Always talk pleasantly and with a flavor of wit but be sensitive to the kind of answer each one requires.

Col. 4:5

Today, in the political atrocities and tension, we need to respect each other and not spend time in the citizen's tax money to promote extremist ideologies and are actions of injustice.

Political

Respecting the birth and development of human life requires peace. Peace is not merely the absence of war, and it is not limited to maintaining a balance of powers between adversaries. Peace cannot be attained on earth without safeguarding a person's goods, free communication among men, respect for persons and peoples' dignity, and the assiduous practice of fraternity. Peace is "the tranquility of order."Peace is the work of justice and the effect of charity.

Individual

Today we have become evolved in God's awareness of what He desires. However, we cannot obsolete children of God called to do His works that have gifts beyond understanding. We need to protect those who have talents and support them, not seek to take otherwise when the innocent or used for what we think is better when it is not God's purpose. Hence, this is why we need to allow the children to be creators of the ideas they were given and protect their freedom.

First is the Love of God. We have to balance our communities in love; however, we need to have the truth and tradition in America to restore her freedom. Open your heart of your eyes, that is why the First Commandment is most important; when we have God's love is first, we have that infinite love. And since God created humanity and building a relationship you will know who and what you are and why you were created.

Divine Message for the people of America
St Bede's Catholic Church, La Canada

God has a gift for the people, and this gift is that He stated for each to "plant a fruit tree because," this is a symbolism of the fruit that we now are being blessed with under the leadership of President Trump and his team; we have had much fruit.

We have been an instrument to save America in following the commands that God has ordered President Trump and the team.

(Follow in God's justice) President Trump and the American Freedom Warriors and Americans have brought fruit to our country, states, communities. People, children, and adults and each one that is to the goodness of what it is to be American and respect America and its justice system. (has brought fruit).

Community

God is infinitely greater than all His works: "You have set your glory above the heavens."[156] Indeed, God's "greatness is unsearchable."[157] But because He is the Free and Sovereign Creator, the first cause of all that exists, God is present to His creatures' inmost being: "In him, we live and move and have our being."[158] In the words of St. Augustine, God is "higher than my highest and more inward than my innermost self."[159]

We find community in unity, DRIVING justice in God, "In Him, we live and move and have our being."

Deliberate *hatred* is contrary to charity. This is essential to speak of, it is the seriousness of the culture and masonry of actions that are against humans. God gives one who is called the gifts to protect the people from this treacherous deceit. We need to be careful because there, masonry and cultural witchcraft are used for their desire to fulfill their emptiness. *"But I say to you, Love your enemies and pray for those, who persecute you, so that you may be sons of your Father who is in heaven."*[cxi]   Mat. 5:43-45

When someone is a human and imperfect and even weak in the eyes of the world, and when they bring a message for a warning for all, I would say this is one of the greatest tests.

Today we as a country need to continue to seek to love when the American legacy and the beauties and beliefs that have been given as a gift from God.

Nation

"Every act of war directed to the indiscriminate destruction of whole cities or vast areas with their inhabitants is a crime against God and man, which merits firm and unequivocal condemnation."[cxii]

Safety is the first to protect America.

Integrated into the solution for each person

Why would we speak about justice?

Because judgment is needed, and we want the truth?

When one wants justice, something is lacking?

Hence, each of us needs to look inside ourselves to how we are not bringing justice. We need to understand and ask ourselves and those who when we pray: "how can I bring justice?"

Give Justice to the Weak (Psalm 82:1-8)

For each of us to integrate into a solution to make justice flow, take heed to:

Pope Ambrose truth and working force of justice: In love is our best defense of justice!

Common Unity

"Love gives confidence even when there is an enemy."

Pope Ambrose

Forgiving for reasons of division and to accommodate in truth for solutions for the best of community is the virtue of love of God's purpose to take care of humanity and the dominion God has given us.

Divine Justice Psalms 72

The s human, giving only what he has received from God. Hence, intercession must be made for him. The extravagant language is typical of oriental royal courts.
The *life* of justice and the *spirit* of right.
When we protect each other, we have life and life abundant.
We need each other for protection and God's love.
I have nothing if I do not have you, America.
https://www.youtube.com/watch?v=FxYw0XPEoKE

ARTICLE 3: SOCIAL JUSTICE

Society ensures social justice when it provides the conditions that allow associations or individuals to obtain what is their due, according to their nature and their vocation. Social justice is linked to the common good and the exercise of Authority.[cxiii]

Justice: is rendering to everyone that which is his due. It has been distinguished from equity in this respect that while justice means merely doing what positive law demands, equity means doing what is fair and right in every separate case.[cxiv]

Because the happenings of the world that are uncontrollable it is irrational to accept that you can measure the strategy for justice in the same process to deliver it.

There has to be a "Divine Grace" of God that has the power to bring justice under the most shocking happening of human trials. (COVID-19 Virus, Disunity of the people, Poverty, Economic Crisis, Environmental Crisis, Immorality of Humans, Breakdown of the wholesomeness of the Culture).

Therefore, what is due is not always accessible to obtains; hence, there needs to be a "Divine Nature" in the "Divine Grace" that God gives to us individually that we can bring His "Divine Power" of God to bring justice if we receive. Everyone, has a certain purpose. It is individually we have this Divine Nature, Grace, and Power of God. An individual is responsible for his or her own life in choosing God or worldly ideas. Hence, the Divine Nature, Grace, and Power of God are then perfected in God and not mixed with worldly or human ideas. I pray we have the same purpose of bringing justice though we deliver it individually, and if we received the Divine, Grace, Nature, and Power in God individually we are guided. All humanity is God's love; He carries even the most powerful in His arms. God tests the power to build their faith to gain another armor. The trickery of others is not powerful and is not the creator of life.

That perfection of his nature whereby he is infinitely righteous in himself and in all he does, the righteousness of the divine nature exercised in his moral government. Note: When they kept on questioning him, he straightened up and said to them, *"Let any one of you who is without sin be the first to throw a stone at her (him)." John 3:7*

At first, God imposes righteous laws on his creatures and executes them righteously. Matthew 6:12 – From the Lord's Prayer – "And forgive us our debts, as we also have forgiven our debtors." God forgives us, ask Him, to help you not to sin with all your being. When you love God with all your being, you turn from sin. And when you love your neighbor, you do not want to sin.

Justice is not an optional product of his will but an unchangeable principle of his very nature. **God never changes; men change. This is why we trust in God.**

His legislative justice is his requiring of his rational creatures' conformity in all respects to the moral law **states,** *"Do not be deceived, my beloved brethren. Every good gift and every perfect gift is from above, and comes down from* **the Father of lights, with whom there is no variation or shadow of turning.** *" James 1:16-17*

His rectoral or distributive justice is his dealing with his accountable creatures according to the law's requirements in rewarding or punishing them (Ps. 89:14). **Now that God has sent the Son of God to take our sin on the cross, we can ask Him for forgiveness, and He forgives us when we repent with all our hearts.**

In remunerative justice he distributes rewards (James 1:12; 2 Tim. 4:8); in vindictive or punitive justice, he inflicts punishment on account of transgression (2 Thess. 1:6).

As infinitely righteous, he cannot do otherwise than regard and hate sin as intrinsically hateful and deserving of punishment. "He cannot deny himself" (2 Tim. 2:13). His essential and eternal righteousness immutably determines him to visit every sin as such with merited punishment. Gen. 49:16

"Dan" — Dan here means he provides justice.[cxv]
Let us all be "Dan," providing justice.

Summa Theology

The knowledge of God belongs only to the good; for Augustine says (De Trin. i): "The weak eye of the human mind is not fixed on that excellent light unless purified by the justice of faith." Therefore, God cannot be known by natural reason. For it is written that "those who instruct many to justice," shall be "as stars unto perpetual eternities [*Douay: 'for all eternity']" (Dan. 12:3). Now, if God alone were eternal, there could not be many eternities. Therefore, God alone is not the only eternal.[cxvi]

[I.16.4] Whether good is logically before the true?

Reply to Objection 3: The virtue which is called "truth" is not truth in general, but a certain kind of truth according to which man shows himself in deed and word as he really is. But the truth as applied to "life" is used in a particular sense, inasmuch as a man fulfills in his life that to which he is ordained by the divine intellect, as it has been said that truth exists in other things (Article [1]). Whereas the truth of "justice" is found in man as he fulfills his duty to his neighbor, as ordained by law. Hence, we cannot argue from these particular truths to truth in general.

G1343 δικαιοσύνη *dikaiosynē*

fair and equitable dealing, justice, Acts 17:31; Heb. 11:33; Rom. 9:28; *integrity, virtue,* Lk. 1:75; Eph. 5:9; in N.T. *generosity, alms,* 2 Cor. 9:10, v.r.; Mt. 6:1; *piety, godliness,* Rom. 6:13; *investiture with the attribute of righteousness, acceptance as righteous, justification,* Rom. 4:11; 10:4, et al. freq.; *a provision* or *mean for justification,* Rom. 1:17; 2 Cor. 3:9; *an instance of justification+,* 2 Cor. 5:21 ˘ *innocence; justice; justification; righteous, righteousness,*

provision or *mean for justification,* Rom. 1:17; 2 Cor. 3:9; *an instance of justification,* 2 Cor. 5:21 ˘ *innocence; justice; justification; righteous, righteousness.*

GK 1468 | S G1345 δικαίωμα *dikaiōma*

pr. *a rightful act, act of justice, equity; a sentence,* of condemnation, Rev. 15:4; in N.T., of acquittal, *justification,* Rom. 5:16; *a decree, law, ordinance,*

Lk. 1:6; Rom. 1:32; 2:26; 8:4; Heb. 9:1, 10; *a meritorious act, an instance of perfect righteousness,* Rom. 5:18; Rev. 19:8* ˇ *regulations; righteous, righteousness; righteous deeds.*

In Ezek 1:24 and 10:5 the sound of the cherubs' wings is compared to Shaddai's שָׁדַד **shadad,** *shaw-dad* powerful voice. The reference may be to the mighty divine warrior's battle cry that, accompanies his angry judgment.) Finally, the name occurs 31 times in the Book of Job. Job and his "friends" assume that Shaddai is the sovereign King of the world (11:7; 37:23a) who is the source of life (33:4b) and is responsible for maintaining justice (8:3; 34:10–12; 37:23b). He provides abundant blessings, including children (22:17–18; 29:4–6), but he can also discipline, punish, and destroy (5:17; 6:4; 21:20; 23:16). Hebrew Strongs 7703. שָׁדַד **shadad,** *shaw-dad´;* a primitive root; properly, to be burly, i.e. (figuratively) powerful (passively, impregnable); by implication, to ravage:—dead, destroy(-er), oppress, robber, spoil(-er), x utterly, (lay) waste. <u>God will strike against as He revealed the geopolitical power that China and the silent Communist and Socialist and the Technological evil workers now being revealed the voting conspiracy and conspiracy against American people. Also, I will repeat, the Elite that wants to save America and the world's freedom are commanded to support President Trump and His Presidency 2020. Elites need to build an intimate relationship with God, more than they have. Now my leaders.</u>
<u>I have another Divine Message while correcting this book. November 22, 2020, I felt earthquakes in the spirit world. I also saw visions I cannot say. God is protecting us. I believe all should pray without ceasing in all and everything you do. Ask God, my people.</u>

Genesis 23:14-20. Prudence, as well as justice, directs us to be fair and open in our dealings; cheating bargains will not bear the light. Listen, America and other parts of the world when "dealings, cheating bargains, will not bear the light," of God. And we are responsible for maintaining justice. Ezek. 8:3; 34:10-12; 37:23b.

PRUDENCE AND JUSTICE AND FAIR

Prudence is it good for America and the world to bring a harvest.

Justice does bring life and truth of God's grandest intention for the freedom and energy of humanity's development. God has given us Divine gifts and mercy. We need to use them always for His purpose.

After the birth of these sons, he set his house in order, with prudence and justice. He did this while he yet lived. It is Wisdom for men to do what they find to do while they live, as far as they can. Abraham lived for 175 years.

Metaphorically, the righteous man is said to "hold to his way" (Job 17:9). One can "grasp" an idea or "take hold" of folly (Eccl 7:18; 2:3). In his grace, God will "take hold of my right hand" as a sign of his guidance and favor (Ps 73:23; cf. Isa 45:1,). Ps 139:10 speaks of God's right hand leading and "laying hold" of the Psalmist. In Deut 32:41, the Lord sharpens His sword "to take hold of justice.

Yes, God has "taken hold of my right hand" because I follow His call. Justice is His, not ours, and He knows the way. He uses us to plant the mustard seed of His truth in the mind, heart, souls, and actions of the people.

<u>See those who work for truth, see God is yearning for the enemy's repentance and forgiveness entering into a personal acceptance of Him, Jesus Christ as their Lord and Savior in the love and mystery of the Holy Spirit living in their heart in the power of the God of Abraham, Salvation. God is calling on them. Because they are seeking to kill, steal, and destroy. Cannot you see just as God allowed the Chinese Virus to spread yet He also healed the world; it could have been worst; God has given us mercy.</u>

IV. ECONOMIC ACTIVITY AND SOCIAL JUSTICE The development of economic activity and growth in production are meant to provide for the needs of human beings. Economic life is not meant solely to multiply goods produced and increase profit or power; it is ordered first to the service of persons, of the whole man, and the entire human community. Economic activity, conducted according to its own proper methods, is to be exercised within the limits of the moral order, and in keeping with social justice to correspond to God's plan for man.[cxvii]

We have to be careful, some of those that are advocate for Justice bravely independent have been secretly oppressed and suppressed; they know the truth with God's clarity, and they have not been accepted perhaps who they are.

ARTICLE 3: SOCIAL JUSTICE Catechism-E(Title) 3

1928 Society ensures social justice when it provides the conditions that allow associations or individuals to obtain what is their due, according to their nature and their vocation. Social justice is linked to the common good and the exercise of Authority.[cxviii]

God has given us "authority" in America to be safe and robust. And a good man *shall be satisfied* in God.

The **virtue** of their royal priesthood, and (those who are rs) added) join in the offering of the Eucharist. 318 (Vatican II) "They likewise exercise that priesthood in receiving the sacraments, in prayer and thanksgiving, in the witness of a holy life, and by self-denial and active charity." Self-denial can also be putting God first in all one does. Love God with all your heart and soul and put no other God's before Him. (First Commandment) God's Eucharist is that from KING DAVID. And that Resurrection Cross of Jesus Christ the Messiah.

God of Abraham sent HIS only begotten SON JESUS CHRIST AND WE, now the Resurrected life in God when one brings all their experience to Jesus Christ in the God of Abraham the First Commandment.

The Eucharist is our life in God and who we are as His people. It is a part of us that God desires. God desires that the original purpose of each person, each humanity He created; He wants wholeheartedly that He even gave His only begotten Son as a redeeming perfect lamb to take upon Him the sin of humanity. In that, we will then be justified, redeemed, and deliver to new life. God is asking you to first love Him with all your heart and soul and life. When you seek to worship God, then you are sanctified in His love and grow in His grace to know His purpose. This is the Divine, Grace, Life, and Power of God we discussed above. [cxix]

Our priest, ministers, and the people of God our leader seek their love and give them God's love in return. They strive for God's justice.

The assumed root of the following.

643a חֹטֶר *(ḥōṭēr)* **branch or twig** (Isa 11:1),

> *There shall come forth a shoot from the stump of Jesse, and a branch from his roots shall bear fruit.*
>
> Is. 11:1

This is the branch of those in humanity that choose to give to God their heart even if they do not understand all things, God will be with them and guide them and heal and redeem them. For those who are do not believe in Jesus Christ, Jesus Christ said if you believe in My works, I will profess you to My Father; His Father is the Father of Abraham, the God of Abraham.

This is the justification that Jesus Christ speaks of He has to be justified by the Father, and we humans have to be justified by Jesus Christ.

This is God's intention of the way humanity and the world is supposed to live and be, then it will be justified by Jesus Christ and then explained by the Father Abraham.

On Him will rest the spirit of Yahweh, the spirit of wisdom and insight, the spirit of counsel and power, the spirit of knowledge and fear of Yahweh: ³ His inspiration will lie in fearing Yahweh. His judgement will not be by appearances. His verdict not given on hearsay. ⁴ He will judge the weak with integrity and give fair sentence for the humblest in the land. He will strike the country with the rod of his mouth with the breath of his lips bring death to the wicked.

Is. 11:2-4

The assumed root of the following.

644 חָיָה *(ḥāyâ)* **live, have life, remain alive, sustain life, live prosperously, live forever. Also be quickened, revive from sickness, discouragement, or even death.**[cxx]

Our America has life חָיָה *(ḥāyâ)when we have justice to live prosperously in the in Jesus Christ. Moreover, here now in God, we can revive all from sickness and discouragement or even death, sustaining life, and live prosperously in the justice of God. Also, live forever promise of eternal life when we accept Jesus Christ as our Lord and Savior.*

Justice in Potentiality

Reiterating each one of us knows in our heart of God in us that God is calling to us, what truth for justice is, and how we can deliver it. *Please, the Chart of Justice.*

I am called to tell you and encourage; God's loves because I am the first that needs to understand; because I search for what I should do in God, because many things I have n and experienced, and have had many trials and failures, and beauties and miracles. I want to continue in being apart of His creation to restore the humanity and gifts that He has given us in America and the world that I seek to do it with you individually yet for God's same purpose.

Since by your obedience to the truth you have purified yourselves so that you can experience the genuine love of brothers, love each other intensely from the heart; ^{23} for your new birth was not from any perishable d but from imperishable d, the living and enduring Word of God. ^{24} For all humanity is grass, and all its beauty like the wildflower's. As grass withers, the flower fades, ^{25} but the Word of the Lord remains forever. And this Word is the Good News that has been brought to you.

1Pet. 1:22

We are responsible for each of us for our own life and our sin. We are individuals; we cannot integrate with space and take and command or control of another person; there is only one life for each person, not for another to incorporate into another to control; Controlling a person is a treacherous sin cutting off life; it is murdering the potentiality of the authentic being of God created in that individual. Even in the curiosity of another person, there has to be respected and allowing each person's identity to be whom God created, even in the prayer and intimacy with God that is for the individual's intimacy with God directs each person to God calling in that person. Contemplate, in each area of life there needs to be a protection of the potentiality of humanity and that is in the respect of one another. That is delivered in the First Commandment and then in the Second Commandment.

All if us, open the eyes of your heart. Cannot you this begins at the first inception of the d of a child, needs to be respected and love to be the potentiality[cxxi] of a human. This is why virtues are the tools of God's truth, and truth in God is the justice we seek and live toward.

Notes: now on potentiality. God allows us to have the potentiality that He created us as our cell make-up already has coded within. We can be an individual in God's specific plan when we seek Him first. Even if we have a falling short when we ask in humble forgiveness and strive to be in God love and bring our sorrows and sins to the Cross.

Then we ask how we can enter in an agreement with the acceptance of these commands of the Ten Commandments, and yet gifts toward justice and continuous restoration of the potentiality and happiness of humanity?

Truth in God's Love in the way of His purpose is for each individual is the greatest of all things because it is love, God's love; God only creates love.

It is a continuous evolution of the acceptance of each individual's potential to accept God's purpose as who was created for. It is the free will choice of good or evil. Remember, though evil uses right, and innocence and even confusion to bring down good; yet, only for a time or detour, God always redeems; sometimes we do not see the gifts of the worldly needs for God's creation, because the good received are eternal treasures, just like Apostle Paul says.

And then realizing there is a history of God and His people, we cannot deny humbling ourselves at the foot of the cross.

Resurrected life in Christ

Resurrection life is this life in us that is nearest to God's love, and we live as human's imperfect and incomplete; He redeems our humanness even if we are good there can be a trial small or severe, yet we can only be redeemed by the Cross of Christ, in God for a resurrected life. Though may I reiterate, God created all humanity, and He decides even when society does not come to Jesus Christ's Cross, He accommodates them. He is yearning for all His creation to accept His eternal love in and with and through to His heart.

The heart cry of David in fearful respect of God's command has a desire and vision to believing Jews and Gentiles unified through worship, and for the entire body of Messiah to be aligned with God's heart for Israel!

Divine Message

Remember, those who have God's gifts cannot be judged by others and even cannot be judged by even believers. [Discussion in prayer and revelation in prayer: Did you ask yourself ever if God's Spiritual Gifts in His people also evolve and become more beautiful of God's truth, just as God allows us to create things in life with what He gives us? God is not limited He is infinite in us.] Remember, I have told you the Divine Messages are for those who have faith in Me of the Divine Messages that My Father has given Me child. These Divine messages are for those who want to know Me more and those who do not know Me, and those who want to know God's truth, life, and way. Jesus Christ is: The Way, The Truth, and the Life, and no one comes to the Father except through Him. John 14:6

Today February 7th, 2016
Holy Family Church at Mass

In prayer and again I was reminded to warn **the people of America and the world that: if we do not seek justice, under God to save America, in the American way, in the precepts of the Constitution, and seek to protect the poor, the lower, and middle class, our children will not be children, deathly they will be, and just be a robotic replica, controlled by the technological powers and powers of the world. This relates to the technical control and group financed by the silent powers. It is a time for the Church to speak. I have, and I will, and I am doing.**

The solution is Jesus Christ and His Authority. The Spirit of God is in the r.

Rev. Robert Clancy, Austria

Divine Message September 9, 2020

The creation of God, all things molecules, atoms, and even the items made by man will also manifest His intentions for His directions and purpose when they are sought in truth. Those things organic especially are supposed to be directed in the way of God's purpose. Therefore, scientists and all peoples in all works again, I proclaim in the directions of the Divine Trinity.

When actions are prepared and worked through and sought to deliver and deliver with the intention of the closest Truth, and when they are in the foundation of the closest truth known, they will manifest the Divine.

PURE JUSTICE IS GOD'S TRUTH. GOD'S TRUTH IS PURE JUSTICE

Remember, even those who do not believe in God, God can use them to bring God's truth through His Word's, Sacraments, precepts, and even daily work. Therefore, we can work together in these times of severe tragedy, and blind division, in our America, and the world, to deliver God's justice. Open our hearts for others; forgive; when we respect the good, they have done, and identify it to justice, as their real persona; then, life will light up in them. The other part of them that does not do righteousness is because they need God's redemption, and God's redemption is justice. God's justice is the action of good toward God's perfect truth.

Divine Message. October. 8 2019 Vision in the heavenly

I SAW MANY MANY MANY HANDS STRETCHED OUT AND THEY EACH HAVE A RING... AND THEY ARE THE BRIDES OF Jesus Christ; the hands were all different colors and sizes; the light is heavenly; Jesus Christ in the Spirit said, "these are My brides of love. [ALSO JESUS SAY: WE ARE GOD'S CHILDREN, AND DISCIPLES AND LEADERS AND PEACE WARRIORS]; Now each person has the door open for their life; when someone is married, there is a new home, a new life, a new house, a new heart, and a union. Awake and arise, when the bride is married to the Bridegroom, the Bridegroom takes care of the bride, and the bride takes care of the Bridegroom; however, there a covenant. They live together, building a home in the living and the heart; Hear, listen this is how America can find the solutions and the answers to their life, the bride of the Bridegroom, God, is a covenant of love in the highest love; not a physical love though, the body has to be seeking purity. Please, America there is a new house; a new heart; a new soul; when a bride is married to the Bridegroom, this marriage is a covenant of the heavenly

So for anyone who is in Christ, there is a new creation: the old order is gone and a new being is there to see.

2 Cor. 5:17

This is a heavenly covenant two hearts in one, is the Bridegroom Jesus Christ, and the believer the Bride. Yet, I am heavenly perfect toward perfectness. planning .. a blossoming a covenant. This is correct of truth always when the bride works in the heart with the Bridegroom, God.

It is the Bridegroom who has the bride; and yet the Bridegroom's friend, who stands there and listens to him, is filled with joy at the Bridegroom's voice. This is the joy I feel, and it is complete.

John 3:29

The Church alone, being the Bride of Christ and having all things in common with her Divine Spouse, is the depository of the truth.

Pope Pius X

But you are a chosen race, a kingdom of priests, a holy nation, a people to be a personal possession to sing the praises of God who called you out of the darkness into His wonderful light. [10]

1Pet. 2:9

He is the living stone, rejected by human beings but chosen by God and precious to him; set yourselves close to him [5] *so that you, too, may be living stones making a spiritual house as a holy priesthood to offer the spiritual sacrifices made acceptable to God through Jesus Christ.* [6] *As scripture says: Now I am laying a stone in Zion, a chosen, precious cornerstone and no one who relies on this will be brought to disgrace.*

1Pet. 2:4

Chapter Three

Restoration

Four Foundational Truths

"Without God, ye can do nothing." John 15.5 ^{cxxii}

Christ Holy Cross has Redeemed and Restored the World.

Even when you live somewhere you plant seeds and get thorns and weeds; and you may even suffer from injustice, violence, and danger from the situation, God, sustains, protects, strengthens, empowers, heals and restores. You do not always see immediately God's Spiritual seeds that you plant sometimes. When you are growing in life, and God wants to use you, you need to walk in darkness to bring God's light. Hence, you will reflect the light because you have a part of His heart when you receive God's light. God's heart to restore creation is in those who seek His love, and obedience to learn and pursue what His Peace and Justice is. God uses even those who do not know Him or even those with different ideologies; We know in humanity's existence that we must always reconcile and meet toward perfect justice to live in happiness; We know there are miracles of restoration and healing.

God desires a heart of love and accommodating His humanity and wants His greatest love to **pour over and into His people. Restoring is God's expertise; God has and knows the molecules, and electrons created of all things and even formed by humanity intentionally or non-intentionally that is not with His plan, He will and may obsolete or redeem and restore.**

Listen, God listens to our prayers. God's quintessential fresh breath restoring compassion, He will forgive us, and we have the never aroma of the scent of God's love, and His tenderness pours over into the heart of our people and our land and has the shimmering Spirit of God.

Divine Message 9.28.20

Vision saw a heavenly place of shimmering platinum with colors of aqua, blue, yellow, green; I could not what was ahead in front of and on the sides. Yet it the shimmering light is infinite and brought a profound mystery and life within my soul. The word came to my mind. I saw myself looking at this place. I am standing in front of it. I was alone, yet the Spirit of God with me. I ask Jesus Christ, what is this? The Spirit of God said, "your life is unlimited in all I have planned for you. Because I am Alpha and Omega, when you are in Me, I am in you, and then you are in My path. (We as a people are unlimited under God's sovereignty; to restore our American and the world. God is a sovereign God; He is waiting for us to ask in prayer and continue to ask in prayer and continue even when we are still waiting. God listens.)

And if we know that He listens to whatever we ask him, we know that we already possess whatever we have asked of Him.

1 John 5:15

For the eyes of the Lord are on the upright, His ear turned to their cry. But the Lord's face is set against those who do evil. No one can hurt you if you are determined to do only what is right; [14] *and blessed are you if you have to suffer for being upright. Have no dread of them; have no fear.*

1 Pet. 3:12-14

"You realize The Truth; you have known the Truth, yet you have been blocked and even conspired against. I this child. I have told you this because of your heart I need to protect it; This is what happened to many

Americans; they realized The Truth and yet have been blocked." This is the time of restitution for all injustices upon the people; I will protect My people and strengthen them more than they realize. "You will finish and deliver My child. Fret not I all those who conspired against you, I will bring victory swiftly."

When someone has the power to help, such as the wealthy monetarily and use these people for their ideas and not of God, God will strike. Hence, we need to continue to protect now under the present directly under the American Freedom Warriors and President Trump to protect the people.

Therefore, we have to be careful and experience and live in God's commandments and commands to take care of our people and land in God's First Commandment and Second Commandment.

And if we know that He listens to whatever we ask Him, we know that we already possess whatever we have asked of Him.

1 John 5:15

For the eyes of the Lord are on the upright, His ear turned to their cry. But the Lord's face is set against those who do evil. No one can hurt you if you are determined to do only what is right; [14] *and blessed are you if you have to suffer for being upright. Have no dread of them; have no fear.*

1Pet. 3:12-14

The Four Foundational Truths are Peace, Justice, Restoration, and Forward Building in Love are the God-given tools to restore and heal America. The Four Foundational Truths all work congruently, supporting each other to bring Freedom and wellbeing. To have Restoration, we need God's Peace and Justice.

ATTENTION ALL AMERICANS

GOD HAS WON VICTORY. HE WANTS US TO TAKE UP HIS LIGHT, GRACE, TENDERNESS, FORGIVENESS, STRENGTH REALIZING His purpose, we have AUTHORITY AMERICA in bringing Peace, Justice, and Restoration in God.
RESTORATION AMERICA IS AN ONGOING URGENCY TO CONTINUE FOR HER TO BE RESTORED: hence, we need to take up the promises of God and realize He has been there for us and never forsakes us through all trials; we overcome.
America our magnificent ship powerful, yet vulnerable, injured yet healed, more abundant in the heart TO RESTORE AMERICA FOR GODS PEOPLES WE, THE AMERICAN FREEDOM FIGHTERS, HAVE ENGAGED INTO A WORK TO RESTORE AMERICA.

LET US OPEN OUR MINDS AND THE TRUTH THAT
"OUR AMERICA OUR SHIP IS BEING RESTORED"
NOW TOGETHER, LET US CONTINUE TO RESTORE OUR AMERICA PRESIDENT TRUMP AND THE ENLIGHTENED AMERICANS AND THE THE FREEDOM WARRIORS
We have overcome the Coronavirus in that we are going to **TRUST GOD.** *God has redeemed us. Let us all return even more open-eyed, and eyebrow lifted to the Truth in HIS LOVE.*

We know the most impoverished or the most vulnerable need to be watched and empowered. Even the politicians and the great peoples of love need compassion and hope for reconciliation.
Of course, with all the magnificent work America is already doing, we need to continue to work together strategically.
Community: Help the Inner Cities, and all our cities and our children's education for America's future. Our children are our future in America.
What do the states and districts need to ask? Enter into a conversation and assessment by local leaders, virtuous and knowledgeable people, and the wise. Since the pandemic, there are changes now, and we

need to WORK to where we left off **and continue NOW; and recover what was lost**. When we empower now, there is not enough time for healing; If we do not empower the people now, it might take too long in every business and life of humanity to heal. That what is injustice needs restoration. Otherwise, it stays the same and even deteriorates. *Take care of the cities and the states. The people need to be subsidized financially; Now, since the Coronavirus, many have had devastating life trials.*

Divine Message October 30, 2020
Pasadena, California
Spirit of the Lord States

1. I cannot pour justice upon the land that IS NOT JUST, even if My people are not just, I cannot pour justice on a land that is not just.
2. Those people that are the leaders and control have done much to help the people and the land; however, it is not enough.
3. There needs to be a complete change of man and woman's transformation toward justice in My Father's love.

Then justice will be balanced; My Father has told Me this, in that I am telling you.

Divine Message I received just this month, August 20, 2020.
Holy Family Church.

I had a vision with Jesus Christ side by side, and I hid under His Robe. **(I hide my life in Christ Jesus.)**

The Spirit of the Lord stated, "This is why I am asking them to come to Me. I want to give them the answers and guidance by sitting with them side by side. I pray with them; I sit with them, I kneel with them, stand with them, walk and run, live in, and with and through them. When they pray and seek Me and want to learn from Me, they are with Me side by side, sitting next to Me. I am redeeming them; I take them to the heavenly garden of life of the Tree of life, and there are leaves of eternal love and growth, and I will teach them the way."

I shall instruct you and teach you how to go; I shall not take my eyes off you.

Psalms. 32:8

Divine Command October 5, 2020

All America and the world essentially are to pray daily for the atrocities against humanity to be restored, healed, and even bring miracles.

We together have to plead with those in control. God shall strike unexpectedly. The human and child trafficking and abortion is the most deformity of humanity's darkness upon society.

I pray, "The humanity, and child trafficking," oh Jesus, I pray that all will be redeemed, and the world unifies together in power and love protecting the people from the abuse of human rights.[cxxiii]

John Paul Rice reveals the atrocities of Human Trafficking: Notes[cxxiv]

1. 40,000,000 humans trafficking
2. 140 Billion dollar history that is very dark and ugly ties
3. Human Trafficking goes all the way up to Wall Street and beyond.
4. The selling of organs is also a violent crime against humanity.
5. 5.5 Million trafficking children around the world do not live past 7 or 8 years old.
6. Banking and Hollywood entertainment rape and tortured boys and girls it is a hidden layer.

7. The sacrifice of people is also hidden "from secret occults."
8. The evil traffickers said this, "Indeed, children human beings are the most useless."
9. They harvest organs.
10. There are now concentration camps for young Muslims in China for the amount of 1 Million; The Communistic party beats and abuses these innocent people, re-indoctrinating them and raping their wives to start a new nationality. Let us pray the billionaire Muslim will help them, God commands.
11. Slave of workers in China.
12. It does not matter whether you are a Democratic and Republican this we to unify to bring a miracle of healing to human trafficking, pipeline to Hollywood, and all around the world in all different countries.
13. Satanic in the music industry, they manipulated it in the consciousness of the kids to do witchcraft. They make it sound fun attracts the children. The singers have diversity and tolerance.
14. The slavery of human beings and child abuse issues is rampant internationally.
15. They offer alcohol, drugs, money to lure them in.
16. Gatekeepers knowledge just doing their jobs. Managers make sure that we do not wake up. It is essential for them. Because they do not want us to have new ideas about things that go outside of the ordinary, orthodoxy of what they want us to know.
17. . It preys on children. They want us to think everything is ok. The Gate Keepers are the one-tenth of 1 percent who control everything, and have the gull to tell us we are the problem or white people are the

problem or black people are the problem or brown people are the problem.

Divine Message October 24, 2020

In God's Four-Foundational Truths: Humans will build something that requires to be achieved by the natural evolving God's intention planned using the pure first substance of the first thinks with the technological times. However, we know that all things that are created to be fair and withhold in society to be built are in the wholesomeness in the community that keeps the American dreams, is to take the tools of human attributes is: vision, hope, faith, hard work, unity, reconciliation, and always working forward to justice, and never giving up, one aspect cannot be without the other. They are essential to use integrating, asking what I do, creating, making, teaching, working for, and living for all these aspects. Because humanity **needs to be kept in the line of the first substance of truth, young yet ancient, contemplative yet fast as the speed of light, renewed yet forward, restored yet building.**

Housing in America many of our Homeless
Divine Message October 5, 2020

Many are homeless across America! The calling of those billionaire women of God's great gifts and the Catholic Church, Christian Church, and those who have influence and heart. God is asking us to work together to help. Now. The people are suffering. Let us help them. For many, there is a heart desire to help the homeless in Los Angeles Across the nation. There are empty housing and buildings within the cities and rural areas developed into stable housing and small entrepreneurial businesses and well-being centers.

Moreover, there can be housing used across the nation in rural areas to build smaller communities. This project will give wellbeing and peace and justice to the homeless and also to all the people. I pray, and the Holy Spirit will open the hearts of the people to make this happen. I ask for a miracle, God.

We, America, under President Trump, have developed programs and housing for prostitution. There is a dark veil of generational deformity in individual families in America. A young girl's golden-brown eyes of hope when you look closely in her eyes, there is a sincere hope of new pure sunlight will be here, but with a hint of the strength of 15 years old, she needs to get food, water, and housing. What skills does she have to work? Nothing? Is there any work for her? Nothing? She is helpless, hopeless, holding on to the little she has. Her small delicate body is bruised and burning sores, especially in her heart. She sells herself for prostitution. Many girls, boys, women, and men are being forced into trafficking victims for many reasons. Skills training, healing, and centering on the beauty of these people as a person to be restored to God's purpose is achievable, and we can bring a miracle.

We, as a people of America, will continue to build in *forwarding the Building of Love*.
We, as a people of America and the world, can bring peace to many victims of trafficking.

"Therefore, as often as problems arise concerning matters of justice or charity, the Bishops should take the greatest care to see that the faithful do not overlook Catholic moral teaching and do not depart from it even a finger's breadth."[cxxv]

Prosecution of Child-Sex Traffickers Plummeted Under Trump
Adam, Klasfeld, July 2019

"Beneath that gloomy surface, however, an even darker picture emerges: federal prosecutions of those who trafficked children for sex dropped 26.7% over the last year."[cxxvi]

https://www.courthousenews.com/prosecution-of-kiddie-traffickers-plummeted-under-trump/

Drugs and Alcohol: Drugs 578 Billion Drugs and Alcohol Direct

America urgently needs to put in the soil America the love of God and we need to keep on this path of "actuality" of the prime mover that is the appropriate form in a given environment that is in togetherness to bring "enjoyment" to the Perfect Divine. We have the potency of God's love and faith in us and the tools to make a path of "actuality" of forwarding Building in Love America.

Divine Message Cal Tech, September 17, 2020

1. Listen while they are creating the curriculum for the History of America. Moreover, the public school system should teach of the History of America; it has to show the USA is a country of four foundational truths, Peace, Justice, Restoration, and Forward Building in Love(Compassion)
2. Make sure the new curriculum develops a small book of Judeo-Christian ethics; the children have to memorize the ethics to understand that the foundation of the American Legacy.
3. They have to learn the Constitution and the Declaration of Independence. (Remember the Judeo-Christian ethics has similar ethics that are in the Asian and Middle Eastern Ethics. They can bring this point across. However, remember an elephant does not need to wear men's pants. We cannot put a different breed of clothing in America; she is not a Socialistic or Communistic Country.
4. America is God's land and protects all peoples and women and children in the Judeo-Christian Ethics.

5. Make sure all other curriculum is correct .... **Some of the curricula are incorrect and** (Communistic, Socialistic, and false documentation and information that is missing)
6. Also, I told you before they did not begin it. Each child has to study the eco-system of choice, Ocean, forest, water, soil, atmosphere, oil, natural gas, coal, gas, etc. Electricity. even and also a choice of a science-related, however, first eco-systems. , Every year they have to have a written notebook report, and each should be for every year of education .. They can do raw studies and also go on field trips ..
7. The children also have to have entrepreneurial skills and learn basic survival, living, and accounting. . spending. They can have stores at their schools where they sell products.
8. They have not begun the Homeless redemption project in Restoration for impure injustices on the people's full force. If they start now, they will bless them a triple, and when there are trials, God will remember our love for others.
9. The water needs to be corrected and the filter systems now so no bacteria and virus are in the water; in the schools, the water fountains need to be filtered.
10. [In Universities and all schools, all studies and projects need to be in the welfare of the people and protecting the development of the mind in the truth of individual] of life. and the Four Foundational Truths, Peace, Justice, Restoration and Forward building in love

"The free market is the only thing that allows the individual to be who he or she is meant to be; it unleashes your spirit, it will enable you to go out and innovate and be creative and be the person who you were set to be by the Almighty. . .it allows you to pursue your dreams. It will enable you to pursue your goals." The Conservatives, Dr. Stephen Bannon, A Young America's Foundational Film DVD 2012

POMPEO WARNS OF CHINESE THREAT TO US COLLEGES, SAYS MANY 'BASICALLY BOUGHT' BY BEIJING

Rep. Gallagher of Wisconsin sends letter to Dept. of Education questioning $10M donation According to Gallagher, the former head of the CP group, Dhanin Chearavanont, is "one of the CCP's oldest and most important friends in the diaspora," citing a diaspora work conference organized by the United Front Work Department in which he was recognized for his "contributions to China's rise."[cxxvii]

Public and Private(NOT IN A COMMUNISTIC INFLUENCE) <u>schools should have vocational training</u>; this is relevant to the school systems and what training the children need to exist in everyday life. Not just theoretical aspects of learning although, relevant daily survival skills, home education, accounting creative a natural flow of k 2COR. 5:1 knowledge, basic science about the eco-systems, and entrepreneur skills of gifts (each child should have training in an entrepreneur business). Note: depending on what area of cultural traditions, it is paramount to understand and seek to have two rivers meeting in the same foundation. Realize America's history and keeping our country safe, and having her identity is a prerequisite to put America first. God has given us this Divine Message that we need to understand the communication of peace and justice to restore America. Judeo-Christian ethics should be mandatory training in the public schools and accepted in a fair business transaction and all of the American life; this is what America's Legacy, and the land are built on. Otherwise, even national voting, and laws, and governmental and local authorities, will **steer away from the standard that should be Judeo-Christian ethics, that is general a general accept ethics internationally in a** globalized world. It is a command to protect our land; it is God's land. We cannot do anything without God.

LET US CONTINUE: TAKING care of our country AND continue to send restoration ships of business TO RESTORE OUR AMERICA.

Ships today are many in America business and economy to renew and fashioned in God's hands of the transformation of Restoration that bring the people a sense of hope in reviewing the paradigm in restoring the city. (Please, Table of Contents eq. Cities.) Some towns have delinquent payments or debt for a variable of reasons. Many of these cities have taken in all the dysfunction of people in need. Let us forgive and surge forward. We are protecting our cities for renovation citizenship and support.

"The Fundamental problems of local government ...... administered services, and obscure relationship with the central government, lack of effective local (and governmental) accountability."[cxxviii] Let us work together to integrate into restoring these communities. Yet, we have to have respect for the legacy of America in her history. The people are multi-cultural and even more ideologies and stronger beliefs and specialized groups. We need a foundation of agreement that has proven to stand up against all things, and has been realized and needs to be continued to be faced. Being face is facing the front of God. He has the answers for Restoration in the people. When we meet God with our life, we then reflect His face in all we do. Remember, some are used specifically for a purpose that no one ever accomplished today. Now that there has been COVID-19 and its detrimental contra-indications in every facet of life, we need to be strategic and patient. When the tragedy of the holocaust to seek to obliterate freedom strikes, the situation is identified even more straightforward. Disasters can benefit from much need improvement because there was no agreement for change for society's benefit, or even hands and arms and feet were locked. Not now. God has said in a Divine Message, "It is the century of restitution."

I had a vision it was at St. Andrews Catholic Church in Pasadena. I was praying in front of the vestibule of the Holy Altar, and the painting of the Father in Jesus Christ; is at the top of the ceiling, and His hands both hands are in front; God is waiting for us to take His hands to do His work and live His life. Then all of a sudden, the face of the Father Holy Sacred Art changed in different faces looking like other nationalities. The Father in Jesus Christ changed back to the original painting, yet still the Father in Jesus Christ. In prayer, I asked what this means the changing of the faces, **"I am the God for all peoples all nations."**

Divine Message February 17, 2020 Pasadena I saw the living heavenly beauty in the given vision of Jesus Christ with the crown of eternal light that has no end in the light it is always. A long beard and the Spirit of the Lord told me: the oil that runs down My beard is like it did Aarons is the anointing I have given to you I saw another face in His beard.

It is free will to choose God or evil; this is also for America when we try to find and believe in God's face, we have His anointing, in the power of the Holy Spirit, that run's down the face of America, and the blessing God is saying to seek His face, seek His love, seek His wisdom, seek His light. Awake , we USA cannot have Biden-Harris would Deal a Huge Blow to Religious Liberty.[cxxix]

Protect our seed of life. Democratic presidential nominee Joe-Biden is vowing to make the Equality Act a priority in his first 100 days in office. ᶜˣˣˣ However, he will not enter into office. The Trump administration has opposed the legislation, saying it is "filled with poison pills that threaten to undermine parental and conscience rights."

Health Care

We Americans should be grateful to receive a Health Care Plan that protects Americans in greater well-being than ever before in history. The Republican Health Care Plan is the greatest in the Times of the History of America and her people. We now will trust in the knowledge that has become the Wisdom of God's intention to take care of humanity in the best way.

Health Care Plan from the Republican Party. September 24, 2020

1. We repealed the individual Mandate
2. We eliminate Obama Care Health insurance medical device AND THE Cadillac tax
3. Expanded Associate Health Plan
4. Increased ability of short-term limited ability duration plans
5. Expanded Health Reimbursement arrangements
6. President Trump, lowered prescription drug prices. Lowest ever Will send at $200 prescription drug to seniors. Largest decrease ever of drug cost than ever.
7. More generic approved saving Americans an estimated 2. 6 billion dollars in 18 months
8. We signed four Executive orders to lower prescription drug prices.
9. Signed Legislative banning gag clauses
10. Took Executive action to price transparency healthcare
11. Required hospital to prices on the internet
12. Modernized Medical more options, more benefits, and lower premiums
13. Improved Kidney Care
14. Lowered price insulin
15. Invested therapy initiative of sickle cell anemia disease
16. 500 Million investment initiative for Child Cancer

17. Drug demand and opium crisis with life treatment of medication assistance
18. Treatment.gov for drug issues assistance
19. Right to try to give patients access to life-saving cures where alternative medicines not been approved FDA yet
20. Launch an initiative for HIV aides America eradication
21. Expand access to telehealth, especially in under-served and rural areas.
22. Signed VA choice legislation a 91 percent approval .. VA accountability.
23. Took action of VA suicide 24 hotline
24. Largest increased of the ability of childcare block grants of approx. 500million
25. At-home dialysis, increase incentives for Kidney disease
26. Produce Medical Supply manufacture in North Carolina, bringing business[cxxxi]

God has answered. GOD COMMANDS TO RESTORE AMERICA IN HIS PEACE AND JUSTICE IN HIS TRUTH. Speak when we know there is treacherous evil upon us.

We, the Freedom Warriors and our present government who in continuing Divine Messages and commands have been accomplished; I continue first to do this work of God.

Please, the first two years of President Trumps Presidency.

SAFETY FIRST OF OUR COUNTRY

PROMOTING JOBS

PROTECTION OF VETERANS
DEVELOPING PLANS FOR THE INFRASTRUCTURE
PROTECTION OF THE SEED OF LIFE
PROTECTION OF CORONAVIRUS AND BRINGING JUSTICE TO TAKE CARE OF THE PEOPLE ECONOMICALLY AND SAFETY
RESTITUTION AND PROTECTION OF FUTURE INTERNATIONAL TRADE OF ALL BUSINESS
PROTECTION FROM PRODUCTS IMPORTED AND MADE IN USA FOR THE HEALTH AND SAFTEY

RESTORATION AND PROTECTION OF AMERICANS SMALL AND LARGE BUSINESS

PROTECTION OF FAIR BUSINESS TARIFFS

OPIOID CRISIS
As Opioids Ravage Communities, Locals Unite in Response
From faith groups to treatment centers, state and local communities start to make headway to reduce deaths.[cxxxii]

I hope . . . that mankind will at length . . . have reason and sense enough to settle their differences without cutting throats; for, in my opinion, there never was a good war or a bad peace.

Benjamin Franklin, In a Letter to Josiah Quincy, 1773

For who is God but Yahweh, who is a rock but our God? This God who girds me with strength, who makes my way free from blame, [33] who makes me as swift as a deer and sets me firmly on the heights, who trains my hands for battle, my arms to bend a bow of bronze.

Psa. 18:31

You give me your invincible shield (your right hand upholds me), you never cease to listen to me, you give me the strides of a giant, (thank you for giving) me ankles that never weaken.

Psa. 18:35 - 36

<u>VIRTUE OF GOD IS VICTORIOUS!</u>

Communities need to be watched closely; remember, since technology causes all movements of life to move faster and at times unexpectedly in imbalance, it can be a detriment impeding the human person's creativity and even pure, original ideas; the heart desires innately to find and know the images to bring for humanity; therefore, if we empower the people in the truth of virtues, we will succeed. God never forgets the home He has given to all peoples. We need to restore now in the continuous heart of God. We are looking and living at life in the heart of virtue. When a person experiences injustices or when a person is disrespectful, or someone in the community is treacherous and even uses trickery, we need to speak up and tell them. Otherwise, they will not be the life of ethics or virtues planted in the community. Continually we need the spirit of the virtuous life in our community. Virtues bring truth, truth brings experience, and life brings love. Awake America, disrespect will be the void of integrity and ethics. There are Masonite; I have spoken loudly and told them of their injustices. We need to speak up, write, sing, and deliver the best we can in peace. Ethics brings Freedom! NOW, NOW LET US RESPECT EACH OTHER. However, in these times of volcanic trial, we need to assess why people's actions have been placed in the environment of their lives. Therefore, assessment and Truth is paramount to have Restoration.

Above all, we must realize that no arsenal, or no weapon in the arsenals of the world, is so formidable as the will and moral courage of free men and women. It is a weapon our adversaries in today's world do not have. Directly in front of me, the monument to a monumental man: George Washington, Father of our country.

Ronald Reagan

America's moral courage of free men and women: Today, for the first time in America's history, have we had to overcome the condition and position she, America is in.

The people work to survive, and many cannot have time to understand and recognize the emergency of the diversity of areas that have been formed against the intention of God's purpose.

WE CAN RESTORE AMERICA
WHEN WE TRANSFORM ARE ACTIONS IN EACH ACTION, DO WE ASK?

OUR ARE ACTIONS IN VIRTUE AND RESPECT?
When we do actions in virtue, we will get better
Virtuous action---- →righteous life
When there are actions in crime-- → there will be a breakdown for those who did the crime
Criminal action-- → criminal life --- →
When we do actions to protect America and humanity, we will get God's promises

PEACE---.>JUSTICE

AMERICA NEEDS TO BE LOVE IN GOD
AMERICA NEEDS TO BE FIRST
AMERICA NEEDS TO BE VIRTUOUS
AMERICA NEEDS TO BE AUTHORITY OF TRUTH
AMERICA NEEDS NOT TO USE MASONRY.

It is politically incorrect to speak of masonry. This chapter is on Restoration and healing. If we do not proclaim and reveal the levels of injustices and masonry are evil, we are not identifying the God Truth. When we disclose and reveal injustices an Masonry, we recognize this is **NOT God's Truth, INJUSTICES AND MASONRY.**

Many have known that there shall be a plague against the Masonite. Moreover, God said, "do not provoke the people, to protect themselves from masonry, because you are provoking Me, and testing Me."

It is proven we need to take care of our America for our Legacy, our children, our families, all of our futures.

Saint Elizabeth's Church Altadena, California Commanded to give the people God of Abraham Loves

I am calling on the Jews to return to their Father, the God of Abraham now! To produce their gifts to God in righteousness and love, God first and love their neighbor; Nebuchadnezzar realized to realized God gave him all he has and live in righteousness, Daniel 4. I have given them in the God of Abraham, America, to take care of and love the Spirit of God. Now we need to restore, rebuild, regain back what was lost from the other countries and return it to the people. The Jews, I am asking to do this now, My child. They, the Jews, are much of America.

Governmental leaders and decision-makers, "in these great state-funded programs should be <u>decentralized</u>. . . Training and Enterprise Councils . . . To take over responsibility for the delivery of these programs. They consisted of <u>groups of local employers, who knew more than any 'expert'</u> what skills were going to be needed."[cxxxiii]

However, a functional, successful city paradigm of a reflective protocol used in these cities and local employers should be an example and foundation for transforming another town that needs to be restored. Each city has different restoration needs; we can bring a miracle of God's ever-flowing beauty.

Upholding America

Healing requires different medicine types and, in some cases, miracles, nutrition excellent, exercise, emotional, physical wellbeing, spiritual, and a relationship with God. The medicine I am speaking of is not the organic actions of the being and the natural environment. The medicine I am speaking of is the Spirit of God within the being, that "ruah," that is the breath of God, THE MESSIANIC BREATH OF LIFE within each human. Correct restoration and healing require something more magnificent than human ideas. Correct restoration requires those things of God to heal that what needs to be transformed to the authentic purpose of the Trinity's at creation. Healing requires those things that the original intent of the being and the first substance needs to be made up of the same and intended being of our content that God created at creation. Yahweh's word was addressed to me as follows, 'Look, I am Yahweh, God of all humanity. Is anything impossible to Me?

Jer. 32:26

However, some may ask that oh we can use a different substance or be to heal or *restore or even create an original purpose; however, is this God's intention? God accommodates to the human and the actions that they take. Sometimes, these actions go beyond recall and destroy the being or substance of its authentic intention, and then it needs a miracle.*

America has given many gifts to many Americans and non-Americans. America has wounds, and we need to heal her, America, NOW WE HAVE TO HEAL

AMERICA NOW SHE HAS WOUNDS.
HEAL AMERICA; YOU HAVE AUTHORITY IN THE VIRTUES OF GOD.
Healing requires defining what is not healthy.
Then the question needs to be asked, what is it meant to be human?
There needs to be a unity of practical understanding of healthy humans. Then there can be transformational healing because we are working in harmony.

Unity:

Unity is forgiving; yet, it is telling the Truth the way you are being treated, good or bad. Otherwise, it will not be revealed, and the people involved in good and evil will not be exposed until God calls another person. Today people have not spoken out because facts are needed, and the facts may not be politically correct. Remember, we always have to speak in peace.

Perhaps, there is fear and abuse and the unsoundness of those not supporting the Truth. Sometimes the Truth is not supported by individual facts immediately; it takes time. Unity requires Truth to speak out what injustices are being deceivingly, destroying, and even killing individuals and blatantly upon one person or many people.

Today we have to consider all cultural and religious traditions, such as Muslims, Christians, Jews, and Buddhists.

Individual:

Ask yourself, do you know of an injustice that is not a natural development or action? Each one of us needs to integrate into the solution to be in unity with God's intention. And if you do not in God, you know things only will work a sure way to exist in the fullness. And even when we understand, there is still a better way; we become closer to the Truth of Restoration because God is infinite.[cxxxiv]

Unity takes courage! To achieve harmony, one may even be in danger. Unity is in the light of Truth and life the best for human flourishing in the highest well-being; this is the catalyst to creativity and authentic development, achieving the intention of the Creator's purpose, for each life, and all of growth and creation. Americans, we want to CONTINUE TO have and be the individuals; is free to think, free to work, open to earn a fair wage, free in family values, free to be protected, free to own land, free to dream and pursue the American Dream. Though I would have to say we always want to speak IN RECONCILIATION AND RESOLUTION, hopefully, we need to talk about Truth. The truth is that those in power need to open their heart to restore and keep America safe continually.

The truth is evident that those that are in leadership and power over those that are working for those in leadership and vice a versa, **PRAYFULLY, I hope they would meet in reconciliation, and they have the same purpose each that is the key. Life will be God's intention and each** person will reach toward satisfaction and beyond, toward all their life in a wellbeing state, is toward developing and achieving. Yet, sustaining is essential. Though empowering to be independent is life and the most vital crucial to life.

The modern movement in America is flowing into the transformation of God's most magnificent beauty to heal, His humanity and all creation.[cxxxv]

Americans understand, and immigrants live in a country that has given them life, respectful and honorable to our America wholeheartedly seek justice in Truth. Their blood, sweat, and tears are the flow of energy that keeps America alive for all those people who want America to keep its legacy as the "greatest country on earth as the Mother of all Nations:"

Virtues of Miracles

"I ask you to ensure that humanity is served by wealth and not ruled by it."

Pope Francis

Yes, we want a government that serves the people and not a government that controls the people. Especially those that have wealth, virtue needs to be in the hands of each America to restore America.

St. Faustina speaks of

Ask the question: do we feel "deep pain" in happenings and experience in life?

Crimes bring "deep pain and even a normal action of the persons to react for protection. WE need to seek to forgive others and ourselves and ask forgiveness and reach in our heart to reconcile and live first toward virtues; then the "crime" is forgiven and washed away in the mind and heart of the person.

When virtue is not put first, there are crimes, correct? The "hell" is the crime here on earth that sins that have not been redeemed and forgiven. My mother once told me, "there is hell on earth here." In reflection of this statement, she has seen deep sorrow, yet her consistent, faithful prayer life has seen and lived miracles. God redeems both the criminal and the victim. He sanctifies the believer and makes Him stronger. And seeds of love are planted in the criminal. When people have to be jailed physically by law for their crimes, this is a form of reconciliation and toward justice, if the conviction is real.

After the convicted has paid for his time, he is then released. (note- this is a vast subject we cannot speak in this context about criminals and freed convicts.)

Our justice system has "mercy," for only specific regulations, severe crimes those convicted are placed in incarceration, and "justice demands it." Listen, there is are other crimes that are not viewed as crimes.

Divine Mercy of Jesus Christ is given to all humans when they accept and receive mercy.

Divine Message Scottdale Arizona

The Spirit of the Lord said you have My mercy. You have given others mercy. You are a child of mercy. Listen, sometimes mercy is carrying other's wounds until God in the Trinity allows it to pass. See, the person that needs compassion cannot hold the weight of sin or human condition whatever it is; they need help in the Trinity, and sometimes God even uses a believer.

Prayer is that mercy in miracle between God in the Trinity and humans and Arch Angels and God's Angels. The Spirit of the Lord said, "I have given America mercy." The vote of some of the people was blinded and not understood, it was voted out of belief or ideology, not justice looking in the future. I have mercy because some do not understand. They need to put justice in their life, righteousness and seek My love. My Father is watching, and He has given mercy, mercy, mercy; I cannot say how long and for each thing He will give mercy.

St. Faustina speaks of purgatory:

"My mercy does not want this, but justice demands it." [cxxxvi]

Question: would you not think that we have to pay for the crimes we have done after death that we have not asked for forgiveness or sought to change or reconciled? Many have suffered, right?

What do you think about this question?

Where do you think you need to forgive, be forgiven, reconcile? Protecting oneself against any form of abuse is not a sin. Remember, life needs life to exist.

The Our Father Prayer is a miracle to receive the virtues!

Our Father, you are our Father; Help us; Show us your ways, Father; Forgive us and help us realize our wrongdoings.

Art in Heaven: You are in heaven, though you have promised to send your Advocate in us through us and with us.

Give us this day our daily bread; please, Lord, help us be Your "bread," the bread of life to our life for You and to bring to Your purpose for others. Families are made up of individuals in communities. Individuals go out to the community and bring what they have learned from families. Family members need to be forgiven. In forgiveness, You empower that what needs *forgiveness, whether intentionally or nonintentional; when you forgive that person, it brings in a miracle; the action of wrong-doing can be stopped and never done again. The one that is forgiving has redeemed that what needed to be forgiven. And then there is life, a creation of beauty. Making the person aware of their wrongdoing identifies Truth; there is the free-will of choice to take up that first-substance of God's life of truth.* **<u>Although remember, humans are sometimes provoked that causes them to do "wrongdoings." Also, God could only judge His people and humanity. Sometimes, there is a specific purpose that needs to be carried through, not in humanity's mind; however, in the Mind and Spirit of God.</u>**

Ask yourself, why is this person in wrongdoing?

Ask the person, why do you do your wrongdoings?

Empower the person to give medicine of God's love that is a miraculous treatment.

<u>*God's love has created life; hence, God's love, received, and death becomes life.*</u>

Many families have lost traditions and values, and Truth because of the deterioration of the family itself.

Also, the meaning of relationships has caused voidness into what is defined as the sanctity or understanding of the necessary respect to the person.

Listen, each action in human form constitutes a connection with another activity; there is the stream of life when there is a virtuous movement with virtue and sanctity for communication life—identity to uplift as an individual, business, relationship, and vocational and personal goals and gifts. Mothers and children have been the greatest victims of the family's deterioration, needing restoration and empowerment. There is a vast difference between parents and children's beliefs because of the technological world. Today we need to heal our families.

Virtues of God and Judeo-Christian ethics in society is a hovering beauty of a miracle that can restore America in the Trinity's Salvation. I think this will help us seek virtues. I know for myself; I need to look at my actions and forgive myself and others continually, and I can concentrate and realize the Truth about any sins, and then my virtues they grow.

Other significant religious groups of Muslim and Buddhist and other traditional groups need to enter into a mediation of peace, and justice that develops individual freedom and safety.

Also, racism is spoken about and argued and protested violently. Today, we need to plan a paradigm of refreshment of that new seed of **"Seth" in the New Covenant in Jesus Christ the Lord and Savior. And for me, to proclaim in the love and truth in the Trinity.**

However, there is a difference between forgiveness and telling, speaking out loud, about the crime done upon you or others essential to be corrected to protect others. Be, truth awake, arise, America, to seek virtues; otherwise, the life actions of attributes in the living are compromised. And virtues will be replaced by accepted crimes. Believers will grow from these experiences and trial; they grow in God's purpose and have realized more how the VIRTUES ARE MOST IMPORTANT IN GOD'S SALVATION AND LOVE **In heaven, St. Faustina tells us:**

"Incomprehensible is the happiness in that soul will be immersed."

The more virtues you have on earth, the more of you in the Spirit of God will be with you on earth as it is in heaven. Let us serve humanity in the wealth of our gifts that God has given us.

WE AMERICANS NEED TO ALL WORK TOGETHER IN VIRTUE AND GRACE TO LIVE IN THE SCEPTER OF AUTHORITY

"The Fundamental problems of local government badly administered services, an obscure relationship with the central government, lack of effective local accountability not only remain; they will get worse."[cxxxvii] We need to work together in agreement on what is best for the people. When we realize virtues and ethics and love, we recognize the Truth, and we have the solutions.

Before COVID-19 and now regenerating to succeed

Jobs are soaring in America (Before the CCP virus)
To supporting and protecting and all the Veterans,
To make aware of the need to Eradicate the Drug War at all Levels Protecting our America.
To empower restoring the Middleclass
To empower Small Businesses in America
To empower all Business and Tax Benefits
To empower our Country against war
To empower our Country from Nuclear Warfare
To empower Fair International Trade
To promoting all General Businesses in America
To empower the Healthiness of the Stock Market
To protect American History in the Public and Private Schools developing Classic and Creative Education and relevant for daily existence for all Children's School
The children are the Life and Legacy of America
The children are the life and Light of America's future and success
The children's education needs to be at the top of the list.

TODAY OUR AMERICA HAS COME OUT OF OUR COCOON HELD BY THE BLINDNESS OF UNRIGHTEOUSNESS. WE REALIZED WE WERE TREATED WITH UNRIGHTEOUSNESS.

<u>AMERICA HAS AWAKENED</u>

TODAY UNDER THE WINGS OF ARCHANGEL MICHAEL, GABRIEL, AND RAPHAEL, OF THE GOD OF ABRAHAM
AND IN THE RIGHT ARM OF GOD IN HIS POWER

Our America has always kindled with God's light, and **the light of the power of God's promise in us.. has NOT gone out**; we remain covered with the Legacy of our American flag of hope, liberty, Truth, all in God's Power. God has called us, all of America; We have answered His request God's call for America: **We have now been uncovering our cocoon, our power, and the strength and gifts God gave America!** Let the children dance, laugh, create, grow beautiful, and shine their light of God upon America! GOD IS OMNIPRESENT IN AMERICA

Let the Mothers be at peace.
Let the Fathers be satisfied.
Let all America lift their heads and hearts high, knowing they are in God's mighty hands.

I will not restrain my lips:

Great America, just as Great King David
We waited patiently for the Lord to bring us out of the pit of destruction, setting our feet firm.
God put a new song in our mouth, our confidence praise to our God.
Now we are keeping America Great and Restoring Her!
We know in science and business and human life in every science of life, when the paradigm is building Truth of Restoration of light for the wellbeing of humanity in view, we make on it!
Let us build on our present leaders under each individual, each family, each community, each foundation, each state., I first, each member of the city Lisa Lucia Arden, with President Trump's promise to seek to keep America Great.

READ ALOUD AND PUT YOUR NAME IN: Let us build on the success of our present leaders under each individual, each family, each community, each foundation, each state, and each member first me, put your name in *I _____ I WILL TRUST GOD; I WILL SEEK HIS LOVE FIRST; I WILL SEEK to keep and continue to restore and keep America Great.*

I have proclaimed glad tidings of righteousness in the great congregation
I have not hidden the righteousness within our hearts.
I have spoken of Thy faithfulness and Thy salvation.
I have not concealed Thy loving kindness and Thy truth.

Psalm 40 (New American Standard)

How can you be a part of the transformational healing and Restoration of America?

>Prayer is the answer, Jew, Christian, Buddhist, Muslims, and all other religious affiliation, and even Atheist. God has called us, all of America: We need to answer His call God's call for America:

Immigration: If we do not take care of the heartless, inhuman immigration catastrophe, we will have crucified wounds on those who pleaded to release the bondage on the adults and children. And God Himself will strike back, as shown in history when evil abuses His humanity. **However, those of us are practically all immigrants need to treat America and her people with respect.** However, remember, we each need grace in our suffering. Each party involved. Also, God will NOT allow America to deteriorate! God wants His America to have retribution: I wrote the message above in 2018 and prayed, and God has answered my prayer:

PRESIDENT TRUMP AND THE AMERICAN FREEDOM WARRIORS ARE BRAVE

Today for the first time in America's history and in a long time, we are addressing the justice and safety for America IN regarding immigrants, economy, trade war, infrastructure, military, small businesses, opioid drug issues, right for life, American jobs, and endless other changes toward the Restoration of America.

TO SPEAK OF ON ANOTHER GRATEFUL AND HAPPY MIRACLE OF

GOD'S PROMISES OF PROTECTION
PRESIDENT TRUMP AND THE ENLIGHTENED AMERICANS AND THE ENTIRE TEAM HAVE ALL THE PROTECTION OF THE WINGS OF THE ARCHANGELS AND THE PRAYERS FROM HEAVEN OF THE PAST PRESIDENTS AND THE GREAT ARCHANGELS OF GOD TO BRING VICTORY TO BRING RESTORATION IN GOD'S TRUTH TO THE LAND OF GOD, AMERICA

KEEPING AMERICA GREAT AND RESTORING HER.

**All need to take responsibility, immigrants, and all those in power.
AMERICA LET US BRING THE MIRACLE OF RESTORATION
God has called us, all of America: We need to answer His call God's call for America:**

If we do not take care of the immigration catastrophe now, we will have a continuous scar with a memory, defacing the beauty and love that we have given to the nations of the world, as being the *"Mother of all Nations."*

Today for the first time in America, the media has shown whether real or not immigration urgencies dehumanize peoples and innocent children.

Ask yourself, has this been going on before President Trump, has gone into office? Yes!

Why have those in power hidden the human deformity of the immigration urgency?

Now that the catalyst of President Trump's calling to reveal the Truth about the immigration problem among URGENCIES AND CRIMES UPON AMERICA together all need to take responsible:

There has to be a structure of regulation and understanding the standard to heal and restore the immigration complexity. It is an international civility responsibility.

AND THERE NEEDS TO BE A RESPONSIBILITY FOR THE CRIMES UPON AMERICA, AND WE NEED TO PUT HER FIRST.

**All need to take responsibility, immigrants, and all those in power.
AMERICA LET US BRING THE MIRACLE OF HEALING**

God has called us, all of America: We need to answer His call God's call for America:

Suppose we do not take care of the conspiracy against the American people to control the votes. Suppose we allow the left, Communistic rule with Socialistic ideology to and allow the control of the people and take away our freedom. America will have a deformity of deep psychological scars., not only in the immigrant children and adults, and consequently in the children and adults across America. They will view this of controlling humanity of immigration as it is accepted. The children and young adults will have to carry this defacing liberty of society upon their hearts into the history of America. Now is the time to form a just law and safety for America and the immigrant.

All need to take responsibility, immigrants, and those in power.
AMERICA LET US BRING THE MIRACLE OF HEALING

God has called us, all of America: We need to answer His call God's call for America: If we do not take care of the immigration catastrophe now, within the long term, there will run through the soul and heart and the mind a sorrow so deep: When the perpetrators open their eyes in sunrise, tears will pour from their hearts. And joy will not flow freely from their life.

It is each one of us that are responsible,

a. The leader of the immigrant country first needs to take care of their people.
b. The immigrant is responsible for bringing children into the world.
c. The country that takes up the immigrant's needs in communication and agreements should uphold justice and fair laws.
d. Those leaders who protect the immigrants need to investigate and study all contraindications and seek citizenship.
e. For those companies and peoples who employ the immigrants, it is essential to treat the immigrant justly.
f. America needs to be respected and protected its borders; that is a Divine Command.

Ask yourself: if your country's leaders and your country's welfare did not give you the tools for the existence to live a life for the felt needs and future, where would you be now?

All need to take responsibility, immigrants, and those in power.

IF WE DO NOT TAKE RESPONSIBILITY FOR ALL OF AMERICA'S FREEDOM'S RESPECTED TOWARD EACH OTHER AND IMMIGRANTS:

When the sun shines at noon, it will not warm the cold-hearted chilling fear heart, and it will run in the psyche of the perpetrators and perhaps even the immigrants. All need to take responsibility, immigrants, and those in power. All need to take responsibility for all the freedoms to keep America for our Legacy and children.

Those who have the power when they help the immigration catastrophe will be shimmering beauty of the moonlight that God gives in the evening for the light; they will see effervescent never forsaking beauty on the soul of God's moonlight night guide. LIBERTY NEEDS TO BE REDEEM.

These are just a beginning list.

When you read this list, you can add other items that need healing in America.

<u>President Trump and the Republican Team have worked on these Divine Commands to deliver to the American people, and some of these points we are still working on.</u>
The right to life and protect our unborn
Dialysis medicine is costly
The regulations for the transplant of Kidney donors
INNER CITIES
Cleaning Freeways
The lottery 94% is used for the controllers, not for the people
Non-Profits fraudulent
Immigrant countries taking advantage of their people
Infrastructure
Credit Cards and the interest rate 18- 27% this should be lower
Opioid Drug Problem
Education System Transformation and Restoration
   TEACH CHILDREN SKILLS NOT JUST HYPOTHETICALS
   EDUCATIONAL SYSTEM IS OUTDATED.

SAFETY- Our country needs to be CONTINUED TO BE SAFE. When a country is threatened in production and self-worth of the individual's production, those whom the beauty wants it, the state becomes in danger. OUR AMERICA NEEDS TO BE CONTINUED TO BE REBUILD AND RESTORE FOR AMERICA FIRST.

I've always won, and I'm going to continue to win. And that's the way it is.

President Trump

Divine Messages and Commands Given
WE NEED TO CONTINUE TO KEEP AMERICA SAFE AND GREAT.
POLICE AMD MILITARY is a protective armor to America's body, and the police and the military are used to uphold and bring a safety foundation; just as the body needs proper nutrition and living components in all environments with simultaneously existing in the variables of the Aristotle categories of life to live; the police and military must be continuously evolving in the variables of life to protect America within her country and even in other countries.

Years ago, in Monrovia, California, at the prayer garden at the Sisters of Maryknoll. Queen Virgin Mary told me for America to be careful of China for they are a treacherous country and also taking our business and for us to do the following:

IMPORTS – When purchasing imports, we give monies from our pockets. Ask where do we get the money from? Not from the people we import, not unless we sell their goods or buy our products. Hence, we NEED TO make our own money from our cistern of America SO WE CAN buy and exchange enough funds to exist? There needs to be a balance between imports and exports. America has to produce as much as she can in her own country. America's first production had to come from America. We cannot stop putting demands on tariffs; otherwise, only the very wealthy will exist for a while in America, and the middle class and poor with not be able to exist at all. Consequently, people will need to sustain life from the government without being empowered for work.

In humanity's nature, they are created to seek with all their senses, and the highest reason is curiosity, when one has gifts. In Genesis, the man was made to cultivate the land and women to bear and take care of the woman prepares her purple cloth to sell in the market. Today life has become modernized. We need to keep jobs and continue developing them so that they can identify each person and all economic avenues of America can be sustained and maintained to be restored and great. <u>Awake, Arise, realize many are controlled not to speak, and reveal truth and freedom. They conspire against those who have light and seek to minimize their accomplishments and use them as theirs.</u>

<u>God will not allow this. There shall be restitution.</u>

President Trump Fights for all Parents in America

To every parent who dreams for their child, and every child who dreams for their future, I say these words to you:

I'm With You, and I will FIGHT for you, and I will WIN for YOU.

President Trump

Notes for Children of America First to Empower and Teach

Education:

    1. Ethics: (Please, Virtues)
We need to put ethics first in the education system.

Virtues should be taught and respect.

The education system has to begin with an ethical value of forming ethics in all actions one carries in life. Because there is a globalized world, and there is a multi-cultural understanding of various beliefs that may not have relevance to one another. Therefore, is it paramount that there be a common ground for all peoples and that the children dynamically experience the basic understanding of ethics?

> God cries from the mountaintops of heaven when His people are deceived because their minds are focused on His peace and love.

God cries from the mountain tops of heaven, may strike as we have natural disasters.

2. Process and delivery of Education:
   Teaching children skills is paramount for them to survive in the future.

Children need to produce regular existence training first, as we stated ethics, healthy bodies nutritionally, and emotionally. In private schools, they address spirituality and a religious foundation for education. There needs to be a strategy for the children's learning, where there is hands-on training to clean and buy groceries. Balances costs of a home, cooking, sewing, producing, organizing a house, accounting balancing a budget, safety measures learn for catastrophes, planting and growing — even learning how to invest in different forms of business — learning and understanding how to purchase a home and start a bank accountant.

There should be a notebook of training and scheduling and all contact numbers. I followed some of these valuable virtues when I was raising the children.

Of course, learn the necessary skills of job interviewing.

Master report of each year and classes should be prepared for each student's interest. Regular field trips need to be taken out in nature and report not just written but hands-on projects that need to be produced. They are eliminating the integration of the vast hours of using technology and reading and writing and critically analyzing what they have learned.

3. **PROTECTION OF OTHER SALIENT ENTITIES FOR CHILDREN, note these are just notes to inspire and prayerfully take care of our children, empowering them.**
   1. Proper filter water needs to be available at each school where the children can receive CLEAN WATER.
   2. Candy and foods with preservatives and sodas should not be in the schools are sold in the schools.

3. All phones and technological computers need to be blocked from pornography.
4. As we also have n in the news, online cheating is found, and assignments have to be surveyed. Handwriting, in some cases, is essential in higher grades.
5. (I know there are schools already that have incorporated these ideas; however, we as a country need to include them more.)
6. Retire professional or skilled peoples can be regular lectures. (I Know schools have professional days. However, proper professionals and qualified people teach the children other than teachers (just) presenting a subject hypothetically and not putting it into action.
7. Our present public education system needs to be relevant to America's history in a globalized world.
8. Our present children need skills training in every area of work. Creative science developed in solving problems in society.
   All the necessary developments of (relevant) information now taught can be applied to a hands-on actual real-life experience for the children.
9. The tests should not just be hypothetical; it should be relevant to what is needed for a person to exist and develop for the individual.
10. Action, bodily and contemplative action with actual tangible delivery as if the child is a skills person. If a child wants to learn about wines, they should make a hands-on report and do the actual skill in wines they are interested in.
11. Children need to study the aspects and characteristics of each natural resource and accomplish a report. There should be an integration of the reasons we use them and the tools and apparatus and tools used to transport them, processes them and store them, and tools that put them to a substance used to bring them to a source for use.
12. Hence, this may take integration with all courses working simultaneously with the projects or one specific project. If the teachers work together on the same subject simultaneously, the children can process the information more dynamically in applying it to skill and actual real-life experiences.
13. I know that some of these solutions are already used and applied; however, this needs to be incorporated in public

schools.
14. Classical music is essential for all peoples, especially children from the mother's womb until all pursued studies.
15. Verbal discussion and story time in that the children form a story and speak out loud about it; perhaps this is where they can be taught ethics and virtues.
16. Subject, manner of skill the student is interested in: each child should have an enormous report or book they begin and work on regularly, and it is given at the end of the semester of school.
17. Schedule, diet, exercise, family thank you, and letters are necessary.
18. Children's daily chores and responsibilities in the home for home care should be taught in the house. Also, there should be home management subject to study at the school; the children can reflect on it. Each family should have a garden. Mothers and fathers both work and it is difficult for sometimes parents to teach children to clean after themselves.
19. Survival tactics for children should be taught.
20. Relationships with boys and girls and being virtuous and celibate.
21. Dress and social skills, table manners and table preparation, social manners, friends, and business. (Ethics)
22. Discussion about what responsibilities a person has children, family, relationships, and living expenses.
23. Remember, remember that people are also suppressed and oppressed for those that the powerful do not want. Hence, we need to forgive many individuals and children. I know of a young woman whose young mother is a political writer and consultant. They oppress even the children of leaders that are not covered by the powerful. Yet God does, and He will vindicate.
24. (In the Divine Message, mothers are supposed to say prayers and read the HOLY SCRIPTURES aloud and sing and hear music while the child is in the womb. Also, for those who in the ROSARY AND CATHOLIC PRAYERS.)

"The Fundamental problems of local government badly administered services, an obscure relationship with the central government, lack of effective local accountability not only remain; they will get worse."[cxxxviii]

The children should accept they have a responsibility to help in the home. The fruit that parents give them is at a certain age to participate in fruit production to care for the family home. Otherwise, they are not providing what they are obliged to provide by nature of caring for the place where you live. Then they will carry this on in the community and expect something without working for it or have others solve the problem. Virtues today are in all of America's responsibilities in **life; treat America with respect**.

Some of these protestors have been treated with injustice, and we all have to be in reconciliation. We need law and order of justice; otherwise, America, a greater evil, will come and destroy us. This is a Divine Command, protect our cities in communities, fund the police of justice and compassion, and strategic communication and safety. Some are forced to act as they do to survive because of dysfunction in life and life emergencies; however, others are aware of what is need yet they do not help. The technological atmosphere of energy causes a rapid movement without any working for answers; I think this has, at times, poured over to other aspects of life. Sometimes, there are periods of scheduling when one has exams or projects; however, children should help in the home. The fruit in the community for the future in their home will be as full. I have experience of this in my life and my not understanding of all things to have a safe and productive, and prosperous home. During this severe tragedy of the pandemic and over 200,000 people have died. Tell the children to draw their family and write about how they feel; applying the ethics and virtues in the education of children how they can be better family members and community members, justice, Truth, hope, love, forgiveness, responsibility, honesty, communication with patience, patience, awareness, sympathy, empathy, brings life and restoration. (Have these people understand these words define them.) Let them have the proper definitions of the virtues not made up by the rhetorical words. Give the children a scenario of how to relate with their friends or people. Just as the caretakers and parents tell children, they should be told what is right from wrong, using the virtue definitions. It is not that we are integrating into the belief systems of the child. There has to be respected for the individuals and communities around them that they respond to. Each child has to work toward an understanding of the definition of ethics toward the same opinion. Therefore, if one agrees when the work from a foundation of constants of proof treating humans to the most significant level of wellbeing, then there will be more of a productive flow, that each individual will be at peace to pursue their characteristic authentic purpose because it is pure in the cell that is pure in the creation of the person, this is why it needs an environment of just ethics to be able to evolve and come to continued life.

Notes on Infrastructure:

Infrastructure: It has been a command also in contemplation prayer that the physical and organizational structures and facilities, buildings, roads, power supplies need to be restored and toward perfect operation of a society or enterprise.

When in and toward productive and just working order delivering freedom and truth, the social and economic infrastructure of our country will then bring safety and the most outstanding products for the human welfare and success in the community and each life.

1. **Water is our most precious resource, and all water basins need to be taken care of and the piping throughout each city and community.**

2. Utilities: all lines and resources used to produce power need to be restored to a safe and highly sufficient for the present and future dynamic electricity use process.
3. <u>Global Warming</u>

The Job One for Humanity Story and the Latest Global Warming Facts

For years, the IPCC, governments, and environmental organizations they influence have told the public:

1. <u>Global warming</u> is still manageable (in the sense that we are currently and will continue to make steady and adequate progress in lessening global warming for the foreseeable future)
2. Global warming consequences will occur gradually,
3. Global warming consequences will remain generally mild until about 2100 And,
4. The worst impacts of global warming will happen after 2100, long after most of us living today are gone.

Nothing listed in items 1-4 above could be farther from the Truth!

1. The public has no idea that we have managed global warming *so incredibly poorly* for the last 35 plus years that it has become <u>out of our meaningful control</u> for at least ***another*** <u>30-50 years</u> with <u>horrific and unavoidable consequences</u> arriving *far sooner* than almost any of us are prepared to deal with.

The rest of this document, plus the dozen reasons that global warming may be uncontrollable for at least another 30-50 years found <u>at the top of this page,</u> will *conclusively prove* to you that global warming is, in fact, now our of our meaningful control.

2. Global warming is now far worse than just now *unavoidable* horrible consequences. In addition to your location, what we do now until 2025 to reduce fossil fuel use will be critical in determining how much time we have left to prepare for what is coming and how much longer more people will live as a massive human, animal and biological extinction event unfolds within the next 30-50 years. Please, the information. [cxxxix]

4. Oceans
5. Forest

6. Cities
7. Electrical and Gas lines streets and infrastructures
8. In the USA in 2018, the number of Homeless is 552,830. In January 2019, over 151,278 homeless and.
9. We can ask if the billionaires can make bond investments between the city to clean these cities and help the homeless and the deteriorating cities. This has been a Divine Command for Billionaires to help the homeless.

GOD HAS ALREADY WON THE VICTORY. HE JUST WANTS US TO PARTICIPATE IN WHAT WE ALL CAUSED BECAUSE NOT FOLLOWING GOD FIRST, WE CAUSED SIN AGAINST HUMANITY. HE HAS GIVEN US HIS PROMISES OF AUTHORITY ASK, AND YOU SHALL RECEIVE TO DO HIS WORK.

10. We can ask if the billionaires and those in power can make ~~bond~~ investments between them to clean these cities and help the homeless. Otherwise, the taxes can that they pay can go directly to these programs. Their money is sitting, why cannot it be used? I had a Divine Vision that I saw the *"builders of compassion,"* walking down the streets and going to the rural areas and seeing the people cared for and also workers having jobs. These *"builders of compassion,"* were given a larger light they seemed talker and the light of God was part of their being and with thick sharp edges that nothing could penetrate them, they were going to bring that compassion of righteousness that God commands from them.

Short Notes:
Drug, Alcohol, and Mental Health

   a. Homes, Streets, Schools, Small Medical Programs, Business, Proven Successful Exercise Programs, Proven Successful De-tox programs,
   b. We can also relocate these people and help those who want help and then clean up certain areas.
   c. In some cases, if they have mental health, they need to be treated appropriately with tenderness and patience.

d. We can incorporate, miraculous science of technology, western and eastern medicine, and environmental exposure to nature and focused identity development.
e. Western Medicine with heavy pharmaceuticals has been a great challenge for many patients with Mental Health Disease that needs to be accessed.
f. Food intake should be pure and a high volume of a raw balanced diet of the cultural foods and minerals and vitamins.
g. Prayers and reading silently and aloud and healing prayers and taking notes and writing questions and answers: 1. What do you need to forgive;2. Who do you need to forgive? 3. What is a goal for your life? 4.How will you accomplish it. What roadblocks do you think you might have? What finances and timing do you need to set up to achieve these goals and timelines.
h. Mind and thought process should be stimulated with religious sermons if they desire, one on one counseling, poetry, meditation, classical music, positive songs, and art forms, drawing, and hobbies
i. Communication groups of speaking
j. Arts and sciences teaching in ways of skills and finances <u>and</u> daily schedules and nutrition and exercise.
k. Structure and Hospital should be in rural areas on ranches having chores and getting out in nature.
l. If their stay is long term, skill classes could be visited and developed; working skills should be concentrated on each individual's interest and the experiences that they have and have not done. Since they have not explored different areas of life, this could impede their healing. The mental disease is sometimes from a catalyst of the false self, where there is a void self,(Winnicottian theory) and the personality and psyche are not fulfilled.
m. Integrated and incorporated Eastern and alternative medicine.

We can hire reliable and knowledgeable professionals first for safety and all other aspects mentioned above.

AMERICA LET US BRING THE MIRACLE OF HEALING

Let us have a metanoia[cxl], a revelation of love.

"A profound transformation in one's outlook."

You know how when you go to a professional for help, they tell you the strategy and have proven history to back up their ideas;

God throughout history has redeemed countries, peoples, and individuals;

Even if you do not believe in God, you cannot deny God has been there for humanity.

You know that when we carry the Truth and seek to deliver it when we work in God's intention, we know we gave our best, and we won in our hearts, and when we win, others win when they are on God's side, and even sometimes not on God's side; because God wants their heart and His warm and powerful love tears yearn for His humanity as a Father.

We are responsible for working toward bringing God's love in His Truth, "*metanoia*," of the revelation of the "revolution of love." When I have said an extension of each other, I am referring to the responsibility to bring God's love; However, we are not all an extension of each other because we are individuals; and many are and have opposite beliefs in God and in life itself. Even when we are in God, we are still an individual and responsible for our lives, and God knows what has happened.

While visiting New York for my daughter's college visit's, we met a Taxi Driver:

An African American has an eye of understanding of the circumference, as a taxi driver from New York, viewing the New York streets and peoples from a distance yet from close up. The mirror observing upon oneself you look upon yourself, and some carry others, and others only carry themselves or the overwhelming purpose. However, we can all carry each other when we seek integrity and work ethic for one common good. (Not throwing the pearls to the dogs. However, as a believer and warrior, God takes us to places to help others. And God will protect us. He will give us the strength to carry on.) That good American, the taxi driver, smells the fragrance, sweet or sour of the streets, clear or blocked, he hears the stories, death or life, knows the people's direction, failure, surviving, or success, and feels the sectioning and separation of peoples, healing toward unity. And the taxi driver knows when there is unity, peace, healing, and justice, and building all in God's love. The taxi driver told us, sitting at the front wheel of realizing the New York people's hearts had a miracle, he spoke with deep compassion and relief. Yet, sorrow was pierced in his heart in the sounds of his vowels speaking, "It took a deathly horrifying human tragedy for the people of New York to become in unity and love toward each other." Now let us also love one another and have the miracle faithfulness to restore and heal our America and the world.

"What the Flag Meant- On September 11, 2001
Why We Stand Young America's Foundation

"September 11, 2001, the end of the world as we knew it. In the aftermath of the attacks, Americans united without regard to a political party, race, ethnic background, or any other matter. Those differences immediately need [heal into love] as we pulled(pull) **together as a nation.**"

Together as a nation <u>we have to obsolete the treacherious plans of the left,</u> Communist: MARK OF THE BEAST

1. We also know that there are conspiracies to kill off many of the people; they want to de-populize the peoples and have less people that is why they build all those coffins at the FEMA compound.
2. Furthermore, today December 10, 2020; they want to give the people a vaccine for the Covid-Virus that the syringe have a tracker in them, the tracker can be considered, "the mark of the Beast." Each microchip has unique I.D. code this would enable them to control the Americans and peoples of the world.
3. "Cashless society. Using cards they can, track, and identify the persons in the techological systems. Even controlling their amounts of income and economic position."

4. "They the people in power, to create the world that they want."
   "The people in power, they want on the digital program."
   "They the people in power, want to use this technology to take back control."
5. Under President Trump and the Team and the American Freedom Warriors: Continue to Control our Economic Systems America First, and Safety and working to putting the American people first.

(See under President Trump we put God first and the American First.)

UNDER PRESIDENT TRUMP AND THE AMERICAN FREEDOM WARRIORS.
LET US TRUST EACH OTHER IN OVERCOMING THESE EVILS OF INJUSTICE.
LET US TRUST GOD IN US.
LET US TRUST GOD IN AMERICA.

OUR AMERICA TODAY IS JUST BEGINNING. WE HAVE
The GREATEST TEAM: THE AMERICAN PEOPLE, PRESIDENT TRUMP WHO IS MAKING AMERICA GREAT AGAIN AND COLLABORATIVE GOVERNMENT OFFICIALS

Proverbs 29:4   The king by justice establishes the land.

It is a command to make justice to keep our land America.
Proverbs. 29:26   Many people seek the face of a ruler,
*   but it is from the LORD that one receives a sentence.*

God will give us justice when we seek His face.

Proverbs. 29: 27   An unjust person is an abomination to the righteous,   and the one who lives an upright life is an abomination to the wicked.
Be careful when there are trials for the righteousness of God the wicked have eyes of satan and the heart of satan to hurt the righteousness of God.

Seek God's Love, Seek God's Power.

We need to ask ourselves: those against each other we need to forgive, did you forgive?
Forgiving is a constant act we need to refresh our persona, attitude, heart, soul, and even our physical and emotional response upon our long past due, past, and immediate time.

The gifts, the living waters that God has given you can make into wine, "God's transformational healing" into the transformational healing of America.

John
2:1-11

1. When you are in the transformation and healing, you are being formed to the image of the authentic person God has created.

2. When having transformational healing, you may feel and experience a high tension and battle between the past and reaching into the present what God's plans are for you. Let go of this tension of the past, perhaps trials, finishing the quest, maybe failure, winning is done and accomplished when and finishing the mission. God knows you gave your best. Be careful, in your zeal to do what is right, you may react in Truth yet not be diplomatic, be calm, and breathe, yet speak the Truth in love. Many do trickery upon and the innocent that have the heart to heal America. Realizing in healing, there are trials to pass through.

3. God wants us live in Truth to transform and then improve in the present, you will grow toward the forming, improving in God's intention, what God's creation expects, and how it works to its real created purpose.

God has control over all things; however, we are tested, tried, and even test and tried again, and again in the strength of God, we can overcome all things.

    MAY ALL OF AMERICA IN THE LIGHT OF JESUS CHRIST SALVATION LOVE AND GOD'S PRECEPTS WILL HEAL AMERICA

Let us not be blinded by the god of this age. Let us the light and glory of the gospel of Jesus Christ, who is in the image of God.

Cor. 4:4

I have hope that NOW America continues to open its eyes, and we all need to ask God.

"Among our tasks as witnesses to the love of Christ is that of giving a voice to the cry of the poor."

Pope Francis

"How can we heal America?" Forgive with God's peace and justice, and then restoration can occur because in forgiving, something is given. Then we can have a forward building in love. When we forgive, it mends and soothes and brings the life of what God created from the onset and for the present, and into the future. Forgiving is speaking aloud about what needs to be restored. And to work for restoration.

"Do not judge, and you will not be judged. Do not condemn, and you will not be condemned. Forgive, and you will be forgiven. **Luke 6:37** *Give us each day our daily bread.* **Luke 11:3** *Forgive us our sins, for we also forgive everyone who sins against us.* **Luke 11:4** When we speak injustice, this is not judging. Open the heart of forgiveness for us all. We need to find the best in each other and hope for reconciliation and action to bring justice.*

Who needs the most healing in America that has given their life?

God has answered my prayer for America's healing. I can see the baskets the multiplying of fish and wine to heal America.

The First Lady of the United States, Melania Trump, initiative

"Be Best."

"It remains our generation's moral imperative to take responsibility and help our children manage the many issues they are facing today, including encouraging positive social, emotional, and physical habits." "Three pillars . . . wellbeing, which includes the social and emotional health of children; social media, and understanding both the positive and negative effects it has on our children; and opioid abuse, and how to protect or most vulnerable from the effects of drug abuse while educating parents about the detrimental effects of opioids." [cxli] America's transformational healing needs to be in the center of the life of our children that are the "most vulnerable," and the future children.

The Veterans that protect our Freedom and our future Legacy

President Donald Trump has given significant donations and promoted Veteran Charities to get money for our Veterans that have given us life and liberty, making our Legacy live.

Nathan Rousseau Smith, Journalist

May 17, 2018, President Donald Trump has donated a quarter's worth of his salary to the Department of **Veterans Affairs**

Our Veterans have given their entire being to protecting the Freedom of America. Our Veterans have to be that human that gives his or her life for America. There is death, scarring, disease, and even loss of home and family in some cases.

We need to be that enlightened force to bring about transformational healing.

1. When that belief in God, there is much light and Truth and transformational healing. They realize that we need continued recovery. Because God is a God that is life and health, He teaches His people who listen. Do we listen, do we look, do we seek the light and Truth?
2. We need to obsolete much lost, much danger, much division; we to follow the ways of God's love; even the innocent, the brilliant, the call, are scarred yet by God's miracle in us, we can heal the wounds and heal the scars of America.
We know a dichotomy from the past.

Our present is more of the transformational purpose of God, that is, life.

3. Reflecting on the first book, Our Need to Give to the World,[cxlii] we discussed in this present book.
What do we need?

What do you need? How can we serve each other?

When we WORK FOR VIRTUES OF PEACE, JUSTICE, to be in the love of God and toward the love of God and our neighbor, we will have RESTORATION.

All need to **treat each other with tenderness and love:**

"When the righteous are increased, the people rejoice." Proverbs 29:2

America will be in more unity and flourishing when righteousness increases.

"A just man [should] never seek his advantage in another man's disadvantage."

Pope Ambrose

What happens when the strong man takes advantage of the Actually, the strong man because less strong, He becomes more like an animal or beast. And the more disadvantaged man becomes faithful if He is a believer.more disadvantage? Actually, the strong man because less strong, He becomes more like an animal or beast. And the more disadvantaged man becomes faithful if He is a believer.

On the side visioning in the telescope of the Mother of America
Nevertheless, we America have embraced many people from all countries that need a mother to be nursed by the breast of the heart of the mother of America.
Let us transform and heal and give back to the health care system for the children.

Let us transform and heal our immigration system. Let us protect the life and the family unit. Let us protect our freedom.

He who trusts in the LORD is safe.

Proverbs 29:25

There are times when one has to be a warrior and shield for others; whether you are of the Trinity or not, God is a sovereign power; we are all His humanity.

4. Let America the light of the gospel of the glory of Christ, who is the image of God. God is here in the land. We know we have a relationship with God, and He has His hand on our nation.

5. Even if they do not believe in the gospel, we can bring God's love when they seek to have the Judeo-Christian ethics together.

6. **Jesus Christ, My Greatest Leader ever, and for me as I have experienced an *"intimate, in a spiritual understanding of His purpose for His creation of love, personal relationship with,"* as the Son of God, Jesus said:**

The great multitude of need - Give them to eat: How many loaves have ye have to go and. Five (Bread) and Two (Fishes). *Here is a boy with five small barley loaves and two small fish, but how far will they go among so many?" Jesus said, "Have the people sit down." There was plenty of grass in that place, and the men sat down, about five thousand of them. [11] Jesus then took the loaves, gave thanks, and distributed to those who were seated as much as they wanted. He did the same with the fish. John 6:10 -11*

7. **All we need to heal America is in God's hands if we have "five," good bread of life of people, and "two" good fishes that seek to catch other fish proclaiming to them God's salvation, that is the of life living; God's Truth fulfilled in all things that you do to heal America.**

It is a complete transformation and change, a thorough renewal of the whole of each human. "What is meant is not a theoretical relearning, but the renewal of the will." (R. Bultmann *Theology of the New Testament*, I,

1952, 211; Reason, art.)[cxliii] *G3628 (mimeomai),* imitate, follow;[cxliv] Having an intimate relationship with God, you will know how to proceed toward the solutions to help heal America.

Intimacy with God Needs to be Believed and Accept His Love

We need to keep our intimate, personal relationship with God. They had a plan for themselves and forgot about what God wanted.

A self-made man I use to work for. I loved him as a friend; he was trying to help me. He was shocked at what happened to me in my position over the years, that it was extremely unbalanced. He finally saw the truth. I lost him as a friend in the for fighting to keep America free and protected.

He told me this about California: *I think they want to take the state over and separate it from the union. They have been planning this for years. We agreed together. They hired different people, and many left certain cities because secret people in power had a conniving strategy. We ask-why was there over 151,000 or more homeless they put human-made ideas first. God told me they would not win because He wants to save the righteous.*

Years ago, the Spirit of God told me there was a Mafia here in California, and they were the ones that try to kill you and oppress and suppress you. They saw your light before and sought to kill you and could not, especially when I brought the article back from Rome on the Economic Holocaust in the USA. I worked on the project "Our Need to Give to the World," Heal America Love in God since 2007. Advocating the urgency of the eco-systems protection and the homeless God spared me. And when I wrote the book to promote the need to restore and heal America and vote in Trump, they tried to kill me then. God spared me. **I am a humble victor in the Trinity;** America and the American Freedom Warriors have overcome this. We shall conquer and protect America as it is a command of God to restore America; it is God's land. Where ever God sends me I will be praying and consulting and advocating for America and humanity's needs of protection and well-being.

They were shocked their plan is off schedule. Now they have trepidation because the world COVID-19 a greater evil. However, some are also involved with the Chinese Virus tragedy. It is the Third World Order that is trying to control.

I have to state this because the Spirit of God commands me. I already said and revealed a third party that is not upheld by the Democratic values that vote Democratic.

I pray day and night for the cities and California and the USA because God will not stand for this. I know He wants to restore America. He told me He loves America, and there are many righteous people that He will not forget. God never forsakes us. Though He, God is sovereign, and He balances justice.

Listen, Millenials, and America, God wants to save His land and His humanity. You want to be free, living, being, and loving in God's Truth. I know you want FREEDOM AMERICANS.

Please, listen, these people that want to take over will not. They are different hierarchies of Masonite. I just came in contact directly with one today. Some do not even know they are being controlled by the Mason's hierarchies, the Third World Order.

Millennials, you want to be free and have your life's existence. You do not want these hierarchies of Masons, of the Third World Order, that are hooked now in this presidential election to the Democrats to control your life. We now have to continue to restore our America under the Republican Party, and the American Freedom Warriors, and all Americans who want freedom.

We need to protect the people from ownership of their land, save their resources, and keep their freedom.

During my studies at La Verne, University, I studied and explored the Third World Order. God always never made me forget it. For our country, the USA to be restored and under God's hand and in the power of God's right arm, we have to continue those who seek His righteousness.

Complete Transformation, Restoration of Man

COMPLETE CHANGE
1. *Epistrephoœ* is used to convert a man that involves a **complete transformation** of his or her existence, the Holy Spirit's influence.[cxlv]
2. Note: This change, "complete transformation," is the acceptance of the Holy Spirit in your heart, mind, soul, entire being, entire life; it does not stop evolving closer to God when you come to Him. Sometimes, this takes much suffering. Some do not realize your time is not yours. It is the Lord's, and when He says to do something, it better be done. Many might of having thought I was "cold," or "ignorant" or "childlike;" no, this is incorrect. There is a working of God. His real purpose is not of this world that we do not comprehend; it is a mystery.

These years and moments are crucial for His mission in me, in America, and the world. We have the choice to choose God. Others have different timing in God's purpose, and each one of us who believes, and even He uses those who do not believe. Many special chosen people have helped me with jobs and housing; I am grateful. Realizing all that I am, and who I am, human and the intimate relationship I have with God in Him, in the mystery of the Trinity in the power of the Holy Spirit. I would have to say I want to share more of my experience of Truth of God's Divine Messages and Divine transformation. I have planted seeds through the power of the Trinity and the mystery of God's love. In God's will and Omni power and mystery, in the heavenly wisdom of the infiniteness God with His "warrior of love in me(and all His people), in Jesus Christ," in our weakness He manifests strength. He knows and directs me(all His people) in an intimate relationship with Him to bring His wisdom in love and transformational healing.

We America need a "complete transformation under the influence of the Holy Spirit," our mind, hearts, souls, bodies, and all our attitudes that have taken apart of our atmosphere needs to be redeemed.

*If you do not believe in the Holy Spirit, ask God to guide you. Judeo-Christian ethics toward justice is paramount to bring back in the educational systems immediately. All forward building has a solid foundation. In a **globalized world in America now,** we need to revisit, restore, and in some cases, redefine for those who do not know the truth about America, her history, her law, and her legacy, of "one nation under God."*

In God, we trust. In God is our truth. In God is our protection. In God is our restoration. In God is our life. In God is our happiness.

REPENTANCE UNTO GOD'S TRUTH

1. **Metamelomai,** however, expresses rather the feeling of repentance of sin, which need not involve a genuine turning of a man to God.
   Today we cannot have just repentance of sin. We need to have a genuine turning of a man and woman TO GOD.
   A *Epistrephoœ* complete transformation.
   How do the leaders today in America conduct business to bring justice?
2. Today in America, we live in a "globalized" world. Most have different belief systems of justice and purpose. Moreover, many do not know the meaning of America's traditional values that need to be restored, relived, and rededicated. America is built on God's truth, in honesty, working together for their ideas on what is righteousness and liberty. Never give up because God is with you.

3. ***Epistrephoœ*** (meta¿noia; cf. Acts 3:19; 26:20). It expresses the conscious turning from sin, a change of mind (Reason, art. nouvß), and the whole inner attitude to life, without which true conversion is impossible. ***Epistrephoœ*** has a wider meaning **than *metanoeoœ*,** for it always includes faith, while ***metanoeoœ* and *pisteuoœ*** can stand together and complement each other (*Faith, art*).[cxlvi]

We Americans and the world need to turn away from sin and change our minds consciously in the whole inner attitude of life of God's love to restore our country.

Sacred Heart consecration

Prayer to the Sacred Heart of Jesus

O most Holy Heart of Jesus, the fountain of every blessing, I adore You, I love You, and with lively sorrow for my sins, I offer You this poor heart of mine. Make me humble, patient, pure, and wholly obedient to Your will. Grant, good Jesus, that I may live in You and for You. Protect me amid danger; comfort me in my afflictions; give me health of body, assistance in my temporal needs, Your blessings on all that I do, and the grace of a holy death. Amen.[cxlvii] When we change our mind toward turning away from sin, our whole inner attitude is directed toward a life of God's goodness. What responsibility do we have, and how can we make it more Truth, more forgiveness, awareness, beauty, and healing around us?

WE NEED TO CONTINUE TO BREAK THIS DIVISION IN AMERICA

There should be no division!

Division cannot be in one household in a nation; otherwise, both sides become weak.

And perhaps another stronger nation comes and takes the country.
The stronger one is another nation.

VOTE TRUMP AND THE AMERICAN FREEDOM WARRIORS TO SAVE AMERICA

God wants His America's love and righteousness with His relationship Praying heart, WE NEED TO CONTINUE TO RESTORE AMERICA. PROTECT OUR LEGACY.

Community

גֵּאוּת n.f. majesty;[cxlviii]

1. *lifting* גֵּאוּת עָשָׁן *column of smoke*; גֵּאוּת הַיָּם *swelling of the sea*.
2. *majesty* of God; גֵּאוּת עָשָׂה *he hath done majestically*; עֲטֶרֶת גֵּאוּת *crown of majesty* (Samaria, on a round hill majestically commanding the country).
3. *pride* דִּבְּרוּ בְגֵאוּת *they speak proudly*.

    גְּאוּאֵל **n.pr.m.** *(majesty of El)* the spy of the tribe of Gad. **BDB (English Content)**

I am lifting in prayer in the mystery of the (Holy Spirit) in the vast love of God's sea of His land, of America and the World. I am a praying warrior, "spy," of God for His majesty. We all need to be that "spy" in praying and keeping our eyes open to truth toward virtues of the Revolution of love and restoration.

God as Creator or Maker focuses His planning and forming the creation as a skilled craftsman.[cxlix]

God is the "skilled craftsman." When weseekGod's relationship, we will know how to heal the community; because we will know God's intention.

> 1. Community is essential. Yet sometimes, a certain one needs to be that voice to awaken the people. There are times when one has to be an introvert to learn and prepare to bring revelations of God's purpose to the world. Hence, it is a fact why it is paramount to have the education (experience) and creative, ethical, and Biblical, and prayerful learning. God also works with us spontaneously, giving us refreshment and hope that He is with us and will provide us with all we need that very

moment to succeed in His purpose. Remember, God knows all sides to the story and past, present, future, and distant future.

2. I will never forget a man, a self-made multi-millionaire, who said this: Keep going if a door does not open up and seek to go through another one.

God has control of all things and has always put truth first.

Daniel 4 Nebuchadnezzar had a Dream a Greatest Wealthy King

The tree grew taller and stronger until its top reached the sky, and it could be seen from the very ends of the earth. ⁹ Its foliage was beautiful, its fruit abundant, in it was food for all. For the wild animals, it provided shade, the birds of heaven nested in its branches, all living creatures found their food on it.

Daniel 4:7-9

Then Nebuchadnezzar lost everything, all his kingdom until he realized and proclaimed, "Nebuchadnezzar, praise, extol and glorify the King of heaven, all of whose deeds are true, all of whose ways are right, and who can humble those who walk in pride."

Daniel 4:34

I have to say, I have gone against the "Socialist and Communist," "politically correct," and the "worldly media," by the command of God, to tell of His truth. I have been commanded from the Lord and Virgin Mary to speak aloud, to Consult, and to write, to be an advocate to reveal the conspiracy and danger, **yet, God has allowed us to disclose the conspiracy**. God has brought His purpose. Each of us needs to advocate peace for America's life of freedom in the present and the future. I pray I am helping the wealthy and all Americans what they want to choose and allow to have those gifts of God. *I pray I am helping them realize what they want to* *choose to be apart of the Third World Order and live in a controlled, non-Godly intention, or live in Epistrephoœ. The conversion of that involves a complete transformation of his or her existence, the Holy Spirit's influence, in the living of God intention.*[cl] California and America can be redeemed to the intimacy and living in God's will first. Remember, it is one great woman or man who can change a city for God's truth.

However, I am a woman in the purpose of God's Truth:

When we continue to love, we can plant seeds to bring healing, justice, and truth to our individuals, communities, states, and nations.

> 3. Of transformations: a clean heart; new heaven and earth (in place of old); change of nature; with double acc. *transform Jerusalem into rejoicing*.

Mark 5:23

Lay your hands-on America: this act for healing is frequent in Mark.
Lay your hands on her, America, to heal her.
Continually now in the community, we can richly and flourish into the truth of the American legacy of our cultural, traditional, and American dream, and even heal now.

"Wise and frugal government... shall restrain men from injuring one another, shall leave them otherwise free to regulate their own pursuits of industry and improvement, and shall not take from the mouth of labor the bread it has earned. This is the sum of good government."

Thomas Jefferson March 4th, 1801

UNDER PRESIDENT TRUMP today, there has been a surge of a miracle to restore America. America's safety, American jobs, significant tax incentives, Veteran care, international trade justice, and many other salient issues to give America the restoration is paramount to continue. America is flowing like living waters, and we have that promise of God's love in us when we have ***Epistrophe, a complete conversion toward God***, to continue to be redeemed and completely healed even after the trials of the China Virus.

When the communities empower each other with virtue, they work together and exchange businesses; they are proud in a humble way yet optimistically to show all and exchange their gifts, building each other up. I know many recognize this though we need to build this up. Small businesses will allow people to flourishes instead of putting the production revenue into one large company; when the individuals are healthy with their financial, emotional, physical, and spiritual, the community flourishes.

Be courteous to all, but intimate with few, and let those few be well tried before you give them your confidence.

George Washington, In a letter to this Nephew, Bushrod Washington 1783

Integration into the solution for each person
Revolution of Love to Heal America
Let us have loved, and love, each one of us toward restoration and virtue and truth and tradition
Let our thoughts be actions for the Revolution of Love and
Peace,
Justice,
Transformational Healing
Forward Building in Love

Revolution of Love:

"Every revolution was first a thought in the one man's mind, and when the same thought occurs in another man, it is the key to that era."

Ralph Waldo Emerson, "History," Essays, First Series, 1841.

God has given the keys to heaven to pray! Listen! Love!
God has given us the keys to America's beauty! Listen! Love!

Remember, there is a time for sorrow to be compassionate for a time taking on the cross of others and encouraging and empowering them to live in the life of God's:
The sorrow of compassion realizing the wrong; yet, heal the wrong with God's justice
The faith of compassion recognizing the injustices; however, remedy the injustice with God's love. Yet, the sorrow, compassion of understanding, and realizing the dehumanizing will be healed with love of restoration of God's life in the miracle of the Holy Spirit.
Let us find where this sorrow is and bring the effervescent beauty of new

life. Set your eyes on the truth!

We as Americans and humanity run to those that are unsafe and sorrowful and lift them on our shoulders, that is my calling.

RECONCILIATION is redeeming and having compassion for others even if someone else caused the problem and sin. We as a people are responsible for bringing God's love.:

> *For this reason, I say to you, whatever you make a request for in prayer, have faith that it has been given to you, and you will have it. ^{5} And whenever you make a prayer, let there be forgiveness in your hearts if you have anything against anyone; so that you may have forgiveness for your sins from your Father who is in heaven.*

> **Mark** *11:24*

Constantly I have to ask for forgiveness and forgive others. There have been many trials, and some I have not acted on them.. properly.

ng. That is our calling, America,

1. II. גֶּבֶר n.pr.m. an official of Solomon.
גֶּבֶר n.pr.

adj. גִּבּוֹר בַּבְּהֵמָה *mightiest among beasts*; מלך גבור; אֵל גִּבּוֹר the Messiah; attribute of God especially as fighting for his people.

3. n.m. *strong, valiant man*, cf. phrases גִּבּוֹר חיל *mighty man of valour*, גבורים לשתות *valiant to drink*.^{cli}

Titus 2:1-15

i. Underlying the admonitions for moral improvement in Ti 2:1-10 as the
ii. Moving force is the constant appeal to God's revelation of salvation in Christ.
iii. With its demand for transformation of life.

In Ezekiel 17:22, "Thus says the Lord God,"
I will also take of the lofty top of the cedar, and will set it; I will crop off from the topmost of its young twigs a tender one, and I will plant it upon a high and lofty mountain:
We America are ready in our righteousness in God. He will take our " young twigs, a tender one," at heart and heal our land.

"In the mountain of the height of Israel will I plant it; and it shall bring forth boughs, and bear fruit, and be a goodly cedar: and under it shall dwell all birds of every wing; in the shade of the branches thereof shall they dwell. And all the trees of the field shall know that I, Jehovah, have brought down the high tree, have exalted the low tree, have dried up the green tree, and have made the dry tree to flourish; I, Jehovah, have spoken and have done it."

Ezek. 17:23-24

We those who are working with God's right arm in the hands of His truth may be smaller in number just as the Israelites were, though we have the power and justice of God in us and with us to be His light of love. America, the people's endurance moment after moment their unfailing devotion. Let us take up faith to transform and heal our America, our world. God accommodates humanity when they turn from their sin and seek humbleness and forgiveness and reconciling to righteousness. God will also provide the falling short of ignorance in the wrong direction from how America has proceeded in each science of strategy, and each part of life whether we did it intentionally or not. It is time now, my brother and sister and friend and family and even enemy, that many aspects of America are in an urgent need to be restored and healed in the purpose of God's love. God's intention is the way things work. God is only holding the beauty of America in balance to this point because of the many that seek to make righteousness, and the wholehearted love, that they desire to do God's will. Making righteousness is making all one creates the closest beauty of peace, justice, and love.

Think about it; each process has a particular way, and there are sometimes new ways because new methods are created and formed. God has the best way and the best intention that makes the best life.

Sometimes, human choice is not good enough to exist under life and future life and even to redeem the necessary experience. God is merciful, they did not see the outcome, so there is a possibility of being failures. God understands this and wants us to come to Him to restore and transform America for the betterment; hence, God will renew America and even of the world when we allow the hand and heart of God giving us His Hand and Heart for His purpose. The Master Creator is God. He knows how to redeem and correct the situation or any entity.

"The greatest leader is not necessarily the one who does the greatest things. He is the one that gets the people to do the greatest things."

Ronald Reagan

For example, from 2007 to 2009, the Spirit of the Lord had me study the recycling issues and sought to promote them. Now today, we are in urgent need to have a process of recycling our plastics. We do not have the engineering and factories to process our plastics. China has these industrial facilities to process the plastics for energy and used mixed waste. I pray that they listened when I promoted America's restoration and healing when America voted in President Trump.

LISTEN, MILLENNIALS AND AMERICANS Today 2020 NOW,

"Piling Up: How China's Ban on Importing Waste Has Stalled Global Recycling" *China's decision to no longer be the dumping ground for the world's recycled waste has left municipalities and waste companies from Australia to the U.S. scrambling for alternatives. But experts say it offers an opportunity to develop better solutions for a growing throwaway culture.*[clii]

Ronald Reagan was in the entertainment business. No matter who we are, we can help America keep her freedom for legacy.

"I ultimately went into politics because I wanted to protect something precious."

President Ronald Reagan, January 11, 1989

Precious is our Children of America
Precious   is   all   our   People   of   America

Justice, love, and truth, is the criterion to all political success.

St. Thomas Aquinas

INTERNAL CONSOLATION Book Three The Thirtieth Chapter:
THE QUEST OF DIVINE HELP AND CONFIDENCE IN REGAINING GRACE

Thomas à Kempis, a friend of the Trinity:

"But now, after the tempest, take courage, grow strong once more in the light of My mercies, for I am near, says the Lord, to restore all things not only to the full but with abundance and above measure. Is anything difficult for Me? Or shall I be as one who promises and does not act? Where is your faith? Stand firm and persevere. Be a man of endurance and courage, and consolation will come to you in due time. Wait for Me; wait — and I will come to heal you."[cliii]

What area do you need to heal? God is asking all of us?

Open up this treasure of wisdom:

Courage--→ Grow Stronger each day in the light-----→ Restoring to full and abundance----→ GOD OMNISCIENT AND OMNIPOTENT--------→ FAITH --------→
STAND FIRM AND PERSEVERE--------→ GRACE ---→ STAND FIRM AND PERSEVERE

TRANSFORMATION RESTORATION AMERICA

The Spiritual Director and Retreat Leader, Pastor Jeffrey D. Imbach, in his book,

The Recovery of Love, Christian Mysticism and the Addictive Society, Julian of Norwich, John Ruusbroec, Meister Eckhart, Dante Alighieri, illuminates the empowerment of God's love:

"*God holds a fragile universe in love. God loves us in our goodness and our poverty and brokenness.*"[cliv]

Julian of Norwich

"Dante saw in the collapse of the major social structures of his day a necessary call. I did not produce in him a sense of victimization, but a call to empowered action."[clv]

Dante Alighieri

God already won the victory! Tasha **Cobbs**

Empowered that is God's gift for His people; when we see him first and love our neighbor with justice and truth toward peace, we have God's power promises.

"Looking up at the stars and planets, we can make a vast movement of rotation. It becomes for Dante a picture of empowered choice. In the place of purified love, all things are drawn together and choose to move harmoniously in a dance, energized by love."[clvi]

To live love is to love justice, the prophet tells us (Mic. 6:8)

We cannot have a division in Democratic that are Socialist and Communist, and Republicans

Government Checks and Balances:

We HAVE A Government to serve the people.

"People are the creators of prosperity. Without human ingenuity and innovation, we would still live in caves and have a life expectancy of 25 years. More people in an environment of freedom and free markets---means more prosperity."

Steve Forbes, April 13, 2009

"For they cast down every man his rod, and they became serpents: but Aaron's rod swallowed up their rods."

Exodus 7:12

God's rod can swallow up all "rods" of life that are not good and heal America.

Aaron's Rod is God's authority in us America we can, through God's authority, "swallowed up all that is not good."

[מִשְׁטָר] n.m. rule, authority.[clvii]

4294. מַטֶּה **matteh,** *mat-teh´;* or (feminine) מַטָּה **mattah,** *mat-taw´;* from 5186; a branch (as extending); figuratively, a tribe; also a rod, whether for chastising (figuratively, correction), ruling (a sceptre), throwing (a lance), or walking (a **staff**; figuratively, a support of life, e.g. bread):— rod, staff, tribe.[clviii]

America's authority is from God's Authority, "the Staff," is in the Word of God.

The "Staff of God, is the support of life, and Bread of life," Jesus Christ.

I am a girl answering God's call, and with GOD'S GRACE, I AM SAVED AND LOVED

In His Authority with the POWER of His Rod and Staff to bring Life and Restore, FOR HIS PEACE, AND LOVE; And to carry His love knowing I can do only with God's love.

Lisa Lucia Arden

AMERICA AUTHORITY IN GOD'S STAFF IS IN HIS HOLY SCRIPTURES AND ACCEPTING JESUS CHRIST AS KING AND SAVIOR.

America makes us be a nation of prayer, faith, virtue, and God's love.
America: From "wounded to healed to raised," and "instructed in the authority of God's rod."
The Book The Imitation of Christ by Thomas à Kempis:

Thanks to You {God} that You {God} have not spared me evils but have bruised me with bitter blows, inflicting sorrows, sending distress without and within. Under heaven, there is none to console me except You, my Lord God, the heavenly Physician of souls, Who wound and heal, Who cast down to hell and raise again. Your discipline is upon me, and Your very rod shall instruct me. [clix]

Unity Renewal by Christ and transformation into the family of God

She, (Family of God) is to be a leaven (Rising of God's love) and, as it were, the soul of human society in its ."[clx]

Let us rise together in agreement and work. When we forgive each other, the love will pour into God's purpose; we will have healing and life of God's intention for all of America.

America's physician is God to heal all things.

"Without God, I can do nothing. John XV.5

Realizing doing truly is only in God's intentions and purpose; everything else is nothing.

All of us in America can hope and change for God's goodness in us and "wipe clean our failures." I can genuinely refresh, regain, restore, and have a new nation's rebirth, free-flowing of America's revival.

Just as the scientist is diligently trying to find answers in their laboratory tests, and they are receiving responses every moment so can the legacy for our children, and ideas can be allowed to be created. However, we cannot force God's purpose.

We can restore in the Spirit of God within the human's inner being soulful, mindful, and physical action movement if we seek God's intention.

God is a merciful God.

The idea of "division" let this be **past tense**: stagnation, tragedy, acceptance of loss. We have a room of prayer of transformation and healing when we pray to God when we repent and seek the face of God's love. We face life with His purpose. We face life in Him toward an endless love of closer in and with and through Him, God, in us.

Rom. 12:2 declares: "Do not be conformed to this world but be transformed by the renewal of your mind that you may prove what the will of God is, what is good and acceptable and perfect." (It is) no mere change of mind or adoption of a new moral outlook. It is a complete transformation and evolution, a thorough renewal of the whole man. "(It is not) is not a theoretical relearning, but the renewal of the will" (R. Bultmann, *Theology of the New Testament*, I, 1952, 211; Reason, art. nouvß).[clxi]

Epistrephoœ (beauty) is to convert a man, which involves a **complete transformation** of his existence under the Holy Spirit's influence. [clxii]

Hence, when we have a "complete transformation renewal of our will that will be God's will; therefore, we will be able to overcome all that is not of God; and become more faithful, and His grace is sufficient for us.

The Spirit of the Lord said, "You put fresh water on a tree to grow. Each American needs to be freshwater, a new life of God's will God *planning, and creation as a skilled craftsman.*

God never changes,
God never forsakes us
God never gives up on the righteousness of His People
God never has the impediment of life
God never stops living. He is Alpha and Omega,
God evolving of His creation is always movement and beauty upon beauty to grow and heal and be sanctified.
God has created a life that is always living, and it never stops growing

Now my America, let us live in God's power and strength and wisdom of His light. To walk in His light, one has to seek His light of love. We are His created humans and can take up those promises and His creation of fresh living waters.

By her very mission, "the Church . . . travels the same journey as all humanity and shares the same earthly lot with the world: she is to be a leaven and, as it were, the soul of human society in its."[clxiii]

"The *epiclesis* {Eucharist] is also a prayer for the full effect of the assembly's communion with the mystery of Christ. "The grace of the Lord Jesus Christ and the love of God and the fellowship of the Holy Spirit" ~~28~~ have to remain with us always and bear fruit beyond the Eucharistic celebration. The Church, therefore, asks the Father to send the Holy Spirit to make the lives of the faithful a living sacrifice to God by their spiritual transformation into the image of Christ, by concern for the Church's unity, and by taking part in her mission through the witness and service of charity."[clxiv]

III. THE CHURCH IS CATHOLIC

Vatican II-E

> Then a great promise and great trust is committed to the disciples: 'All things are yours, and you are Christ's, and Christ is God's' 208

CHAPTER V

May all those who are being down with poverty, infirmity, and sickness, as well as those who must bear various hardships or who suffer persecution for justice's sake-may they all know they are uniquely united with the suffering Christ for the salvation of the world.

"To satisfy the demands of justice and equity, strenuous efforts must be made,

without disregarding the rights of persons or the natural qualities of each

country, to remove as quickly as possible the immense economic inequalities,

that discrimination. Likewise, in many areas, given the unique difficulties of

agriculture relative to the raising and selling of produce, country people must

be helped . . .to increase and market what they produce, introduce the necessary development and renewal and also obtain an adequate income.

Otherwise, as too often happens, they will remain in the condition of lower-class citizens.

Let farmers themselves, especially young ones, apply themselves to perfecting their professional skills, for, without it, there can be no agricultural advance

"Let also workers themselves, especially young ones, apply themselves to perfecting their professional skill, for, without it, there can be no business or vocational or individual advance." [clxv]

The way of Christ "leads to life"; a contrary way "leads to destruction."The Gospel parable of the two ways remains ever-present in the catechesis of the Church; it shows the importance of moral decisions for our salvation: "There are two ways, the one of life, the other of death; but between the two, there is a great difference."[clxvi]

1. We have to find the purest, most just paradigm with a long-term significance of healing for every science and working knowledge of the community.
2. We find it in following the
   4 Foundational Truths
   1. Peace
   2. Justice
   3. Transformational Healing
   4. Forward Building in the love of humanity.

One cannot work without the other they need to be all incongruent.

[I know sometimes one has to step back and assess what is front of them to accomplish a transformation and restoration, many times in history it is the unexpected who directs." Of course, you have to have the tools—belief with understanding, peace, justice, and forwarding building in the love of humanity. Furthermore, you also need an agreement with others.

There are times when one has to seclude themselves to enter into revelation of secret or unknown knowledge and wisdom to bring to the present that is waiting to take birth or to naturally heal, because what is present and needs restoration it is against life created intention, of the Trinity and needs restoring and to be given to the messenger to bring it so that those things that need restoring can and will be restored. God is asking for you to be in unity with Him, give Him your heart, and know His wisdom that carries the "handmaid" of knowledge about the solutions in you to find the answers to heal America.

Job 28:28 And unto man(humanity) he said,
Behold, the fear of the Lord, that is wisdom;
And to depart from evil is understanding.
What is the life of the most divine *peace*?
What is the life of the most living *justice*?
What is the *healing* that needs to be redeemed?
What is the *Forward building in the love of humanity* that is most important?

"Salvation in the Lord the God for those who are believers in Jesus Christ, our Lord, and Savior."

Pope Benedict XVI

Do not follow who modernizes God in Jesus Christ's Salvation.
Do not you go away from the truth.

Note: I use the definitions and the study of the words to seek the truth of God's purpose and His intentions.
I seek to use the information that brings love and also warning for protection, with Wisdom.

If one form of need in the community is weak and imbalanced, the strong seek to support it in their intentions or God's intentions. Though the strong keep growing, and if there is a Socialistic or Communistic influence many are suppressed and oppressed. We need to find those things in the community that needs healthiness. If the vast majority of people are controlled, enslaved, treated with injustices, without any identity, there will be no one to exchange with including relationships, economics, culturally, and even psychological expression, and in some cases spiritually, life will be bleak without emotions. Awake to restoration in justice and peace for a smoother experience of the masses, otherwise America will be not that *Mother of Love*. Again, God cannot pour good upon evil

AMERICA GOD'S YOUR:

> PEACE
> JUSTICE
> HEALING
> FORWARD BUILDING IN LOVE

LET US CONTINUE TO RACE AND WIN TO BECOME INDIVIDUALS OF FREEDOM TO EXPRESS OUR CREATED BEING AND EVERY DAY EXISTENCE WITHOUT INJUSTICES UPON EVERY STREET IN OUR CITIES AND EVERY WAY IN OUR LIFE.

LET ALL OF US PRAY FOR PEACE OF
Vatican II-E(English)
Part1 CHAPTER III

For God's Word, through whom all things were made, was Himself made flesh and dwelt on the earth of men. Thus, He entered the world's history as a perfect man, taking that history up into Himself and summarizing it. He, Himself revealed to us that 'God is love' (1 John 4:8) and at the same time taught us that the new command of love was the fundamental law of human perfection and hence of to world transformation.[clxvii]

Praying is receiving God's love

Praying is receiving God's love in the Trinity because the Trinity was together at creation, creating all things; God's love can overcome all things and heal all things. God can redeem all things. When we pray, there are miracles. Our body changes even at the molecular level in a transforming spiritual healthiness in God's will. Moreover, our body, mind, soul, and atmosphere are transformed into God's will when one receives it. Remember, there might be a time that is needed to wait for the answered prayer. Our authentic creation that He intended that He fashioned with the omnipotent Words is living. For each person to repent, to know, and continually seek righteousness in God and His precepts, through the power of the Holy Spirit, there is God's love that will be manifested in love. We are given His love in our being, that we receive from the Trinity, and even Virgin Queen Mother Mary, and the Saints, and the heavenly Angels of and the Arch Angels of God.

Divine Message December 6th, 2019 Pasadena

I was taken in the Spirit of God to the heavenly in prayer. I rested and slept in worship. I was in a realm of the heavens, taken to a place of great light and piece yet majesty. I felt life and peace and miracle intensely, perhaps more than I ever have. Then I saw Jesus Christ's cross. It was bright platinum rays of pure light coming from it; it was close to me; I ask what this bright cross of light signifies? The Spirit of God said, " I have given My life so others can have life abundant." I have given My life on the cross to redeem the sins of the Sacrificial lamb. I was resurrected after My crucifixion. I have saved the sins of the world; When those whom come to Me and ask for forgiveness and seek to do righteousness even when there are mistakes, I have a grace that has been given to Me by the Father; and I give it to humanity whom calls upon Me and humbles themselves and asking for forgiveness for their sins then I bring the sin up and it is resurrected; when we repent and ask for forgiveness, the sin disappears and is erased by The blood that I shed on the cross for humanity's sin; then the cross in heaven is the victory the light of the Greatest love to give your life for a friend; [however, Jesus Christ also is the Son of God only in Him is the overcoming sin, of humanity, of culture, and evil. We are not slaves; we are His friends in Christ when we accept Him as our Lord. Even though we are a servant for Him and His humanity, we are not slaves. We are His friend.]

The lighted Cross in Heaven is the victory over sin, and when we turn away from sin, our life is even more extraordinary in God. The more we come to Christ Jesus in the Trinity, the more we pass through crosses of life redeemed by GodBECAUSE I HAVE JESUS CHRIST'S PROMISE HE WILL TAKE CARE OF ALL THINGS; I FORGIVE THIS MOMENT ALL THAT HAVE HURT AMERICA. We need to keep on keeping America great. Under President Trump, he has sought with the team to keep America great and work for THE AMERICAN PEOPLE'SSAFETY, developing all sides from infrastructure to business to education to the right to life ongoing work of liberty to restore America. PROCLAIMING AND CONSULTANTING AND ADVOCATING AMERICA'S PROTECTION OF HER LAND AND LEGACY, I have had much violence; God in the Trinity has protected me.

Though I cannot say many things, I was told to keep it quiet; I Love in the Trinity and Mary and the Arch Angels, America, and the world.

AS AMERICAN LEADERS, WE NEED TO STAND, STAND WHAT GOD'S JUSTICE IS;

REMEMBER IF WE ARE TRICKED BY DECEIT OR STEALING IN THE ACTIONS OF OTHER'S AGAINST US, GOD WATCHES US WITH HIS EYES, AND HE WILL TEACH US THE THINGS YOU NEED TO KNOW AND HOW AND WHAT YOU NEED TO DO

We America, have God's covenant to love America "causes us to stand" firm. In strength, we stand! Insecurity we stand in security; we stand WITH stability;
Making our country, we stand firm!

The Holy Spirit stands at our side, ask for His Guidance and Wisdom.
America follows God to freedom.
The Cross of Jesus Christ is in the life trials and sin to redeem all that needs love and new life.
America calls upon Jesus Christ; He is your Savior.
The God of Abraham is jealous of God He will not accept any God's before Him.

Amad, "to stand", hence, "to cause to stand." It means that the makes the nation "stand firm," with "standing firm" is a figure for strength, security, and stability. Cf. NCV "makes his country (the nation CEV) strong. In investigating term= (*}amad*, "to stand"), Here when we have a just leader, "King," (*and*, "to stand"), "to cause to stand," and "stand firm," he or she "makes his/her country strong.

(*{aœmad*), q. Stand, take one's stand, stand still, stay; hi. Set up, station, appoint, restore. Be presented, be set upright (H6641).[clxviii]

I have arisen with Jesus Christ because I have accepted Him as my Lord and Saviour, I have spoken, I am coming on the scene. I am here writing and speaking and praying and acting in that I am proclaiming the truth. Remember, let me reiterate, one word of the Holy Scriptures is the Christ personified, and it has and will bring a miracle for the restoration of America. I have been sending Divine Messages and Divine Commands on Social Media daily to protect, and warn, and give hope for America and the world that are given me to from the Spirit of God. The people have listened, and their faith is excellent and pure, and they have humbled themselves, and the Divine Messages and Commands many have been fulfilled.

The verb o *(amad,* "to stand") may denote "to arise; to appear; to come on the scene" (e.g., Ps 106:30; Dan 8:22, 23; 11:2–4; 12:1; Ezra 2:63; Neh 7:65); cf. BDB764

Even if there may be trouble, we know we have eternal life in heaven and with God Almighty. Praying the Holy Scriptures, "The Word Became Flesh, Jesus Christ," is with us, silently, meditatively, always without ceasing of miracles prayers that heal the entire human being. *To change the external form, transfigure;* mid. *to change one's form, be transfigured,* Mt. 17:2; Mk. 9:2; *to undergo a* spiritual *transformation* Rom. 12:2; 2 Cor. 3:18. ˇ .clxix

Let us have a transformation to restore America in peace, friendship, happiness, prosperity, health, salvation, and restoration.

Baskets of Restoration of God's love

I had a vision of a basket sparkling foaming light. There were many hearts within the basket. The hearts were moving, and unlimited colors of red, pink-red, and maroon and their movement reflected love and healing. When we are in the heart of God, we have His Sacred Heart. When we give our heart, we will multiply the hearts like God multiplies His love. Jesus Christ fed the 4,000, and in the faith, He had for the Love of His Father and humanity. Jesus Christ used seven loaves of bread and two fish to feed the 4,000. Mathew 14: 13-21 We can, in God's love America restore her. Give America your heart in love.

*Restoration is defined as peace, friendship, happiness, prosperity, health, salvation, and happiness. Speaks first of God's anger and punishment, but then God alters his plan and brings healing and comfort. The word of God

has life-giving power and thus brings comfort in affliction (Ps. 119:50). A faithful friend is described as an elixir of life (Sir. 6:16).[clxx 6]

A loyal friend is the elixir of life and those who fear the Lord will find one. ¹⁷ Whoever fears the Lord makes true friends, for as a person is, so is His friend too.

Sir. 6:16

There have been times I have had "God's anger" because I can feel and understand Him in the Trinity, that we as a people have to seek restoration, and there may be a warning for danger ahead if we do not seek His face of peace, justice in His love. Even if we do not believe in God, we can seek love. We know what pure love and peace, and justice is. The Holy Spirit, in the midst, the action of justice is, and the Holy Spirit is yearning to kindle the love directly in the soul, heart, and body of the person.

Jesus is the King of Society
Sanctity of Marriage and love

Restoration:
With individuals
With children
With families,
With home life
With businesses
With Communities
With Country
—Disciples empowered to heal (Matthew 10:8)

We America, the Disciples, to heal America.

Do not make your way to gentile territory, and do not enter any Samaritan town; go instead to the lost sheep of the House of Israel. And as you go, proclaim that the kingdom of Heaven is close at hand. Cure the sick, raise the dead, cleanse those suffering from virulent skin-diseases, drive out devils. You received without charge, give without charge. Provide yourselves with no gold or silver, not even with coppers for your purses, with no haversack for the journey or spare tunic or footwear or a staff, for the laborer deserves his keep.

Matthew 10:6-1

Divine Message Holy Family 2020
The Spirit of the Lord told me to do this. These are all Biblical Passages.
Put your
Hand on your throat and neck Four……(Wrap the Word of God around your neck. Proclaim and sing of His Healing Love.)
Put your
Hand on your head…. Four……(the Chief Authority of His Wisdom). (humbleness is authority God realizing God is Almighty).
Put your
Hands-on your feet Four…(My Light is your path.)
Put your
Hands-on your arms and hands. Four…(You have the right arm of God's Strength and you are in and with and Daughter through MY POWER AND LOVE the hands of God

You are in My Heart.

Standing in front of the Church, I heard the Spirit of Mary say; I hold the baby Jesus because of the … love of God; I have Jesus Christ at my heart daughter .. I have Jesus Christ at my left arm..

 This is symbolizing love. I have in the Trinity. For humanity, this is for all Christians.

All Christians are supposed to be like that.
Baby Jesus Christ said,
I am on the footstool here, a daughter that I use the enemy as my footstool in the right way.. it allows me to show goodness over evil, and then they will open their eyes to My father's love.
If they try to water the tree with poison, it will kill the tree, and they will not have fruit or even anything on the tree. This is why they seek to take from others even if they are rich in material goods; they do not have God's fruit.
When I water the tree, it will bring fruit.
 I use the enemy as My footstool for them to receive God. "Using the enemy's footstool is showing them what God gave them is a blessing from

God, and it will and can be multiplied in love when it is shared in God's purpose. Not by force, not by abuse, and not by masonry or witchcraft."
I am with the children at school as them to call upon me when they need help.

Little Jesus said, "If they call upon me and ask me to help them;I will be there. when they seek."

Strength and Power for Restoration

411.δύναμις; *dunamis, dunameōs, hē*; (from Homer down); the Septuagint for *ḥayil, gĕbûrâ, 'oz, koaḥ, ṣābā'* (an army, a host); *strength, ability, power*; a. universally, *inherent power, power residing in a thing by virtue of its nature, or which a person or thing exerts and puts forth*: Luke 1:17; Acts 4:7; 1 Cor. 4:20; 2 Cor. 4:7; 12:9 (*hē dunamis en astheneia teleitai* (R G *teleioutai*)); 13:4; 1 Thess. 1:5; Heb. 7:16; 11:34; Rev. 1:16; 17:13; *idia dunamei*, Acts 3:12; *megalē dunamei*, Acts 4:33[clxxi]

    We America, when we receive God's purpose, we, plural and also, I singular have the power of God in virtue. **δύναμις** "power residing in a thing by virtue its nature," to restore. First, it has to start with I have the **δύναμις** "power residing in a thing by virtue of its nature," to restore, we do this for "we," God's people. Even we are growing, and learning and imperfect and incomplete God can still use us.

Of course, we need to understand our mistakes and learn from them and turn away from our sins, yet, we need to give the sorrow of this to God at the foot of the cross and lay our burdens upon God's heart. Then you will receive God's love. See when burdens and sins are not forgiven and changed by God's Cross and truths are not searched then God's life does not live. Sometimes it takes someone that can see what needs to be redeemed because they have experienced it and know the Wisdom of God's purpose. However, many times this is someone clear and pure at heart and not of the world.

Consequently, it will take much or a minute to wake up to the truth for the people to arise to the fact. Either way, God does not give up. He relies on us to bring His message of truth and the carrier of His light of His love. We are His light when we are in His truth.

1410. **δύναμαι;** *dunamai*, deponent verb, present indicative 2 person singular *dunasai* and, according to a rarer form occasional in the poets and from Polybius on to be met with in prose writings also (cf. Lob. ad Phryn., p. 359; (WH's Appendix, p. 168; Winer's Grammar, sec. 13, 2 b.; Veitch, under the word)), *dunē* (Mark 9:22f L T Tr WH; (Luke 16:2 T WH Tr text); Rev. 2:2)

Rev. 2:2 ᵃ" 'I know your works, your toil and your patient endurance, and how you cannot bear with those who are evil but have tested those who call themselves apostles and are not, and found them to be false.ᶜˡˣˣⁱⁱ

<u>Be careful; the ones closest to you may use evil upon you.</u>
Just know you are forward; building in love can overcome all things.
Remember, we are all becoming closer to God and need forgiveness though we need truth.

Love is always patient and kind; love is never jealous; love is not boastful or conceited, ⁵ it is never rude and never seeks its own advantage, it does not take offense or store up grievances. ⁶ Love does not rejoice at wrongdoing but finds its joy in the truth. ⁷ It is always ready to make allowances, to trust, to hope, and to endure whatever comes.

1 Cor. 13:4

Love never comes to an end.

1Cor. 13:8

'Do not give dogs what is holy; and do not throw your pearls in front of pigs, or they may trample them and then turn on you and tear you to pieces.

Matt. 7:6

America in God's heart "Love never comes to an end."

Sometimes those who need to be healed need to have an awakening, and they need an escalation of the senses; therefore, the delivery has to be dominant in God's truth.

tēs anasteseōs tou Christou, the **power** which the resurrection of Christ has, for instructing, reforming, elevating, tranquilizing, the soul, Phil. 3:10; *tēs eusebeias*, inhering in godliness and operating upon souls, 2 Tim. 3:5; *dunameis mellontos aiōnos* (*aiōn*, 3), Heb. 6:5; *to pneuma tēs dunameōs* (*pneuma*, 5), 1 Pet. 4:14

I may know Him and the power of His resurrection, and may share his sufferings, becoming like him in his death. We need to **"become like Him," love like Him.**

Phil. 3:10

4982. σώζω sozo, *sode'-zo;* from a primary σῶς sos (contraction for obsolete **σάος saos**, "safe"); to save, i.e. deliver or protect (literally or figuratively): — heal, preserve, save (self), do well, be (make) whole.[clxxiii]

1407 [1295] διασῴζω, **diasǫzō**, v.

[1328 + 5392]. save, spare, bring safely through a dangerous or distressing situation, with a focus that the rescue is complete or full; to heal, with a focus that the injured or sick person goes from the danger of ill health to the safety of a completely restored or healthy life.[clxxiv]

23.138 ἴαμα, τος *n:* (derivative of ἰάομαι^a 'to cause to be well again, to heal,' 23.136) the capacity to cause someone to become healed or cured — 'the power to heal, the capacity to heal.' ἄλλῳ δὲ χαρίσματα ἰαμάτων ἐν τῷ ἑνὶ πνεύματι 'and to another man the same Spirit gives the power to heal' 1Cor 12:9. In some languages, it may be difficult to speak of 'giving the power to heal.' A more natural form of expression is 'cause to be able to heal.'

23.139 θεραπεύω^a; **θεραπεία**^a, **ας** *f:* to cause someone to recover health, often with the implication of having taken care of such a person — 'to heal,

Divine Message August 30, 2019

> Mary said, "when the children are being breastfed, there should be no phones used or any, technical devices or computers the experiences and attitudes and all other items. will be exposed by the infant and are detrimental to the brain. There should be prayers of the rosary and the bible verses and prayers of the God of Abraham. The baby will remember these Holy Divine Words, they are the closest experience of God's infinite teachings that the infants can come into contact with besides the Holy Spirit and the sacraments and the believers themselves and the Saints and Angels. Also, the infants will develop the more heavenly brain of God's replication of His purpose when listening to these prayers, rosary, songs of God. While breastfeeding. Just as the milk is the nutrition of the infant to live and develop by at this essential time so is it essential the infant knows the Holy Scripture Prayers and songs. Of God of Abraham.
> Tell President Trump and the leaders, if they pray my rosary, I will lead them and guide them and they will know their successes will be in God and they will know that it is Me who has guided them. They need a Spiritual Director. They will know the difference and it is not from them, because the correct way is in God's way and I am in God and He is in Me. The Son of God is in the Father and I am in the Father My flesh bore the Son of God and We are in the Sacred heart together; I am in Him the Son of God and He is in Me.   Therefore, the Holy Scriptures are also in

Me, because I am in the Father and in the Son and in the Holy Spirit. My veil is the greatest protection of the Holy Spirit. Mary also stated, something about the clothes.. though I did not get .. all of what she wanted to say, she said the clothing is important what we wear. The dye and chemicals they use to make the clothes needs to be safe.

Acts 5:12-16 HEAL THE SICK

Revival REALIZING A REAL SHIP WITH GOD IS:

Messages of the prophets are not just warning of sins, most important is: " <u>God's grace and restoration, especially God's transformation of the human</u> heart (e.g., Jer 30–33, Ezek 36–37). (Exile: History)" [clxxv]

God has redeemed us when we receive Him.

Transformation of the human heart is the answer to healing America,

<u>Remember, I am called to bring His purpose, God's purpose, to bring His love for the people. Yes, we are all called to bring God's love to the people. We can restore America to the truth to help those in the future.</u>

Children and Young Adults Educational Authority of Truth in the private and public schools

1. Program to study ethics and respect and peaceful communication.
2. Program for the self-sufficient understanding of basic accounting needs for daily living. And the entrepreneurial project for the production of purpose or trade. Also, investment understanding of stock and other types of commodities.
3. Required to study their choice, humanity and the eco-system and natural resources and all those things related to humanity each year and keep a notebook of study, raw research, not just theoretical, all year long and each year throughout their research. The courses the students can choose from can be anything related to the eco-system, and natural resources, water, ocean, sand, rain, rivers, forest, plants, mountain ranges, soil, lakes, and all w*ater bodies of water*, atmosphere, electricity, gas, windmill power, microwave, solar power, recycling, sewage, and agricultural, foods, and production of foods, climate, pharmaceuticals, alternative

medicine, insects, animals, nutrition, exercise, sound, and health of the human body.
4. All students are required to study the periodical table and understand how all things are related to life.
5. Already underway is a program to study American History and its legacy and founders and developers.

<u>The more I seek to run the race of God's calling;</u>

<u>The more I see God tries to plead to answer God's call:</u>
<u>Whether it is to be the most generous friend,</u>
<u>Whether it is to be the wisest servant to give God's love,</u>
<u>Whether it is that person to forgive and also save others from death,</u>
<u>Whether it is to be a mother of the highest respect and patience,</u>
<u>or the father to be the honesty and strength and tenderness to all humanity,</u>
<u>or to be the President of the United States and Government officials to be the heart and mind and righteous, just servants for God's people of America,</u>
<u>all are called, all are drawn together as the same purpose yet individual in God, and only in God can we truly bring God's justice and God's love.</u>

In the enlightening book the *Authority*, magnificently, eloquent Lloyd-Jones D. Marlyn heralds the solution for transformational healing of America:

"Let us remind ourselves that day by day and many items during the day; we will spend our time before God pleading for revival. But, foolish as we are, we will never do so until we have come to the end of ourselves and of our own resources. We will do so only when everything else has failed, and we have realized our utter bankruptcy and impotence, and we had come to that our Lord spoke the simple truth when He said, <u>"Without God, ye can do nothing. (John XV.5)</u> [clxxvi]

The Lord God told me, "Claim what I have given you child."

America claims what God has given us the authority to restore America, the land of God's love, America.

HEBREW IS AN ANCIENT HOLY LANGUAGE THAT GOD SPOKE WITH HIS PEOPLE AND GAVE THEM DELIVERANCE, AND TODAY GOD SPEAKS WITH US AND HAS DELIVERED US[clxxvii] LET US ALL STAND

MAKING OUR COUNTRY STRONG *AS LEADERS OF GOD*

Prov. 4:1   Hear, *my* sons, the instruction of a father,
And attend to know to understand:
Prov. 4:2   For I give you good doctrine.
Prov. 4:1   Listen, my sons, to a father's instruction.
pay attention and gain understanding.
2   I give you sound learning, so do not forsake my teaching.
3   When I was a boy in my father's house,

still tender, and an only child of my mother,
4   he taught me and said,
"Lay hold of my words with all your heart.
keep my commands and you will live.
5   Get wisdom, get understanding.
Do not forget my words or swerve from them.
6   Do not forsake wisdom, and she will protect you;
Love her, and she will watch over you.
7   Wisdom is supreme; therefore, get wisdom.
Though it cost all you have, get understanding.
8   Esteem her, and she will exalt you.
Embrace her, and she will honor you.
9   She will set a garland of grace on your head
and present you with a crown of splendor."

Prov. 4:10   Listen, my son, accept what I say,
And the years of your life will be many.
11   I guide you in the way of wisdom
And lead you along straight paths.
12   When you walk, your steps will not be hampered.
When you run, you will not stumble.
13   Hold on to instruction, do not let it go.
Guard it well, for it is your life.
14   Do not set foot on the path of the wicked
Or walk in the way of evil men.
15   Avoid it, do not travel on it;
Turn from it and go on your way.

16		For they cannot sleep till they do evil;
		They are robbed of slumber till they make someone fall.

Prov. 4:18		The path of the righteous is like the first gleam of dawn,
		Shining ever brighter till the full light of day.

Prov. 4:20		My son, pay attention to what I say;
		Listen closely to my words.
21		Do not let them out of your sight,
		keep them within your heart;
22		for they are life to those who find them
		and health to a man's whole body.
23		Above all else, guard your heart,
		for it is the wellspring of life.
24		Put away perversity from your mouth;
		keep corrupt talk far from your lips.
25		Let your eyes look straight ahead,
		fix your gaze directly before you.
26		Make level paths for your feet
27		Do not swerve to the right or the left;
		keep your foot from evil.

We now have taken up the wisdom of God Our Transformation of Restoration has been Sorrow turned to Joy because of the Enlightened American People

President Trump

Collaborative Government Representatives

I PLEAD LET US TAKE UP THE LOVE OF GOD IN TRUTH AND IN AUTHORITY

I plead and pray upon my knees for America with tears within and upon the heart and give my heart even though I know only of me is dust, the only life, light, truth, and love of me is in God.

I am in joy, overpouring joy, everlasting joy, knowing today all is well with America because even if we go through trials, God is with us.

Writing this moment, I am deeply yearning that we receive the love of God, knowing God never forsakes us, as He promises us in Holy Scriptures, that are the life of God and His people Jeremiah and Esther are true peoples of God in the life of humanity.

In the "Book of Consolation," Jeremiah *looked forward to when God would give joy instead of sorrow (Jer 31:13).*

*When in the days of **Esther**, the threat of persecution and death was lifted,* **sorrow is turned into joy, a time of mourning into a time of feasting."**

Esther
clxxviii 9:22

America, let us CONTINUE TO bring our country to the restoration
AMERICA, WE HAVE BROUGHT SORROW TO JOY IN PUTTING
AMERICA FIRST AND GIVING HER OUR DEDICATION AND LOVE

PRESIDENT TRUMP, GOD FEARING AMERICANS, AND THE TEAM
HAS RESTORED AMERICA FOR TRUTH AND TRADITION
WE NEED TO CONTINUE THE JOY AND HAPPINESS TO RESTORE AMERICA.

Cannot you SEE God's love relationship with His people, is still living from ancient times, proves God is alive in Jesus Christ in the power and mystery of the Holy Spirit?

Say, Yes, to God, and have a relationship.

The Lord God told me, "Claim what I have given you child":

"Wherever and whenever the Church is persecuted, the Lord hears and answers the prayers of His persecuted children. He is the blood of the martyred saints, and trumpets of judgment warn the wicked. (Chapters 8-11),

The struggle on the surface- between the Church and world, always indicates a deeper struggle between Christ and the dragon (chapter 12-14). For the impenitent, bowls of final wrath always follow trumpets of judgment (chapter 15, 16). That is true today; it was true yesterday; it will be true tomorrow, whether you live in Africa, Europe, or America. **Satan and all his helpers . . . are always defeated.' (Chapters 17-19; also 20-22). P. 34**

Truth and Tradition:

Spinoza warns us of the salience to keep America's freedom and life:

America is the original foundation of her country cannot be changed to a Socialistic or Communistic rule. Utmost caution, life or death: "even dominion should retain its original form, and indeed cannot change it without danger of the utter ruin of the whole state." [clxxix] The ONLY RESTORATION IN PEACE AND LIBERTY GOD WILL ACCEPT.

Let us warn each other America, let our fighting be only for PEACE AND LIBERTY,

NOT FOR GOD'S GLORY.

"After the kings acquired sovereign power, the fighting was not (is) longer for peace and liberty, but glory; accordingly, we find that they all except for Solomon (whose virtue and wisdom would be better displayed in peace than war) waged war, and finally a fatal desire for power gained ground, which, in many cases made the path to the throne a bloody one.[clxxx]

We as Americans for the transformational restoration of peace and liberty, not for war. In gaining peace and pursuing the truth.

We need to continue to for restoration as individuals and as a unity of agreement a covenant. The 'entirety" is the purpose of God's intention.

PERFECT FAITH AND LOVE TOWARD JESUS CHRIST WE HAVE MADE OUR COVENANT IN TO LOVE IN GOD.

"None of these things escapes your <u>notice if you have perfect faith and love toward Jesus Christ.</u> For these are the beginning and the end of life: faith is the beginning, and love is the end, and the two, when they exist in unity, are God." Everything else that contributes to excellence follows from them."[clxxxi]

"The tree is known by its fruit." "For the Work (Rom. 3.3) is not a matter of what one promises now, but of persevering to the end in the power of faith." [clxxxii]

Divine Message 2020 Justification

You will go into the room of justification.

I shall justify you because of the sin that has been done upon you.... You will be justified.
What is justification?
Though the Spirit of the Lord said justification is love.
The room was all blue.
I have evil on every side against me though God has redeemed me.
The Spirit of the Lord just told me.
Old is not measured by years, it is measured how much life of God one has in them.

February 20, 2020

Virgin Mary the Voice of the Queen of Heaven and Earth of the God of Abraham

TRUTH path is living in God's will, Mary said, "Though to help one has to take a detour into the darkness to bring the light of God;because the light needs to be in the darkness child.

How will you be able to help people if you do not go into the darkness, my child? They need to experience the light; however, you cannot be abused. You do need to use the tools of protection when you go into the darkness. This is why you have them. They need to wake up and come to the truth that there is darkness, and when they are shocked in the light of God, they are then awakened. It takes a change in the mind, child, and for them to hear the truth, there needs to be a catalyst. Sometimes, force is even used. This is why you need to protect yourself and all those in the light toward sanctifying God's truth; when those attempts to place and promote and instigate and even put into law those things that are not of the wholesomeness for humanity.

"It is to be regretted that the rich and powerful too often bend the acts of government to their own selfish purposes."

President Andrew Jackson

Your minds, then, must be sober and ready for action; put all your hope in the grace brought to you by the revelation of Jesus Christ. [14] Do not allow yourselves to be shaped by the passions of your old ignorance, [15] but as obedient children, be yourselves holy in all your activity, after the model of the Holy One who calls us, [16] since scripture says, 'Be holy, for I am holy.' [17] And if you address as Father Him who judges without favoritism according to each individual's deeds, live out the time of your exile here in reverent awe. [18] For you know that the price of your ransom from the futile way of life handed down from your ancestors was paid, not in anything perishable like silver or gold, [19] but in precious blood as of a blameless and spotless lamb, Christ. [20] He was marked out before the world was made, and was revealed at the final point of time for your sake. [21] Through Him, you now have faith in God, who raised Him from the dead and gave Him glory for this very purpose—that your faith and hope should be in God.

1Pet. 1:13

When we told you about the power and the coming of our Lord Jesus Christ, we were not slavishly repeating cleverly invented myths; no, we had n his majesty with our own eyes. ¹⁷ He was honored and glorified by God the Father when a voice came to him from the transcendent Glory. This is my Son, the Beloved; he enjoys my favor. ¹⁸ We heard this voice from heaven when we were with him on the holy mountain.

Pet. 1:16

"*History and experience tell us that moral progress cannot come in comfortable and in complacent times, but out of trial and out of confusion.*"

President Gerald Ford

Because God never forsakes His people; He is a jealous God, and He will not allow them to be overcome by evil. God's New Covenant in Jesus Christ to restore humanity through the power of His Cross.

Divine Messages First week of February 8th, 2019

I saw a room of the student individually sitting at a chair and table in the heavenly. The colors were shimmering platinum and white and light yellow.

The Cal Tech students are the students that need to realize God has given them gifts that are paramount to use for the justice and compassion of humanity. Each student should be also a student of God. Of course, there is a teacher, though the teacher has supposed to already manifested God's purpose in their life in the course they are teaching and also have a continually evolving and deliver it to the student. They are given the secrets of God's intention when they seek to ask in righteousness and devotion to do the best for humanity, God is there in, with, and through the student and the professor. The secrets are gifts that are revealed to humanity to enjoy and create in God's intention when the student and teachers seek the best toward the justice and righteousness in God's purpose. Though God does want the student and the Professor to ask Him and seek in prayer and righteousness upon their knees, "Guide me God of Abraham in Christ Jesus in the love and righteousness for God's intention to bring the creation and learning of your purpose for humanity that is a gift you have given me and I give it back to humanity all in your powerful right arm yet tender compassion for the greatest beauty and purpose."

God has given you a great responsibility to take up His intention and apply it to the greatest purpose for humanity for the earth. You need to ask Him what is it that you want me to know and deliver and help me to learn. All are privileged to learn. When we cannot learn we are not living. When we are learning and evolving and expressing our gifts we are living. This is why it is paramount that each individual find the gift God has given them when they were created then they are living.

I ask Jesus and Mary once what was all the Saints doing in heaven, " The Saints are preparing assignments for the believers and helping the believers, and to call in to the heart and salvation in Christ Jesus, those who do not know Jesus Christ, and those who they guide.

Chapter Four

4 FOUNDATIONAL TRUTHS

Four: Forward Building in Love

> *As it is, these remain: faith, hope, and love, the three of them, and the greatest of them is love.*
>
> 1Cor. 13:13

America, you are the blossom of a new fresh flower of the first blossoming of the season.
America, your smile glistens so brilliantly with distinct kissed by God.
America is a unique beauty, a breed of flower-like no other that stands and shines even in the storms and always comes to life and becomes even more beautiful and never turns back to the old.
America, Yes, the pristine and illuminating shimmering smile of your rare fragrant blossom speaking:
"I know the wisdom of the way
    I know the Your loving Light
    I know the Your Precious Peace
    I know the Your tender Truth
    I know the Your luring love
America, Yes, the beauty of your smile receives the Holy Scriptures of the living Truth of God:
    I will love,
    I will forgive
    I will receive,
    I will ask,
    I will believe,
    I will listen,
    I will embrace,
    I will hear,
 And I know I am the child of the King of Kings, Jesus Christ my Lord.
Yes, I will take up the living waters of God's love gift to bring life to America and love to America and Peace to America and Justice to America to keep her blossoming of the fragrance of the Holy Spirit of God in the heart of America.
Poem by Lisa **Lucia Arden**

Lord, make me an instrument of your Peace.
Where there is hatred, let me sow love.
Where there is injury, pardon.
Where there is doubt faith
Where there is despair, hope
Where there is darkness, light
And where there is sadness joy.

>St. Francis

My declaration to you to tell you we, as Americans, have God's promises when we have uprightness and heart integrity, we receive the "the continue faithful love of God."

Solomon replied, 'You showed most faithful love to your servant David, my father when he lived his life before you in faithfulness and uprightness and integrity of heart; you have continued this most faithful love to him by allowing a son of his to sit on his throne today.

>*1Kings 3:6*

Sitting on the throne can signify the authority of a country. We the people, when we seek God's faithful love with the integrity of the heart God, God of Abraham in Jesus Christ, and the power of the Holy Spirit will "continue to give us His most faithful love."

God of Israel, there is no God like you in heaven above or on the earth beneath, as loyal to the covenant and faithful in love to your servants as long as they walk wholeheartedly in your way.

>*1Kings 8:23*[clxxxiii]

Remember, even if one does planting of God, and is not accepted, it will be "rewarded" in God's purpose. On the other side, remember, God does not reward working dissension, masonry, violence, injustices, and evil. Eventually, someone in God's love will have to plant the mustard seeds of God's redemption. Pay is just not always with money. Sometimes God has a calling for someone to do His work urgently

and timely to bring about the hopefulness of God's purpose and urgent Forward Building.

Paul, I did the planting, Apollos did the watering, but God gave the growth. ⁷ In this, neither the planter nor the waterer counts for anything; only God, who gives the growth. ⁸ It is all one who does the planting and who does the watering, and each will have the proper pay for the work that he has done. ⁹ After all, we do share in God's work; you are God's farm, God's building.

1Cor. 3: 7-9

When our Lord says, "Lovest thou Me?" He uses the Greek word agapas;

John 21:16-17

Agape is love of the unconditional love of God; only God has unconditional love. When we dedicate our lives to Him, we are, in a dynamic powerful wise flicker of God's Light; we can light a candle of life where it is needed to be; God's agape love in a sense, giving unconditional love in that we accept what we receive, yet we have peace, love, and justice knowing and experiences God's promises when we live in, with, and through Him. Yet, only God can fully give us unconditional love. Humanity needs love, and God's love to exist. However, we know truth and love are the hands of the body of life required to be together for there to be the truth and there to be love. When we know there are injustices, injustices have to be revealed; and we then can release a vision of justice to build in a forward building in love. Otherwise, these injustices become ingrained in life and are accepted as life; however, they are not life. Consequently, there is a deformity of the injustice that becomes evident.

We can do nothing without God's love.

40. **ἅγιος hagios,** *hagʹ-ee-os* (physically, pure, morally blameless or religious, ceremonially, consecrated): — (most) holy (one, thing), saint.[clxxxiv]

America, we need to seek to be sacred (physically, pure, morally blameless or religious, ceremonially, consecrated) in God.

In the land, if there is planted something, not of God's intention within the soil of the community, the child, the warrior, the servant, the believer, the wise, of God needs to come in the power of the Holy Spirit and pour God's love upon it for forwarding building.

God cannot cascade good upon evil. God's s intentions and Mother Nature cannot put life upon that what is evil; evidentially, if there is a massive imbalance, there will be a movement caused by the differences of good and evil.

God's intention will fight in His mystery, even using His people to protect His love for all humanity, for even someone He is searching for their heart for their salvation.

5.39 θώραξ[a]**, ακος** *m:* a piece of armor covering the chest to protect it against blows and arrows θώραξ[a] is also used figuratively in the NT to indicate the protective values of certain Christian virtues: ἐνδυσάμενοι θώρακα πίστεως καὶ ἀγάπης 'we must wear faith and **love as a breastplate'** 1Th 5:8.[clxxxv]

In virtues of God in the people, it brings protective values and brings *forward building in love*. In the breastplate of God's eternal candescent light reflects and shimmers love upon the hearts to give love, agape love, everlasting love. In the faithfulness to believe in God's love, God pours upon His Divine Love to sanctify the human love and sorrow, anointing it with the eternal resurrected life for that what needs to be redeemed. Just as the sunlight shines upon the land to give life, giving love beauty and happiness, so does the light of God's love shine upon the people's hearts to give life, giving love beauty and joy. Just as the moon accepts the light of the sun across the world to give light in the darkness, a faithful soul agrees with the light of God in enlightening the soul to the light and knowledge of God's love and protection for another miraculous day ahead to the forward building in love.

Open your eyes America, "the **protective values** of certain **Christian virtues:** ἐνδυσάμενοι θώρακα πίστεως καὶ ἀγάπης 'we must wear faith and **love** as a breastplate' 1Th 5:8

Be very careful, as you value your life, to love Yahweh your God.

Josh. 23:11

St. Thomas Aquinas a great Saint known as the Angelic Doctor.

"*Thomas appears to hold that there is a kind of divine idea for the prime matter. There is a perfect divine idea for prime matter only insofar as it is realized together with its appropriate form in a given composite. This is because ideal pertaining to matter only insofar it is so realized.*" [clxxxvi]
St. Thomas.[clxxxvii]

Envisage and comprehend God, "Perfect Divine," for the "prime matter," can only realize together what is the appropriate form of a given composite.

But what Saint Thomas Aquinas states are that God has redemption and love for us humans that are "imperfect or incomplete."

Apprehend, in the most delicate capillaries of God's breath in your heart that gives you existence proving we can restore in a *"Forward Building, in Love."*

Because, even though we are imperfect and incomplete being, God, "The Perfect Divine," of the "prime matter," taken in itself," the imperfect and the incomplete beings (humanity) realize together and appropriately with "enjoyment."

Breathe that purest part of peace and love you have ever felt in your life; God's love is existing in every part of your cell makeup and persona and spirit when received and at all different levels understood and not understood; this is where we must get our quintessential "happiness," and surreal and blissful moment; because it is the "Perfect Divine," in the prime mover, to realize, in (unity) together with the imperfect and incomplete beings (humanity). The concept of potentiality, in this context, generally refers to any "possibility" that a thing can be said to have. Aristotle did not consider all possibilities the same and emphasized the importance of those that become real of their own accord when conditions are right and nothing stops them. Actuality, in contrast to potentiality, is the motion, change, or activity that represents an exercise or fulfillment of a possibility when it becomes real in the fullest sense.[4]

Potentiality

Dunamis is an ordinary Greek word for possibility or capability. Depending on context, it could be translated "potency", "potential", "capacity", "ability", "power", "capability", "strength", "possibility", "force" and is the root of modern English words "dynamic", "dynamite""dynamo".[5] In early modern philosophy, English authors like Hobbes and Locke used the English word "power" as their translation of Latin *potentia*.[6]

Actuality is often used to translate both *energeia* (ενέργεια) and *entelecheia* (ἐντελέχεια) (sometimes rendered in English as *"entelechy"*). "Actuality" comes from Latin *actualitas* and is a traditional translation, but its normal meaning in Latin is "anything which is currently happening".

The two words *energeia* and *entelecheia* were coined by Aristotle, and he stated that their meanings were intended to converge.[10] In practice, most commentators and translators consider the two words to be interchangeable.[11][12] They both refer to something being in its own type of action or at work, as all things are when they are real in the fullest sense, and not just potentially real. For example, "to be a rock is to strain to be at the center of the universe, and thus to be in motion unless constrained otherwise".[2]

Interesting to note that "action or at work, has its own type," hence, there is an intention specifically of all actions or work.

<u>**This is why we need to have "actuality," not just "potency,"**</u>

<u>**God gives us the potentiality first all the tools for the freewill the possibility to choose the actuality of motion, activity, and fulfillment of the possibility in the real and fullest sense, this living toward God's life, God's intention, this is Forward Building in God' love.**</u>

<u>**God has created both actuality and potency in the human and the life of existence in perfect order. Life is love, and love is actuality and potency of truth. And love is the most pre-imminent and the most pre-imminent is God. Hence, when we build will build forward toward love. The actuality is life, and even if there is it has to be toward God's more honorable purpose, not ours; Humanity is incomplete and imperfect. Consequently, education in the purest form is God's intentions**</u>

Education in relationship to Actuality and Potency

1. Education, in many instances, is only "potency; it is only a "possibility."
2. The education that should be in the Restoration of America "actuality," where there is the "fullest sense," of activity in motion representation. Necessary skills need to be in the educational system. (Please, the list, visit the table of contents, education). Education should be relevant to daily existence and specializing in natural resources and entrepreneurial endeavors, sciences, and arts raw study not hypothetical.

God is gracious that He gives us a choice even though we are imperfect He provides us with the decision if we are appropriate to realize Him together.

Divine Message

February 27, 2020 St. Andrews Church California

I ask the Lord what should I tell them; they do not listen:

He said, "tell them this child they are like ants working, and they are made of dust. I am Alpha and Omega and when they do not have My thoughts and those who chose to make their intentions will not be of My created blessings." Jesus Christ told me to look at His head. He had me look at the floral designs on His Halo of majesty, He said this, "their thoughts are not the child of my thoughts. Tell them to pray and get on their knees and ask Me I will guide them into all truth. I created the heavens and earth and the universe. If they use their thoughts, they will create something that has sin, and will not be in My fullness. When they seek My thoughts and prayer and humble themselves, I will give them My creations to the fullest."

I AM IN MARY CHILD JUST AS I AM IN YOU. THOSE WHO ACCEPT ME AS THEIR LORD AND SAVIOR, THE SPIRIT OF GOD IS IN THEM. BECAUSE I AM IN MARY, WE ARE ALSO ONE FLESH I AM FROM HER WOMB
THE CHILD. I AM... IN HER ARMS ALSO WHEN SHE CARRIES ALL THE CHILDREN OF THE WORLD...." WE CARRY THEM TOGETHER CHILD.

WE CAN DO NOTHING WITHOUT GOD.
OF THE AMERICAN PEOPLE
PRESIDENT TRUMP AND HIS TEAM
THERE IS THE GREATEST FRUIT AMERICA HAS EVER HAD

Jesus Christ tells us He will send us the Paraclete revealing all truth to us. The Paraclete is the Holy Spirit.

John 16:13

Each individual needs to ask themselves what they want for their lives and their children and their community?

Of course, most would want happiness and good and success and love.

We know now with humanity has been on earth for a while, we have our best, we have our trials, we have our failures, we have our victories.

Now today is the most significant time in history. We have all information at our fingertips. We also have many chances to succeed and many tools to succeed.

However, because we have voluminous aspects of life and knowledge of life at our fingertips, and simultaneously working with tools in the technological realm that practically go at the speed of light, there is a rapidly changing world; Defining what it means to be human today is complex; Family, individuals and protection of the appropriate teaching and information to the children and the globalization, and multi-cultural traditions and ethnic groups and differentiation of moral values and relationships has made defining what means to be human complex is and even caused chaos and beauty of life and love.

In my book, *Our Need to Give to the World, Heal America, love in God*,

I introduced how America **was in** a grave "economic holocaust," and severe human rights problems and all other issues of America;

Today under President Trump, we have recognized the economic holocaust and have swiftly corrected every office of America and her country and the world.

Today under President Trump, we will continue VICTORY even though we have had **a silent war of the Chinese Virus;** we will continue VICTORY AND FORWARD BUILDING IN LOVE.

Let us continue to BRING GOD'S TRUTH IN
Forward building IN love in action,

I AM OPTIMISTIC IN GOD'S FAITHFUL HE GAVE DAVID IT IS ESSENTIAL TO REALIZE TO CONTINUE TO
We need to ask ourselves, is this
THIS IS WHY
PRESIDENT TRUMP AND THE TEAM AND THE AMERICANS FOR GOD'S PURPOSE FOR AMERICA'S LEGACY

IN THE PAST Gen. 11:4 And they said, Come, let us build us a city, and a tower, whose top may reach unto heaven, and let us make us a name; lest we are scattered abroad upon the face of the whole earth.

IN THE PAST Our America has been scattered of HER GIFTS OF GOD because America has chosen to reach for human-made heaven, with a different name.... to MAKING a name of human ideas intentionally and or non-intentionally SCATTERED ALL AMERICA'S GIFTS OVER THE FACE OF THE WHOLE WORLD instead of GOD'S IDEAS.

God has given us information beyond our scope of understanding during this technological period in humanity.

OUR NAME IS AMERICA IN GOD LET US CONTINUE TO WORK FOR forwarding BUILDING IN LOVE

Hence, our America in the past builds their ideas to reach their human-made identification of heaven, not of God's ideas. And even the innocent people of God have been scattered although they carry God's powerful cross; they are the American Warriors of everlasting waters of God's love.

IN THE PAST

This is evident in America's past danger in all areas in her position, from employment, production, economy, military, trade, businesses, and all areas of her land.

Consequently, IN THE PAST, we lost much of our America in all aspects. Though because we open the door to orphans and the homeless of other countries and have been righteous unto the Lord's will, He will redeem us.

At one time, we were all orphans, except the Indians were already in the land in parts of America. We need to respect one another. I know Indians have claimed much of their land; however, other parts were distributed; Consequently, now both Indians and other peoples from across the world have assimilated and inter married, so identifying the land is the *Mother of All Nations*.

NOW TODAY
THE OF THE AMERICAN PEOPLE
PRESIDENT TRUMP AND HIS TEAM
THERE IS THE GREATEST FRUIT OF AMERICA
America now is being restored to her beautiful and fullest.
Even in ancient Hebrew filling and baring children, to make worth and fulness in actuality is needed.
Today can restore America as did in the ancient days. God has continued to keep humanity in a flow of living waters of life.

4392. מָלֵא **male', *maw-lay';* from 4390; full (literally or figuratively) or filling (literally); also (concretely) fulness; adverbially, fully:—x she that was with child, fill(-ed, -ed with), full(-ly), multitude, as is worth.[clxxxviii]

We America each one of us that want to restore America, "with child " let us be "fully, filled in the multitude, as is worth."

The facts show our America now is FORWARD BUILDING IN LOVE
Refer to the achievements of President Trump and the Team in this book.

You already know of the achievements; because it has been in actuality.

It is living proof in the life of the people.
It is living proof in the life of the land.
Of course, we need and have tumultuous work to do to restore America.
However, we cannot stop with the work we are accomplishing.
Each American
Each Governmental Representative with President Trump.

Each individual of America, let us bring the fruit in your baskets and multiply them as Jesus Christ multiplied the fish and bread.

With the potency of His gifts for you and bring it to the "actuality," of the realization of the "Perfect Divine," in the "prime mover," we can of a motion of

4. אֵב **'eb,** *abe;* (Aramaic) corresponding to 3:—fruit. [clxxxix]

OUR FRUIT אֵב IS THE FAITH IN THE LOVE OF THE PEOPLE OF THE HEART OF GOD KNOWING WE WILL

CONTINUE TO MAKE AMERICA GREAT
OUR FRUIT IS SHOWN IN THE SUCCESS UNDER
PRESIDENT TRUMP AND THE AMERICANS THAT LOVE AMERICA'S LEGACY

> 155. אַדֶּרֶת **'addereth,** *ad-deh´-reth;* feminine of 117; something ample (as a large vine, a wide dress); also the same as 145:—garment, glory, goodly, mantle, robe.

When we multiply the fish and the bread of God's love, we wear that glory of the garment of the ample good in God. That garment we have a covering in the mystery of the Holy Spirit to cover the Eucharistic table of God that is the life of multiply the fish in the bread in His Holy purpose to bring all things to redemption.

The holy table cloth upon the Eucharist table is that garment, of the glory of heavenly righteousness from Jesus Christ in the power of the Holy Spirit to bring Forward Building in Love.

That "garment of God," covers over America in the power of the Holy Spirit.

Yes, that it that "garment of peace and love," in the mystery of the sanctifying love of the Eucharistic table and with the Saints and Virgin Mary.

Mary is the large vine of God in His glory and goodly mantle robe אַדֶּרֶת that has protected and guided America; she has overcome the serpent. Mary is the builder of Truth of God, and the builder in Truth in God is the builder in God's love because love is the greatest of all things.

Divine Message California Technology, Pasadena California 10/02/20

GOD
PREIMIENT IS LOVE
LOVE IS CREATION
IMAGE OF GOD HUMANS
IMPERFECT AND INCOMPLETE BEING HUMANITY
DOMINION OF LAND AND ANIMALS
IMAGE OF GOD PERFECT NOT KNOWING GOOD AND EVIL BEFORE THE FALL
GOD KNEW THAT THE HUMANS WERE IMPERFECT AND INCOMPLETE HENCE THAT IS WHY HE DID NOT WANT THEM TO EAT FROM THE TREE OF GOOD AND EVIL

GOD KNEW THAT IT WOULD NOT BE GOOD FOR THEM

HENCE, WE AS HUMANITY NOW HAVE TO PARTICIPATE IN HELPING TO BE PERSON OF GOOD NOT EVIL AND WHEN EVIL IS DONE, IT NEEDS TO BE REDEEMED

I ASKED HOW DO THEY KNOW THEY ARE NOT DOING EVIL OR WRONGDOING OR EVEN THE INTENTION NOT OF GOD. WHEN THEY ARE IN THE INTENTION OF GOD, ALL THINGS HAVE TO BE FOR LOVE. NOT FOR THE MOTIVE OF THEIR IDEAS; YET OF COURSE IF THEY

WANT TO BE REALIZED AND IDENTIFIED AND DESIGNATED, YET FOR LOVE OF HUMANITY AND ALL THINGS RELATED.

HOW CAN I TELL THEM WHAT LOVE IS AND GOD'S INTENTIONS ARE ALL THINGS THAT ARE DONE SHOULD HAVE PEACE, JUSTICE, HEALING, AND FORWARD BUILDING ALL IN LOVE.

(AND OF COURSE, THOSE WHOM IN GOD AS THEIR LORD AND SAVIOR)

THEN THEIR WORK WILL BE IN GOD'S INTENTION AND IF IT IS INCORRECT FOR CERTAIN REASONS THEIR WORK AND INTENTIONS .. GOD WILL REDEEM BECAUSE THEIR INTENTION WAS TO DO GOOD AND TO DO LOVE IN PEACE, JUSTICE, AND FORWARD BUILDING ALL IN LOVE.

REMEMBER, SOME ARE FORCED OR ONLY HAVE A PORTION OF TOOLS TO BRING GOD'S PERFECT INTENTION; HENCE GOD ACCOMMODATES TO THIS. AND HE REDEEMS.

ALL GOD'S CREATION WAS MADE AND IS FOR LOVE AND LOVE FOR CREATION. ANYTHING LESS IS NOT THE INTENDED GOD CREATION. THEREFORE, IT NEEDS TO BE REDEEMED.

If the work is not done in God's intention, even if it is thought to be good, it is still not God's intention only if He IN HIS sovereignty of choice decides to redeem at that time. Remember, we want freedom; we do not want control, and God does not want that either. Hence, this is why He has been merciful to us because those in power to control and our gifts and will not allow that He will Redeem them; It is the time of God's Restitution, and all of us have to decide what side we have to go on, God's or the darkness of Satan. I am being blunt and forward, we need to be. Our Name is America in and with and through the power of God. We do not want Communist or Socialistic control, and we do not want even those who pose to be for the people to use our ideas and work for their name and their treachery.

God has me write these points of wisdom because, for the present and future of humans, acceptable and perfect intentions are paramount in a globalized world where many actions have a vast reaction and response to the world as a whole.

For example,

1. **The Chinese Virus .. people had such evil** that
this was totally against humanity; consequently, it is evil the preparation of the virus had the non-God intention at the beginning that possibly was even clearly evident toward the onset. Again, I write these points because it paramount now that all scientific studies, and productions of manufacturing, and all business has the code of God's intention ethics, that it is proven to bring Four Foundational Truths, of Peace, Justice, Restoration if what you are making or creating there is a command of Restoration or healing what you create, is command to create in love.
The first, Commandment is to love God with all your heart and soul.

2. **NOTES THE ELEMENTS ALL ON THE PERIODICAL**
All the elements of the periodical table have a particular reason and intention to participate in God's creation... as we know, they all react together with each other individual or together in twos, or more or groups, then making new substances, recreating, and also breaking down of the essence, and all are affected by the Aristotle Categories.

    Hence, we, as a people, need to seek to create in love the best way we know toward always asking
    Does it bring Peace?
    Does it bring Justice?
    Does it bring Restoration?
    Does it bring Forward Building all in Love?

One is not with the other they all need to work together to make the intention of God's purpose.
And if we do not do this .. we have missed the best way and God's intention
We are not slaves; we are friends of the Creator.
Sharing the table in God is the Eucharistic Table. When we sit at the table with Him and share His friendship and love... we are also that love of His in the God's intention living as His Father has told Him respect of God loving God and the sharing in the redemption of the universe in redeeming love
..

DIVINE MESSAGE Jesus Christ of the Sacred heart the Eucharistic Adoration April. 18, 2019 ..

Saints Peter and Paul Maronite Church, Simi Valley
Jesus Christ said, this at the Eucharistic Mass.
The Eucharist is the book of life.
The Eucharist is the book of life on earth and from heaven
Those who . have accepted Jesus Christ as their Lord and Savior and Redeemer are in the book of life.
And the Book of Life is in heaven yet it is on earth. Because, though God's redeeming power, through the Eucharistic the body and blood of Christ.. they have life and life abundant from heaven and on earth..

The Book of life is also the Holy Scriptures.. child on earth.
Each, page ..of the Holy Scriptures should be as your life a day should be as of each page of the Holy Scriptures should be a page of The book LIFE ....daughter.
I have allowed those to come to me in their free will; though there are times when I control those who do not believe, to protect My people and THE life OF MY PEOPLE, MY children. However, I still seek for them to accept Me a child.
The Eucharist is the light of the world My daughter, and when one has the Eucharistic they are sanctified continually in the and through the body and blood of Christ...
The Eucharist is in those who take it and receive and are a light to the world .. and will bring the light in the darkness to be the temple and body of Christ Jesus. My child...
The vision was of a book and the cover of the book was the Eucharistic Table of the Last Supper and the side were pages of the Holy Scriptures. And then I put The Book of Life The Book of the Holy Scriptures in my

heart.. that is where it needs to be and working toward continually for each one of us.
[When we receive]We each carry the cross of Christ, and we each have the Sword Spirit that the Book Life and the Book of the Holy Scriptures through Eucharistic mass of God redeeming.. give life and life eternal.[Remember, the Trinity is the foundation of the Eucharistic mass in the redeeming Cross of Christ. When we are in the Trinity we are continually sanctified in the Eucharistic mass.]

Through the [Jesus Christ's] Cross has power over sin. Men have to humble themselves first to accept that I have died for their sins and have given them new life and a resurrected life.

It not by works you are saved but by faith.
The vision I say the rings at each book they are gold.. this is the Book of life in heaven...
Then I ask Jesus of the Sacred Heart what are these rings of the Book of Life. Also, the Book of the Holy Scriptures that are from heaven.
Jesus Christ said this of the Sacred Heart this.. these rings are the rings those who have accept Me as their Lord and Savior Child those are the Brides child I am the Bride Groom as I have told you in the Scripture the wedding party that .. those who I call to come to the Wedding. feast and make sure that the oil lamps are ready .. .. for the Wedding Feast.. the oil lamps are our bodies as Brides of Christ t DIVINE MESSAGE Jesus Christ of the Sacred heart the Eucharistic Adoration

April. 18, 2019 ..
Saints Peter and Paul Maronite Church, Simi Valley

Jesus Christ said, this at the Eucharistic Mass.
The Eucharist is the book of life.
The Eucharist is the book of life on earth and from heaven
Those who. have accepted Jesus Christ as their Lord and Savior and Redeemer are in the book of life.
And the Book of Life is in heaven yet it is on earth. Because, though God's redeeming power, through the Eucharistic the body and blood of Christ they have life and life abundant from heaven and on earth.

The Book of life is also the Holy Scriptures child on earth..

Each, page of the Holy Scriptures should be as your life a day should be as of each page of the Holy Scriptures should be a page of The book LIFE ....daughter..

I have allowed those to come to Me in their free will; though there are times when I control those who do not believe to protect My people and THE life OF MY PEOPLE, MY children. However, I still seek for them to accept Me a child.

The Eucharist is the light of the world My daughter; and when one has the Eucharistic, they are sanctified continually in the and through the body and in the blood of Christ.

The Eucharist is in those who take it and receive and are a Light to the world .. and will bring the Light in the darkness to be the temple and body of Christ Jesus My child.

The vision was of a book and the cover of the book was the Eucharistic Table of the Last Supper and the side were pages of the Holy Scriptures. And then I put The Book of life, The Book of the Holy Scriptures in my heart that is where it needs to be and working toward continually for each one of us.

[When we receive] We each carry the cross of Christ and we each have the Sword Spirit that the Book Life and the Book of the Holy Scriptures through Eucharistic mass of God redeeming give life and life eternal.

Through the cross has power over sin. Men have to humble themselves first to accept that I have died for their sins and have given them new life and a resurrected life.

It not by works you are saved but by faith.

In my vision I saw the rings at the binding of the book they are gold, there are many rings that I could not count; this is the Book of life in heaven...

Then I ask Jesus of the Sacred Heart what are these rings of the Book of Life also the Book of the Holy Scriptures that are from heaven?

Jesus Christ said this of the Sacred Heart; these rings are the rings those who have accept Me as their Lord and Savior Child those are the Brides child; I am the Bride Groom; as I have told you in the Scriptures, the Wedding party that those who I call to come to the Wedding feast and make sure that the oil lamps are ready . .. for the Wedding Feast. the oil lamps are our bodies as brides of Christ the Bride Groom and the . . the oil is the Holy Scriptures the Eucharistic. .. mass the body and blood of

Christ of Jesus and the .. this is here and now child. For those who believe in Me to be in the Holy Spirit anointed by the Spirit of God in the temple of their oil lamp their body of Christ that the oil is the Eucharistic Mass and the. the Holy Scriptures and then the Book of life from heaven is on earth. because My believers have brought life through Me child truth and truth is life.. in Me. Amen
I am the way the truth and the life and no one comes to the Father except through Me. The Bride Groom and the .. . the oil is the Holy Scriptures the Eucharistic. .. mass, [Holy Spirit and even the Spirit of Christ in the Trinity] the body and blood of Christ. Of Jesus.. and the .. this is here and now .. child.. for those who believe in Me to be in the Holy Spirit anointed by the Spirit of God in the temple of theirs. oil lamp their body of Christ. That the oil is the Eucharistic Mass and the Holy Scriptures and then the Book of life from heaven is on earth.. because My believers have brought life through Me child truth and truth is life.. in Me. Amen
I am the way the truth and the life and no one comes to the Father except through Me. Matthew 25;, Matthew 22:1-14,

At the Wedding Feast
In the Book of John 2:5, Virgin Mary states, She has always said, "**Do what your father tells, you to do."**

God will turn water into His living body of the sanctification of His giving His life on the Cross so that we may have life, and the water will be miraculous turning into wine, the living Eucharist that redeems all things, in the cisterns of our bodies individually, families, communities, states, nations, and the entire universe. The water is the begetting of life and it is multiplied in God's Eucharistic bodies of the Resurrected life when we believe and seek after righteousness. That is why Virgin Mary the Mother of Jesus was faithful enough and believed knowing that Jesus is the Creator, the Sanctifier, and the Sustainer of real living waters of life. Hence, in Jesus Christ's life through the Eucharist life is sustaining of truth of God's intentions of what life should be in the way it was created.

> *Then he told them, "Now draw some out and take it to the master of the banquet."* **John 2:8**

We as believers have "draw some out," the wine of pure life, the Eucharistic life, and given it to the people good and evil, to receive when they believe. However, recall God is a sovereign God and decides what will happen. Remember, He does have a heart for His people just as He listens to Moses and pleading, so will He listen to us in your pleading for our country and the world.

Proverbs Do what your father tells you, my son, and never forget what your mother taught you.

Work your miracles of grace in us, so that we may be a glory to the Blessed Trinity. Who created, redeemed, and sanctifies.

Proverbs 6:20.

Sentence of the Prayer to the Immaculate Conception.

We who in God in Christ Jesus has this goodly mantle robe for protection. And remember, even those who do not have confidence in God He protects all humanity; God is a sovereign God, and His excellent mantle robe, they may be even wearing it because they are Forward Building of Love and God is waiting for them to accept Him as their Lord.

Let us continue to BRING GOD'S TRUTH IN
Forward building IN love in action,
OUR NAME IS AMERICA IN GOD LET US CONTINUE TO WORK FOR forwarding BUILDING IN LOVE
None can fulfill perfection, only Jesus Christ; however, we can Love and live intentionally to love God with all our heart and soul.

Divine Message God's Ideas to the fullest

The Spirit of the Lord has commanded me to write these things to warn all of us, the people of America, to continue and forward humanity's building in God's love. Moreover, if we continue to seek righteousness, God will continue to redeem our America and CONTINUE TO return our country back to its growing fruit. America has enough fruit for all those in need; however, we have to disperse the fruit properly in God's intention. "Christian, either individually or collectively, if they wish to remain faithful to their vocation, may not foster enmities and dissensions between the classes of civil society. On the contrary, they must promote mutual concord and charity. The social question and its associated controversies, such as the nature and duration of labor, the wages to be paid, and workingmen's strikes, are not simply economic in character."[cxc]

Realize we cannot have a break down in finances. It causes deformities in the living, the family, and education and home life and stability and even impedes the gifts God has given us and His mission.

However, I know that He overcomes and FULFILLEST in us His beauty and glory even when we are rejected, oppressed, and suppressed by the world.

Epistrephoœ *God's faithfulness I am never forsaking to the sweet little birds of the air, bringing the manna of sustaining trust. .. Let my doubt be transformed into trusting faithfulness reaching to others sharing in the manna of the Trinity's and Virgin Mary's love.*

God's promises bring hope to the sweet little fawn in its disparity from the horror of the hungry hideous hyenas... Let my heart be Your hands of hope for the hearts of the precious little children of despair. Whether powerful men and women of the world or innocent and destitute of humanity.

God's light of the sun for the day and the moon for the darkness bringing eyes of vision, arms of warm and trusting expectation for all creation.... Let my light be love and lifting of the darkness in these little island homes of the hurting hearts.

God's joy brings a new day, and the leaves on the trees are clapping in a glistening melody of worshiping and joy singing: "The Spirit of the Lord has come in the hearts of our little island homes."

God's wisdom is in those who look for him in the heavenly morning prayer in the refreshment for the mind of hope and goodness.
God's love is in the moonlight gleaming pouring the love of the Paraclete in the almighty God of the Trinity. Ask Him to give you love.

God's hands are almighty to uphold you, America to be strong in power for love.

Lucia

And if someone is POLITICALLY INCORRECT in the world, ask what are they revealing?
The attributes toward God's intention for Peace, Justice, Restoration, and Forward Building and Protecting:
UNBORN
CHILDREN
TRAFFICKING
EDUCATION FOR THE CIVILIZATION IN 2019 AND ONWARDS
INFRASTRUCTURE
INNER CITIES REBUILD
SAFETY OF AMERICA
AMERICA FIRST
AMERICA BUSINESS
ETHICS

Let us come together with the bright, brilliant, and humble, find them, to build America in the forward building in love.

Even though America ms that it has lost from the COVID Virus and all other secret and revealed barbarisms, evil try to hide the eternal jewels of God's promises on earth has it is in heaven evil and its demons (3) an evil, non-material being (**Demon**, evil spirit)[cxci], **lost;**
2.55 χαλκεύς, έως *m:* (derivative of χαλκός[a] 'bronze, brass, copper,' 2.54) one who makes objects out of brass, bronze, copper, or other metals — 'coppersmith, metalworker.' Ἀλέξανδρος ὁ χαλκεὺς πολλά μοι κακὰ ἐνεδείξατο 'Alexander, the coppersmith, did me great harm' 2Tm 4:14.[cxcii]

The coppersmith has done me a lot of harm; the Lord will repay him as his deeds deserve.

2Tim. 4:14

> *But the rest of the human race, who escaped death by these plagues, refused either to abandon their own handiwork or to stop worshipping devils, the idols made of gold, silver, bronze, stone, and wood that can neither nor hear nor move.*

Rev. 9:20

When God's people love, they seek to proclaim the truth and for forward building in love. Truth brings God's Forward, Building in love.

America the right arm of strength to the Lord has gained in the hearts of those who love America; their love is never forsaken because it is in the hands of the Lord

The love of God has sustained America, the lovers of America.

America, it has God's love greater than any time in history. That is how is being sustained. WE MAY BE A SMALL ARMY YET WE ARE THE POWER AND LIFE OF GOD.

The enemy God laughs at and He will to this:

> *Now Yahweh is going to say this to them, 'Sav lasav, sav lasav, kav lakav, kav lakav, zeer sham, zeer sham.' So that when they walk they will fall over backwards and so be broken, trapped and taken captive.*

Is. 28:13

We know in the humanity of the powerful force OF GOD who seeks to bring truth, there is always a tension and opposite forces that need to be addressed and balance in God's purpose.

Americans have experienced this great danger and chronic danger and even for those close to physical death. God has spared us, and the Angels of God and the Virgin Mary continue to watch over us.

Get Divine message Protection and angel of God
October 15, 2019
Church of Saint Teresa, Alhambra, California

St. Teresa Said this:

"Many things shall be revealed soon (that people are doing against each other)."

Things people are doing to each other. Then it came to my mind.

In each office of the government, there are problems. They needed to be revealed. He will not know until revealed. The Chinese Virus conspiracy of a silent war and vast corruption in the government and the world.

Divine Message Dec. 3, 2019

Spirit of the Lord speaks
When darkness is acquired in the world, it takes more for My Angels of God and Me to hold back the evil in the world, that it does not become infiltrated with more sin. Many are innocent and can easily be targeted and deceived by some half-truths of the person acting unjustly and with deceit. You have experienced this in the city vastly. This form of life cannot be tolerated for My purpose of humanity. I am a compassionate God; however, I will not let deception and injustices to continue.
My humanity needs to seek a purer heart, a pure purpose in all they do.
Go now, daughter, do your work I will tell you more.

Alleluia! I am filled with love when Yahweh listens to the sound of my prayer, [2] when He bends down to hear me, as I call. The bonds of death were all round me, the snares of Sheol held me fast; distress and anguish held me in their grip, [4] I called on the name of Yahweh. Deliver me,

Yahweh, I beg you. Yahweh is merciful and upright, our God is tenderness. ⁶ Yahweh looks after the simple, when I was brought low he gave me strength.

Psa. 116:1-6

TRUTH IN RIGHTEOUSNESS FORWARD BUILDING America in God's name as Abraham "And in you [Abraham] all the families of the earth shall be blessed." Gen. 12:3

<u>We cannot reach Justice in our strength and purpose. It is only in God's purpose in power</u>. Otherwise, our life in America will be scattered! *In the PAST we gave our business to the other parts of the world; we gave our jobs to other parts of the world. We shared a part of her heart.*

It is a fact actually that those in the PAST SOUGHT TO MAKE DECISIONS

REGARDING AMERICA FOR THEIR DECISIONS ON BUSINESS VENTURES NOT CONSIDERING AMERICA'S LEGACY AND FOR THE IDEOLOGIES OF THEIR NARROW DIRECTION OF NOT KEEPING AMERICA'S LEGACY

NOW AMERICA IS BEING HEALED

TODAY THERE IS GOD'S SPIRIT STRONGER THAN EVER

CONTINUE TO HEAL AMERICA NOW.

HOWEVER, THERE IS NOT TO SAY WE HAVE PERFECT SAFETY WE HAVE TO BE FAITHFUL AND KNOWING GOD WILL REDEEM US AND WE HAVE ETERNAL LIFE WHEN WE IN HIS SON JESUS CHRIST AS OUR LORD AND SAVIOR.

When a person s in God the mystery of the Trinity and Saints and even Angels of God is able to do a good work in them.

Even if a person does not in the Trinity and in the works of Christ:

JESUS CHRIST PROMISED, "IF YOU BELIEVE IN MY WORKS I WILL PROFESS YOU TO MY FATHER."

To reiterate those who do not in God, many are intellectuals as such and they receive their strength by their own power and knowledge; at this vein of thought, hypothetically, would not you think then they would there is an intention of a specific order of all things, likened to their opinion by their endeavors?

They do not realize God is holding them together and has given them by nature their goodness that they accomplish. There is a working mystery of God and humanity that cannot all always be revealed. God has a connection with each human being.

Those who seek to keep America great have always gone forward in love.

Hence, America has accepted all peoples from all countries as the *"Mother of all Nations."* It is time to continue to restore America with the stability of just laws for immigrants and America. The foundation needs to be continually strengthened. Yet, protected

Much has been sold and given in our America.

When Mother Nature is NOT taken care of in nature it is intended to be, it becomes less than what it is, and eventually, it loses its identity likened to

THE PAST DESTRUCTIONS OF AMERICA:

**NOW
PRESIDENT TRUMP AND AMERICANS AND THE TEAM
ARE WORKING ON THESE URGENCIES**
There are lists and lists. I am just encouraging you and helping you realize the Restoration we have done before the Chinese Conspired Virus of a silent war.

Global Warming urgencies need to be respected, and nature needs to care with the greatest minds of generalists and scientists with ethical Judeo Christian training.

Our oceans are the incredible beauty of God

The way food is processed synthetically, or pharmaceuticals are processed,

or how water is not cared for as if it were infinite liquid of precious diamond of the most extraordinary beauty; And how the light of the brilliance of the mind needs to be flowing, upon the minds of our children; And how the middle class and the lower class has been subjugated to chronic anxiety and depletion of all their worth to be able to pay their bills.

At the birth of America: REMEMBER MOST OF CAME TO AMERICA AS LOWER AND MIDDLE CLASS.

Please, the Our Need to Give to the World, Heal America Love in God.

We were not evolved in all sciences of understanding! Hence, we need to allow our America today to blossom and build forward and live and love.
Ask ourselves, do we respect the gift of life and dream of America and treat each other with Justice and Truth and love?
Do we respect those at the highest accord, the Veterans that have saved our life?.
Do we protect America and love her, or act upon for Justice?
Do we always protect the unborn?
Do we remember how the strenuous labored hands kissed by the Light of God cultivated the land while they sang for a miracle of deliverance?

Do you remember the backs of strengths and knees embedded rooted in the ground to bring the food of life to bring the life of food to the people and cotton and harvest of all life in the past and the present?

Do you remember the immigrants in the coal mines and industry of the industrial revolution and after?

Do we advocate how we always need to respect just laws and rights in the Constitutional purity of and for the people with pure laws to give to the people?

Do we seek to help stop the trafficking and mental disease victims to create a miraculous strategy for their healing and new foundation?

Do we seek to clean up the inner cities of the drugs that treacherous humans have poured into these cities?

Do we make sure large companies protect their employees and treat them with fairness even if they have to give more than what must be due? Remember, inflation and the highest incomes are only dispersed to an extremely small number of people.

Do we need to make sure the water companies keep our water pure?

AMERICA FINALLY HAS THE FLAME IN OUR HEARTS TO CHANGE TO BRING AMERICA BACK TO THE NAME OF GOD.

We will never forget that God is in America and in those who have Justice flowing and living in the veins of their life and their hearts.

I have addressed these issues to take care of America First.

We now need to continue working in faith, prayerful solutions in power, tenderness, reconciliation, and love.

To wait in working in strategy and work to expect to look forward to.

We know that when we do what is right, we expect goodness.

We know that when we do what is right, we will wait in action in hunger to thirst after righteousness until it is God's right timing.

I have to say I have been impatient for Justice in Peace and action even under great danger of life-threatening living. I have a calling to speak of Justice to:

We, America, have been impatient in Peace and action.

We have been impatient, rightly so.

We have not always loved it. Let us, love, let us love, and continue to bring America to the arms of God's purpose.

We, America, have not always loved it. We have forgiven and have reconciled.
We have been taken advantage of and conspired against and used. We, America have been provoked.
We, in our actions, now, are opening those doors of truth and finding Justice and bring life.
We saw God's Light! Now we are giving life back to America.
We heard God's voice! Now we are Justice.
We felt the sorrow of those in need! Now we bring them safety and a home.

I have been raw and to tell the truth even when politically incorrect by media standards!

We, America, have been raw to tell the truth even when politically incorrect by standards.

I have to speak aloud because those same people who love America are saving the children and her legacy.

Now, is the time! The time is now!

Now we have the *"Revolution of Love, purity of love!"* A love of unity, we are a people, a people who has opened their heart to each to have life and life abundantly in America! Let us take up our gifts and unity to care for one another in Truth and Justice. There is much land, rural land that can be developed for those who need a home. I that great men and women will walk upon the earth God has given them; they are waiting in their search for life to create and this is truly waiting for God to use them, to give to humanity to work in and for and through for a life of empowerment to those in need. Now it is time to bring formally recognized citizenship to those Dreamers. Now is time to check each part of the governmental process to develop a strategic plan for legal citizenship. We will not turn our backs on and the neglect that we have caused and have used people for our desires and plan, we will face it and bring Justice. Whether it is the immigrant, we will not turn our backs; we will face it and bring Justice, whether it is the middle class not supporting their needs, we will not turn our backs; we will face it and bring Justice, Whether it is the protection of American jobs, we will not turn our backs, Whether it is the safety of America, we will not turn our backs. We will face it and CONTINUE TO bring Justice.

We have experience in America when we deliver goods, we have a good flow.

I prayed and pleaded with the Virgin Queen Mary to tell me what I need to give to the people. While being lifted to the heavens, **_Mary told me President Trump will be and needs to be to keep America great and continue the Restoration of America._** Today while correcting the book ... to publish

THERE IS A DIVINE MESSAGE We, as people, need to work toward restoring America for our legacy to exist in freedom. We have enough time and resources, and we have all we need; however, those who have used America for their life the home, foreign investors, international students, and all Americans need to bring their life to the heart of America, and that is God's Truth. Toward truth, we all need to walk; hence, we need to forgive each other continually. However, we need to speak in the reconciliation of working to bring greater Justice. Remember, righteousness lives, and evil is death.

> *For this reason, I say to you, Whatever you make a request for in prayer, have faith that it has been given to you, and you will have it.* ²⁵ *And whenever you make a prayer, let there be forgiveness in your hearts if you have anything against anyone; so that you may have forgiveness for your sins from your Father who is in heaven.*
>
> **Mark 11:24**

A Reconciliation (40.1–40.7)

40.1 καταλλάσσω; καταλλαγή, ῆς f; **ἀποκαταλλάσσω; συναλλάσσω**: to reestablish proper friendly interpersonal relations after these have been disrupted or broken (the componential features of this series of meanings involve (1) disruption of friendly relations because of (2) presumed or real provocation, (3) overt behavior designed to remove hostility, and (4) restoration of original friendly relations) — 'to reconcile, to make things right with one another, reconciliation.'[2cxciii]

Reconciliation, Restoration, Propitiation, Atonement'

So we are ambassadors for Christ; it is as though God were urging you through us, and in the name of Christ we appeal to you to be reconciled to God.

2Cor. 5:20

Reconciliation means the Restoration of a good relationship between enemies. To achieve this good relationship in the confrontation of God and man, it is necessary that the factors that produce the enmity be removed. This is achieved by atonement. These various aspects involve the use of the three groups of words dealt [Vol. 3, p. 146] in this article. (*ex-*)*hilaskomai* and its derivatives belong to the cultic realm and chiefly denote actions that are supposed originally to make the gods favorably disposed of and, later, to expiate sin. The group of words around *katallassō*, on the other hand, comes from the secular world and indicates the improvement (*allassō*, to change) of a negative relationship. *apokatastasis* is a technical term in politics and eschatology, meaning a partial or universal restoration. In the NT the cultic term *hilasmos*, the political term *apokatastasis,* and the ordinary term *katallagē* are all comparatively rare, but they occur in crucial passages.[cxciv]

ἀποκαθίστημι G635 (*apokathistēmi*) and **ἀποκαθιστάνω** G634 (*apokathistanō*), re-establish, restore; **ἀποκατάστασις** G640 (*apokatastasis*), restoration.

CL 1 The vb. *apokathistēmi* (Xen. onwards) meant originally to restore to a previous state, and then generally to restore. It is found at first in a literal and non-religious context: of the giving back of what has been lent (Xen., *Respublica Lacedaemionorum* 6, 3), of the renovation of a canal (W. Dittenberger, *Orientis Graecae Inscriptiones*, I-II, 1903-5, 672), of the **Restoration of a sick person** (Dioscorides, *De Materia Medica* 1, 64, 4); later, more generally, of **the renewal of the world** (Lactantius, *Divinae Institutiones* 7, 18).[cxcv]

Redemption, Loose, Ransom, Deliverance, Release, Salvation, Saviour

Whenever men by their own fault or through **some superior power have come under the control of someone else,** and **have lost their freedom to implement their will and decisions,** and when their own resources are inadequate to deal with that other power**, they can regain their freedom only by the intervention of a third party.** In the NT, depending on the aspect envisaged, the Gk word-groups associated with *lyō, sōzō, rhyomai*, are used to express such intervention. *lyō*, to free (42 times in the NT) is used **to express liberation from bonds or by payment of a ransom (*lytron*)**, but it has other shades of meaning which are also discussed here. *sōzō* (106 times in the NT) is the commonest term and has the widest range of meaning. **Predominantly it means to <u>save, preserve and rescue</u>.** The least used, *rhyomai* (16 times), has the narrowest range of meaning, i.e<u>. to rescue, deliver, and thus save from a threatening or acute danger. *sōtēr*, derived from *sōzō*, means deliverer, savior, and was in general use to denote someone who so acted</u>.

We are filled with exultant trust in God, through our Lord Jesus Christ, through whom we have already gained our reconciliation.

Rom. 5:11

It is all God's work; he reconciled us to himself through Christ and he gave us the ministry of reconciliation.

2Cor. 5:18

I mean, God was in Christ reconciling the world to himself, not holding anyone's faults against them, but entrusting to us the message of reconciliation.

2Cor. 5:19

διαλῠτός, όν, *capable of dissolution*, Plat. From διαλύω **II.** *a change* from enmity to friendship, *a reconciliation, truce*, Hdt., Ar.; in pl., Eur.; διαλλαγαὶ πρός τινα Dem.

διαλλακτήρ, ὁ, *a mediator*, Hdt., Aesch.; and διαλλακτής[cxcvi]

I am a mediator to bring reconciliation in writing this book and working toward awareness of America and the world, and Peace.

GIVING HER JOBS
GIVING HER SMALL BUSINESS
GIVING HER LARGE BUSINESS
GIVING HER NEW RELEVANT EDUCATION IN ETHICS AND FINANCE FOR FOR CHILDREN AND ENTREPRENEURIAL SKILLS
GIVING HER THE PROTECTION OF ALL HER NATURAL RESOURCES
GIVING HER THE PROTECTION OF HER NATION
GIVING HER THE RESTORATION OF THE INNER CITIES
GIVING HER HISTORY AND THOSE WHOM: GONE BEFORE US TO SPEAK OF THEM IN THE SCHOOL SYSTEMS TO MAKE THEM PROUD OF OUR AMERICA THE MOTHER OF ALL NATIONS.
GIVING HER OUR HEARTS OUR FIRSTFRUITS OF OUR GIFTS.
GIVING HER OUR PEACE AND LOVE TOWARD ONE ANOTHER FOR FORGIVENESS.
GIVING HER PROTECTION OF HER NEW D OF LIFE
GIVING HER THE PEOPLE TO ALLOW TO BE PROTECT BY THEIR RELIGIOUS BELIEFS
 And we better CONTINUE NOW to all work to get back on top. First, me since I have known God's sorrow, God's anger, and God's love. First, me since I know QUEEN VIRGIN Mary's deep sorrow, deep love, and profound

power to protect with the Angels of God. Though, all have different missions of God. WE HAVE ONE PURPOSE, AND THAT IS TO LOVE.

I KNOW IT MS TO YOU THAT LOVE IS USED SO MANY TIMES IN THE BOOK. WE NEED TO ECHO IT IN OUR MINDS, OUR HEARTS, OUR VOICE, OUR ACTIONS, OUR THOUGHTS, OUR PLANS, OUR WORK, AND OUR PURPOSE FOR EACH ONE OF US AS AMERICANS.

LOVE OVERCOMES ALL THINGS.

AND WE HAVE BEEN CRYING OUT IN PRAYER AND KING RIGHTEOUSNESS.

Forward Building for those rs and those who and those who are Curious:

I have Spiritual Godly experiences where the Light of God is in the natural sun of the day, and it prompts me to pray. The light is brighter than the regular sunlight, and IT has a love of GREATEST QUINTESSENTIAL BEAUTY. God is using the miraculous holy sunlight from heaven to give me a message and also healing.

Divine Message 2020

I have experienced miracles of the (Sunlight) the Light of Christ Jesus with the Arch Angels and Virgin Mary, calling me throughout the day to listen to **the Divine Messages for the people's messages**. For healing for direction and intercessory pray for America and the world. After the prayer, I receive guidance from the Light of Jesus Christ; the Arch Angels are in the Light and Virgin Queen Mary.

1. We are called to be His children, God, He is the light of the world, and we as believers carry that light, thru, in, and with God and in Christ Jesus. We need forgiveness for our actions and others. If we realize our small followings, we can help restore America the way God wants us to with His intentions.

2. Even if we do not in Jesus Christ as the Savior of the World, we know that He is a healer; when He came to earth, and now many can there are miracles and love in His people, and even experience

all Godly experiences is evident and alive in the people. I have experienced miracles. God in the Trinity in the Arch Angels of God and Queen Virgin Mary and the saints are here with us more than ever before in history to help us.

3. We know He is a man to bring Peace and Justice.
4. We know that those who in the resurrected Son of God, Savior of the world, find all injustices can be brought to the Cross of Christ Jesus and forgiven, and there is a new Resurrected life for all humanity in Christ Jesus.

    And we know to have Restoration, one needs to show and give redemption to that needs to be healed.
5. If one man or woman in the community works forward to build the love of God in America for the Restoration of America, one man or woman can help heal America.
6. I know there is a deep desire in America's soul; when we have forgiveness, our soul is God's and then He will work a good work in us.

7. When we forgive ourselves and realize our incorrect actions and all levels of humanness, we will open our hearts to God's true intentions. Though I would have to say God is unexpected, and He expects our love. And He s and knows the most beautiful in us remember we have His breath. Genesis. 2:7

    Yahweh God shaped man from the soil of the ground and blew the breath of life into his nostrils, and man became a living being.

    Genesis 2:7

    Only He God knows our potential, not ourselves or anyone else. God knows us the best. This is why there can be redemption and miracle and Restoration and healing in each individual in America in our entire America and world. Remembering, we are a reflection of God's love and Justice.

8. To be that we as Americans can redeem and heal America for another man or woman's neediness to be a full living human being, without sin, suppression, oppression, poverty, trickery, and bringing miracle in God's miracle.

America, we will not give up; we will expect in a forward building in love and confidence, looking forward to what is useful and beneficial. We know what is good deep down in our souls. Let's live in America and forward of building.

When we hope and integrate with the right actions, we have confidence, knowing hope in expecting love and shall reign in humbleness and the most astounding quintessential beauty. Leaders are servants of God

"

"Build yourselves cities for your little ones and sheepfolds for your sheep, and do what you have promised."

Num. 32:24

Here, God tells us to take care of our children and make cities. We need to restore our inner cities for our "little ones."

Let us all be as Moses leaders that have led the people of God out of the land of Egypt by God's Arm.

Number 33.1

Leading the people to a place of righteousness and truth and empowerment to forward build in love. And accept the happiness the "enjoyment" the Perfect Divine has when He helps us in our imperfect ways an incomplete person and life.

God prompts us to His purpose. When those things are not smooth and in turmoil and people against people and city against city and state against state and ideology against an ideology, the voice prompts us and even warning of God to turn back and restore what has been lost. Restoring is causing us to come forward.

Going ahead is going forward and advancing though it is taking the majority with you. The majority does not have to be in number; it is, in truth a people that desire to grow. It is the analogy to be spoken of if the power only restore their selves they only take with them a portion of the trees at harvest and leave the other trees non-nutritious .. and soon those trees of mighty strong will become unnatural and even perhaps burden, not unless these few mighty trees are toward the perfect intention of God. Open your eyes. Can you this is presently happening with the Democrats' ideologies and the Republicans and the government and powerful control. We need first to put the people first, the majority first. The governmental powers and powers need to open their eyes and become aware of the warning God has given in the mere fact of the devastations of natural disasters, family dis-unity, community dis-unity, economic uncertainty, and even future health for our county's moral and educational hope for our children.

Our President and the team are making America great again; however, we cannot waste time and money pointing fingers at whether someone had a personal encounter or not. We need to forgive rapidly. Each one of us has some type of scandal in our life, faithful or not accurate. Remember, there are different forms of human iniquity. Let us forgive rapidly. Then we ask who is affected by this chronic monstrosity of confusion and battle between governmental figures? It is the weakest, and those even the most powerful. This disunity breeds discord and also brings something that was supposed to be not to be. Today we have all we need to CONTINUE to make America great again. Let us look at the good that has been accomplished under President Trump's leadership and his team and the senate and house.

Enemies cannot live under the same roof. also spelled ἐκκοπή, pr. *an incision,* e.g. a trench, etc., cut in the way of an **enemy**; *an impediment, hindrance,* **1Cor. 15:25** For God's wisdom and the one who has received a specific mission will be directed to make the **enemies** the footstool, [26] and the last of the **enemies** to be done away with is death, for he, God has put all things under his, God's feet. God uses warriors of wisdom and virtue to help Him.

God will use what He made of each person of His good to create restoration and *forward building of love*. Because the good of your enemy is that love of God that never dies.

The leaders of the nation's rally to the people of the God of Abraham. The shields of the earth belong to God, who is exalted on high.

Psa. 47:9

The shaft of (her) spear was like a weaver's beam, and the head of his spear weighed six hundred shekels of iron. A shield-bearer walked in front of (her).

1Sam. 17:7

(She) put on saving Justice like a breastplate, on (her) head the helmet of salvation. (She) put on the clothes of vengeance like a tunic and wrapped (herself) in jealousy like a cloak.

Is. 59:17

The American justice system has been created for checks and balances. However, there has not been checks and balances **in the past**; therefore**, a new strategy** in some ways has to be used to clean up and cure and restore the loss of Justice to bring Justice. Remember, America is a young country yet evolved and the most extraordinary country globally, and we need to use different yet experience strategies to restore her. Much is evident in what has to be done and how to accomplish it. It is just that some want their intention and not God's purpose.

To reiterate, ladies and gentlemen, there is a particular intention and mechanism and process for each part and science of life that, when used correctly it will bring the fullness to what is needed to be restored. Because much has been lost and needs to be restored, remember, our American is a young country.

Therefore, whom would you get the information or the answer from to restore her? Then you would ask what brings the most life and Restoration for any experience in life? That would be love.

Then you would ask who has the most incredible love? God has the greatest love. He made life and all of nature and humans that created His **most** magnificent things.

God, He covers you with His pinions, you find shelter under His wings. His constancy is shield and protection.

Psa. 91:4

Now go to Him ask for His love to restore America; you have the God-given capacity and all the answers. , there is a plan He already had. He is waiting to give it to you. Because He created humans and is even in sorrow for what has happened that something, He made has fallen short and needs to be redeemed.

Go to God and ask. Then we ask. Ask Him? Yes, just as a student asks a teacher, learns, contemplates, and creates and brings life. Going to Him is first is prayer and contemplation and fasting and retreat and searching the Truth in Holy Scripture and forgiveness, looking at accommodation to the situation you are dealing with. Of course, it is [He wants to speak to you; He wants to tell you. God wants America and the world to be restored and loved by those who care and those who need to care. Then you ask, would not you think that He wants to care for what He created. He wants America redeemed and cured and healed and restored; it is His creation in the people given the freedom to be the individual and live in a land to be whom God created one to be. Urgently, let us be thankful that there has been a brave man and government official to work to save areas in our American country that need to be changed:

Otherwise, the brilliant and bright that are not powerful and do have the supernatural strength of God can be lost in America and that is our children, our legacy.

There is no room for self-delusion. Any one of you who thinks he is wise by worldly standards must learn to be a fool in order to be really wise. [19] For the wisdom of the world is folly to God. As scripture says: He traps the crafty in the snare of their own cunning [20] and again: The Lord knows the plans of the wise and how insipid they are. [21] So there is to be no boasting about human beings: everything belongs to you, [22] whether it is Paul, or Apollos, or Cephas, the world, life or death, the present or the future—all belong to you; [23] but you belong to Christ and Christ belongs to God.

1Cor. 3:18 -23

Time is at hand, let us take what has been good and honest, show respect and thankfulness. Let us now work together for unity. God knows the heart of the treacherous technological evil. Evil finds what is good and tries to change it. God will strike them soon. He did tell me this is a decade of restitution. The problem is not just certain beliefs and ideologies in Justice; there are motives and power struggles. **Do not bring upon the book of American history the battle between the government representatives and the people. The American children and people suffer the most. The government is to serve the people. And the people do help the government with respect and just order. The government services the people.**

President John F. Kennedy said, It is not what your country can do for you, it is what you can do for your country.

The American people should not be used at the expense of ideologies or ideas to certain people's defamation. It is time to recognize the division and seek ways to mediate into solutions that benefit n American people and those that need citizenship and fair and just protection of our country on all sides.

Now when I came to you, brothers, I did not come with any brilliance of oratory or wise argument to announce to you the mystery of God. ² I was resolved that the only knowledge I would have while I was with you was knowledge of Jesus, and of him as the crucified Christ. ³ I came among you in weakness, in fear and great trembling ⁴ and what I spoke and proclaimed was not meant to convince by philosophical argument, but to demonstrate the convincing power of the spirit, ⁵ so that your faith should depend not on human wisdom but on the power of God.

1Cor. 2:1

Since in the wisdom of God the world was unable to recognize God through wisdom, it was God's own pleasure to save believers through the folly of the gospel.

1Cor.1:22

Forward building for humanity

Great companies such as

Winsupply "under Rick Schwartz's leadership-eventually as president, CEO, and chairman of the board of directors Winsupply was structured into a company whose headquarters now consider now considers itself an entrepreneurial support center for each of the 600 local companies."

Winsupply, "provides the critical services around finance, IT, legal, marketing, and other back-office responsibilities that often make starting and running a small business cost-prohibitive. . . Winsupply companies can get fast access to top-quality products from 130 vendors through Sourcing Services."[cxcvii]

Let us be unlimited and open up the magnificent of America's hearts, communities, states, and country in the unity of the same purpose to keeping America's freedom and restoring her in giving restitution to her people and her land and for the future in that love of God will flow.

"When you open your heart to patriotism, there is no room for prejudice. The Bible tells us how good and pleasant it is when God's people live together in unity. We must speak our minds openly, debate our disagreements honestly, but always pursue solidarity."

President Donald J. Trump

We **20.** ἀγαλλίασις; *agalliasis, agalliaseōs, hē* (*agalliaō*), not used by secular writers but often by the Septuagint; *exultation, extreme joy*: Luke 1:14,44; Acts 2:46; Jude 1:24; Heb. 1:9 (from Ps. 44:8 (Ps. 45:8)) oil of gladness with which persons were anointed at feasts (Ps. 23:5), and which the writer, alluding to the inaugural ceremony of anointing, uses as an emblem of the divine **power** and majesty to which the Son of God has been exalted.*

Let those that "write," those that write their calling and perform the actuality to
"Fairer, stronger, purer, and brighter with the luster of distinguished virtues."

Pope Pius X

Jerusalem in Jesus' Day: In Jesus' day, the city of Jerusalem had only recently been transformed into one of the most magnificent cities in all the Roman Empire. A glorious new Temple now stood over the city, along with a new palace, stadium, theater, and other public buildings constructed during Herod the Great.

Let us build not a "Temple" of a worldly heart toward God.

Let us build a "Temple" inside of us of God's heart. I met this American man for the first time. I will never forget when he stepped up in my presence. The light was shining from his spirit. I think he does not realize

God has carried him; because, he has given his life for others as a warrior of protection and love. He was (and shill is) a man that reflects God's love in his heart. I did not anything else, except his heart of God. When I was working on the first book I was called to write, "Our Need to Give to the World," *America love in God, Heal America*. And my calling and quest are to bring God's love. I have been called to me in unity in prayer for years to receive God's love and grace, yet as a warrior of His Truth.

The Trinity and Virgin Mary and the Saints are closest to me and the Angels Michael Arch Angel, Gabriel, and Raphael Arch Angel.

He is an American Veteran and has given his life for the people. Shill to this day, even though he has deep scars, I pray he goes forward building in love to help other Veterans. Even though our America has deep wounds and imperfections, we can mend them up by giving Truth and Justice the essence of love. , he as America at times does not realize God and Mary love them, and because of them helping others has kept them in their heart. I am a *confidant* of the Trinity in Virgin Mary and the Arch Angels of the God of Abraham.

The essence of the solution to heal America for the forward building is in God's love of humanity. And my calling and quest are to help mend in the wounds of God's society in America and the world. God carries the scars of all that is not good. Each one of us is called to this, "mend the wounds of humanity" and mend them in God's love. We can only heal and restore, and structure or work or form our nation in God's love; his intended purpose that He has given humanity does begin with the 10 Commandments, the Judeo-Christian. No matter what religious upbringing, truly, those who wholeheartedly love America and are patriots of goodness will build America forward in love toward humanity. Though God does not want His people to be abuse, and used, and provoked, and scandalized, and oppressed, and suppressed by others; there will be a time that not only will He come as an unexpected miracle in the night at the "Second Coming." However, He will come with His Angels of God and Saints to redeem His people any time and any moment. Many of times **the Spirit of the Lord has said,** "I am with you and in you child, right here with you."   as warriors of light, we have to work and walk through the valley of darkness because we are literally,

"warriors," of God, we become warriors through God's righteousness, though none of us is perfect. We repent and ask for forgiveness and seek not to sin.

Warriors of God are:

to bring His Light in the darkness to heal those who want healing,
to bring the good news of God in Christ, expose the darkness that is deceiving and others think it is true, to bring and work in the power of God in the Trinity and all the Saints and heavenly Angels and Michael Arch Angel, Gabriel and Raphael Angels. Remember, we know that sometimes God does not reveal all things because we would be anxious. Also, we are here to help the sick. Moreover, we need to enter into the darkness to bring God's light.

While praying the first week of August 2- 4th**, 2018 at the Mount Carmel Our of Lady, I saw the cry of Christ Jesus of the tears run down His Holy Face, in a vision.**

Vatican II- E (English Content) 78

Consequently, as it points out the authentic and noble meaning of Peace and condemns the frightfulness of war, the Council wishes passionately to summon Christians to cooperate, under the help of Christ the author of Peace, with all men in securing among themselves a peace based on Justice and love and in setting up the instruments of Peace.[cxcviii]

Community

I have experienced this:

From time to time some are not accepted in their own country though they plant God's Truth and love and even pray for the country's protection no matter where they are. they are God's friend and are the knight, warrior at the Eucharist table to bring life and protection to humanity. Or they are there for a specific time and then will be called back. God knows the better plan, and some that humbled themselves even do not know what is next in God's gift and are honored to do God's work.

Psalms 66

1. In the first part (1-12), the community praises God for powerful acts for Israel, both in the past (the exodus from Egypt and the entry into the land [6])

    Use the prayer journal for

a.[Explain with the daughter. God promises us when we seek His face and Love Him, He will live with all our heart and soul, He will redeem our land and save His people. He has never forsaken us! Knowing we have His strength and love and eternal life even unto persecution. I died ultimately and came back to life. Actually, in front of a physician.

This was not a prayer of a Divine Message and lifting my body up to the heavens. My body was taken up to the high heavens. I saw a tall, magnificent, oval-shaped door with effervescent beauty; the color was yellow shimmering gold, and white. And I wanted to stay; then I remembered my children.

Divine Message God's' face: When you look upon God's face through the Holy prayers and asking for forgiveness and or through the goodness toward God you find the truth to all things that he allows you to; because you are facing God. In meeting God, there is truth, and even redemption because of His only begotten Son Jesus Christ has given His life to bring new life to all things that have been less than what He intended in His creation. Though remember, He desires a friendship because of the love He has for humanity. This friendship has an ongoing plan.

"Sing forth the glory of His name." Psalm 66.2

> I always want to sing and praise the people that God has created and those who accepted Him and know Him God Almighty. I have to say I sing out when I feel the Spirit of God in the people or when He prompts me.

> Even if one does not accept the Trinity, they do not realize the Trinity is in their presence, waiting for them to ask, k, and knock. I have sung spontaneously in many places, from Cal Technology in Pasadena, where the married couples take pictures, to La Canada, Rome, Glendale, South Pasadena, to Montecito, Pasadena, Altadena, San *Marino,* and Arcadia

Perceive when we praise we understand... and have realized the deliverance is from God, not ourselves.

And in the present (deliverance from a recent but unspecified calamity [8-12]). In the second part (13-20), an individual from the rescued community fulfills a vow to offer a sacrifice of thanksgiving.

God has given us all we need to build forward ahead in love with humanity.

Each individual within the community brings a gift of Restoration to heal America.

As often in thanksgivings, the rescued person steps forward to teach the community what God has done (16-20).[cxcix]

Let us each one be able to teach the community what God has done to solve the urgencies needed for each city.

A person needs to be only in the presence of Christ Jesus and listen and use the Trinity power and Godly and heavenly purpose for the mission that is God's in that person or peoples In the Trinity, God is not a God of normality and stagnation or even regularity in a world now of "upheavelness," He is a God of revolution of love in Peace and Word.

Though those who are strong, humble, gifted, and bright are sometimes used in the way men think and not how God thinks. Though God always redeems. Hence, this bright and talented m as if they do not have sound judgment though they are suppressed and oppressed. Though we know in history with God and His people, it is the heart of love for God that brings God's glory for humanity. And in God's strength in the Spirit of America, we will conquer God's will.

Remember, nothing is too hard for the Lord God, we ask these things and become to the purpose. Remember, if we are carrying out God's purpose and intentions in His time He will make sure that we do even if we are persecuted. It may take a generation [8years, Jesus was in the Church at 8years learning] though it will be corrected in His time. God accommodates us.

His Spirit fills us with power, love, and the ability to understand how to make wise decisions' 2Tm 1:7. It is also possible to realize in 2Tm 1:7 as moderation and sensible behavior (88.93).[cc]

Humans of integrity and work ethic and honesty of actions is indirectly the beauty and love of God's true purpose. God will

President Trump Primrose Speech before the China Virus

Economic turnaround of historic proportion, 1.5 million prime-age Americans were working than 8years before. We lost 200 manufacturing jobs under the previous presidency. More than 10 million Americans have been added to food stamps in the past years. Now America is leading the entire world in the economy. We added 3.7 million new jobs since the election, and it has increased. (Before the Chinese Virus), We were in the job growth streak in history. Unemployment reached its lowest level in almost half a century.

We will continue even with the temporary silent war of the Chinese virus. We are finally putting America first. Everywhere we look, we the effects of the economic miracle.

Trust in the Lord with all your heart and soul.

Analysis and Synthesis

The ancient Greek mathematicians use the difference in "analysis" and "synthesis". Most sources characterize synthesis as working from givens to the desired conclusion, and the analysis starts from a decision and working back to its cause. What would be an example of the Greeks doing this? It ms that all arguments I have read in Euclid's *Elements* would be synthetic.

Analysis

What analysis involves is the finding of appropriate principles, previously proved theorems, and constructional moves utilizing which the problem can be solved (the desired figure constructed, or the relevant theorem proved).[cci]

https://hsm.stackexchange.com/questions/5629/analysis-vs-synthesis-in-greekmathematics?utm_medium=organic&utm_source=google_rich_qa&utm_campaign=google_rich_qa

There is a particular way and purpose of Unity.

We ask ourselves, why do we look up these words of ancient Greek? In linguistics, we understand, words change over time because of what environment they are used in and how humans and even animals respond to them. And new words are always developed. Furthermore, words shape the society and culture and traditions, and the individuals become assimilated by the culture. Words become action and the formation of human life. Wake up and Arise America, analyze cannot you the words have become action and life that the Divine Messages and Commands have been followed. All the other brilliant strategies to restore America in trusting God have become a reality under President Trump and the American Freedom Warriors.

We seek to know, we strive to understand, we seek to accomplish, we seek to redeem, we seek to be sustained.

LET US ALLOW OUR LEGACY OUR AMERICA TO BE EDUCATED..This is what the Creator has done for our. Language has words that we speak and are identified with our actions.

Word---Speak-------- Contemplation----Analysis----- Synthesis---- ------------ Action to solve the solutions.

to separate, set apart, Plat.:—Pass *parted from the throng,* of **two heroes coming forward as champions,** Il.; *to be separated and brought* under one name, Thuc.[ccii] Let our name be only in the God of Abraham.

Let us be champions, "heroes," working together they are "separated," yet they are "under one name. "Under one purpose, "under God's name." Let us be "under one name," in God and in God we trust.

"The Church, 'like a stranger in a foreign land, presses forward amid the persecutions of the world and the consolations of God' announcing the cross and death of the Lord until He comes.' By the power of the risen Lord it is given the strength that it might, in patience and in love, overcome its sorrows and its challenges, both within itself and from without, and that it might reveal to the world, faithfully though darkly, the mystery of its Lord until, in the end, it will be manifested in full light."[cciii]

ὠφέλησις, εως, ἡ, *a helping, aiding;* and so (generally) like ὠφέλεια, *use, service, advantage,* Soph.; and ὠφελητέος.[cciv]

Moving forward through trial and tribulation, the Church is strengthened by the power of God's grace, which was promised to her by the Lord, so that in the weakness of the flesh she may not waver from perfect fidelity, but remain a bride worthy of her Lord, and moved by the Holy Spirit may never cease to renew herself, until through the Cross she arrives at the light which knows no setting.

Therefore the promised Restoration which we are awaiting has already begun in Christ, is carried forward in the mission of the Holy Spirit and through Him continues in the Church in which we learn the meaning of our terrestrial life through our faith, while we perform with hope in the future the work committed to us in this world by the Father, and thus work out our salvation.239

Vatican II-E

Best economy in decades

Lowest Unemployment for Blacks, Hispanics, Women in decades in 18years.

Rebuilding the military

July 18, 2018

Our Lady of Mount Carmel..

While preparing to take the Eucharistic mass:

Divine Message I gave myself to Jesus Christ to enter into the heavenly to receive

I had a vision..Though I was in heaven... I saw Jesus Christ in a white Robe light blues .. around Him.. and the form of the quorum to the sides.. shimmering platinum shinning majestic eternal and His robe sitting at the table in heaven.

Jesus Christ told me these things..

1. "Tell the Leader's and governmental Leader's in America and the world when they are making decisions in My intention and righteousness, they are at My table in the highest heavens with the quorum the and their these decisions will be in Me and My purpose for humanity."
2. "If Leaders and governmental Leaders do not lead with righteousness to care for humanity they will not be at the highest table in the heavens it will be a lower table and there will not be a restoration or healing." While Jesus Christ was speaking of this, I saw a table. vaguely and the light was not bright it was dim.
3. Then I went back up to the high heaven at the quorum and was healed and strengthened and humbled.

Montecito after Church Eucharistic

The Son of God called me outside to bring me in the light of heaven to receive the Divine Messages

" The Leaders and Governmental leaders of America in the world. I can heal their land if they humble themselves and live and work in righteousness in and for humanity. I can heal their land with the miracle of life and their varied being, their varied atmosphere, and all things from people to people, to land and all of life. Even if there is no hope with the numbers and statistics of problems, I will make a miracle and those things of the world will not have any power, the healing and Restoration will be in the faithful righteousness and love in humanity in My love in them, child. I will heal them with the substance that I created with My child."

Then the two doves came that are with me. and showed themselves to me. in the Son Light of healing and redemption.

"Tell the American people and those of the world this is for all people they are at the table of God in the highest heaven when they work and live in the love and truth and righteousness of humanity."

ὠτ-ἀκουστής, οῦ, ὁ, (ἀκούω) *a listener, spy*, Arist.[ccv] This is understood even in the times of Aristotle, 300-500 years before Christ.

We have brought fruit in America; our country has opened its eyes to the truth of our condition this is why there is an imbalance. Because the truth is being revealed. I am a spy of the Trinity, to make seek with all my heart to understand what is hidden to be brought to understanding or protection and ask: what is hidden that I do not understand to bring love humanity.. and of God salvation to the people.

Look up *leading on the seasons,* or *bringing on the fruits in season,* h. Hom.[ccvi]

ἀ-αγής, ές, (ἄγνυμι) *unbroken, not to be broken, hard, strong*, Od., Theocr.

God never breaks His love for humanity. (It is to say how much are we at God's heart? We are also tested). He is always at our heart and love to honor Him. Just as the moon and the sun are whole we as His people seek to be whole to give us all we need to be a part of His creation and omnipotent plan of His quintessential beauty. Just as the human cells work and support each other in the flowing of the blood flow within the veins and capillaries and body, so do we as the body of a human is connected to His mystery and omniscience of humanity and creation and His **ἀ-αγής**, ές, (ἄγνυμι) of His love for humanity "unbroken, not to be broken, hard, and strong."

ἄ-απτος, ον, (ἅπτομαι) *not to be touched, resistless, invincible,* χεῖρες ἄαπτοι Hom., Hes.

God's love in the human soul cannot be broken it could not even be fractured. God is a perfect God and His Spirit is, "not to be touched, resistless, invincible."

Love forgiveness

The soul of America is in the invincibility of God, "not to be touched."

Now we are in forwarding building we are identifying, that our humanness is being, "perfected," and we are allowing, God's Truth, to bring Justice.

Now we are in forward building we are identifying, that our humanness is being, "perfected," and we are allowing God's love to bring Peace.

Now we are in forwarding building we are identifying that our humanness is being, "perfected," and are allowing God's forgiveness to bring life to its fulness.

Yes, all of us can when we stop and wake up to God allows the world and creation to work beyond all human failures and successes and to bring that natural human being of the ocean of magnificent gifts! Yes, God always, redeems,

"And the surviving remnant of the house of Judah shall again take root downward and be a fruit upward."

Isaiah 37: 31

"As President Regan stated, "Let us do all that can be done. Let us be inspired by the example of our forefathers and their courage, strength, and wisdom. Let us be inspirited by the genius of the Constitution and does8u preservation of the individual and the civil society. Let unleash an American renaissance in which liberty is celebrated and self-government is cherished. Let us together, we, the people restore the splendor of the American Republic."*ccvii*

THOUGH WE CANNOT FORGET THE IMMIGRANTS AND WE NEED TO MAKE A JUST LAW AND NEED TO TAKE CARE OF THOSE IN DACA AND WE NEED TO WITH NO FURTHER ADO RETURN THE CHILDREN BACK TO THERE FAMILIES.

March 2, 2020 Pasadena

Divine Message Virgin Mary
All Boarders have to be watched closely. All borders have to be watched so nothing is missed.
Those who vote need to take care in that they have the most righteous decision that God will make

אבב*(fresh, bright)*. **[אב] n.[m.] freshness**, fresh green; concr., pl. *green shoots.*ccviii

America, now today we have brought, new green "shoots," small branches of truth!
Even though there is tension this brings truth to the surface and opens the eyes of all the people.

America, Now, we are freshness we have brought the bright truth
America, Now we are freshness we have brought the bright Love
America, Now we are freshness we have brought the bright forgiveness

America, Now we are freshness we have brought the bright happiness

We Americans are in the truth to raise to Justice in forwarding building, in the love of God's humanity. We Americans are now being, "fresh, and bright," we have a "fresh green, green of shoots," of the most beauty and power of the branches of God. Please, know my friend, even if you are an atheist and do not in God, God's base foundation is from the His truth, Truth, and Truth is love and love is Peace and Peace is Restoration, and Restoration is Justice. Even if we have some differences we can work toward goodness for America and the world. Our children will be "fresh and bright as new green shoots of the greatest beauty, greatest life ever in America." The door is open of God's love to be carried through to continue to heal America. when we are asking for Peace, Justice, Restoration, forward building in the love of human life, we know there needs to be a "new fresh, shoot, branch of "green," plants of the Creators "אבב*(fresh, bright*" of life, of America.

Truth brings Love
Love brings forgiveness.
Forgiveness brings happiness.

"Whatever I command you, you shall be careful to do; you shall not add to nor take away from it."

Deut. 13:32

Know that God s the future He desires of His humanity's life; he knows what the future should be. However, we have free will; we can choose. Even if those who do not choose to take up the building of America, in truth, the people of God will build in love as they will have victory in God's will.

Divine Message August 21, 2018, Montecito, California

I will give you answers, daughter. Always ask the questions:

Does it bring the most generous Justice?
Does it bring the most incredible Peace?
Does it bring the most extraordinary Restoration?
Does it bring the most miraculous Forward Building in the compassion of humanity?

What do we need to restore in America specifically Justice, Peace, Restoration, and Forward Building? How can you help in your life whether to bring virtues.

When great countries of God through history had tragedies, downfalls, and confusion, God of Yahweh always directed them.

Those who God can then think that God can also direct us in our tragedies, downfalls, and confusion. God will bring Justice, Peace, Restoration, and forward building. As we know, we are the people of the Beatitudes, and we have listed them.
I have numerous Divine Messages and Commands that I have received
This Divine Message and Command is salient for the future.

1. In each government office, there should be a notebook of the history on a weekly or monthly bases for the following items:
   a. Federal and State Government what areas of work do you think have been outdated with all the other variables that this area of work or office comes into contact with for everyday life and how can we improve it in the Four Foundational of Truth.
   b. Ask what areas are putting out the highest costs and what costs need to be trimmed or even changes if adding or subtracting.
   c. Ask: the costs that are going out is it just those receiving the funds or payment is it and promotes the Four Foundational Truths
   d. What areas of work are irrelevant to the check and balances of your office and delivered to you in unnecessary information?
   e. In each transaction, what is the most essential and what is not most fundamental?
   Ask the questions?

- f. Government spending has to be corrected in that it is in the correction of
  the increase of jobs decrease the less social services
- c. We cannot allow companies to abuse employees, environmental issues, Federal and State benefits in that it hurts the middle or lower class or the poor.
- d. On the other hand we need to give the Large and Small Companies the benefits for deductions and benefits. In doing, we will have a competitive edge even if our goods are more expensive, not using imported goods where they're in some cases, "slave workers." We can then increase the hourly wage because housing and all daily costs of living are outrageous.
  - e. With the increase of manufacturing with competitive pricing, we have fewer imports; however, we cannot have more inflation, and if we do, we need to raise the income of the daily wage. Many Americans live on two jobs, one full-time job and then one part-time job. Concluding, there is an inflation of 1.3 percent.
- f. We need to allow the people that have entrepreneurial work and small businesses.
  They are sharing and exchanging small businesses and even trading businesses for payment.
- g. Proven by the fact the Federal, State, and Communities have allowed an imbalance of the distribution of funds and rules and regulations.
- h. We cannot balance the budget. Increment by increment, we need to make wise changes and move swiftly.
- i. The evidence is that the individuals who have great power and even influential jobs connected with those who can control our country's economy have used their gifts and have evolved to the quantity of more in their pockets. We now need to consider America first with all we do that we think and an act of business virtues that promote and make Forward Building in love.
- j. This is human nature to increase and increase to the best out of funds, and even intentions are mingle Justice to produce and keep America and their families and goals. It has to be revealed it has not been that way this
  Is proven by the fact that we [HAVE BEEN 4TH IN PRODUCTION]

NOW OUR PRODUCTION AND OUR COUNTRY IS THE IN THE RESTORATION EVERY UNITED STATES HISTORY.
NOW FINALLY WE AMERICA UNDER THE PRESIDENCY UNDER PRESIDENT TRUMP WE HAVE INCREASED IN:
Trump's First Two Years.

WE NEED TO KEEP ON THIS LIFE IN AMERICA OF
AS PRESIDENT TRUMP AS WORK TOWARD
"MAKING AMERICA GREAT AGAIN."

> *There is nothing wrong with men possessing riches. The wrong comes when riches possess men.*
>
> Billy Graham

God in Jesus Christ, is our redeeming Savior and Guide to continue for Forwarding Building.

Divine Message October 2,3, 4, 2020 Pasadena
This Divine Message and Command is salient for the future Technological Warnings

All top universities and schools and private businesses or

areas that produce and share information national of science and or

the extensive and relevant information that can be a danger to humanity

needs to be investigated; whether funds and information that was shared

with conspicuous or illegal counterparts nationally or internationally.

The technical information and secrets necessary for protection and proper use are the most dangerous that can control all things and even bring catastrophes from technology to nuclear today by day happenings. Therefore, all need to be protected in Peace, Justice, Restoration, and Forward Building in love.

I am a listener and a warrior of America and the world for God's peace and love it is by the Spirit of God that He makes a good work for Him in me for

His glory. I seek to live in God's Holy Scriptures, that is God's Light and Wisdom. I am a warrior; I am a messenger of the Divine Messages of the Trinity and the Saints for America and the world for God's glory. I am a friend of God to seek to prevent and purpose and in the listener's ear and Divine Messages. I am a lover of humanity; I find out what is not acceptable and expose what is not Truth and Truth. However, people have to listen to and carry out the Divine Messages. Ask God what we need to be to help Forward Building America. We need to be a friend of God of ourselves that nothing seeks to hurt our America and continue to forwarding Building. And realizing what is happening in all our actions in life is it Peace, Justice, Restoration, and Forward Building? America and the World need to be people of God's friend to continue forwarding Building in Love our America and the World. Then we need to speak aloud in truth. Things that we do not realize are and could be treacherous or impede us that we do not learn, God will make visible to protect us when we seek righteousness.

For me, and the living history of humanity, most necessary knows Jesus Christ as your Lord and Savior, and He will guide us and lead us unto all truth.

Because Jesus Christ is the greatest love ever in a human person and from heaven sent from Abraham's God. He Jesus Christ is the way the truth and life and through Him, all things shall be redeemed on earth as it is in heaven.

Forwarding Building in Love is forward building in God's love for eternal treasures.

Mathew 6:19-21

Jesus Christ proclaims:

I am in the Father and the Father is in me, or else, because of the works themselves. ¹² Amen, amen, I say to you, whoever s in me will do the works that I do, and will do greater ones than these, because I am going to the Father. ¹³ And whatever you ask in my name, I will do, so that the Father may be glorified in the Son. ¹⁴ If you ask anything of me in my name, I will do it. ¹⁵ "If you love me, you will keep my commandments. ¹⁶ And I will ask the Father, and he will give you another Advocate to be with you always, ¹⁷ the Spirit of Truth, which the world cannot accept, because it neither s nor knows it. But you know it, because it remains with you, and will be in you. ¹⁸ I will not leave you orphans; I will come to you. ¹⁹ In a little while the world will no longer me, but you will me, because I live and you will live. ²⁰ On that day you will realize that I am in my Father and you are in me and I in you. ²¹ Whoever has my commandments and observes them is the one who loves me. And whoever loves me will be loved by my Father, and I will love him and reveal myself to him.

John 14:11-21

So we have confirmation of the words of the prophets; and you will be right to pay attention to it as to a lamp for lighting a way through the dark, until the dawn comes and the morning star rises in your minds. ²⁰ At the same time, we must recognize that the interpretation of scriptural prophecy is never a matter for the individual. ²¹ For no prophecy ever came from human initiative. When people spoke for God it was the Holy Spirit that moved them. 1Pet. 1:6 This is a great joy to you, even though for a short time yet you must bear all sorts of trials; ⁷ so that the worth of your faith, more valuable than gold, which is perishable even if it has been tested by fire, may be proved— to your praise and honor when Jesus Christ is revealed. ⁸ You have not n him, yet you love him; and in him you in him and so are already filled with a joy so glorious that it cannot be described; **⁹ *and you are sure of the goal of your faith, that is, the salvation of your souls.***

2Pet. 1:19

He is the living stone, rejected by human beings but chosen by God and precious to him; set yourselves close to him ⁵ so that you, too, may be living stones making a spiritual house as a holy priesthood to offer the spiritual sacrifices made acceptable to God through Jesus Christ. ⁶ As scripture says: Now I am laying a stone in Zion, a chosen, precious cornerstone and no one who relies on this will be brought to disgrace. ⁷ To you rs it brings honour. But for unrs, it is rather a stone which the builders rejected that became a cornerstone, ⁸ a stumbling stone, a rock to trip people up. They stumble over it because they do not in the Word; it was the fate in store for them.

1Pet. 2:4

"Governments do not make ideas, but ideas make governments."

President   Calvin Coolidge

But if you faithfully obey the voice of Yahweh your God, by keeping and observing all his commandments, which I am laying down for you today, Yahweh your God will raise you higher than every other nation in the world, ² and all these blessings will befall and overtake you, for having obeyed the voice of Yahweh your God.

Deut. 28:1

Our Lady of Mount Carmel Montecito 12.31.18 and January 1, 2019
Jesus said of the Sacred Heart
Praying in the Front of Jesus Christ Sacred Heart

1. Do you lock your doors a night child?

2. Those who have brought drugs into the country have caused many to be destroyed the innocent and the weak and the poor.
3. Those who have caused the immigrants to leave their country because (for all sorts of reasons) and their own country has caused them to find life and existence in another country.
4. Those responsible for the child that they bore need to consider "who will take care of the children? Parents need to take responsibility. Of course, we know we can be the best parent though something happens on the way that our child has death threatening deformities to their authentic character.
5. The Republicans and the Democrats have taken advantage of these peoples, and they need to set a strategy with the checkpoints and laws that Queen Virgin Mary and Jesus Christ of the Sacred Heart have demanded... Jesus Christ said, " Give Caesar what is Caesar's." However, in the Justice of the people. They have not given proper Justice. I know the minds of men and their motives child...
6. This is what Jesus Christ told me first of the Sacred Heart of Jesus told me and showed me the titration report's vision. [Jesus Christ told me to look it up. Today I did. January 1. The contamination of the samples may interfere with the result of the titration. The amount of acid added would be more than required. A few steps can be taken to avoid errors. We have not neutralized we have allowed human faults and human survival of the fetus to be imbalanced.] This is what Jesus Christ has said.
7. Now is what is happening this is.. Now is what is happening this by dripping and dripping of the titration in the life of America and become changed in the Ph of nature of America is not the color changes in a Ph color

Suppose to be this is why there needs to be a change .and protected in. not in the nationality however, in the Justice of how to treat human beings.

8. I asked Jesus Christ. this: we have a Divine Command and Mary told me this .. do as your Father tell you

9. January 1, 2019 Virgin Mary

Jesus of the Sacred Heart told me this: there is a home of America that I have given.
I have allowed enough in the House of America to be sustained. First, I have given (you) enough to be sustained. "Meaning each one of us.
You need to help him, (the President) My daughter, there is a verse in the bible that Jesus brought to my mind; and I heard his words also regarding to those the way that their thoughts are. "Respond to those as they need to be responded."

President Trump is a businessman and is bringing restoration building to My America.
My home that God has given [us as believers and those whom He created.] I am in America brighter and pure wisdom when they call upon me; I am Mother Mary Queen of all Mothers and the Mother of God. I am the Mother that bares children sorrows, hurts, and needs and even close to death, guiding them and protecting them to Jesus Christ. I am here when those call upon me, working toward righteousness to do what is right, even though they may not know what is correct because the future is uncertain in men's eyes, not God's. I accommodate the child. All have to be redeemed toward redemption child, in Jesus Christ. Tell them to follow my light in Christ Jesus the light of the world, the Lord and Savior. God has accommodated to American child At this very moment, He has accommodated America. Sit still and listen child (I wanted to knell**) You need to fight for him in peace child President Trump. I want him in Child..." I asked Mary please let me hear your voice clearly at this moment. .. Find the good things he has done and allow the people to it**... Stay seated child you are in the Quorum of heaven. Tell the people what truth they can bring to their life to restore America. You have had to enter into the darkness with the power in God's light to help places that need light.

10. You have been given in the body of the Trinity new life. I have given you many lives to be sustained on earth.
11. When Mary told me this there was light upon her feet an in front of her

12. Then I prayed to the higher heavens she said, prepare the Trinity is Mary ahead....
13. During my prayer, I saw.... Great white of her love....
14. Great begin... Jesus Christ and Mary gave me their blessing together I was looking at them both.
15. Now looking up I saw lights on both sides of Mary.. Mary told me, " you have lights on both sides... " I know what this is; however, I will not say.
16. All these things are for the glory of the Lord.
17. Jesus Christ said the Angels of light of the Trinity will protect us from the angels of the darkness.

July 29, 2019, Praying to Jesus Christ.

Kissed and loved Him.. with My whole heart. He made me pull my shoulders up strong and holding what He has given me for Him and His glory I stand in His love and power and relying faithful upon in Him.

I bowed down.. we exchanged love and love. He is in Me and I and in Him. I gave Him all I could give that I understand. And He accepted. and I am honored.

> Divine Message October 30, 2020
> You are in Me, and I am in You.

America and the world, and you are sure of the goal of your faith, that is, the salvation of your souls.

2Pet. 1:19

Chapter Five

Wisdom and the Wise

Do not desert her, she will keep you safe; love her, she will watch over you.

Prov. 4:6

I love those who love me; whoever searches eagerly for me finds me.

Prov. 8:17

I in a loud voice of love, I sing:
In a loud voice, I sing:

In my vision, I heard the sound of an immense number of angels gathered around the throne and the living creatures and the elders; there were ten thousand times ten thousand of them and thousands upon thousands.

Jesus Christ the Messiah ….. "Worthy is the Lamb, who was sacrificed to receive power and wealth and wisdom and strength and honor and glory and praise!"

Revelations 5:11-12

In God through Christ Jesus, America:
America, you are God's land of Wisdom.
America, you are God's land of Peace
America, you are God's land of Justice
America, you are God's land of Restoration
America, you are God's land of Forward Building in Love

I serve you to bring a brief discussion on "Wisdom and the Wise."
True Wisdom is only of God; Wisdom of God is only comprehended
God is asking all of us to pray and ask how we can receive His first intention
of Wisdom, and receive His Wisdom and knowledge to have the solutions
to heal America and continue to keeping America Great again.

<u>*When I say "Wisdom," we receive in God, it is the grace He gives to understand His purpose and His love.*</u>

How rich and deep are the wisdom and the knowledge of God! We cannot reach to the root of his decisions or his ways. ^{34} Who has ever known the mind of the Lord? Who has ever been His adviser?

Rom. 11:33

A mere Word of God is like an ocean that reaches across the seas upholding all the ships and passengers on their journey of life.

Even though there are differences, we Americans can bring truth; because the light of God has been revealed and is brilliant upon America NOW AND FOREVERMORE.

Love uprightness you who are rulers on earth, be properly disposed towards the Lord and seek Him in the simplicity of heart

Wisdom.
1:1

We know that not one individual is perfect. We need to seek the best of each other. And when we find the truth in the Wisdom of God, we need to seek God's face, and for me, that is the Word of God and His truths and in prayer and song and proclamation.

<u>We need to vote for the protection and life of our country and our people. Even though we know that there are unanswered questions, fabrications, and discrepancies, and even human injustices, we need to who will do the best job to protect our country, protect our life and legacy of America and her people, and protect our future seed of life.</u>

The truth will ultimately prevail where there are pains to bring it to light.

George Washington

Do not let anyone claim the tribute of American patriotism if they even attempt to remove religion (The Pure Covenant with God) from politics.

George Washington

Robert Welch, in the book The Politician, Proclaims,
Eric Hoffer's in his book, The Truer,

Any man of real faith, or beliefs, or principles, to which he is willing to pay anything more than lip service (is not the greatest Justice); It cleverly holds up to ridicule those thousands of Americans, of whom this writer hopes he is one, who not only **there are certain eternal truths which should guide the human race but are willing to fight for that belief and to die for it if necessary.**[ccix]

Remember, to proclaim in "God's Words of Truth," is to bring life to its fullest.

I have been grateful that God has merited me this job. Many do not know me; I plant the miracle of a mustard d of faith. However, I am known by the Trinity and in the guidance and protection of the Trinity, Virgin Mother Mary, and the Arch Angels.

The LORD is my shepherd, I shall not be in want. . . He leads me beside quiet waters, He restores my soul. He guides me in paths of righteousness for his name's sake. Even though I walk through the valley of the shadow of death, I will fear no evil, for you are with me your rod and your staff,

they comfort me. And I am given your rod and staff to bring your truth. You prepare a table before me in the presence of my enemies.
You anoint my head with oil; my cup overflows. Surely goodness and love will follow me all the days of my life, and I will dwell in the house of the LORD forever. **Psa. 23:1 -6**

The Mother of all Nations

America, the Mother of Liberty, the Statue of Liberty
Standing for freedom and life is Mother, America that bears the
Legacy to Keep America Free in the Light and Wisdom of God
American Mothers of Freedom Bring Life and Proclaim Truth

"The Statue of Liberty Enlightening the World" (is) a gift of friendship from the people of France to the United States and is recognized as a universal symbol of freedom and democracy. The Statue of Liberty was dedicated on October 28, 1886. It was designated as a National Monument in 1924. Employees of the National Park Service have been caring for the colossal copper statue since 1933.[ccx]

American Mothers of Freedom of Life:

You know mothers carry in their womb the miracle of life holding God's child and nurturing the d of life of the greatest gift of God to humanity is a child.

Queen Virgin Mary is the Liberty of the Light of God

The Mother of God has a significance that exceeds anything human and natural. She is the "Mother of the eternal Divine Logos," the Mother of God.[ccxi]

You America, are that child at her immaculate heart, Queen Mother Mary, the Mother of God.
Let her guide you to all Wisdom as she did Jesus Christ, the Son of God.
Queen Virgin Mary is the "Original Mother of Man."[ccxii]:
She is the Son of God's mother and guided Him to the Holy Temple to find Wisdom in God.

'Ask, and it will be given to you; search, and you will find; knock, and the door will be opened to you. ⁸ Everyone who asks receives; everyone who searches finds; everyone who knocks will have the door opened

Matt. 7:7

*O Lord, you are great and greatly to be praised: great is your power and your **wisdom** is without measure.*

St. Thomas Aquinas

Finding Wisdom:

"*The outer room of the sanctuary may be referred to in some languages as simply 'the first room of the Holy Temple' or 'the first holy room of the Temple.'* **The 'holy of holies' may be referred to as 'the holiest place' or 'the second holy room of the Temple' or 'the Temple's interior holy room.' What is important here is the degree of holiness**, *not the actual location within the temple. For this reason, for the 'holy of holies' many translators use* **'the most sacred place'** *or 'the very, very **sacred** room.' In this type of context, the term '**sacred**' may be rendered as 'dedicated, especially to God' or 'consecrated to God.'*[ccxiii]

When we ask and give ourselves to God we are "dedicated especially to God" and "consecrated to God." In being consecrated to God, we have His blessings and ongoing sanctification. *However, we are warriors of love and need to put on the Armor of God.*

In experiencing and knowing God's Wisdom, we have God's armor

Growing strong in the Lord. . stand your ground, with truth a belt round your waist, and uprightness a breastplate, ¹⁵ wearing for shoes on your feet the eagerness to spread the gospel of peace ¹⁶ and always carrying the shield of faith so that you can use it to quench the burning arrows of the Evil One. *¹⁷ And then you must take salvation as your helmet and the sword of the Spirit, that is, the word of God.*

Eph. 6:14 -17

You might as why does she have so many verses in writing. The Word is the characteristics and miracles of God. These Words are pure truth, pure Wisdom of God.

America is dedicated to God of Abraham.

God is the "Holy One," *Haq-qadosh. Yahweh is God and is not man. Precisely why, like man He is moved by the self-giving quality of love that is centered upon the* Hosea learns from the Holy One that a certain kind of love possesses the virtue of healing, saving, and life-renewing *Da'at Elohim,* " the knowledge of God" (Hos 6:6), discloses to the prophet that *agape* constitutes the core of holiness.[ccxiv]

Yahweh Sabaoth will brandish a whip at him he struck Midian at Oreb's Rock, will brandish his rod at the Sea as he raised it on the way from Egypt.

Is. 10:26

Awake, Arise, in Truth of God's Wisdom, because of God's never forsaking love for His people, Jesus Christ raised the rod of God's Wisdom to heal America.

America:
American Awake anew, America Arise, America in truth anew
Jesus Christ has given us a life of redemption with the God of Abraham's in the hearts of the people that will RESTORE OUR BEAUTIFUL COUNTRY OF GOD, AMERICA.
Again all that does evil shall be exposed. See God wants to protect the children.

In reiterating this book is not an intellectual presentation; it is guided by Divine Command of Proclamation Wisdom and of Truth to uphold the freedom for the American People.

America her gifts are for God's intention; this allows freedom like no other freedom because it is then the creation of God's purpose that is natural to God's creation. Therefore, if one chooses God's Wisdom in his or her heart, there will be freedom of living waters. Living waters are watering others naturally, not taken by force though naturally flows from God's love. However, those who give living waters to God also need to be sustained. Even after Jesus healed the sick, He rested. He did not tolerate money exchange or bargaining of gifts that God gave the people.

It is by him that you exist in Christ Jesus, who for us was made wisdom from God, and saving Justice and holiness and redemption.

1Cor. 1:30

Jesus then went into the Temple and drove out all those who were selling and buying there; he upset the tables of the money-changers and the seats of the dove-sellers. [13] He said to them, 'According to scripture, my house will be called a house of prayer; but you are turning it into a bandits' den.' [14] There were also blind and lame people who came to him in the Temple, and he cured them. [15] At the sight of the wonderful things he did and of the children shouting, 'Hosanna to the son of David' in the Temple."

Matt. 21:12

America is the temple of God for those who in God's love; and with Wisdom and redemption, *"you have been washed clean, you have been sanctified, and you have been justified in the name of the Lord Jesus Christ and through the Spirit of our God."*

1Cor. 6:9

When the children America healing the people and land they will shout for joy, the violet sun-kissed mountains will roar, the oceans held in God's hands will be at peace, the birds will sing, and soil will be the most beautiful harvest of heavenly fruit to heal the land and her people. Hence, each American will love each other in truth and respect. Each business transaction at all levels will be fair for their work and in the amounts deserved in the powerful world even if they do not have a title. Moreover, those who have gifted the power should not monopolize them and abuse them, from brilliant ideas to human trafficking artists.

"Titles don't mean anything."
Talal Al Murad

Remember, there is a purpose for the gifts God gave America and each person. "Do not pour your gifts (pearls to the dogs)." (However, some are forced into a conspiracy and slavery.) There has been a Divine Message God will strike unexpectedly. Let us continue the subject matter in any working strategy of life when we finish one job and mission. We then seek to maintain it and keep it healthy and then go to the next. God's message: we are not here to heal the healthy but the sick. Erstwhile, an individual with the Wisdom of God has to be that Cross, and though they do, they are pouring the Spirit of God upon with heavenly hope, faith; It is an urgent message to tell of Jesus Love to redeem now. Listen, we know timing could change all things. However, God can reverse time and save time. If we now cannot face the truth and speak out in peace and first pray and face our God, our America will not have freedom and life. <u>Each of us needs to pray, face God, listen, and ask for a miracle for our legacy, our Millennials, and our children.</u>
<u>Look, God's Wisdom is Righteousness, Holiness, and Redemption.</u>

But there is one thing, my dear friends, that you must never forget: that with the Lord, a day is like a thousand years, and a thousand years are like a day. [9] The Lord is not being slow in carrying out his promises, as some people think he is; rather is he being patient with you, wanting nobody to be lost and everybody to be brought to repentance.

2Pet. 3:8

*It is because of him that you are in Christ Jesus, who has become for us **Wisdom** from God—that is, our **righteousness, holiness**, and **redemption**.*[31]

1 Corinthians 1:31

Moreover, God uses the weak of the world to open the mind and hearts of the world's powerful.

1Corinthians.1:27

First, to proclaim for the Wisdom, we need to heal America and to be a reflection in the world of righteousness. Hence, we have to treat humans and all creation with peace, justice, and God's love. Then we need holiness, and that is developed in the grace of God's redeeming power of the Cross and continuing to be sanctified in His love professing sin and sin no more. It is also doing and living in holiness.

In the past, as stated a multiplicity of times in this book, we Americans have neglected and disrespected America's needs. [ccxv] America is supposed to be the reflection of the house of God.

Each one of us has to what is passionate in our heart to bring God's Wisdom.

"And Jesus entered the temple and drove out all who sold and bought in the temple, and the other tables of the money-changers and the seats of

those who sold pigeons. ¹³ He said to them, "It is written, 'My house shall be called a house of prayer,' but you make it a den of robbers.

Matt. 21:12

. . . You were living by the principles of this world, obeying the ruler who dominates the air, the spirit who is at work in those who rebel.

Eph. 2:2

Today even the information and work made by others is even taken without fair pay and Justice. God will not allow this. The technological controls are vast. It is a present future urgency that we as a people in the entire world, adapt and perform and create measures of knowledge and grace of God's wisdom to protect humanity from its piercing poisons of deforming the human beauty and life.

Nothing passes the eyes of the Lord. A blink of His right eye can blind the traitorous technology of the entire universe. And then His eternal light in His left eye could bring salvation and peace to the whole universe.

It is the duty of all nations to acknowledge the Providence of Almighty God, to obey his will, to be grateful for his benefits, and humbly implore his protection and favor.

George Washington

America, the land is God's gift to the people; America's skills are God given to the people for God's purpose. America is the temple of God's heart. And the people who are the temple of God. Therefore, our gifts need to be treated respectfully and for God. Even in a sense to find and observe what the children and adult's offerings are, they can learn and develop and form that authentic person they are created for.

Yahweh God shaped man from the soil of the ground and blew the breath of life into his nostrils, and man became a living being. **נְפֵ֫** breath (*yāpēaḥ*), **witness (H3641).**

Gen. 2:7

"And God gave Solomon **wisdom** and understanding exceedingly much, and largeness of heart, even as the sand that is on the seashore."

1Kings 4:29

The person will be at peace when they are working toward and in their purpose, even with or without the danger, the "robbers," the "deceivers," and those who try "to kill." In God's peace, they cannot danger the soul, cannot be robbers of God's gift, and cannot kill the heart. Let me reiterate we do not want a Socialistic or Communistic rule. Socialism and Communistic government destroy humans' innate drive of curiosity and achievement and cultural diversity to express their authentic being, own land, own businesses, and fulfill a dream of beauty in each individual that brings happiness. God is most happy when the people live, be, work, learn, build, respect in compassion, share the best for more beauty, and reconcile the worse for a new life.

Grace be with all who love our Lord Jesus Christ with love undying.

Ephesians 6:23-24

I know I keep mention Jesus Christ, name, and referring to all His teaching. , He is the best human and the best that can guide to Wisdom that I know. And it is proven over time through others applying and living His precepts. We are in a time of America's history that none of us should hold back the living waters of beauty that life of wholesomeness and pouring compassion on all things destroyed to healing, blindness to light, and living to miracles. And Jesus Christ is the Son of God, the King of Kings from heaven above entered into the world to give us pure life.

Awake, Arise, in Truth, America, whether you in God or not, He has given gifts to you your talents. All gifts are intended to be pure; gifts are purest known; they are from heaven, and they cannot tolerate the one measurement of imbalance. God will not tolerate violence; nature cannot tolerate abuse. Hence, God sustains those who are His people and gives them the strength to do all things in His Right Arm of Power in His hands.

Remember, God is a warrior. However, God's warrior carries the Light of God in the battle of darkness that God fights with Michael Arch Angel, Gabriel, and Raphael and the Angels of God to bring the Light of God's truth and His Salvation. Gifts from a child or adult or priest and mother nature will cause God's heart to strike when someone tries to sabotage.

Because we are imperfect humans, we do not have regular freedom; and if we do have a large amount of democracy in ways of life, we still have the variables of others around us and all the happenings of life that we cannot control. When we have God's Wisdom in our hearts, then our freedom can flow even under the variables of the imperfection of others and ourselves, because He the God of Abraham in the Trinity is a Redeemer and a Savior bringing all things new. However, sometimes others have to carry the Cross.

My grace is sufficient for you. 2 Corinthians 12:8

It is my calling to bring the love of God's Wisdom of truth to help you open up the authentic Wisdom God has in you. **Americans, have we used God's given knowledge for good, for the freedom of America and the world?**

Has there been justice and freedom? When there are injustices, it must be revealed only in peace; otherwise, we are not putting God's truth first. Speaking and proclaiming crimes is protecting and bringing a warning to those who are doing wrong. Wisdom has a fountain of forgiveness that is redemption, that allows God's Wisdom to flow continuously; forgiveness has the hand of God's heart of His knowledge.

Wisdom in God is a warrior of what is the truth, even when speaking out a warning, and those who do not want to hear it will bring persecution on the warrior of truth. **Each person has their Wisdom in God that is in their cell makeup that makes them wise. The individual can receive God's Wisdom in their cell makeup and in their life and be in the right relationship with God; therefore, this is living waters of life and living in God's intention.**

For God so loved the world that he gave his only Son so that everyone who s in him might not perish but might have eternal life.
John 3:16

Prayer one cannot describe it is beyond human knowledge; it is God's voice of the most beautiful soothing song when He answers, even when He is silent, there is a quintessential melody in the soul of peace-king to know God. Go to Him and ask Him.

'"Behold, I stand at the door and knock. If anyone hears my voice and opens the door, [then] I will enter his house and dine with him, and he with me. ^{21} I will give the victor the right to sit with me on my throne, as I myself first won the victory and sit with my Father on his throne. ^{22} "'"Whoever has ears ought to hear what the Spirit says to the churches."'

Revelations 3:20

In each person is created in the image of God.

God created man in the image of himself; in the image of God, he created him, male and female He created them.

Gen. 1:27

God knows you best. Ask Him to guide you for Wisdom.

Depending on what is needed, many go-to professionals for help when they need help. The Creator in the Trinity has given you life and knows you the best, for life and eternal life; Ask God in humble prayer, for you, to who you are, and what you are created for, and how to develop God's Wisdom in your heart and deliver it, as a gift of the wise. Even if you do not in God, reach Him, call Him up in a pray as if you would call a professional, ask God, seek God, knock at God's door of the most incredible Wisdom of Heaven.

From my experience and realized only through God can I be toward His purpose and intention, and then knowing who I am in the journey of my life and even recognizing He is with me in happiness and trials. God loves us all, and we make the choices and free-will choose. Remember, some do not have free-will because the powers of the darkness secretly in the community seek to hurt them and use them. God is more powerful and will redeem them; even if they suffer many dangers, God will save them. Knock at that door of heaven of the greatest love, of the omniscient Wisdom, of the omnipotent life in God.

We need God's thoughts to do what is life and the indecent eternal beauty that gives and allows all things in life to be lived and to be love.

> *For my thoughts are not your thoughts and your ways are not my ways, declares Yahweh. ⁹ For the heavens are as high above earth as my ways are above your ways, my thoughts above your thoughts.*
>
> Is. 55:8

To recollect your memory, I am writing as if I was writing this book to a child and an adult who has a childlike faith that is how God's truth and Wisdom are given. All of us need to seek God as a pure child FAITHFUL yet BRAVE and seek God's Wisdom as an adult. I am always praying and want to know and understand and be and give AND FORGIVE AND BE FORGIVEN. Therefore, God has listened, He gives me His ear, and He hears me, and I hear Him; yet, I am quiet and listen in prayer; I also cry out to God to help America, and most of the time I listen in prayer. I also speak out in fervency when many have gone against me because of my protection for truth. Even take the "Sword of Truth and Strike," only to overcome evil in the power of God's Right Arm.

As we some people, God gives excellent worldly knowledge, and they do not recognize Him and respect Him. You know that sooner or later, some of the knowledgeable of the worlds will question God, and we hope and pray to God, the person will accept God and receive Him. However, you know some do not in the Lord as God and Savior. When this knowledge takes the Wisdom of God, they will be able to solve the solutions. God is sovereign, as we already mentioned; He makes the choices. And if they do solve the answer, they can bring peace and redemption in God's Wisdom. We need to start optimistically first. Even if there are roadblocks and even dangers on the treacherous journey of life, we can overcome knowing the Holy Spirit is with us and will manifest strength in our weakness.

When we contemplate in humble yearning to do God's will, and when we step aside and take a look at the needs in society and life to help with, we can be in the right relationship with the Creator and even be directed by the Holy Spirit; we can have many living revelations about ourselves of our true Wisdom of God, in us and deliver it, and we will have inner happiness that will never leave us and will be able to overcome all trials. You know that is the Holy Spirit in you. For prophecy never had its origin in the will of man, but men spoke from God as they were carried along by the Holy Spirit.

2Pet. 1:21

For us to restore America, we need God. We can do nothing without God.

When we know God and seek Him first, we will restore America when we love God. The First Commandment is to love God with all your heart and soul.

But it is as scripture says: What no eye has n, and no ear has heard, what the mind of man cannot visualize; all that God has prepared for those who love Him.

1 Cor. 2:19

America and the world, we all need the Wisdom of God in you to be wise in your gift with God's intention; otherwise, it is not what is God's choice.

What is God's Wisdom in the relationship in God and humanity?
Ask God for yourself?

I want to bring a message of God's truth; I am called to show and proclaim in the foundation of God the truth and how to apply it to our life, on earth, and our relationship with God and humanity. The truth is the Word of God.

Jesus Christ is the way, the truth, and the life, and no one comes to the Father except through Him.

John 14:6

In our humbleness and surrendering freely to His love, God can work and manifest His purpose.

The owner of all 'He who is sufficient,' 'our Great Father,' 'the Highest One,' 'the Great Spirit,' 'the Unending Spirit,' 'the Commanding Spirit,' 'the Great Chief,' 'the Self-Existing One,' and **'the truly Sacred One.'**[ccxvi]

God 's Grace is Sufficient for the UNITED STATES OF AMERICA. 2 Corinthians 12:8

Again, to be a moving force to realizing that we need: First, to identify the pure because it is closest to God's intention: Pure is Wisdom. Wisdom is the truth. Truth is forgiveness. Forgiveness is healing. Healing is forward building in love for freedom. Wisdom of the Creator is to defined and restore and continue to keep America great Freedom of God's Wisdom at her heart, hands, and life among the people and the land. These "Words" are of the nature as a child of hope. However, we know there are trials and tribulations and tests and even dangers when bringing God's Justice. Awake protects ourselves and learns from the experiences, yet a human truth can only be pushed so far before they react.

<u>When you give something that is a *"Sacrifice for Justice in Love,"* such as to save a child, and you gave all you had, and someone did not follow the agreement. God redeems when we seek righteousness and trust Him.</u>

<u>WISDOM OF GOD TO PROTECT AMERICA'S FREEDOM</u>

NOW WE HAVE TO CONTINUE TO PROTECT AMERICA'S FREEDOM TO PROTECT AMERICA'S JUSTICE

And God will use them to proclaim Justice. God will redeem an abnormality to bring it health when we seek His Wisdom in righteousness and humbleness.

God's thoughts are not human.
America, we can ask now; God gives us your Wisdom.
Moreover, nothing can overcome the Trinity. Even in the community's higher powers, the cultural dark practices and s and ideas of men and women cannot defeat God's purpose for His people. What will happen to them will be death if they do not change because the darkness is death.
 We will persevere in remaining healthy and trusting God to redeem us.

μένω G3531 (*menō*), remain; **ἐμμένω** G1844 (*emmenō*), stay or remain in, persevere, abide by; **ἐπιμένω** G2152 (*epimenō*), stay, remain, continue (in)[ccxvii]

We know for sin and life tragedies can only be redeemed by a Savior of the pure, perfect life in God's Wisdom and unconditional love. In God, Jesus Christ is the pure human without sin and the transcendent Son of God that as a human redeem sin because of His perfect body and self and in doing, resurrect all things so that they again will have life. He showers away from the sin and death with His blood. And then, He delivers that why needs to be delivered to new life.

America that is us. We are what He has delivered, is delivering, and will deliver.

Pray, and in praying and God in the First Commandment, you will have His Wisdom and His righteousness, holiness, and redemption to restore America in His love.

*And you may be sure that anyone who tramples on the Son of God, and who treats the **blood** of the covenant which sanctified him as if it were not holy, and who insults the Spirit of grace, will be condemned to far severer punishment.*[ccxviii]

Heb. 10:29

129. **αἷμα haima,** *hah'-ee-mah;* (the juice of grapes) or specially <u>**(the atoning blood of Christ);**</u> by implication, bloodshed

Even if the enemy seeks to defeat God's people, it is just for the temporary treasures, not heaven's eternal treasures on earth. **<u>Today IS(ARE) the days of restitution.</u>** And we most know the heavenly treasures on earth bring the greatest love, life, and freedom on earth and in heaven.

He it is who came by water and blood, Jesus Christ, not with water alone but with water and blood, and it is the Spirit that bears witness, for the Spirit is Truth.

1 John 5:6

*It was by faith that he kept the Passover and sprinkled the **blood** to prevent the Destroyer from touching any of their first-born sons.*

Heb. 11:28

*I pray that the God of peace, who brought back from the dead our Lord Jesus, the great Shepherd of the sheep, by the **blood** that sealed an eternal covenant,*

Heb. 13:20

Harkening in Song, I have many songs truly to tell you: God wants the greatest in their worldly power to enjoy the gifts God gave them under the foundation of heavenly treasures that bring peace, justice, restoration, and forward building of love. You are honored and merit to have these gifts, and they will flow among the land when used in His Wisdom.

Remember, the God of Abraham is a Warrior, and all things come first in His eyes. Each of His people is a warrior and has a place in their mission that God has given in their gifts to bring His wisdom.

Globalization
Divine message 2012-2020
Please *Our Need to Give to the World, Heal America Love in God*

<u>More than ever, God's Wisdom will only allow certain life actions because of globalization and China's Conspiracy for Geopolitical control, and *the 'Gate Keepers,' the Elite that wants to control. Though I that many Elite will the truth of God's Wisdom, they have been entrusted with great gifts, and God deeply desires their heart and an intimate relationship to bring His righteousness. Because they know if the Socialist and Communists take over little by little, so will their businesses be broken down.*</u>

Cashless Society

For example, the cashless society is reflected in areas of society. [ccxix] We need to be careful. A cashless society is a transition of the future that the people of power desire and work for. However, we together can trade business in small businesses. And trust in God. We can make entrepreneurial businesses and exchanging business. Though we can adapt and work to exchange funds.

The real reason for a new force in our economy for the technological transition of finances. The gap between rich and power has gotten more. **.1percent control the funds in our America.** Although, we can work together and seek to take control of our own actions. We have to take control in cities and states to obsolete the cashless society.

America's #1 Futurist Issues Bold Predictions George Gilbert also s massive shift taking place. Secure.investedbetter.com. [ccxx]

As Americans, we need to find that unity what America was built on and work toward that Wisdom, the Wisdom of God, in God, is what America was built on.

Today, for many respect, what America was built on the Judeo-Christian ethic in the Trinity. Deep down in their soul and their psyche, they were called to America. They must be searching for God of Abraham; because the land of America has the Holy Spirit of the Trinity hoovering over every city and community, more than ever. We know innately, men are searching for God. In devastation, they received when they search in themselves and not God directly.

Humans are imperfect and incomplete beings, made in love in God's image. God will not humanity go; he loves humanity and wants to share life with humanity in society. Sharing experience with the community is working through, in, and with each individual.

Divine Message June 14, 2018 Holy Family Church South Pasadena California

I love Mary with all my heart we are together in the Sacred Heart. I

Praying at the higher heaven in the heavenly room, I listened with my love e all my soul, heart, and being:

The Spirit of Queen Mary told me," there is 10 Wisdom of God's truth:

1. God of Abraham
2. Jesus Christ
3. Holy Spirit
4. Virgin Queen Mary

5. Holy Scriptures
6. Saints
7. Arch Angels
8. Church's teachings
9. Spiritual Experiences proved by the Word of God
10. Spiritual Writings and writings have proven and supported by the Word of God
11. I saw files that were ten in color.

1. Yellow
2. Sky Blue
3. Red
4. Light Green
5. Royal Blue
6. Light Purple
7. Aqua Blue
8. Green
9. Purple
10. Gold
11. Platinum

My daughter God chooses what shall be. Be strong. The Spirit of the Lord guided me and the Holy Spirit to go to St. Peter... Sacred Art. St. Peter loves me, and I love him with all my being..

1. I can say: It is about God's will. I will wait until it comes to the past... because it is needed to help America. and God's glory in the world.
2. When St Peter's spoke, St. Peter is strong, vivacious, fervent, with authority in God in heaven and earth ... He was speaking to me for me and God's plan and all the believers and all the people that the Trinity is to come to their heart...
3. **<u>There is a plan, and men will not change the plan that the Trinity and all the Saints in heaven and earth have planned, and only God knows all the plan.</u>**
4. <u>the plan that is immediate men think they know what is correct though only God knows what is right. this is why St. Peter prepared me.. to tell me this..." will happen and all shall</u>

be shocked and surprised. **God will make a good ... work in you. (in us). "** <u>This is why each one of us needs to get closer and closer to God to know our purpose for America and the world for His, God's Glory.</u> [though we cannot abuse humanity.].

5. I went into heavenly. and was also healed and came unto a quintessential unity of pureness with Jesus Christ in the Room of heavenly.

When we pray, we are in Jesus Christ in the Trinity. Pray is the life of God, and He gives us the Wisdom to deliver His righteousness, the holiness we become all on different levels, and redemption to help provide.

Jesus Christ ... has an infinite love to give... to Him regularly go . . . in prayer.

Listen, for all of us, we cannot forget the legacy of who built the communities and who planned is America. When we fail those, who made the communities and protected them, we are neglecting and ignoring God's commands to "take care of My people." "Feed My Sheep." In praying for America. I pray that many will open their eyes and the truth. From the Veterans to the fieldworker, each professional, the mother and father, and each supporter, we cannot forget. If one does not , we need to seek together and find common ground to rise and continue to restore America and the world. We need to practice those virtues in love that we have discussed in God's love in life that are the essence of living to the fullest toward the well-being of humanity together. Awake, arise; in truth, practicing the virtues and loving God, and your neighbor will guide you to Wisdom.

How can this help you? God's Wisdom, you will be able to find, and know, and live <u>toward the authentic person in God's power He created you for.</u>

Where are you to bring truth?
The Fountain of Life God tells us in the Holy Scriptures:
Fear of Me of God is a Fountain of Life, fear in Hebrew means respect, and

we have respect for the Creator; we seek toward the righteousness of His intentions. Of course, we will always not known God's intention swiftly; otherwise, we would be anxious.   (Some are persecuted for Justice; they are justified in God.)   The fountain of life is to bring God's truth.
Even if you do not know God He has the world in the palm of His hands.

"Whoever acknowledges me before men, I will also acknowledge him before my Father in heaven. ³³ But whoever disowns me before men, I will disown him before my Father in heaven.

Matt. 10:32

Hear, He loves you and wants you to come to His heart; He accommodates you.

Therefore, do not feel you are not interested, or you do not need Him, or you may feel not worthy; whatever it is, He can redeem it and make you understand grace and heal you to that person you were created for. Pray now and ask Him to guide you, whether you are a believer or not.

NOTHING IS TO DIFFICULT FOR THE LORD.

You are saying about this city, 'By the sword, famine, and plague it will be handed over to the king of Babylon; but this is what the LORD, the God of Israel, says: ³⁷ I will surely gather them from all the lands where I banish them in my furious anger and great wrath; I will bring them back to this place and let them live in safety. ³⁸ They will be my people, and I will be their God. ³⁹ I will give them singleness of heart and action so that they will always fear me for their own good and the good of their children after them. ⁴⁰ I will make an everlasting covenant with them: I will never stop doing good to them, and I will inspire them to fear me, so that they will never turn away from me. ⁴¹ I will rejoice in doing them good and will assuredly plant them in this land with all my heart and soul.

Jer. 32:36

Many are frustrated, or search for life in other things, or forget, or do not realize; first, go to the source of where that authentic stream of consciousness is of where the foundation of life was created from, and it will be most beautiful. It will be more like His image, and then we have more of a chance to be into unity even in our diversity. God is merciful and grace that is generous to understand us and forgive us; He knows our life trials.

God Giver of Great Wisdom

Awake, arise, look, listen, hear, ask, know, and knock and push open that door.

At least, if there is a Creator, He gave this quintessential earth and universe to us. And since He has given us to have dominion over and take care of His creation, He will provide us with the Wisdom that is of God to take care of His nature.

He is the Giver of the Great Wisdom of the God of Abraham.

These intentions of respect toward God in the Trinity will have your gift given to you pouring freely of a Tree of branches of life and the where the wind of the Holy Spirit will sing of peace, justice, and joy and the song of love of Wisdom of the Giver. The Great Wisdom from the hands of God in His right arm of His strength and His Sacred Heart will pour upon your branches of life.

Wisdom --→ Love-→ Life and Happiness

God's Heavenly Love

God is the Giver of the "Heavenly of Love" over you and watches over you with His eyes, and He will teach you the things you should know. God's "Love," over you in the Holy Spirit, in, and through, and with you, to give you that Wisdom that He deeply with His Sacred Heart of love wants you to accept so that you can be part of the redemption to bring all of humanity back to His heart. you are in His image, and you are His vessel when you receive the Giver of the Great Wisdom of the Trinity in the power of His Salvation.

, we bring up the word salvation. Most things that need restoration need a savior to bring salvation. In most peoples, work, and the life they are restoring and giving and bringing love, salvation life to God's creation toward God's intended righteousness.

The God of Abraham in the Muslim, Judaism, and Christianity is a God of Redemption and His people. And I know the other religious beliefs also respect the truth of life and Justice and compassion when they and experience it.

However, the world's darkness can deceive; hence, we need to ask to reflect God's light and show and have miracles to take care of humanity and its injustices so those others will turn to the truth.

ὀδόω, f. ώσω: aor. 1 ὤδωσα: (ὀδός):—*to lead by the right way*, Aesch.; c. inf., τὸν φρονεῖν βροτοὺς ὀδώσαντα *who put* mortals *on the way* to **wisdom**, Id.: of things, *to direct, ordain,* Eur.:—Pass. *to be on the right way, be conducted,* Hdt.[ccxxi]

Our fearlessness towards him consists in this, that if we ask anything in accordance with his will he hears us. *15 And if we know that he listens to whatever we ask him, we know that we already possess whatever we have asked of him.*

1 John 5:14

Therefore, you are that Giver of the Great Wisdom of God when you are righteousness in the Trinity. Even if you do not God remains the sovereign God and has the universe in the palm of His hands. Yes, we can restore America and the World in the Giver of the Great Wisdom of God in the hearts of the people of Jesus Christ's Sacred Heart.

The sovereignty of God is illustrated by this root's only two occurrences. As Creator and Provider, he causes the wind to blow (Ps 147:18), and the expiration of his **breath** can consume grass and flowers, but just as easily, people (Isa 40:7).

Blowing (**breath**, wind) *Yahweh God shaped man from the soil of the ground and blew the breath*נְשָׁמַת *of life into his nostrils, and man became a living being. Genesis 2:7*

Sacred Heart Divine Message

Whoever s that Jesus is the Christ is a child of God, and whoever loves the father loves the son. ² *In this way we know that we love God's children when we love God and keep his commandments.* ³ *This is what the love of God is: keeping his commandments. Nor are his commandments burdensome,* ⁴ *because every child of God overcomes the world. And this is the victory that has overcome the world— our faith.*

1John 5:1

Warrior of His Kingdom is by a supernatural force in the Holy Spirit of Peace and Justice living in the r's heart, soul, and life. Yes, God is a Warrior of His Kingdom by free-will of the force of the Omnipotent Spirit of His might in that He gave His life on the cross so that we can be saved and have Salvation in His love; and then giving His Sacred Heart, we receive, and our heart is in His Sacred Heart. Jesus Christ's Sacred Heart is Sacred, the only perfect and pure Spirit of all humanity to redeem sin. Including Jesus Christ, a Warrior to overcome satan through the Cross, of Christ, the Virgin Queen Mary, and the Arch Angels and God's Angels can defeat satan also in the mystery of God's glory to overcome evil.

If Pharaoh says to you, "Display some marvel," you must say to Aaron, "Take your staff and throw it down in front of Pharaoh, and let it turn into a serpent!"' ¹⁰ *Moses and Aaron went to Pharaoh and did as Yahweh had ordered. Aaron threw down his staff in front of Pharaoh and his officials, and it turned into a serpent.* ¹¹ *Then*

Pharaoh, in his turn, called for the sages and sorcerers, and by their spells, the magicians of Egypt did the same. ¹² Each threw his staff down, and these turned into serpents. But Aaron's staff swallowed up theirs.

Ex. 7:9 '

Who can overcome the world but the one who is that Jesus is the Son of God?

John 5:5

He it is who came by water and blood, Jesus Christ, not with water alone but with water and blood, and it is the Spirit that bears witness, for the Spirit is Truth.

1John 5:6

Divine Message December 6th, 2019 Pasadena

I was taken in the Spirit of God to the heavenly in prayer. I rested and slept in prayer.

... I was in a realm of the heavens .. taken to a place of great light and peace yet majesty I felt life and peace and miracle greatly, perhaps more than I ever have.

Then I saw a cross it was bright platinum rays of light pure coming from it was close to me.

"I ask what this bright cross of light signifying is. The Spirit of God said, " I have given My life so others can have life abundant." I have given My life on the cross to redeem sins as the Sacrificial Lamb.

I was resurrected after My crucifixion. I have redeemed the sins of the world; and when those who come to Me and ask for forgiveness and seek to do righteousness even when there are mistakes, I have Grace that has been given to Me by the Father, and I give it to humanity who calls upon Me and humbles themselves and asking for forgiveness for their sins; then I bring the sin up. It is resurrected.. the sin disappears and is erased by The blood that I shed on the cross for humanity's sin; then the cross in heaven is the victory the Light of the Greatest love to give your life for a friend." Your word is a lamp for my feet, a light on my path.

Psa. 119:105

Jesus Christ also is the Son of God only in Him is the overcoming sin, humanity, culture, and evil. , we are not slaves; we are His friends in Christ when we accept Him as our Lord. Even though we are a servant for Him and His humanity, we are not slaves; we are His friend.

> *I shall no longer call you servants because a servant does not know the master's business; I call you friends because I have made known to you everything I have learnt from my Father. You did not choose me, no, I chose you; and I commissioned you to go out and to bear fruit, fruit that will last; so that the Father will give you anything you ask him in my name. My command to you is to love one another.*

John 15:12-17

The lighted Cross in Heaven is the victory over sin, and when we turn away from sin, our life is even more significant in God. The more we come to Christ Jesus in the Trinity, the more we pass through crosses of life redeemed by God. I do not know why I was extraordinarily upset this man.. walking on the street did something. I spurted out something I do not want to say .. I have responded incorrectly .. Because I know what he was trying to do. Putting this all together. I think down deep in my soul.. I have never forgiven what the leaders and people in power have done to America in the past... We need to keep on keeping America great. **I have forgiven now.**

Under President Trump, he has sought with the team to keep America great and work for her safety, development on all sides to planning to do on the infrastructure to business to education to the right to life.. and endless work of liberty to restore America. I have had much spiritual warfair. God in the Trinity has protected me. Though I cannot say many things. I was told to keep it quiet. Love in the Trinity and Mary. America and the World.

Bishop Barron states:

"On the [August 22] Feast Day of the Queenship of Mary; Mary the Queen is associated with Christ the King. And in the Israelite tradition, Christ and his queen mother are warrior figures. They do battle with the enemies of Israel. And so now Christ and Mary, his Queen Mother, are warriors in the great spiritual struggle."

The concept of spiritual warfare points to the fact that though we cannot it, life on earth is a battle against Satan's work and his demons, even as we count on the victory of Divine Grace and the aid of angels and saints.

"Does anyone doubt that the demonic power has been at work in this terrible time? I think you'd be naïve in the extreme to deny it,"

Bishop Barron

"What's our job?" he asked. "Get in the army. Get in the army of Christ and Mary the Queen Mother, and fight with them for the purification of our Church: through prayer and penance, through abstinence and fasting, through raising of one's voice and calling of the bishops—whatever means you want to use, cooperate with Christ the King in His cleansing and purifying work. That's the spiritual call of our time."[ccxxii]

His people are Warriors of His Kingdom by force in power of His love, in Peace, Justice, restoration, and forward building in love in the heart that we have in the Sacred Heart of Christ. Listen, because God's heart is Sacred, it is pure; therefore, it brings Peace and Justice and Restoration and love.

Wisdom

"I came forth from the mouth of the Highest and covered the earth like a mist. I dwelt on high, and my throne was in a pillar of cloud. I made a circuit of heaven and walked in the depth of abysses. I ruled over the waves of the sea, the whole earth, and every people and nation."

Ecclesiastes (24.3-7).

May 10, 2018, Huntington Library
Divine Message

1. At creation, there is the Wisdom of each process that is needed for the fullness of each authentic entity, and there is Wisdom for every entity of existence that is intended to be directed and lived by that was when each entity was created at creation.

2. Wisdom of the Creator has a sovereign most beautiful His intention; when Wisdom is not followed for each entity of creation of life, it will actually cause stagnation, even deformity, and even death; however, other objects and spiritual gifts are given by God and upholds these entities so that they can be sustained. However, this stronger human that confirms that there are weak entities in human life that are not following the Wisdom of God's creation needs always to keep growing, maintaining, and growing and evolving toward God's Wisdom; otherwise, they cannot sustain the weaker. If the stronger of God's Wisdom has worldly boundaries and seeks righteousness, God will redeem, and the stronger will learn in a different way than the world cannot .

3. It is not by force or integrating into the space of the stronger one of a specific gift. It is only free-flowing what is received naturally by the heart of God's Sacred Heart. If it is received in force, the receiving will not be of God, and it will be non-pure and not create the life of God's intended purpose. Aware and be faithful, the "witchcraft, Masonry, and Church Masonry (organizational abuse)" and the power of darkness of the world cannot overcome God's stronger warrior. (We can do all things through God who strengthens us 4:13) Ensure we have to speak about it and make it aware that it is evil in the world. I have

experienced these types of peoples against me, and I have overcome them in God's strength. I am a messenger and a warrior in the Holy Spirit.

4. I take the whole armor of God, withstanding the evil day and having done all to stand. And I gird my legs with truth, and having the breastplate of righteousness, and upon my feet with the gospel of peace and I have the shield of faith that I quench the flaming darts of the evil. And the helmet of salvation and the sword of the Spirit, that is the Word of God. Praying at all times in the spirit, alert, perseverance, and making supplication for of God's Saints, boldly proclaiming the mystery of the gospel an Ambassador in of His love; that I will declare boldly as I ought to speak. (Ephesians 6: 13-20)

5. We cannot have organizational abuse. This is evil, and God will not tolerate it. Sometimes, the stronger one suffers much, and even God has to accommodate His plan because of the people's stubbornness.

6. It is not to abuse the body; it is to bring the Spirit of God in gentleness and love and power. We each are individual bodies. No one should abuse the body. Remember, there are different aspects; some are stronger in one part of life than the other. If there is injustice upon the stronger in the Wisdom of God, there shall be a warning first, then if there is not Justice brought, God shall strike back; because this is logical not just because the Stronger in God's Wisdom is born to bear His pure intentions and if the people do not listen, God, Himself can only and will only accommodate for a certain amount of time. Remember, the law of nature is God's intentions will only, and His timing is sovereign.

7. Evil cannot be hidden; it needs to be exposed. (Even evil is not considered evil sometimes because sin is here to kill, steal, and destroy. Also, it is a deceiver. God is in control. He just has given us a little honor and merit to help Him. Because He wants to help us and save us from

all evil and sin.) When corruption is exposed, detected, and revealed, it restores truth; When one knows there are evil or even injustices, there needs to be proclamation. Always, there will be retaliation. Hence, pray and remember the deadly vengeance will soon pass. Think of it as precipitate that soon will dissolve. (Sometimes, those who had evil against them also have to be forgiven because they were causing problems in society; yet, someone had to expose the corruption. You that verse, Jesus Christ, carried the sin for us. In some ways, that is what happened to America. **We were sinned against and had to carry the burden, and now the evil is exposed. Many Americans and the world now , are Awakened and have Arisen to the Truth. Yet, no one is perfect if you have not sinned, then cast that stone. Mercifully, this is God has told us to forgive each other continually; we all imperfect people. Yet, someone needs to speak up for God's truth in justice and love.)**

8. (I proclaim this; because, at this very moment, my faith needs to be higher than ever. Though Lord will protect from my enemies, making them my friends. I need to get this message to the people as soon as God commanded for the American Legacy. In Christ, He told me to work now for the people of His humanity. I have worked for years and have prayed and assessed and inter-acted and worked and interceded in prayer and actions of philanthropic works and have made solutions to help America. I am not boasting I am just saying I love God, and I love humanity. There is an urgent call that we all worked together in our differences.)

9. (I have proclaimed to expose evil and to bring Justice. Sometimes others will not realize and understand the one who seeks to expose evil and bring Justice. Sometimes in their actions, others think of them as not of God's Wisdom; to do God's will is the first and most important.)

10. (If in awareness, there is an attitude of the soul and human spirit in God's creation that has the miracle of bringing new life. And evil becomes afraid because evil only exists by using the goodness or another's life or energy for existence; this is why when one exposes corruption... one will know.

    When evil is exposed, it shows corruption (of all sorts); this is not life, and even evil has an ear and can hear and is being redeemed by the Cross of the Crucified Jesus Christ.)

11. " The prophetic moment in the consciousness of evil is the revelation in an infinite measure of the demand that God addresses to man."[ccxxiii]

    "The prophet does not "reflect" on sin; he "prophesies" against it. "But let us indicate first what is said in the utterance that we have called the confession of evil in man by the religious consciousness."[ccxxiv][ccxxv]

12. For us, it is not just 'religious consciousness". We need to have consciousness of the heart to overcome all those aspects of life that are not of God. "Religious consciousness" are the tools that are to be used with the genuine relationship of humanity in the heart. In the fullness of the "religious consciousness," there is the heart that is transformed the most magnificent beauty of love mystically; Love God with all your heart and soul and your neighbor as yourself. This Wisdom is the Wisdom of God that is the greatest love it is beyond the most knowledge of the world; this is the eternal and living truth of what life is and will be manifesting God's Wisdom. Though loving your neighbor, in speaking the truth and seeking in prayerful truth.

13. Divine Prayer: June 19, 2018

14. . God' Highest Wisdom ------------→ God's Highest Wisdom Gives------→

    The High Knowledge ----------→The High Knowledge Gives -------→

Knowledge Gives-----→ Man's Knowledge from God to know in God's Wisdom in Righteousness God's Wisdom Gives + Man's Knowledge that God's Wisdom in Righteousness Gives ---------→ This will Restore America

> *I want you to know how much I am struggling for you and those at Laodicea. For all who have not met me personally. My purpose is that they may be encouraged in heart and united in love so that they may have the full riches of complete understanding, so that they may know the mystery of God, namely, Christ, in whom are hidden all the treasures of wisdom and knowledge.*
>
> Col. 2:1-3

We in love together and can have resolutions in God's Wisdom for America.

We can find the jewels of Wisdom and the
It is evident we need excellent training of God's Wisdom and those things that have made of the purest form of understanding that brings life. We need actual and faith as a child

> *But God chose the world's foolish things to shame the wise; God chose the weak things of the world to shame the strong. ²⁸ He chose the lowly things of this world and the despised things—and the things that are not—to nullify the things that are, ²⁹ so that no one may boast before him. ³⁰ It is because of him that you are in Christ Jesus, who has become for us Wisdom from God—that is, our righteousness, holiness and redemption.*
>
> 1 Corinthians 1:27-31

In God's Wisdom, Aristotle's Categories will respond appropriately to each entity's highest purpose, each movement of life created by God or developed by man in the heart of the Wisdom of God.

If we do not seek the highest purpose, we do not have the fullest

freedom. However, God accommodates to our weaknesses and is tender with us. And He forgives us. Remember, some have to be that servant of long-suffering (Beatitudes Matthew Chapter 5) to bring the sanctifying full sleeve of Christ's to pour over the land to bring freedom.

15. Hence, we Americans need TO CONTINUE to take up that Wisdom of God, His intended way to take care of creation.
16. Those who do not, you know there is a particular way best in the entities of each part of your life. You know there are paradigms in the present that are not the best for the people's well-being; you know that these paradigms become obsolete to significant production and freedom of you and your community's well-being. Cannot you in all forms of life that there is Wisdom to follow every entity of life? Though we are searching for this always to do better.
17. And life will question all of us. You know there are God's Pearls of Wisdom of unknown paradigms, not understood, hidden, and perhaps smothered because of all different human reasons. Because humans have many trials and live in and underworldly ideas, it is difficult to reach the Pearls of God's Wisdom. Although, we know that there are miracles, and we can **and do** enter in God's heart, the Pearls of Wisdom of God.
18. Spirit of the Lord has brought to my heart:

    Many have not helped you because of fear of losing their purse, perhaps of self of power, jealousy, [powers and principalities of satan] and all forms of reasons. My child, your life has been trial after trial; I have allowed .. you to be thrown in the lions den.. to grow, My child and have tests. Now know. Do not listen to what men say; just listen to me, My child. Remember, whoever they are, the greatest men of God in the world only listen to Me, Jesus

Christ, in the Trinity, in Mary and the Saints that I bring to you. This is for everyone else child too; now, this is for every one child. The first will be last, and last will be first! You know the child what you have to do. I have told you. I will guide you; remember as I told you the four foundational truths<u>**: Peace, Justice, Restoration, and forward building of love.**</u>

19. We can this in the way of life, from humans to mother nature. Even to synthetic creations, when we do not take care of them properly, injustice, there becomes a loss, and even a transfer, from one land to another, and from one hand to another, against the innocent and righteous. However, it is not God's will. Hence it does not bring God's life.
20. America needs your continued help to restore, return, renovate, regain what was lost, truth, honor, merit, and for God's land America. Help is directing them and giving them the Divine Messages.
21. "Being wise is virtually equated with being righteous."

    However, all Wisdom of God is not of the practical ideas it is to take care of the world in God's way.
22. God did say that restitution will be made for the things that happen to me.. and all the **information** I have given will be recognized and what conspiracy has done upon me .. there will be justice. God needs to make peace when injustices were done, He cries, and His heart weeps for the innocent, and even those who are powerful yet have intentions that all do not always align with God's. God is Merciful.

Salt is a good thing, but if salt has become insipid, how can you make it salty again? Have salt in yourselves and be at peace with one another.

Mark

9:50

Awake, Arise to Truth
Awake, Arise, Awake, Arise, Awake, Arise in Truth
It is time; we have heard God's voice
It is time, call upon God's Wisdom
It is time; the life and healing of America is in your heart
It is time; you know the answers when you let God guide you.

After saying this, He breathed on them and said: Receive the Holy Spirit.

John 20:22

The Spirit of the Lord Tells us this in His Holy Scriptures:
Just as the flower grows to the most vibrant, beautiful colors each year and season when cared for, my friend can continue to grow in the dynamic, glorious life of the most outstanding beauty God created for each American.

Just ask with every essence of your being.
Prayer
"Wisdom 's dwelling in heaven. And God brings Wisdom to us on earth. Know that Wisdom is gifts from heaven."

This is why God tells us to pray because 'Wisdom's dwelling place is in heaven.' Some go to the higher heavens to pray there; there are different heavenly levels and different rooms. Some do not realize when they pray they are in the holy places and rooms, though God blesses them.

The Trinity, Virgin Mary, Arch Angels, and the Saints reach you on earth in prayer. They are with us. Some say it is not biblical to Pray to Mary. I know President J.F Kennedy did. And I know President Trump and the First Lady respect Virgin Queen Mary. There have been, and there are facts, that the Virgin Mary, the Mother of Jesus Christ, answers prayers and has shown her image in the Light of God to earth to the witnesses of the countless witnesses today. We reverence Queen Virgin Mary.

I listen, and hear, and many times when I pray to the Virgin Mary, I feel Jesus is with her. I asked her, and she told me, "yes, Jesus is always with Me, child. We are together in the Sacred Heart."

I know the truth in God! I know the fact that Queen Virgin Mary a living, Holiest, Pure, and Powerful to hear our prayers and guide us. I am just one of the billions who believe in her. And I am only one of the millions with continuous guidance, in Queen Virgin Mother Mary. Virgin Mary speaks to each one of us differently. When we listen, even if we do not know all the plan thoroughly or answers, the quintessential Mother of the highest Wisdom after Christ, and the Trinity redeems and guides us. Ask as if you ask your mother; seek her love.

It is essential to love and do the Sacraments, and the Holy Scriptures should always be loved garments upon your entire being. Yes, please, listen, these garments are different holy colors, of a pure substance, depending on God's purpose in your life. Remember, Wisdom is infinite. Therefore, the holy, Sacred garment you wear of Wisdom is infinite of God's purpose and in the infinite is known tools that your authentic being in the **θῡμός**, ὁ, (θύω B) *the soul:*

I. like Lat. *anima, the soul,* **breath**[ccxxvi]*, life* breath of God in you will direct you.

"She (Wisdom) came down to earth to live among the sons of men, but found nowhere to stay, so she returned to heaven and took her seat among the angel (1 En 42: 2; cf Bar 3.29, 38).

This is why we need to pray to reach the Sacred God's rooms to hear and receive His Wisdom.

Yes, Wisdom does come down from heaven.

For us, as rs, I need to state: Wisdom is through Jesus Christ through the Eucharist promised, Messiah, and gives us the covenant and having that experience Jesus is through, with, and in us; as when we see and live in a righteous relationship with Him

"Born again," America, we need that new birth, that "Born Again," purpose of restoring and **bringing** God's Wisdom to her and our American Legacy.

God has sent the Advocated the Holy Spirit RECEIVE the Salvation of Jesus Christ. **The Holy Spirit is the Wisdom of God.**
SEVEN GIFTS OF THE HOLY SPIRIT
The **seven gifts of the Holy Spirit are Wisdom, understanding, counsel, fortitude, knowledge, piety, and fear of the Lord.**

The Holy Spirit is part of the Trinity. In this book, we will only touch upon the Holy Spirit. In another writing, we will speak on the Holy Spirit

May 11, 2018, Huntington Library, Pasadena
Divine Message
1. When you put your clothes on, your Clothes America knows that they are the Robe of Righteousness.
2. Your Heart America: is the heart of God, the Sacred Heart.
3. Your Wisdom America: you are the Mother of Wisdom of all nations under God.

"She, [Wisdom] is the mother of all things (*Qu in Gen* IV, 98)[ccxxvii]
Ἀθήνη, ἡ, *Atheneé,* goddess of **Wisdom**, warlike prowess, and skill in the arts, often called Παλλὰς Ἀθήνη, also Ἀθηναίη.[ccxxviii]

θῡμό-σοφος, ov, *wise from one's own soul,* i.e. *naturally clever, a man(woman) of genius,* Ar., Plut[ccxxix].

Not from self but God are we really 'clever, and genius.'

The Wisdom is skilled in "skill in the arts," this is an skilled in the arts.
This is the warrior we are in the Trinity of Peace, Justice, Restoration, and Forward Building in Love. The gifts of God's Wisdom in us is the "skill in the arts," that is your gift. Arts are any gift God gives you.
It is not by might but by the Spirit of God, we conquer the quest; we are given and sustained.

"Thou shalt recognize the totality of the power indwelling thee, producing from the emotion of love a disposition which determines the total direction of thy life, and placing thy whole personality, לְבָב, heart (H4213 / H4222) and נֶפֶשׁ, **breath**, life, desire (H5883) in the service of the relationship to Yahweh, i.e., a thoroughly personal relationship (אֱלֹהֶיךָ)."[ccxxx]

Breath, of life, Wisdom, and Love, all are related to God and His people and humanity. The guarding of eternal light, fresh beauty of the table clothe on the Eucharistic Table. You, the fragrance of the Holy Spirit, sends love most blissful ecstasy for all the people. There is a mixture of God's love in the Trinity, the His Wisdom, His love, His Justice, His Reconciliation, His Life, His Redemption, His New Creation for the repentant, and it is mixed with cell makeup of individual of the person and even the land and the living to bring a greater Light of redemption, of God. Hence, when the people are in repentant beauty of humbleness to seek God's Wisdom, Love, Justice, Redemption, their heart, and entire being is and becomes that Light of God more beautiful in the Holy Spirit. Then all that one faces in life becomes toward the Creator's more perfect intention of Truth and Wisdom and Love and Justice.

ὤψ, ἡ, (ὄψομαι, fut. of ὁράω) *the eye, face, countenance,* Hom., Hes.; εἰς ὦπα ἰδέσθαι τινί to look one in *the face,* Il.; and absol., εἰς ὦπα ἰδέσθαι Od.; but, θεῆς εἰς πα ἔοικεν in *front,* Il.[ccxxxi] In front is Queen Mary the Mother of God. She guides Americans that ask her toward God's truth.seekthe face of God in front of Him, then our countenance will be the face of God's Wisdom.

Oh, the depth of the riches of the wisdom and knowledge of God! How unsearchable his judgments, and his paths beyond tracing out!
Rom 11:33

Know one understands God's paths and why He even allows the way the world has been directed. Though we know that God gives free will to humans. God also accommodates His creation. God also gives greater and more gifts to those who carry through and believe in action to do His glory not of the world yet for humanity in the world for God's intentions.

Ὦ **βάθος** πλούτου καὶ σοφίας καὶ γνώσεως θεοῦ

Oh, the **depth** both of the riches and **wisdom** and knowledge of God![87]

"Who has known the mind of the Lord? Or who has been His counselor?" For from Him and through Him and to Him are all things. To Him, be the glory forever! Amen.

Rom. 11:33-36

WE CANNOT DO ANYTHING WITHOUT THE LORD.

23.187 πνοή[b], **ῆς** *f*: the process of **breathing** — 'breath, capacity to breathe.' αὐτὸς διδοὺς πᾶσι ζωὴν καὶ πνοήν 'it is he himself who gives life and **breath** to all people' Ac 17:25. Rather than rendering Ac 17:25 as 'gives life and **breath** to all people,' it may be better to say 'causes all people to live and breathe.' However, in some languages, 'to breathe' is synonymous with 'life,' and therefore, to say 'to live and to breathe' is to be both redundant and repetitious. One may consequently translate 'who causes all people to live.'

Nor is he in need of anything, that he should be served by human hands; on the contrary, it is he who gives everything—including life and breath—to everyone[ccxxxii]

Acts 17:25.

However, God does give us hands to do His purpose; we are honored and merited to use our hands to do His bring His love and life and breath.

May the God of our Lord Jesus Christ, the Father of glory, give you a spirit of wisdom and perception of what is revealed, to bring you to full knowledge of Him.

Eph. 1:17

πνεῦμα **σοφίας** καὶ **ἀποκαλύψεως** spiritual **Wisdom** and **revelation**
When experience God, we have the Wisdom of God. spiritual **Wisdom** and **revelation**
, the Spirit of the Lord, gave us a Divine Command.
Divine Message God I prayed wholeheartedly, Jesus Christ told me .. "you know Me."
He was saying, what He is commanding and messaging in the Divine Prayers are to Know God and to know what He wants.

<u>**Mentioning happiness is a gift that Wisdom delivers; love and love are truth and truth is justice and justice is life.**</u>

You know Aristotle says that happiness is the end in all that is good and all that should be.

The face of your gift is the truth of God's Wisdom. We, the warriors of God to bring His Wisdom, "vigilant, observant," to cherish the blessings of God, that has been given the beauty of life and to restore America. However, always being cautious to God's truth.

B Socio-Religious (11.12–11.54)
11.12 λαός[b], **οῦ** *m:* a collective for people who belong to God (whether Jews or Christians) — 'people of God.' ἔσται δὲ πᾶσα ψυχὴ ἥτις ἐὰν μὴ ἀκούσῃ τοῦ προφήτου ἐκείνου ἐξολεθρευθήσεται ἐκ τοῦ λαοῦ 'anyone who does not listen to what that prophet says will be separated from God's people and destroyed' Ac 3:23.[ccxxxiii]

People of God Reverence or Worship God

11.9 σύσσωμος, ον: a person who is a member of a group, with emphasis upon his coordinate relation to other members of the group — 'co-member.' τὰ ἔθνη ... σύσσωμα καὶ συμμέτοχα τῆς ἐπαγγελίας 'the Gentiles ... are co-members (with the Jews) and share along with them in the promise' Eph 3:6.[ccxxxiv]

The concept of 'being a co-member' may be expressed in some languages as 'a person who is counted along with others,' so that in Eph 3:6 one may translate 'the Gentiles are counted along with the Jews in sharing in the promise' or even 'the Gentiles along with the Jews share in the promise.'

The phrase 'people of God' may be rendered in some languages as 'the people who belong to God' or 'the people whom God possesses,' but in a number of languages the relationship between the people and God must be expressed in terms of **reverence or worship, for** example, **'the people who worship God' or 'the people who reverence God.' also 11.27.**

The biblical narrative maps out divine action in history; biblical law maps out God's will for human behavior; biblical prophecy maps out God's covenant people; biblical **wisdom** maps out how persons are to fit into God's created order, etc.[ccxxxv]

President Reagan states, "there is nothing to difficult that we cannot solve.".

Wise ἵστωρ or ἵστωρ, ορος, ὁ, ἡ, (οἶδα) *a **wise** man, one who knows right, a judge,* II.**κᾰκο-ξύνετος**, ον, ***wise*** *for evil,* Thuc.[ccxxxvi] I chose this text for those who are not rs or skeptics to God and the wise of good, and wise of evil.
There is wise **ἵστωρ** for a man who knows right, a judge
There is also a wise for evil **κᾰκο-ξύνετος**.

It is wise of who knows right and it is wise that is for evil. This source is an older source from, "Thucydides," historian from 411 BC; this is proving it is good and evil, and there is a particular God who chooses the good, judge the one knows right. Therefore, let us recognize that we who chose well are of God, and those who chose evil are from the serpent. However, we need to bring peace, and in so doing, those who are evil will and awake and arise to God's truth in Love of His Wisdom.

If we choose toward peace in truth and wisdom, we can then reflect the wise, God's good in us to the wise of evil.

, please, this is an ancient text that evil does exist:
There is also evil as n, and we need to vigilant and guardians to protect the Wisdom of God.
  II. of things, κέδν' εἰδυῖς **knowing her duties**, Od.; κ. φροντίς, βουλεύματα sage, **wise**, Aesch**.; of news, good, joyful,** Id.^{ccxxxvii}
  II. as Adj. **knowing**, Hes.; ἵστωρ τινός knowing a thing, Soph.^{ccxxxviii}

  II. of persons, vigilant, observant, Xen.; φ. ἐγκλημάτων **cherishing the recollection of** them, Arist.
  2. (from Med.) cautious, Id.

φύλαξ [ῠ], ᾰκος, ὁ, (φυλάσσω) **a watcher, guard, sentinel**, Lat. excubitor, Hom., Att.; οἱ φ. The garrison, Thuc., Xen., etc.; φύλακες τοῦ σώματος body*guards*, Plat.;—also as fem., κλῇς ἐπὶ γλώσσῃ φ. Soph., Eur., etc.

  II. *a **guardian, keeper, protector**,* Hes., etc.;—c. gen. object, φ. δορός *a protector against* it, the spear, Eur.
I am the guardian, the keeper, the protector that carries Jesus Christ's Cross and Scepter to do His will!

Ask God what your gift of Wisdom is?
 2. *an observer,* τοῦ δόγματος Plat.; τοῦ ἐπιτατομένου Xen.
 3. of things, φύλακες ἐπὶ τοῖς ὠνίοις, of the ἀγορανόμοι, Lys.^{ccxxxix}
We, the American people of God's Wisdom in our hearts and lives, are the **"guardian, keeper, protector against injustices and evil."** Yet, we are and **"watchers," and "diligent," and cherishing** God's Wisdom. To win and

trumpet κέδν' εἰδυῖς **knowing _her duties_**, Od.; κ. φροντίς, βουλεύματα **sage, wise, Aesch.; of news, _good, joyful_** in Victory, for My God.

The first principle of wisdom is the fear of Yahweh, What God's holy ones know—this is understanding

                                                                                   Prov. 9:10.

Fear in Hebrew is respect, and respect is love and faithfulness and trust in God. And I better follow what the Spirit of the Lord states and Queen Virgin Mary. Sometimes, I feel underneath my feet the earthquake of the imbalance of the creation. Sometimes I think of the spiritual fight in the atmosphere of the powers and principalities of satan. I pray for many and first myself.

Though I go to the foot of the cross of Christ and at His heart,; I stay at the power of His right arm and holding me in and through, and with me, I ask Him to guide me. 11.11 ὁ ἔσω[a]: (a figurative extension of the meaning of ἔσω 'inside,' 83.13) a person belonging to a so-called 'in-group' (in other words, not being a member of the out-group in question) — 'insider.' τί γάρ μοι τοὺς ἔξω κρίνειν; οὐχὶ τοὺς ἔσω ὑμεῖς κρίνετε; 'why should I judge outsiders? should you not judge the insiders?' 1Cor 5:12. also 11.10.

We all are God's people. I am not judging; I am the first to speak of I need toseekGod's redemption, love, justice, truth, and Wisdom. Even though I m to be an "insider, with the Church of Jesus," I am not. I am an insider with the Trinity and Queen Virgin Mary and the Arch Angels, Michael, Gabriel, and Raphael, and even Queen Mary's Angels and St. Peter's Angels.
[17] But anyone who attaches himself to the Lord is one spirit with him.

the powerful, and those who have position have used my Divine Messages, Commands, and work for their purpose. It is for America and the world, yet they could of and should have quoted me or paid for my services. It is like the Olympic runner that prepares for years and gives up everything to prepare and then runs the race and wins the first prize yet does not receive the recognition.

Divine Message October 10, 2020

Those who take ideas from innovators and first substance ideas without recognizing and paying for their services. Will also have others take from their information.

When you fear the Lord God, you then receive joy and even consolation by His spoken words. I remember He has complimented me. "You did the good child. a you will receive...... " When I followed through on the information I was given. , the Spirit of the Lord knew I need to be identified. I keep on forgiving and rising higher to the purpose. Yet, God will only allow so much mercy to those he will enable to have the First Substances of ideas. I have been working for years to help America. You can look at my writings. I am thankful. The Spirit of the Lord has got me on another path soon. I am thankful. He loves me that much He wants to fulfill good work in me.

All things will work together for good.

I am concerned for these people. Because many Divine Messages, the Spirit of the Lord and Virgin Mary told me is coming are true.

Firstly, " to bestow a favor on," "oblige," secondly, "to be thankful," *return thanks,"* and thirdly **"to pray."** The noun contains the meaning of "thanksgiving primarily." In the Septuagint, the term is found only in rare instances and only in the Apocrypha (Eucharistic Sacrifice), not in a translation in Hebrew.[ccxl] Thanksgiving of God gave His only begotten Son that we may have life. First, we are favor and chosen and accept Jesus Christ as our Lord and Savior. Second, we are thankful that Jesus Christ is the Eucharistic Sacrifice, and He loved us first, and we return Him thanks in loving Him first, with all our life and being and soul and spirit and worshipping Him and His purpose. Thirdly, we pray, and in prayer, we are transformed and build a supernatural relationship with Him.[ccxli]

The soul is not a portion of God but is created by God's goodness and is the proper Divine Love object. In Philo (giving thanks is), "the public act of making known the virtues and deeds of another" to "an expression of an interior sentiment and only consequently a verb of praise."[ccxlii]
[Mother of all things can bring guidance and direction.]
With a part., οὐκ ἐλλείπει **εὐχαριστῶν** *he fails* **not to give thanks,** ap. Dem.[ccxliii]

"In Heres 15 (on Ex. 14.14 f), Philo summarizes the reason someone addresses God; it is "about the request for the aversion of evil or about the thanksgiving for imparted blessings." In this, the two categories of communication with God are summarized: the plea for help and the thanksgiving for received help. Here, the thanksgiving is a verbal ac in Heres 31 (on Gen 15.1), Abraham's question is n as the expression of "οὐκ ἐλλείπει εὐχαριστῶν *he fails* not to give thanks, because the question, for Philo, is what man can expect which has not been given already.[ccxliv]

"In Plant. 130 Philo describes God's work as Creator, to which the appropriate reaction of creation is "to give thanks εὐχαριστῶν, for they have nothing else to give (13). The " thanksgiving" for they have nothing else to give (130). The "thanksgiving" (to should never cease to be offered by voice and in writing prose and poetry. Philo then emphasizes the value of harmony in praise of the Creator (131). **_The attitude of comprehensive thanks and appreciation Philo expresses in Qu. Gen. IV 130 (on Gen. 24. 52f) with the statement: "it is necessary to begin every pure action with the thanksgiving and honor of God."_**[ccxlv]

God's Divine Guidance to His people: Only God has the eyes to watch all things. Hence, God wants you to protect yourself in relationship to His eyes, not men's; though be respectful and utmost, and in His eyes, you will know the truth and the solutions in your responsibilities; Endless occasions, you are that Cross for others, that He is calling on. And you will mingle be to the world, blind and even deaf; however, that sweet peace will penetrate deep in your soul. Because, you will feel, and know, and , that they have been fed by the eternal love of God, of His Wisdom, from the breast of your heart, in the Sacred Heart of Christ Jesus.

America in your heart in your gifts, and has the authority to heal America. In righteousness, you will have the authority to heal America. When in righteousness, you are of authority is given to ask and receive the solutions. Each in the Wisdom of God and obtains Justice in America has the authority to ask for answers. Sometimes people do not realize they have it; they are just doing God's Wisdom in righteousness. When it becomes evident, there is an extra faithful responsibility, mysterious I cannot speak of.

God's Light of America, your light the light of God will go before you.

You have been the Peace of God.
You are righteous in America when you follow God's Wisdom.
You will know America because the follow of healing will continue
You are righteous America when you bring Truth for Freedom

Only in righteousness can you have the Wisdom.

"Being wise is virtually equated with being righteous. Wise men are a distinct group[that is anyone who asks God], and their significance is summed up at 6.24: " a multitude of wise men(women) is the salvation of the world."

" The goal is the vision of God, a mystical experience which Philo, in notable anticipation of St. Paul, describes as "ing and being n" as "drawing near to God who has drawn the mind to himself. In this vision, the mind is at rest, delighting in joy at the contemplation of God's immutable being in wordless mental prayer that has passed beyond all petitions. "[ccxlvi] Because you have a relationship in Mind, Body, and Soul, and there is "Power in the Name of Jesus."

Keep Making America Great!
May 11, 2018

Divine Messages

1. Just as the blood flows in the body and to each organ and cell to keep it alive and even heal it when needed, one cell is stronger than the other and upholds the weaker cell.
2. The blood flows through and gives life to the body and even helps heal the weak cells when the blood is healthy and pure.
3. My Spirit daughter flows to the body of America when it is righteous. {God does accommodate to man's sin; although he can strike any time..)
4. And in only righteousness may My Spirit flow through America; the Spirit of God of Wisdom flows in the person of America when he or she is righteous.
5. What is righteousness? It is the 4 Foundational truths and virtue.

PEACE, JUSTICE, RESTORE, FORWARD BUILDING

IN LOVE

Turning to God is by free-will, and thus, man is bidden to turn himself to God. But free-will can only be turned to God, when God turns it, according to Jer. 31:18: "Convert me and I shall be converted, for Thou art the Lord, my God"; and Lam. 5:21: "Convert us, O Lord, to Thee, and we shall be converted."[ccxlvii]

We a people of America, converted in God's love July 28, 2018 July 29, 2018 Judeo Christian Ethics

It is not that I am attempting to promote in Divine Matters to change America; The past was changed of America by those leaders that sought to change America to Communistic and Socialistic ideas.

"Every dominion should retain its original form, and indeed, cannot change it without dange of the utter ruin of the whole state."[ccxlviii]

"After the Kings (Politicians or Powerful) acquired sovereign power, the fight was no longer for peace and liberty, but glory (their manmade glory)."[ccxlix]

We need to REDEEM AND CONTINUE TO MAKE AMERICA GREAT.

Americans, we need to be careful of reflecting the "French Revolution introduced permanent and absolute revolution. Its nature is "pure and clear-cut emphasis on the principle of evil. For that reason, it is useless to want to overcome the revolution with political measures. "Revolution is not ended through a constitutional document." Nor is revolution ended through mechanical power. There is "only one power that can end the revolution. That is Christianity."[ccl]

"Two ideologies are struggling together in a fight to the death; modernism wants to build up a world out of the natural man and to build this man out fo nature; and on the other side everyone who kneels in reverence before Christ as the Son of God wants to preserve the Christian heritage for the world, to lead it by virtue of this heritage towards, a still higher development."ccli

There should be a class that the students learn about what righteousness is.

Judeo-Christian ethics is what is toward righteousness when it is followed and acted upon and virtue. (I will write about this in another context). The Bible now should also be in the schools just as another religious study.

Saint Thomas Aquinas, <u>Summa Theologica</u> Brief Discussion

[I–II.109.4] Whether man without grace and by his natural powers can fulfill the commandments of the Law (are Peace, Justice, Restoration, and forward building in life and virtues. The Ten Commandments)?

Only through God's grace are we saved. Only through God's grace can we bring the fullest peace, justice, restoration, and forward building in life and virtues.

There are a miraculous grace and healing in the mystery of God in prayer and beauty and the Eucharistic healing.

"But in the state of corrupted nature, man cannot fulfill all the Divine commandments without healing grace. Secondly, the commandments of the law can be fulfilled, not merely as regards the substance of the act, but also as s the mode of acting, i.e., there being done out of charity. And in this way, neither in the state of perfect nature tolerance nor in the state of corrupt nature can man fulfill the commandments of the law without grace. Hence, Augustine (De Corrupt. et Grat. ii) having stated that "without grace, men can do no good whatever," adds: "Not only do they know by its light what to do but by its help they do love what they know." Beyond this, in both states, they need the help of God's motion in order to fulfil the commandments, as stated above (Articles [2], 3)."cclii

"The preparation of the human will for good is twofold: the first, whereby it is prepared to operate rightly and to enjoy God; and this preparation of the will cannot take place without the habitual gift of grace, which is the principle of meritorious works, as stated above (Article [5]). There is a second way in which the human will may be taken to be prepared for the gift of habitual grace itself. Now so that man prepares himself to receive this gift, it is not necessary to presuppose any further habitual gift in the soul. Otherwise, we should go on to infinity."

"But we must presuppose a gratuitous gift of God, Who moves the soul inwardly or inspires the good wish. For in these two ways, do we need Divine assistance, as stated above (Articles [2], 3). Now that we need the help of God to move us, is manifest. For since every agent acts for an end, every cause must direct is effect to its end, and hence since the order of ends is according to the law of agents or movers, **man must be directed to the last end by the motion of the first mover, and to the proximate end by the motion of any of the subordinate movers; as the spirit of the soldier is bent towards the victory by the motion of the leader of the army—and towards following the standard of a regiment by the motion of the standard-bearer.** *And thus, since God is the First Mover, simply, it is by His motion that everything seeks to be likened to God in its own way. Hence Dionysius says (Div. Nom. iv) that "God turns all to Himself." But He directs righteous men to Himself as to a special end (work of fulfillment in God's completion), which* they k, *and to which they wish to cling, according to Ps.* **72:28**, "ccliii

, God is the "First Mover" that moves men, and that is the Wisdom of God in the hearts of men; some realize, and some do not. "Since God is the First Mover," it is by His motion that everything seeks to be likened to God in its own way.
America realize God is the "First Mover," and everything should be likened to God in its own way. God decides!
He is the "First Mover, with the last end in motion.
We have had grace and continuous grace, and God has accommodated to
Divine Message from Mary and Jesus at Mount Saint Carmel
Tell the Leaders .. this to President Trump

"**Man by himself can make no wise rise from sin without the help of grace**. For since sin is transient as to the act and abiding in its guilt, as stated above (Question [87], Article [6]), to rise from sin is not the same as to cease the act of sin; but to rise from sin means that man has restored to him what he lost by sinning."ccliv

God commanded us to work and live and pray to restore America, whether we were the culprit that caused her torn wounds. We need to mend them NOW WITH URGENCY IN EVERY CORNER OF OUR HEARTS AND HOMES AND COMMUNITIES.

"Now man incurs a triple loss by sinning,. . . Stain, corruption of natural good, and debt of punishment. He incurs a stain since he forfeits the luster of grace through the deformity of sin. Natural good is corrupted, inasmuch as man's nature is disordered by man's will not be subject to God's; and this order being overthrown, the consequence is that the whole nature of sinful man remains disordered."[cclv]

America, we lost by sinning, stain, corruption, and even disorder. The disorder is that in the PAST, AND FORGIVEN; we were losing on financially, morally, safety, and even individual development and loosing what we build, selling America to many other than her legacy and forgetting about who worked blood, sweat, and tears, giving their heart to her, America.
, not putting America first caused a disorder and wounds that need to be restored.
I wrote these ideas and foundations of America's problems before forming this chapter in prayerful union with God.

I use the secondary sources to seek to open the eyes of intellectual leaders who have the power to change things for the Restoration of America. Also, for the people, I write using the secondary sources to show you now with this present leadership under President Trump, he is working to bring America to safety in all ways again in America's vast beauty and production.

We as Americans need to Keep America Great!

"The **Industrial Revolution**, now also known as the First **Industrial Revolution**, was the transition to new manufacturing processes in Europe and the United States, in the period from about 1760 to sometime between 1820 and 1840."[cclvi]

: <u>American system of manufacturing</u>, <u>Interchangeable parts</u>, <u>Economic history of the United States</u>, <u>Technological and industrial history of the United States</u>, and <u>Industrial Revolution in the United States</u> "The late 18th an early 19th centuries when the UK and parts of Western Europe began to industrialize, the US was primarily an agricultural and natural resource producing and processing economy.[167] The building of roads and canals, the introduction of steamboats and the building of railroads were important for handling agricultural and natural resource products in the large and sparsely populated country of the period.[168][169]

Important American technological contributions during the period of the Industrial Revolution were the <u>cotton gin</u> and the development of a system for making <u>interchangeable parts</u>, the latter aided by the development of the <u>milling machine</u> in the US. The development of machine tools and the system of interchangeable parts were the basis for the rise of the US as the world's leading industrial nation in the late 19th century.

<u>Oliver Evans</u> invented an automated flour mill in the mid-1780s that used <u>control mechanisms</u> and conveyors so that no labour was needed from the time grain was loaded into the elevator buckets until flour was discharged into a wagon. This is considered to be the first modern <u>materials handling system</u> an important advance in the progress toward <u>mass production</u>."[33]

A Scientist that is researching for a Cancer cure and other urgencies from California Technology, said, "America is an evolved country, and it brings difficulties." I SAID, "Even though we are an evolved country, we are young and fresh a new birth because we have realized the urgency to restore America and address the issues."

When we apply:
Freedom of human empowerment of safety, jobs, daily needs, and education to sustain and develop, we can continue to bring the new birth, new d, new life, of America.

We call "divine providence" the dispositions by which God guides his creation toward this perfection:

> "By his providence, God protects and governs all things which he has made, "reaching mightily from one end of the earth to the other, and ordering all things well." For "all are open and laid bare to his eyes," even those things which are yet to come into existence through the free action of creatures."[cclvii]

Remember, our production and global manufacturing scorecard was threatened for production in the world.

NOW UNDER President Trump came into the Presidency, he is strategic to work toward Keeping America Great!

That being said, we have to be careful because it is the human nature of other leaders that desire America's gifts will come at us to want to take her. Remember, that statement was written before the Pandemic and China conspiracy to destroy America and even the world.

I have shown and proven to you in the work that the President of the United States, Trump, and the Americans and the Team has taken the right arm of the strength of God to put America first in safety. references on President Trump.

We, Americans, need to continue to bring Peace, Justice, Restoration, and **forward building.**

> "(Men's sin) can be restored (only) by God. Since the luster of grace springs from the shedding of Divine light, this luster cannot be brought back, except God sheds His light anew: hence a habitual gift is necessary, and this is the light of grace. Likewise, the order of nature can only be restored, i.e., man's will can only be subject to God when God draws man's will to Himself, as stated above (Article [6])"[cclviii]

"Thus so that man rises from sin, there is required the help of grace, both as regards a permanent gift, and as s the internal motion of God."[cclix]

The Motion of God is that most infinite light Alpha and Omega. Motion is energy, and the Motion of God is His hand on the life of the universe.

Be on that light of the eternal Motion of God to help redeem America and keep America free.

Hence, this is why we need God's grace to restore the good of justice in the Motion of God's light. As rs, it is the Cross of Christ that redeems us, saves us from our sins, and we have new life because He gave us His life to redeem our sins that we now are forgiven when we realize that we have sinned, and we turn from our sins.

Now, that is loving God, turning from our sins, and asking forgiveness, and realizing that only in God's love of His Wisdom in our hearts, we have grace, and we now can CONTINUE TO HEAL America.

If you do not in God, we as a people can work together in Love. , America is unique! Her land is God's miracle, cannot you, all the people she has given life, America has brought perfect love from hopeless cases.

Some use their violent craft to justify their ideology if they think a person is not agreeable with their thinking. Be careful; those whom you would never expect leaders of Government and Groups and Religious affiliations are jealous or violently indifferent of a humble servant's power to know, to hear, to bring God's truth.
"Government and other leaders who attempt to control minds are accounted tyrannical, and it is considered an abuse of sovereignty and a usurpation of the rights of subjects, to prescribed options should actuate men in their worship of God."[cclx]

The soul is not a portion of God but is created by God's goodness and as such is the proper object of divine love.[cclxi] We, the American people of God's Wisdom in our hearts and lives, are the "guardian, keeper, protector against it, the spear." We are an "observer," and "vigilant," and cherishing God's Wisdom. To win and trumpet κέδν' εἰδυῖς <u>knowing *her duties*,</u> Od.; κ. φροντίς, βουλεύματα sage, wise, Aesch<u>.; *of news, kind, joyful*</u> in Victory, My God.[cclxii]

This is why we need God, "the First Mover," to redeem our America. We need His grace! We need His true intention of how each responsibility we have as Americans; The Holy Spirit, while praying, brought to my mind a city with specific purposes of organization and working that it is intended just as the body does.

The human body has all the internal organs inside and outside it has all the limps the protection of the skin; the skin protects the foundation of the internal organs; in naturally working in the intention of purpose. If the body has aliments or disease, we seek to treat it with the most efficient medical treatment plans, and prayer is the most miraculous. Moreover, the body withholds the *"ruah,"* the breath of the Messianic life within its being; it needs to be that authentic spiritual being that God created. Even if we do not realize our spiritual nature in God is most healthy and to the fullest of life when our physical body can receive the highest Wisdom of God in the person living.

And the environment has been given to the human to have dominion over and use for the fullest living.
"The possessors of sovereign power have rights over everything, and that all rights are dependent on their decree, I did not merely mean temporal rights, but also spiritual rights."[cclxiii]
Ask what you need. Ask in prayer with your entire being; When you give your whole being, the prayers that God answers are not always your expected answer.

Is it the forgiveness from your actions and even trials and forgiveness of others that is the first step to seek that Wisdom of God in your heart?

Because God is sovereign and reigns all things; when one forgives oneself and others, they can receive that authentic fullness of their purpose. Accommodation to all human injustices or sin is also in the house of God's heart for reasons He decides, since He is sovereign.

" I wish; however, first to point out the religion acquires its force as law solely from the decrees of the sovereign. God has no special kingdom among men except in so far as he reigns through temporal rules."[cclxiv].

The body analogy was given to me to tell you; the city has a specific intention that God has given to us that each one of us has a responsibility to live toward and investigate and make it our primary goal of life so that we can correct it, in the power of God's sovereignty.

In some cases, God will answer others quickly. He will wait until it is His timing. Although when asking, go in the highest love, ask first for any forgiveness of yourself of others.

He will work with you while you are working. Sometimes it takes training and sanctification and transformation of the person who is asking, depending on the mission and the person. Listen, since God is the creator of the first intentions of all things, how they work and live and evolve, and you are working with His highest plans toward learning His Wisdom, He will be present even more. Again, the **Aristotle Categories one, the category may be out of line with His policy, keep ongoing. As you know, we need to produce on earth with the world; therefore, it is occasionally too difficult for the people to change to a paradigm that takes faith.**

Sometimes it takes one to step out into an old environment, and because we bring the Church OF GOD WITH US to the people, there have been times the Spirit of the Lord, individual messages, for His workers and servants. These messages have to be listened to. Especially those who need to bring an URGENT MESSAGE TO HELP RESTORE AND KEEP THE FREEDOM OF AMERICA.

"Religion revealed by the prophets might have the force fo law among the Jews it was necessary that every man of them should yield up his natural right, and that all should with one accord, agree that they would only obey such commands as God should reveal to them through the prophets."[cclxv]

And even those are working for the Divine Justice. He will be there for you. I know the Trinity will be right there with you when He plans the strategy and mission in you and delivers it.

Aware, there is timing, that is His. seekwith all your heart and soul regarding the timing, ask, ask, ask, in prayer. God's timing usually offends the world and the community; because you cannot relate to the ordinary, the clock is changed, and the ordinary is not present.

The Divine Command to restore the inner cities has been on my heart and soul:

I have asked and prayed unceasingly.

The inner cities we need to correct. The cities that need help the cities that are in turmoil, and even cities that have specific areas of required Restoration.

The inner cities need to follow after those cities that have accomplished a balance to their businesses and the well-being of their people.

When a town _that "God turns all to Himself." But He directs righteous men to Himself as to an individual (work), which they k, and to which they wish to cling, according to Ps. 72:28_, "

God's Wisdom directs Righteous Men

Righteousness is also part of the promised deliverance of the reign of God. It is often to parallel with justice, signaling that fairness and justice have almost identical meaning."[cclxvi]

And Justice in God is God's Wisdom.

God creates by Wisdom and love

God created the world according to His Wisdom.[141] It is not the product of any necessity whatever, nor of blind fate or chance. We that it proceeds from God's free will; he wanted to make his creatures share in his being, wisdom, and goodness: "For you created all things, and by your will, they existed and were created."[cclxvii]

"Righteousness," of men, "God turns all to Himself." Those "Righteous," men are **"direct to Himself as to a special(work)," and that " "they wish to seek and cling**."
When one has a unique work in God, there is always a battle. This why it is essential to "to seek and cling, to God."
When performing and working toward the "work in Christ," when there is deceit or danger or cause of physical harm upon a person, one should not let his body, mind, or spirit be put in damage, destruction, danger, pain, or injury. They can protect themselves from bodily harm.

<u>**Inner Cities Restoration Mandatory Righteousness**</u>

The Divine Command of teaching Judeo-Christian Ethics is essential for people in the community, "to seek and cling righteousness, "and then they will be **"directed" to Himself as the particular (work)"** will be and the inner cities shall be restored.

Righteousness essence of Judeo Christian Ethics
This writing will not discuss Judeo-Christian ethics; although we know that it is based on the Ten Commandments and the Holy Scriptures and Wisdom writings.

Righteousness the Ten Commandments
The Ten Commandments are the bases of being a Judeo-Christian ethic. The Ten Commandments are the bases of righteousness.

Do not you the buildings they erect so high perfect all the architecture of all the Cathedrals of highest heavenly beauty. St. Peters, in the Vatican.

Pantheon of Rome all that is Sacred to God[cclxviii]
When I entered into the beauty of history and reality of people, here in this history, Italians have been used by the heart of God to lead the Western Civilization for all Sciences and love of God's Gifts upon the heart of the people to flourish and give their gifts to others, this is the Italian light of the of God that cannot be forgotten.

America, We have likened in that way; we are the leader of many gifts from God.
First, we discussed we are the leader of God's Wisdom :
America the Mother of All nations
America, the leader of the Industrial Revolution
America, the leader of the technological secrets, given
America, the leader of the Gifts of God vast and infinite love

When I entered the Patheon it as if I was called to the history of my heritage of Italian descent
I have been warned, "to seek God first IN all that you do child."
Let us help each other America to seek God first
Let us help each other America to hold God's light on the hearts of the people.
Let us help each other America to keep the freedom, keep the peace, keep love, keep the beauty, keep the life

And the Patheon, the columns has the structure that has been a "standard exemplar (paradigm, example)," for classical styles.

The Pantheon's large circular domed cella, with a conventional temple portico front, was unique in Roman architecture. Nevertheless, it became a standard exemplar when classical styles were revived and have been copied many times by later architects.[6]

The name "Pantheon" is from the Ancient Greek, before Christ (pan- / "παν-" saying "all" + theion / "θεῖον"= meaning "of or sacred to a god").[7]

Pantheon All that is Sacred to God
As a people clinging in righteousness, "ALL THAT IS SACRED TO GOD ABRAHAM IN TRINITY we restore America.

The **Pantheon** (UK: /ˈpænθiən/, US: /-ɒn/;[1] Latin: *Pantheum*,[nb 1] from Greek **Πάνθειον** *Pantheion*, "[temple] of all the gods") is a former Roman temple, now a church, in Rome, Italy, on the site of an earlier temple commissioned by Marcus Agrippa during the reign of Augustus (27 BC – 14 AD). It was completed by the emperor Hadrian and probably dedicated about 126 A. In Greek, it also means **"all that is sacred to God."**[cclxix]

In the Pantheon, there is the History and the mystery of the Spirit of God of the beauty of life and love of God and His people.

St. Mary and the Mary and the Martyrs:

Today: The best-preserved of all Ancient Roman buildings, in large part because it has been in continuous use throughout its history and, since the 7th century, the Pantheon has been in use as a church dedicated to "St. Mary and the Martyrs" (Latin: *Sancta Maria ad Martyres*) but informally known as "Santa Maria Rotonda."[5]
https://web.archive.org/web/20150916002619/http://www.vicariatusurbis.org/SantaMariaadMartyres/

First, humble, or superhuman or even excellent, is to bring peace in the Wisdom of God's love.

We! When we are a people toward righteousness, we are "superhuman" or "excellent!" It is not always necessarily physical strength; it is the Wisdom that God directs us and pours upon us when we seek and cling to Him. The first two Commandments are to love the Lord with all your heart and soul and mind, and to love your neighbor as yourself is the "righteousness," of God.

AS DID VICTOR EMMANUEL II UNITED ITALY

In the Pantheon is: The second niche has a 15th-century fresco of the Tuscan school, depicting the *Coronation of the Virgin*. In the **Victor Emmanuel II** (Italian: *Vittorio Emanuele II*; full name: *Vittorio Emanuele Maria Alberto Eugenio Ferdinando Tommaso di Savoia*; 14 March 1820 – 9 January 1878) was King of Sardinia from 1849 until 17 March 1861, when he assumed the title of King of Italy and **became the first king of a united Italy** since the 6th century, a title he held until his death in 1878. The Italians gave him the epithet of ***Father of the Fatherland*** (Italian: *Padre della Patria*).[cclxx]

Wisdom is righteousness. The soul is not a portion of God but is created by God's goodness and is the proper object of divine love.[cclxxi]

Godfrey and Hemsoll maintain that the word Pantheon "need not denote a particular group of gods, or, indeed, even all the gods, since it could well have had other meanings.... Certainly the word pantheus or pantheos, could be applicable to individual deities.... Bearing in mind also that the Greek word θεῖος (theios) need not mean "of a god" but could mean **"superhuman," or even "excellent."** [cclxxii]

WE AS AMERICANS WANT TO BE FATHER'S AND MOTHER'S TO UNITE AMERICA

We the people, are the rightful masters of both Congress and the courts, not to overthrow the Constitution but to overthrow the men who pervert the Constitution.

Abraham Lincoln

It is impossible to govern the world without God. It is the duty of all nations to acknowledge the Providence of Almighty God, to obey his will, to be grateful for his benefits and humbly implore his protection and favor.
George Washington

Father of the Fatherland: AS DID VICTOR EMMANUEL II UNITED ITALY

In the Pantheon is: The second niche has a 15th-century fresco of the Tuscan school, depicting the *Coronation of the Virgin*. In the second chapel is the tomb of
King Victor Emmanuel II

VICTORY AND GOD are WITH US. AMERICA. LET US BE MOTHERS AND FATHERS TO UNITE AMERICA AS DIE VICTOR EMMANUEL UNITED ITALY.
w
Victor Emmanuel II (Italian: *Vittorio Emanuele II*; full name: *Vittorio Emanuele Maria Alberto Eugenio Ferdinando Tommaso di Savoia*; 14 March 1820 – 9 January 1878) was King of Sardinia from 1849 until 17 March 1861, when he assumed the title of King of Italy and **became the first king of a united Italy** since the 6th century, a title he held until his death in 1878. The Italians gave him the epithet of **Father of the Fatherland** (Italian: *Padre della Patria*).
https://en.wikipedia.org/wiki/Pantheoun, Rome

God's Wisdom Given to His People

Let us bring our gifts as the Magi did to the Son of God and also let us accept the Eternal Father in the leadership of Moses

To the sides are paintings (1661) by Francesco Cozza, one of the Virtuosi: ***Adoration of the Shepherds*** **on the left side and** ***Adoration of the Magi*** **on the right.**

The stucco relief on the left, *Dream of St Joseph*, is by Paolo Benaglia, and the one on the right, **Rest during the flight from Egypt, is b**y Carlo Monaldi. On the vault are several 17th-century canvases, from left to right:

Cumean Sibyl by Ludovico Gimignani; **Moses by Francesco Rosa;** *Eternal Father* **by** Giovanni Peruzzini; *David* by Luigi Garzi; and *Eritrean Sibyl* by Giovanni Andrea Carlone.
https://en.wikipedia.org/wiki/Pantheon, Rome

Communities are the heart of the People where that live and bring Gods' Wisdom and life

Grace in the Person and Grace in the City:
There is a center of understanding of a city shall be built.. and He has told us it is in His love ... and Grace. Just as the Lord gives us grace individually, He provides us with the beauty for each city to heal it and for it to receive God's heart the Wisdom of truth.

Grace when .. the... It needs to be redeemed... We need grace. His Grace God grace to restore and heal our America ... in accepting God's Grace is loving Him.. and realizing ..that only through His love can we redeem our mistakes.

We cannot correct our mistakes alone; we need God first to redeem us to change us.
When we recognize that God's love can and redeem America, we realize we need to change, our America will be restored.

The olive tree does not heal itself alone, it needs good soil and the sun and water and Mother nature's love and mystery of her spirit to have sovereign love for her land. God

Enoch and the Chosen
"He will condemn and punish the mighty kings and the exalted, who will fall before him and petition for mercy from him (62.9).

We human disease and death, **AND NOW WE MIRACLE OF NEW LIFE**
We Mother Nature we cannot control **AND NOW WE HEALING AND ANEW FRESH DAY**
We nations falling and (being) destroyed, **AND NOW WE THE PEOPLE , AWAKENED, ARISEN TO TRUTH**

Correcting this book on September 5, 2019, the Dorian Hurricane devastated and destroyed many lives.
God is here to protect us and warn us of His love.

Perhaps, there is war in the spiritual system, the rulers of the darkness of this world, against spiritual wickedness in high places," that Godseeksto protect in a warning.

"For we wrestle not against flesh and blood, but against principalities, against powers, against Ephesian 6:12 KJC

We can be His "Chalice of Love."

You can be an instrument of a "Chalice of Love" vessel to help heal America. We as people are love in America; that is why she is pouring out the

"CHALICE OF LOVE," now to bring:

MAKE OTHERS A COMMUNITY TOWARD PEACE
MAKE OTHERS A LIFE OF TOWARD JUSTICE
MAKE OTHER A TRANSFORMATION OF RESTORATION
MAKE OTHERS A LEGACY OF forwarding BUILDING TOWARD LOVE.

CHALICE OF LOVE OF THE SPIRIT IN GOD'S HEART

Think, answer this question?

We the love and the creation of humans.
We the love and beauty of Mother Nature that gives us all we need when we seek justice, and God's intentions as the Divine nature should be; otherwise, the heart of the Spirit of God cannot allow the disruptions and feed the life with His life. It will not accept it, that is why we have some of these natural disasters in nature, the weather, the people's hearts, and even in the people's life.

A(God intention of all Creation) + B(Human Intentions of life) = A + B

$<a + >b = <a>b$ Hence, we have less of God's intention = LESS LIFE
$>A + < B = >A<B$ Hence, we have more of God's intention = MORE LIFE

America, we love overcoming sin and trials to bring life when we have more of God and less of us.

America, we will CONTINUE to give our hearts to heal America and be a reflection of God's love to the world.

When we injustice, we speak out in love. I would have to say that I have used physical force like those who exercise to release stress. My release was composed and contained in my environment.

To love toward truth, you have to be in forgiveness. Hence, body, mind, and spirit need to be toward well-being.

Protection of God's creation is paramount to sustain that what is pure, that what is innocent, that what is developing, that what has been restored, that what has been peace, that what is being justice.

We, as people, need to protect God's jewels of America, even if it takes us to have rules and regulations of justice to enter into an agreement of being an American. Both parties are protected since the prior agreements used have been abused on both sides.

America is a body of life that needs the RESTORATION of her land.

AMERICA NEEDS HEALING IN THE Hands of God's love with the right arm of His strength.

AMERICA RECEIVE THE medicine of GOD'S TRUTH and the soothing of the powerful yet sweet incense of the Holy Spirit of God to continue to be THE FORCE of the MIRACLE to restore her of the WOUNDS BECAUSE AMERICA HAS GIVEN HER LIFE TO OTHERS and KEEP AMERICA FREE AND BEAUTIFUL

When there is a person that has an exceptional gift in a specific area that is less common, they are accepted, such as the football player, basketball player, or the Olympic swimmer or Olympic runner.

Listen, open your ear today. Some have gifts that seek to hide them that are of the God of Abraham that help heals and restore the communities and souls of the people. They are human yet carry a different purpose that is rare.

When they are exposed, they are thought of as imbalanced. They are not imbalanced they have discernment, that knows what God needs and wants and has been waiting for.

Aware, this all relative to all sciences of understanding and movements of life. When you do not use the purest tools of your mission's authentic purpose, you will get less or nothing. Be aware of the tools you need to conquer solutions and make a life that is contrary to what needs to be corrected. That is why you need to fix it because it is not in the first substance of the being of God's purpose.

It is relative even in an argument; there is a difference in subjective beliefs.

When the tools used to restore the solution are correctly used, they have a period where there is imbalance and even disruption until that what needs to be changed becomes changed by the tools of God's first intention of being of life.

Therefore, some tools may be n to be imbalanced, yet eventually, they will overcome that what needs to be fixed or restored.

God's creation is the same for the human and the same for the families communities, states, and the nation.

When I am saying, heart, it is that gift of you have of you in yourself, have the heart to bring truths of:

PEACE	OF EACH NEED OF INDIVIDUAL'S WELL-BEING
JUSTICE	OF EACH NEED OF INDIVIDUAL'S THAT EMPOWERS A HEALTHY HOMES
RESTORE	OF EACH NEED OF INDIVIDUAL'S SOUL, HEART, MIND, GIFTS OF PERSON, RELATIONSHIPS
FORWARD BUILDING	OF EACH NEED WHETHER PERSON, COMMUNITY, FAMILY,
LOVE	NATURE

"He will be the light of the nations and the hope of those who grieve in their hearts
[I grieve for America and the world] (Isa, 48.4, using Is 42.6;49), and in His name, the holy and righteous will be saved (62.13). After his final judgment, evil will be abolished, and the righteous will live with Enoch in paradise (71.16-17).

Freemasonry should be disbanded in America because our organization has been infiltrated by the Illuminati and they have bad intentions for America and the World.

George Washington

There can be neither Jew nor Greek, there can be neither slave nor freeman, there can be neither male nor female—for you are all one in Christ Jesus. ²⁹ And simply by being Christ's, you are that progeny of Abraham, the heirs named in the promise.

Gal. 3:28

Them that are called, both Jews and Greeks, Christ the power of God, and the Wisdom of God. ²⁵ Because the foolishness of God is wiser than men, and the weakness of God is stronger than men.

1Cor 1:24

"The development of Wisdom was also related to the existence of social subgroups."[cclxxiii]

Wisdom is already a pre-existent figure in the book of Proverbs (8:22f). Where she is a staff of life to all who grasp her (3:18)[cclxxiv]

Wisdom in God, America you are pleasantness, and Peace and a Tree of life, happy that she has in the Temple in her land. Prov. 3:17

Wisdom in God, America, you are a Counselor with sound knowledge. Prov. 8:14
Wisdom, in God, America, you are in understanding and might.
Wisdom in God, America, kings(His people) reign and princes (His people) decree justice.   Prov. 8:15
Wisdom in God, princes rules Prov. 8:16
By me [4]princes rule, And nobles, *even* all the judges of the earth. Prov. 8:17
I love them that love me, And those that seek me [5]diligently shall find me. Prov. 8:18

Riches and honor are with God, America
    Yea, [6]durable wealth and righteousness.
[19]   My fruit is better than gold, yea, than fine gold;
    And my [7]revenue than choice silver.

Prov. 8:20 I walk in the way of righteousness,
    Amid the paths of justice;
[21]   That I may cause those that love Me to inherit substance,
    And that I may fill their treasuries.

Prov. 8:32 Now, therefore, *my* sons, hearken unto ME;
    For blessed are they that keep my ways.

I KNOW I AM ASKING SO MUCH FROM EVERYONE.
I WE CAN ACCEPT AND
"HEAR THE INSTRUCTION, TO LOVE AMERICA!"

Prov. 8:33 Hear instruction, and be wise,
    And refuse it not

Please, America, we need to work in love and truth
Prov. 8:34 Blessed is the man that heareth me, (GOD)
    Watching daily at my gates,
    I was waiting at the posts of my doors.

JESUS, this man this wisdom, and these [17]Mighty Works [5]
<u>**Christ performed miracles with His hand, AND WE ARE IN HIS HANDS, AND WE HAVE THE STRENGTH IN HIS RIGHT ARM: Mark 6:2; MATT: 13:54**</u>

<u>God is asking you to take His hand in His Right Arm of strength.</u>

I envisioned and saw your hand reaching out to me from your heart. Your hand is reaching out in a way that it wants to be held grasped and united in oneness your hand already.. almost carries all it needs. It is waiting to be finished being filled in the dream if you for us to fill you and I united with you on your journey will become my journey and my dream and my journey will belong to your dreams.

Will you bring your hand to me while on your journey finding your dreams my spirit unites with your spirit or are you..that is bonded by weariness fear emptiness of life.. The freedom you run with are you finding your dreams. Do you flight?

Follow the path of God in Holding in the palms of your hands His love and Wisdom of life on earth and in eternal life.

After that I saw that there was a huge number, impossible for anyone to count, of people from every nation, race, tribe and language; they were standing in front of the throne and in front of the Lamb, dressed in white robes and holding palms in their hands. They shouted in a loud voice,

Rev. 7:9

When the Sabbath came, He began to teach in the synagogue; and the many listeners were astonished, saying, "Where did this man get these things, and what is this Wisdom is given to Him, and such miracles as these performed by His hands?

MIGHTY WORKS ARE IN HIS HANDS, AND WE ARE IN HIS HANDS.

Happy are thy men, and content are these thy servants, that stand continually before thee and hear thy wisdom.

America:

"God Its source is in the unconditional election of God, and it requires an unconditional response. As the source of covenantal love and purpose. God remains faithful even when there is unfaithfulness in response."[cclxxv]

America God is calling on you to go to the Sacred place in prayer to hear and receive His Wisdom to Restore America and receive the gifts to keep America's Freedom for America's legacy.

America:

Our hearts will be comforted, they being knit together in love, and unto all riches of the ¹full assurance of understanding, that they may know the mystery of God, ²even Christ, ³ in whom are all the treasures of Wisdom and knowledge hidden. ⁴ This I say, that no one may delude you with persuasiveness of speech. ⁵ . . . I am with you in the spirit, joying and beholding your order, and the steadfastness of your faith in Christ.

Colossians 2:2-4

Chapter Six

Naturalization Oath of Allegiance to the United States of America
Immigration and All Citizens of Americans

Notes of Contemplation and Action

We will briefly discuss the covering of protection that upholds America and her people's justice system of the Naturalization Oath of Allegiance to the United States of America and other pertinent aspects involved.

The prophecy of one who hears the words of God, of one who knows the knowledge of the Most High. He s what Shaddai makes him , receives the divine answer, and his eyes are opened.

Number 24.6

Introduction

America is the Mother of All Nations. The following short chapter on immigration is a brief explanation and ideas regarding America's immigration issue today. These relevant statements delivered here serve you to open your view about the urgencies of immigration issues and spark a catalyst to how we, as great American people, can work together to bring the Four Foundational Truths: Peace, Justice, Healing, Forward Building in Love.

The alien living with you must be treated as one of your native-born. **Love** him as yourself, for you were aliens in Egypt. I am the LORD your God.

Lev. 19:34

True justice must . . . be between white and black Americans and (immigrants and citizens)

Their destiny is . . . (depended on our responsibility to bring God's truth and love) up to us with our destiny

Their freedom is inexplicitly (depended on our responsibility to bring God's truth and love) for our freedom, and we cannot walk alone.

Martin Luther King, Presidential Speeches Ronald Reagan[cclxxvi]

Biblical Immigration

Religion that God our Father accepts as pure and faultness is this; to look after the orphans and the widows in their distress and to keep oneself from being polluted by the world.

James 1:27

These are the Divine Commands

The American People will come first once again. My plan will begin with safety at home - which means = safe neighborhoods, secure borders, and protection from terrorism. There can be no prosperity without law and order.

Donald Trump

Protection is in the hands of the Lord. God has given us the land to be a caretaker of truth. God gave His people law and order so that we would know the truth and covenant of agreement. Prosperity is the Salvation of the Lord in the Trinity. And His love. Of course, His love is to take care of our land, people, and restore all things.

I pray with all my being for America: My people who bear My name humble themselves, and pray and seek My presence and turn from their wicked ways, then I will listen from heaven and forgive their sins and restore their country.

2 Chronicle 7: 14

Also, many know of Our Lady of America of Immaculate Conception. We are protected by her and pray the Rosary.[cclxxvii] Ask in pray, "I consecrate myself and America and to Jesus Christ, my Redeemer, Our Father in Heaven in the Mystery of the Holy Spirit, and Our Lady of America, Mary."

Immigrants

In all lands immigrants enter, there are covenants, laws, and respect for the country and its people.

Let us remember the Indians their motherland are the plains of the United States of America. She America is a Mother of All Nations because she is the heart of God that all those that need to have a place to live in Truth, Justice, and love of God.

The Trinity and Virgin Mary and the Arch Angels watch over us.

Mother Nature sings in the morning holy sunlight of the anew day of another miracle of life given by God Almighty.

The Spirit of God calls in the holy morning sunlight of Jesus Christ in the Trinity the Son of God and Virgin Mary and the Arch Angels

And promises I will give you more life come to my eternal heart of love

Mother Nature sings in the afternoon promise of anew harvest of another miracle of the strength of the people to have dominion over the land the promise of God.

The Spirit of God calls in the afternoon promise of the harvest, what shall now you do with your gifts, I will give to you more joy that passes all understanding.

Mother Nature sings in evening serenity the moonlight of God's covering the Omnipotent Spirit of eternal love protecting America.

The Spirit of God calls in the evening serenity I will give you that quintessential soothing of the sweet Holy Spirit so your life and your family will be happy and fulfilled of all God's good gifts for humanity.

I pray that there is a peace of God that is in the heart and roads of life of veins that flows through each mountain, each ocean, each river, each forest, each field, each harvest, each city, each state, each family, each person, each child, and the air that we breath.

The naturalization of an immigrant becoming a legal citizen in America *entirely renounces and abjures all allegiance and fidelity to any foreign prince, potentate, state, or sovereignty with another country's laws. The citizen now* is dedicated and follows the rules and obedience to America's Constitutional rights. "Citizenship is a unique body that unites people around civic ideals and a belief in the rights freedoms guaranteed by the U.S. Constitution." "Be a person of good moral character." "Be able to speak, read, write, and understand the English Language." [cclxxviii] Demonstrate responsibility to the principles of the Constitution and "well position to the good order and happiness of the United States."

When the immigrant or citizen or government officials do not follow the oath, there is a complete breakage of the oath. The people and the land's heart comes from the oath, that is their life source. It is as if there is an earthquake and it cannot be stopped only by the hand of God.

Americans Keep the Oath of Allegiance to the United States, Arise to Truth

Naturalization Oath of Allegiance to the United States of America

"I hereby declare, on oath, that I absolutely and entirely renounce and abjure all allegiance and fidelity to any foreign prince, potentate, state, or sovereignty, of whom or which I have heretofore been a subject or citizen;

that I will support and defend the Constitution and laws of the United States of America against all enemies, foreign and domestic; that I will bear true faith and allegiance to the same; that I will bear arms on behalf of the United States when required by the law; that I will perform noncombatant service in the Armed Forces of the United States when required by the law; that I will perform work of national importance under civilian direction when required by the law; and that I take this obligation freely, without any mental reservation or purpose of evasion; so help me God. [cclxxix]

"I A DISCIPLES so help me God," the *oath* are codified in Section 337(a) in the oath that incorporates the substance of the following:

1. Support the Constitution;
2. Renounce and abjure absolutely and entirely all allegiance and fidelity to any foreign prince, potentate, state, or sovereignty of whom or which the applicant was before a subject or citizen;
3. Support and defend the Constitution and laws of the United States against all enemies, foreign and domestic;
4. Bear true faith and allegiance to the same; and
5. A. Bear arms on behalf of the United States when required by the law; or
B. Perform noncombatant service in the Armed Forces of the United States when required by the law; or
C. Perform work of national importance under civilian direction when required by the law.[cclxxx]

I.   Oath
1. In an **"oath,"** we have a promise to seek and fulfill. The beautiful aspect is to an oath in commitment; you have a journey and even absolute happiness to conquer a quest to deliver. And both parties must agree.

2. When the **"oath"** is fulfilled even with traitorous and unexpected severe trials, "the quest becomes real and flowing, and happiness succeeds, in the power and wisdom of God."

3. When the **"oath"** and the quest is broken, and there is a death of life and even perhaps lost from the past that was gained, loss of the present, and loss of what would have been. We know God has always redeemed America. Now many have awakened, arisen to the truth to restore America in God's love and truth.

4. When the **"oath"** is not fulfilled or not fulfilled for a short time legitimately, inadvertently or intentionally, there needs to be a reconciliation in peace, not reconciliation in violence. (we will fix and restore the oath, those who are oath keepers, in the Trinity, even if one side breaks it, "He who in me is more powerful than He who is of the world.")

1. Promise OATH TO KEEP THE NATURALIZATION between the Immigrant, the Citizens, and the Country to follow the oath.

There is only one way; there is only one truth; there is only one oath.

'Listen, Israel: Yahweh our God is the one, the only Yahweh.

Deut. 6:4

There is only one Constitution and Laws developing in peace, justice, restoration, and forward building in God's truth and love, that will uphold land and people to live in freedom and safety and happiness.

II. Constitution and Laws

1. In the "**Constitution and Laws,** there is an understanding and a treasure chest of jewels always brilliant to wear upon the oath of the heart of the people and the immigrant and citizens and leaders alike.

2. When these **Constitution and Laws** resilient jewels when used to conspired against or for any other reason of human tragedy, upon the heart of the oath in the immigrants and citizens and leaders, Americans in God are the brave warriors and unstoppable; the Spirit of God works in them to for fight for peace and laws of the land, and there is life, peace, justice, restoration, and forward building of the oath.

3. When these **Constitutional and Laws** resilient jewels are used not for good upon the heart of the oath in the immigrants, and citizens, and leaders, there is the death of life that will be redeemed; and even lost from the past that will have restitution that was gained; and loss of the present, that will arise to God's truth; and loss what would have been will be even more; because, when we give ourselves for God's purpose, He always gives us His love without measure.

4. <u>**L.A.W. and ORDER is the essence of keeping a country safe and living. Just as it is a law in nature to water a tree with water, not tar or thick, filthy oil, we as Americans need LAW AND ORDER TO PROTECT OR NATURALIZATION OATH OF ALLEGIANCE TO EACH OTHER IN THE OATH TO BE LIVING IN PEACE, JUSTICE, RESTORATION, AND FORWARD BUILDING IN LOVE IN GOD.**</u>

<u>*NO PROTESTING IN VIOLENCE! NO PROTESTING IN VIOLENCE! PEACE, PEACE, PEACE, JUSTICE, JUSTICE, JUSTICE, RESTORATION, LOVE RECONCILIATION, REGAIN, FORWARD BUILDING IN LOVE, LOVE, COMPASSION*</u>

2218. ζυγός zugos, *dzoo-gos´*; from the root of ζεύγνυμι zeugnumi (to join, especially by a "yoke"); a coupling, i.e. (figuratively) servitude (a **law** or obligation); also (literally) the beam of the balance (as connecting the scales): — pair of balances, yoke.[cclxxxi]

458. ἀνομία anomia, *an-om-ee´-ah;* from 459; illegality, i.e. violation of **law** or (genitive case) wickedness: — iniquity, x transgress(-ion of) the law, unrighteousness.[cclxxxii]

We will not be unequally yoked ζεύγνυμι **zeugnumi**; our yoke has been broken from the wickeness *ἀνομία anomia,* of the people of the hatred of America's legacy in the violence of violation of the law of righteousness; Our yoke has been broken from and wickedness, ἀνομία **anomia** and even not putting America first in the past. **We are Americans that are with, in, and through God of *nomos*, righteousness to the laws, and *nomoi*** <u>recognize the rules of Laws of Divine Command of God that have Divine Authority in our land and in the entire Cosmos.</u>

The social life of man requires structure and commonly recognized rules of conduct. Within this context, the Gk. Word with the widest range of meaning is *nomos*, which originally denoted a system for distributing property, based upon the collective agreement. Then it acquired the more general sense of a commonly agreed public order, or, in the plur., the laws that regulate life. However, *nomos* or the plur. *nomoi* has a religious basis, being anchored in transcendence and therefore claiming absolute validity, either as authoritative divine commands or as cosmic principles.[cclxxxiii]

The American People will come first once again. My plan will begin with safety at home - which *means safe neighborhoods, secure borders, and protection from terrorism. There can be no prosperity without law and order.*

Donald Trump

Remember, in America, the people's laws and words and life are inherited in humanity's existence in the community and life of the nation; this is the history of our America. We are a history at the beginning of the "Law given to Moses on Mount Sinai."

6.61 πλάξ, πλακός *f:* (Ten Commandments) a flat stone on which inscriptions could be made — 'tablet.' αἱ πλάκες τῆς διαθήκης 'the tablets of the covenant' He 9:4. In the N.T. πλάξ is used to refer to the tablets of the **law** given to Moses on Mount Sinai.[cclxxxiv]

Thought we as a people a people weight and balance, 2218. **ζυγός zugos,** *dzoo-gos´;* from the root of **ζεύγνυμι zeugnumi** (to join, especially by a "yoke"); a coupling, i.e. (figuratively) **servitude (a law or obligation)**; also (literally) the beam of the balance (as connecting the scales): — pair of balances, yoke.[cclxxxv]

Do not be unequally yoked. Break the yoke of injustice. It is our "law of obligation," to be the beam of balance. Serve God of the Trinity.

Pray in the Spirit receive the Heavenly Manna from heaven to earth to earth to heaven.

> *America belongs to (Almighty God Most High) the gold altar of incense, and the ark of the covenant plated all over with gold. In this were (is) kept the gold jar containing the manna, Aaron's branch that grew the buds, and the covenant table.*
>
> Heb. 9:4

America: Arise to Truth the "Constitution and Law," is that covenant that we have with each other, and the Manna is the bread of life it brings when we agree to keep the oath, and our "branch" grows buds of each immigrant and each citizen and receiving that great fragrance of the incense of life, liberty, and justice for all "in God."

For rs, this is the Eucharistic Table of Jesus Christ, the altar on the "ark of the covenant" in heaven as on earth. The incense of the Holy Spirit given to those who in Jesus Christ as our Savior that is the bread of life, "Manna."

God is the vine

> *I am the true vine, and my Father is the vinedresser. We are the branches of America, and the buds are America's righteous growing immigrants and citizens.*
>
> ***John 15:1***

Where ever we go, we are the righteousness of God's Palm Branches, of His Kingdom on earth as it is in heaven, to bring the message and the Light of His love and peace and Salvation to the world.

III. *True Faith and Allegiance*

> *We have to abide in the **"oath,"** in **True Faith and Allegiance** by **Constitution and Laws**, to fulfill our **oath**. We have **"true faith"** is trusting in our nation in the **Constitutional and Laws** and each other to be **allegiance**, respect to the oath, and the **Constitution and laws** in ... in God's Divine Commands and Divine Authority and Divine Conduct.*

"Al·le'giance, *allegiance* may exist under any form of government, and, in a republic, we generally speak of *allegiance* to the government, to the state, etc. In well-conducted monarchies, *loyalty* is a warm-hearted feeling of fidelity and -obedience to the sovereign. In cases where we personify, *loyalty* is more commonly the word used; as **loyalty to the Constitution**; *loyalty* to the cause of virtue; *loyalty* to truth and religion, etc."[cclxxxvi] First, loyalty to God of the Ten Commandments follows, and then loyalty can be given to the individual and the community and the states and the nation.

> When true faith and allegiance work honestly, resilient jewels *are used upon the oath's heart in the immigrants, and citizens, and leaders; there is life, peace, justice, restoration, and forward building of the oath. Each part of the Constitution and the and laws need to have the Four Foundational Truths; that is of why I have repeated them; it is a Divine Command.*
>
> When true faith and allegiance *resilient jewels are not used upon the heart of the oath, God still redeems. We need to Arise to Truth and realize to protect our America in righteousness in the truth and the power of God.*

God's truth is translucent and is for all the people to work in liberty and justice for all. **No trickery or hidden masonry or wicked violation should be accepted. God is watching the powerful, and God will only accept righteousness; otherwise, God may strike; He is Alpha and Omega. Daniel 4.**

There are cities in America that readily accept trickery and masonry; the problem is they are deceivers and the facts are not always to easily proven. Sometimes, it takes over time and experiential life complexities and seeing that the actions are completely incongruent with God. We as a people need

<u>to pray for this. One thing I do know. God wants to redeem these masonite and cultural witchcraft ideologies.</u>

And I blessed the Most Highest, praising and glorifying him who lives forever, for his empire is an everlasting empire, His kingship endures, age after age. And helping those who need.

Daniel 4:31

And now I, Nebuchadnezzar, praise, extol and glorify the King of heaven, all of whose deeds are true, all of whose ways are right, and who can humble those who walk in pride.'

Daniel 4: 34

I am commanded to tell; I am not judging I am just telling you what I have been called to do to proclaim these Divine Messages, Commands, and Warnings. Because my strength comes from the Lord, and anything that I know that is good is from God.

So stand your ground, with truth a belt round your waist, and uprightness a breastplate,

Eph. 6:14

Let us not abuse our American people. Let us not accept the violence or trickery or masonry or power to abuse. Let us now work in peace of a path of flowing beauty of a river of the incense of life in the mystery of the Holy Spirit.
God gives us Spiritual Weapons for protection to receive the sweet incense of God's Wisdom and completion for each mission in our life.

That is why you must take up all God's armor, or you will not be able to put up any resistance on an evil day or stand your ground even though you exert yourselves to the full.

Eph. 6:13

This is also a warning because in the history with God and His people, He does retaliate when we are disobedient to the covenant of truth. God does not want us to allow the darkness and those who have become assimilated to the ways of the world to abuse His people. Abuse can be at any level.

When we seek to reconcile in word, deed, and action, we seek truth and reconciling.

Reconciliation is paramount to heal America and her people. The reconciliation has to be in God's love and truth, not ours.

Bear with one another; forgive each other if one of you has a complaint against another. The Lord has forgiven you; now, you must do the same.

Col. 3:13

We know though that God does not accept evil.

*Lord, Lord, **Almighty** King, everything is subject to your power, and no one can withstand you in your determination to save Israel.* America

Esth. 13:9 [17b]

Truth and allegiance, we protect each other in fact and fidelity. However, in accepting the protector's protection and not returning the truth, to the protector, in the oath, there will eventually be reconciliation and restitution in God's plan because of the Divine Plan, Divine Providence, Divine Law, and God's Divine Truth and the Divine Authority. Protector needs safety and a clear path, though God will do good work in the protector.

We have briefly reviewed all these Divine characteristics of God in this book. Nothing unseen by humans that other humans do is of truth does **not go unseen** from God's eyes.

While you still have the light, in the light so that you <u>may become children of light.</u>

John 12:36

Trust in God.
Today, God brings Jonah, Daniel, and all the prophetic characteristics to different areas to redeem and plant seeds of miracles.

In many languages, it is difficult to speak of 'light' in the t sense of the **truth** that comes from God. Such **truth** is not to be equated with knowledge, but with the principles and practices of right moral behavior. Because of these difficulties in speaking of '**truth**' as 'light,' several translators have preferred to use the expression 'people of God' for the phrases [p. 124] υἱοὶ τοῦ φωτός, υἱοὶ τῆς ἡμέρας, and τέκνα φωτός. In some instances, however, it is possible to employ 'light,' if this is described as 'light that comes from God' or even 'the true light from God.[cclxxxvii]

Truth is the light of God, and in having the light of God, the Holy Spirit lives in, through, and with you.
Nothing passes God's eyes.
He wants everyone to be saved and reach full knowledge of the truth. **1Tim. 2:4**

In God's mysterious way, the person works, and life will be toward truth and allegiance, and if it is in the correct direction of the Constitution and law, it will be toward God's truth. When we are a leader in God, it is not always in a monetary position. We are here to help keep pure His Ten Commandments and bring the fresh always flowing stream of anointing love of His Salvation.

Remember, we the participants of humankind's redemption, waiting for the redeemer to arrive for the Second Coming. Yet, we now have the Holy Spirit in and through and with us as rs of Jesus Christ as our Savior. We also already discussed the sovereignty of God and works everything for good for those who love God.

God will teach you everything you need to know.
America God Trust You

You have the peace in your heart of Me

You have the love in the veins of your soul of Me

You follow the path of My light to overcome all darkness

You have the light in your eyes to My Truth

You have the life in Me that is in you to bring My love to My Creation.

Often the Holy Spirit is named by phrases which explain something of the nature and activity of the Spirit: πνεῦμα (ἐκ τοῦ) θεοῦ 'Spirit of God,' πνεῦμα ἅγιον 'Holy Spirit,' πνεῦμα αἰώνιον 'the Eternal Spirit' (often called 'the unending spirit' or 'the spirit that never ceases'), πνεῦμα τῆς ἀληθείας 'the Spirit of **Truth**,' that is, 'the Spirit who communicates **truth**' (sometimes rendered as 'the Spirit that communicates the **truth** about God'); πνεῦμα τῆς δόξης 'Spirit of glory,' that is, 'the glorious Spirit' or 'the wonderful Spirit'; πνεῦμα τῆς ζωῆς 'the Spirit of life,' that is, 'the Spirit who brings life' or 'the Spirit that causes people to live';[cclxxxviii]

Everything has been entrusted to Me by My Father; and no one knows the Son except the Father, just as no one knows the Father except the Son and those to whom the Son chooses to reveal Him.

Matt. 11:27

*To your hands, I commit My **spirit**, by you have I been redeemed. God of **truth**,*

Psa. 31:5

Divine Message 9.9.2020

The creation of God all things molecules, atoms, and even the items made by man will also manifest His intentions for His directions and purpose when they are sought in truth.

Those things organic especially are supposed to be directed in the way of God's purpose.

Therefore, Scientist and all peoples in all works again, I proclaim in the Divine Trinity's directions.

When actions are prepared and worked through and sought

delivered and delivered with they are in the foundation of the closest truth, know they will manifest the Divine. (In the Trinity)

IV. *Perform Work of National Importance*

1. When these **Perform Work of National Importance** gifts are used upon the heart of the oath in the immigrants and citizens and leaders are lived, there is life, peace, justice, restoration, and forward building of the oath. All the people benefit and oath is living and the utmost truth and allegiance in, for, and with the people in God.

2. When the **Perform Work of National Importance** gifts are used upon the heart of the oath in the immigrants and citizens, and leaders not lived, there is the death of life and even perhaps lost from the past that was gained, loss of the present, and loss of what would have been. When not lived to perform work of national importance, the truth of allegiance to the oath then deteriorates, and the people received or apart of the injustice. God will redeem everything in His time. I walk in the Light as God walks in the light.

3. **Performance Work of National Importance America First**
   Divine Command and Messages delivered
   President Trump and the American Freedom Warriors and Republicans people have now put America First:

Fair Business Trade and Tariffs
Production and Manufacturing in the U.S.A.
Small and Large Business Tax Benefits and safe de-regulations
Onset now and Future infrastructure development
Military protection for America
Many other America First in Performance Work of National Importance

Business in America

Then the disciples, every man according to his ability, determined to send relief unto the brethren.

Acts 11: 29

I pray that your fellowship in faith may come to expression in full knowledge of all the good we can do for Christ.

Philem. 6

V. I take <u>this Oath obligation freely, without any mental reservation or purpose of evasion, so help me, God</u>

  1. When these are used<u>, without any mental reservation or purpose of evasion</u> upon the heart of the oath in the immigrants and citizens and leaders are lived, there is life, peace, justice, restoration, and forward building of the oath. All the people benefit and oath is living and the utmost truth and allegiance in, for, and with the people in God.

  2. When these are used <u>mental reservation or purpose of evasion</u> upon the heart of the oath in the immigrants and citizens, and leaders <u>not lived</u> there is the death of life and even perhaps lost from the past that was gained, loss of the present, and loss what would have been. When not

> lived to perform work of national importance, the truth of allegiance to the oath then deteriorates, and the people received or apart of the injustice.
>
> 3. <u>Mental reservation intentionally or forced,</u> <u>can cause an inhibiting to speak in free speech,</u> **<u>and invasion</u>** <u>could cause us to be "led, like sheep to the slaughter."</u>

If the freedom of speech is taken away, then dumb and silent, we may be led, like sheep to the slaughter." – **Let us bring life and love and keep America's Freedom.**

George Washington

> 4. **No Mental Reservation for freedom of speech** Before and during and after writing my book Our Need to Give to the World, Heal America, Love in God to Awake Americans regarding our position and vote for Trump, I was in great danger. When I began this calling from God to proclaim to the people Awake, Arise to Truth so Americans will not be "sheep to the slaughter." God has spared me.
> 5. **Purpose of envasion are hidden**

a. *Conspiracy – China Virus and Geo-political envasion attempt*

[7] In a number of contexts, ἐπιβλέπω involves not only sight but a considerable focus upon an accompanying **mental** activity, so that one may classify ἐπιβλέπω not only as meaning **'<u>sight</u>'** but as indicating 'paying attention to' or even '<u>**concerning oneself with**</u>'

b. *Crimes of immigrants and citizens and investors*
c. *Socialist and Communistic Not putting America First*

24.32 σκοπέωᵃ: to continue to regard closely — **'to watch**, to notice carefully.' 'take careful notice of those who cause divisions and upset people's faith contrary to the teaching which you have received'ᶜᶜˡˣˣˣⁱˣ

d. Protestors in violence and those whom financed them
I urge you, brothers, be on your guard against the people who are out to stir up disagreements and bring up difficulties against the teaching which you learnt. Avoid them.. **Rom. 16:17**

e. Governmental leaders and local leaders and influential powerful Elite

24.59 ἔχω οὖς: (an idiom, literally 'to have ear') to be able to hear, with the implication of being expected to hear or having the **obligation to hear** (with a further implication of related **mental** activity) — 'to be able to hear, can hear.' ὁ ἔχων οὖς ἀκουσάτω τί τὸ πνεῦμα λέγει ταῖς **ἐκκλησίαις 'if you can hear, listen to what the Spirit is saying to the churches'**

Do not do evil or withhold mental reservation of information because of a reason for human desire for more power or any other human sin or to do good with a good intention. Yet, do not throw pearls to the dogs. And those whom have the information that made it should deliver it, not another. Otherwise, it does not have the benefits intended that God has in store. The person that has made information and created it with the Creator is the maker and it will always stay with the right part of the maker that is what is in God.

Furthermore, do not assimilate cultural masonry or cultural craft to justify what is needed in society or even human greed and curiosity or evil. Only stay in the truth of God's purpose. Hence, this takes us back to virtues, purity, and loving the Lord The God with all your heart and soul, and loving your neighbor.

Be thankful, for what we have,

are matters we accept, always and everywhere, with all gratitude. **Acts 24:3**

God will give us more when we live, and seeking His Truth in different ways when we hear, listen, have sight in His purpose what the Spirit of God is saying.

In rendering the idiom ἔχω οὖς in Re 2:7, the implication is that the individuals involved ought to be able to hear and pay attention.[ccxc]

And that I take this obligation freely, without any mental reservation or purpose of evasion; so help me God."[ccxci]

Let anyone who can hear, listen to what the Spirit is saying to the churches: those who prove victorious I will feed from the tree of life set in God's paradise."

Rev. 2:7

Conclusions points of truth

In our Country of America we need all these aspects of importance to have our freedom, our life, our land, for the people.

If one part of the oath is lacking all may be lost. If one is more substantial and the other one weaker, the stronger can uphold the more vulnerable without abuse. Also, to protect is to have allegiance when there is an evasion of the oath and the conspiracy of the Constitution and laws working to guard the nation, so help me God.

Yes, God protects us when we follow this oath in Him toward Truth.

Naturalization Oath of Allegiance to the United States of America

Cor. 6:14 Do not harness yourselves in an uneven team with unbelievers; how can uprightness and law-breaking be partners, or what can light and darkness have in common? ¹⁵ How can Christ come to an agreement with Beliar and what sharing can there be between a believer and an unbeliever? ¹⁶ The temple of God cannot compromise with false gods, and that is what we are—the temple of the living God. We have God's word for it: I shall fix my home among them and live among them; I will be their God and they will be my people. ¹⁷ Get away from them, purify yourselves, says the Lord. Do not touch anything unclean, and then I shall welcome you. ¹⁸ I shall be Father to you, and you will be sons and daughters to me, says the almighty Lord.

All required to have a country that is Living, in <u>*Truths Peace, Justice, Restoration, and Forward Building in Love*</u>

The American citizen and the immigrants into naturalization are like the Israelites who respected the "covenant" of Yahweh and His people, obedience to the law. The Israelites were saved by Yahweh, God, and directed by Moses to be released from the slavery of Egypt's Pharaoh. Moreover, Yahweh and Moses led the Israelites out of slavery to the land of Sinai. And God gave them Divine Providence.

Your future generations may know that I made the Israelites live in shelters when I brought them out from the land of Egypt. I am the LORD your God.

Leviticus 23:43

In Mish. Heb. and Aram. תּוֹשָׁב is used to **mean immigrant or settler**. As a technical term, גֵּר תּוֹשָׁב refers to one **who renounces idolatry** and **accepts the seven commands of Moses**, as opposed to the גֵּר צֶדֶק, who is the true proselyte.[ccxcii] Gentile converted to Judaism, or a pagan converted to Christianity is a *proselyte*.

Thus the *pesaḥ-maṣṣôṯ* was early associated with the salvation from Egypt, the Feast of Weeks with the making of the covenant and the giving of the commandments on Sinai, and the Feast of Tabernacles with the journey through the wilderness.

(Exod. 12:12, 17; 19:1; Lev. 23:43)[ccxciii].

That night, I shall go through Egypt and strike down all the first-born in Egypt, man and beast alike, and shall execute justice on all the gods of Egypt, I, Yahweh!

Ex. 12:12

This verse is serious, and we all need to open our eyes and mind, many who go against God, He will not tolerate. I have prayed and pleaded with God when He gives me warnings for cities and peoples with practices that are unnatural and evil causing demonic oppression and violence and deception. And simultaneously they use political and social control. Many suffer at the hands of these mastermind masonite deceivers. Awake and arise those who trust in the Lord and even innocent will overcome all things in God's power, yet they need to expose these "gods of Egypt," to protect our people and children.

Yahweh commands to have no "gods of Egypt," and in return, God will take care of the Israelites and give them a land, a Promise Land, and Divine Providence when they are obedient to the Covenant of the Ten Commandments.[ccxciv]

Today: The New Covenant is now in Jesus Christ. He is our Saviour, Lord, and Savior for those who . <u>As the Son of God in the Trinity, he will not allow His country to be filled with "gods of Egypt,"</u> pagan gods of darkness. Otherwise, He is a jealous God and will strike.

God wants freedom and safety and life for His people.

Yahweh, your God among you is a jealous God; the wrath of Yahweh your God would blaze out against you, and he would wipe you off the face of the earth. ¹⁵

Furthermore, America, as immigrants and citizens alike, we are a land of peace, justice, continuing restoring, and forward building in compassion regarding the Constitution, nation, state, and local laws.

That is why, ever since the day he told us, we have never failed to remember you in our prayers and ask that you should reach the fullest knowledge of his will through perfect wisdom and spiritual understanding.

Col.

1:9

Do we take care of America as she is a gift from heaven? As a people, we know that God has given us America as a gift of OUR home. Sometimes I think we all m to forget for a moment or never even think that America is a gift of God, and we need to LOVE AND RESPECT AMERICA!

Note: God has the answer in His heart in you.

Ten Commandments most two Greatest Commandments

Loving, respecting God with all your heart and soul is the First Greatest Commandment.

Loving and respecting your neighbor is the Second Greatest Commandment. Since ethics have many definitions regarding how we treated a person and accepted drugs and smoking, and even relationships, we have to speak out in truth.

Questions Ethics

Americans, every country we know, has evolved in a particular formation under God's sovereignty. The body of America and its heart has specific characteristics created with great of God's intention.

America has been built on Judeo-Christian Ethics, and that is what is planted in the soil of her land. She will not live only when that is the necessary foundation.

Foundation is paramount; we need to have a basic understanding of ethics to have a working country. Ethics is safety; safety is regulations and laws to protect the people present and proven in the Constitutional scrolls of justice. Ethics is reconciliation and fairness toward peace and forwarding building.

There is enough fruit in America to stretch across her land and more

Bible

For if ye thoroughly amend your ways and your doings; if ye thoroughly execute justice between a man and his neighbor; [6] *If ye oppress not the* ***sojourner,(immigrant)*** *the fatherless, and the widow, and shed not*

innocent blood in this place, neither walk after other gods to your hurt: [7] *then will I cause you to dwell in this place, in the land that I gave to your fathers, from of old even forevermore.*

Jeremiah 7:5-7

We, as a people, have given the foreigner to live more than justice! Truth in the justice of the peace is the essence to protect the homes and cities, and businesses, and the safety of Americans who have entered America. Truth in compassion is the essence to protect the immigrants for proper citizenship and fullness of life.

If the freedom of speech is taken away, then dumb and silent, we may be led, like sheep to the slaughter.

George Washington

Let us bring life and love and keep America's Freedom.

Let not the children be separated from the parents in the immigration policy. There should be no excuse. These are the people that have given their backs and life for the growth of America. IN AMERICA, we have the most incredible wealth, the greatest minds, the most extraordinary hearts of America, and we can work together to bring justice.

Questions of Ethics of Immigration:

Do we ask why people are migrating to different countries?

There are various reasons why.

1. The immigration experience of countless has been a trial and a great chance and, in some cases, life-threatening and, in most

situations, a miracle of life to live in a land of the greatest love for humanity.

America is the *'Mother of All Nations.'* She has given all peoples from all countries a place to lay their heads.

2. "47 million immigrants have entered into, the **United States**, larger than any immigrant population in any other country, this represents 19.1% of the 244 million international migrants worldwide and 14.4% of the **U.S.** population."[ccxcv]

Immigration has been a major source of population growth and cultural change throughout much of U.S. history. Because the United States is a settler-colonial society, all Americans, the small percent of Native Americans, can trace their ancestry to immigrants from other nations around the world."

God takes care of the birds in the air, and He has planned to take care of His humanity. America is the hand of God and has taken care of nurtured all peoples; she is a *'Mother of all nations.'*

Owe no one anything, except to love one another; for the one who loves another has fulfilled the law.
Romans 13:8

And I heard a loud voice from the throne saying, " the home of God is among mortals. He will dwell with them as their God; they will be his peoples, and God himself will be with them."

Revelation 21:3

When the Mother Prays

When the mother goes to the water well and searches for water, and there is none, she looks up to pray to God, and He sends her to another land.

When the mother goes to the field for harvest, there is none she looks up to pray to God, and He sends her to another land.

When the mother goes to the town, there is not a home. She looks up to pray to God, and He sends her to another land.

Immigrants: There must be a search in their being, deep down in their soul, knowing where they lived in their mother country is not taking care of their needs.

Countless individuals have experienced solemn and life-threatening aspects on various levels of the (chronic immigration system of severe abuse to humanity when there is not a protected border. One out of every 4-5 people are severely abused.), injustice, fear, and many dangers. (I have experienced this violence.) However, others and most have made a life in America of living and a substantial new life of careers, homes, community, education, health care, and family formation. We, as a people, have a godly requisite to be compassionate to human natures thus far. To redeem and restore the immigration system, we need to all work with strategic honesty. Some will have to carry the burden more than others. Remember, we are all responsible for bringing justice to both the immigrant and the people involved and our America. This short writing will only discuss a few points to reveal and help the people illuminate truth being a catalyst to peace, justice, healing, and forward building in love.

3. It is by human nature one has curiosity as discussed n the highest sense. Curiosity, also used, of course, when one needs the survival of the fetus.

    They go and see and hoping to find; they knock and hoping the door is open; they ask and hoping to be answered. America has been the womb of a Mother and guidance of both Mother and Father, of parents to nurture, guide, and empower all her people. As we know, each parent is responsible for directing and giving the child the exact needs, respect, and covenant in return. This is what America has been as our parents; the land of God needs from her children to have respect and a covenant to take care of her land. And her natural resources are jewels as if they were from the Garden of Eden. Remember, the Our Father: Our Father art in Heaven hallow be thy name thy kingdom come thy will be done on earth as it is in heaven.

    , God does bring to earth heaven. Bringing heaven on earth, God gives His promises when we seek in prayer and love in Him.

4. Their country does not fulfill their life at a certain level, or they need to relocate for work, or they may have a calling. Perhaps the person needs a fresh new start. I have n many have grown out of where they live, and the Creator needs to take them to another place to help them grow.

    Therefore, for various reasons, humans want to migrate to other places to hear, feel, learn, live, conquer, and proceed forward in creating and developing. However, in entering into the nature of life, there is the specific intention and taking, working, receiving, and giving in return to the experience of the Creator, just as the tree does not provide you with fruit not unless it has soil, water, sun, proper nutrition, and adequate care.

5. Then we need to ask why has their country not taken care of them? I once discussed this with a lovely, profoundly honest, highly informative professional woman from Mexico. She explained that she is visiting here in America for work; however, she lived in Mexico. Her eyes began to tear up, and her smooth skin upon her forehead had started to form a line of deep sorrow between her eyes, and the hurt in her eyes reflected the life and death of the dreams of the immigrants. She, with a tone of authority and yet ashamed and sorrow, stated,

"In my country, there are many leaders and people that are in power that are corrupt, and they do not help the citizens. They use them and also to transfer drugs from one place to another. The leaders are not creating enough work and safety for the people to live in Mexico."

I was quiet and listening intently with my entire being. I could fill her deep sorrow for her people. These people are my people also. I am close to God's heart and Virgin Queen Mary; they want us to protect America for justice and protect the immigrants. We know that many countries have caused injustices and even violence against their people.

Please, the book "Our Need to Give to the World," Heal America, Love in God.

Even America in the past did not put America first and her people. NOW PRESIDENT TRUMP, THE TEAM, AND THE FREEDOM WARRIORS

AMERICA FIRST FOR AMERICANS.
WE ARE BRAVE AND CARE ABOUT AMERICA TO PROTECT HER AND THE IMMIGRANTS.

If I were an immigrant at this time, I would also want a better life <u>for</u> myself and my family. It is human nature of the fetus's survival to live, to be, to grow, to evolve, to build, to feel, to hear, to know, all toward truth.

"To make the President look bad,

Democrats and the anti-Trump media are rewriting the definition of the word racist.

The Epoch Times

We need to ask who is going to address the chronic neglect of the immigration issue? President Trump one of the first to address these issues. We need to work strategically for a justice system for immigrants and Americans. What is "strategically?" Ask, and you shall receive, knock, and the door shall be open, k, and you shall find. (Mathew 7:7)

God has given you gifts of understanding; you have it in your cells, your authentic being. I am not a socialist; I am not a communist; I am not here to control or to put the Truth of God on you to manipulate. It is your free-will to choose from.

If we all can BALANCE THE TIME, WE ARE using our phones and all the technological devices and act and work in a balanced lifestyle; we will find ourselves even deeper who we are that God created us to be.

First, let us pray for those peoples to live in peace. Pray for those who try to use conspire against others just because they respect our President. Today I spoke out in anger of truth, not in violence, yet in anger, of the truth of peace. My heart bleeds for the wholesomeness and peace for humanity and the truth not to abuse someone just because of their belief to keep America free and protect the children and their future legacy.

Arise is the issue we are responsible for in our country. Our President works for America. Our President works for the American people putting them first.

The children are God's greatest gift to us!

NEVER IN THE TIME OF AMERICA'S HISTORY HAVE WE AMERICA HAD TO SOLVE AN IMMIGRANT PROBLEMS THIS SEVERE.

We need to take care of innocent children that are here in America and the adults. However, we need to respect JUST LAWS AND COMMUNITY. When a person of violence conspires against the protector for the children to bring about God's Divine Commands, Solutions, and Messages and Miracles, they will be first asked to change and repent. If they continue to abuse the people of God, they will be judged by God now, not just after death.

America and the Crimes related to Illegal Immigration

The Epoch Times September 5, 2019

DENEEN BORELLI The Epoch Times September 5, 2019
"They are helping these smugglers, and these traffickers like nobody would," Trump said.

"They know it. They know exactly what they're doing, and it should be stopped," Trump said. "Because **what's** going on is very unfair to the people of our country, and they violate the law."

ILLEGAL IMMIGRATION AND ISSUES CAUSED BY

Respecting America in all issues and complexities is paramount to keep the strategy of a healthy country and safe country for all the people and the immigrants

Judge Strikes Down Law That Penalizes 'Inducing' Illegal Immigration
MATTHEW VADUM

A federal judge in Kansas who formerly worked for an open-borders group and whose sister currently heads one of the nation's leading open-borders groups has struck down a federal law that prevents people from "encouraging" or "inducing" illegal immigration, finding that the measure unconstitutionally infringes First Amendment free speech protections.

The jurist, in this case, is Judge Carlos Murguia of the U.S. District Court of Kansas, who was appointed to the bench by former President Bill Clinton in 1999.

The judge's online biography acknowledges he previously worked as "the immigration coordinator for El Centro Inc." El Centro Inc. is a left-wing activist nonprofit based in Kansas City, Kansas, that identifies UnidosUS as an affiliate on its website. UnidosUS is the new name for the National Council of La Raza ("La Raza" is Spanish for "the race"),

We have to be careful we need to consider other aspects of countries that we have opened doors to immigrants and people. Yet, we need to protect our borders.

Immigration is a God-given gift of the land that He has given His people internationally.

However, it is paramount that we protect all the people. Safety first.
The Epoch Times September 5, 2019
A SMALL SPECK OF FENTANYL OPOIOD CAN KILL

CHINA THREAT
  China Using Fentanyl as Chemical Weapon Against U.S.

Fentanyl, a synthetic opioid 50 times more potent than heroin, is (WAS) killing tens of thousands of Americans each year.

China also uses the money generated by the importing of fentanyl to effectively "influence political parties," according to Nyquist.

"It opens doors for Chinese influence operations, Chinese People's Liberation Army, and intelligence services so that they can get control of certain parts of the U.S.," he said. Trump called out Chinese leader Xi

Jinping, accusing him of not doing enough to stop the flow of fentanyl, which enters the United States mostly via international mail.

Behind the deadly opioid epidemic ravaging communities across the United States lies a carefully planned strategy by a hostile foreign power that experts describe as a "form of chemical warfare."

It involves the production and trafficking of fentanyl, a synthetic opioid that caused the deaths of more than 32,000 Americans in 2018 alone, and fentanyl-related substances.

Because we are a country of God's people, He brings to the front people to help heal and restore and bring miracles to our legacy.

Mike Lindell: the Pillow King
From drug addict to multi-million-dollar business owner, Lindell is(has) launching a nationwide network to combat drug addiction. A86 (Note wrote this first draft book in 2019)

America spends 578 BILLION on Economic Costs from Drugs and Alcohol, Direct and Indirect. [ccxcvi]

Billions of -Dollar Grants was given: As part of the Trump administration's latest efforts to combat the opioid crisis, the U.S. Department of Health and Human Services (H.H.S.) on September 4 announced nearly $2 billion in funding to states.

According to a release, the funding would expand access to treatment and support near-real-time data on the drug overdose crisis.

In announcing the move, White House counsel Kellyanne Conway told reporters in a conference call that their administration is trying to interject the word "fentanyl" into the "everyday lexicon" as part of their efforts increase awareness. Data suggests that of the approximately 2 million Americans suffering from opioid use disorder, about 1.27 million of them are now receiving medication-assisted treatment, according to the H.H.S.

"Central to our effort to stop the flood of fentanyl and other illicit drugs is our unprecedented support for law enforcement and their interdiction efforts," she said. Conway then brought up the D.H.S. seizures of fentanyl in 2018, totaling 1.2 billion lethal doses.

"Ladies and gentlemen, that is enough to have killed every American four times," she told reporters. Just weeks ago, the White House released a series of private-sector advisories aimed to help businesses protect themselves and their supply chains from inadvertently trafficking fentanyl and synthetic opioids.

The four advisories aim to stem the production and sale of illicit fentanyl, fentanyl analogs, and other synthetic opioids. The advisories focus on the manufacturing, marketing, movement, and monetary aspects of illegal fentanyl.

In March 2018, the Interior Department created a task force aimed to specifically combat the crisis on tribal lands. **Since then, the department has arrested more than 422 individuals and seized 4,000 pounds of illegal drugs worth $12 million on the street, including more than 35,000 fentanyl pills.R**

Conway, on the conference call, described the epidemic of pain relievers as an "opioid and fentanyl crisis."

There are various complexities of immigration. We have n one of the most devastating violence of a country that we have to open our doors to for immigration has treacherously abused and used our American people **as a Chemical Weapon Against U.S.**

As Americans and people of ethics, a country of God, we need to look at the bigger picture and the circular dysfunction from generation to generation. What does it bring the immigrants and America not to have proper citizenship and entering into the country? Companies and private employers, and immigrants sometimes neglect the system for taxing. In the long run, it is NOT advantageous and NOT just laws to NOT TO GIVE the immigrants proper citizenship, proper work identification entering into the system.

Not only do we want to protect the immigrant from having JUST LAWS AND and EMPOWERING them to have a life in society, but we also want to preserve the respect of America.

<u>WE KNOW AS PEOPLE WHEN THERE IS A CHRONIC ACTION OF INJUSTICE THAT IS DONE AGAINST HUMANITY THAT AFFECTS MANY OR EVEN A FEW PEOPLE WE HAVE CONTRA-INDICATIONS A CURRENT AFFECT GOOD AND BAD.</u>

THE INJUSTICE OF THE IMMIGRATION HAS TO BE REDEEMED BEFORE THE IMMIGRATION CAN BE RESTORED.

HOW, can it be redeemed to be that American God intended you to be?
WE ASK GOD TO DIRECT US AND GUIDE US.
NOW WE ARE WARRIORS OF PEACE OF GOD IN AMERICA:
THE GOOD ARE STRONG WARRIORS AS THE ISRAELITES .. AND WE AMERICA ARE WARRIORS OF LIGHT OF GOD

Someone has to carry that burden to correct and restore and heal the immigration problems, that someone is each one of us, citizen, local politician and local leaders, employer, immigrant, and state politician and state leaders from each country involved.

Our children need to be protected and live in a healthy and empowering environment with safety AND NEW FORMS OF EDUCATION THAT ARE ACTUALITY FOR THEIR POTENTIALITY THAT IS RELEVANT FOR DAILY EXISTENCE, NOT JUST THE HYPOTHETICALLY. OF COURSE, KEEPING THE CLASSICAL TRAINING SIMULTANEOUSLY. We have mentioned this subject that is the d of a crafting a new Tree of Education that is mandatory for the changing world; and in doing keeping their innocence toward creative thinking, flourishing; Yes, our flourishing harvest now working legacy that President Trump and the Administration and Freedom Warriors of America our succeeding in.

Our people need to be protected and live in a healthy and empowering environment with safety and restoration for drug addictions.

1. Do the immigrants take responsibility for their actions of family, work, and health? Do they take responsibility to realize who will pay for the cost of their life and their children? Do the children have a place to live? These are various questions, and there are different issues with human life and immigrant to enter America. The variables are endless because the social conditions are complex and are changing with the environment and daily living and circumstances in parallel to the technical course that at times to move at the speed of light.
2. The bravery of President Trump, the Team, the Enlightened Americans, and those all involved need to CONTINUE TO seek the truth and justice to forward building in compassion. Compassion is truth; because it has an understanding of the needs of a human and then guides the human through and to an answer that proceeds to restore the human and finds a solution to build a new and living life of truth.

Peace of Truth

Compassion is the responsibility to realize that if **there is no peace** in a specific situation because it in the actions and results in people's lives and the contra-indications. Then work needs to proceed.

Ask is the human's well-being healthy? If not, then there needs to be justice swiftly proceeded. Ask what has changed?

<u>Justice of Truth[ccxcvii]</u>
In regards to each life action, there are the Aristotle categories. All the activities to create a different environment. The responses of humanity, and even the environment, plant, animal, and even necessary architectural infrastructure has significant signs to reveal those things that need to be assessed and ascertain the changes and what peace, justice, restoration, and forward building performed.

Then you ask what sentence is for all is? Justice is not ideologies of specific motives; justice truth is identification that those are living toward peace.

<u>Restoration of Truth Forward Building of Truth</u>

You look at humanity. Is humanity toward good well-being, are they safe, are their tools to empower them to learn? What are the rules, regulations to uphold for the protection of the people? Since there is such a diversity of socio-economic, multicultural beliefs and traditions, it is, in essence, toward a perfect foundation. The ideal foundation is given by the natural law of the existence of life of God's mind, body, spirit, and connection between each other, our responsibilities, and actions toward the dominion of life. It is not just the people, but it is the foundation of what the country is built on. That is the truth to keep a nation alive and to obtain that well of fresh water to keep on flowing. For a country to flourish towards justice in fact and the tradition of America reaches toward each person, the government has to be treated with respect. She is a newborn child that you desire to give birth to and have a devotion to with your entire heart. We Americans will not abort the beauty of our new legacy of each child's life; we will take the American heritage of each inside our hearts to in the natural law of God's purpose for humanity.

Let me tell you again. God wants you to ask Him how and when we should create together to help the immigration problem.

1. Form places within states and cities, offices to obtain a form for citizenship, and form questions appropriate, as any other citizen has had to enter the country. However, for those who are afraid that perhaps they will deport them if they turn themselves in, there has to be a rule so that immigrants are not afraid to step forward
2. The people that are still crossing over give them a period to become a citizen. Protect the borders is essential.
3. I children should not be separated from their parents, whether either one is not an American citizen.
4. I think those as immigrants in the country now should be able to apply for citizenship as an American citizen. With restrictions in place that are beneficial to the immigrant, yet they have responsibility for American regulations. Responsibility of incorporating into health insurance depending on their income.
Taxes Classes on American history and Judeo-Christian Ethics (Note: these are just first notes).
5. Many Americans hard-core criminals should not be given entrance to America unless they have been free of their convictions; Also, those inmates released need to have been free of their convictions.

    However, the probationary time to maintain these criminals is costly at all levels for Americans. Immigrants and crime is a diatribe of a dichotomy that is a severely complex issue. It should be reviewed extensively and ongoing since immigration and types of crimes evolve and change.
6. I immigrants and citizens alike should take ethics. Many of

these children and if just one is used for human trafficking, and we as a nation in God need to protect the innocent. First, discussing the responsibilities to raise a child. The bird will do anything she can to save her children; that is why many people migrate. Our land is a land of the bird does not have the appropriate environment to build a nest and find branches; she does not lay her eggs in that region. And in some cases, she does attempt to make her nest, yet she needs to relocate her nest; because it is not conducive to the natural well-being of the new baby birds.

7. **The** Temporary Protected Status, or T.P.S., was established by Congress through the Immigration Act of 1990. T.P.S. is intended to protect foreign nationals in the U.S. from being returned to their home country if it became unsafe during the time they were in the U.S. and would put them at the 2010 earthquake in Haiti, T.P.S. status was designated for Haitian nationals living in the U.S. at the time, to protect them from having to return to an unstable and unsafe country should be protected.

I this should be reviewed and reinstated and developed and the following with all the above stipulations:

President Trump's Immigration Reform

Our America before Trump entered into office was broken down and in danger at every side. Not, just by statistics, but by the actual life of the people. In the prior Presidencies, 3,7 million women came into poverty.

All in danger were: Employment, safety, business, manufacturing, terrorist, war on drugs, health, protection of the d of life, human trafficking,

Illuminati control and Elite control, Communistic and Socialistic treacherous influence, Secrecacy to destroy America, and countless other aspects that are discussed in this book. Now there is the Chinese Virus, and hence, many immigrants and people from entering in the country there are regulations.

With the Chinese Virus across the world and one of the greatest tragedies by another country can do upon the world. Ask yourself, is it mandatory to protect the country now?

America needed to be put first to be able to take care of its people and others.

I once America is on her feet, running stronger, and by the Grace of God, she is on wings on an Angels, that we America will be able to help more people around the world.

Oh Lord, I pray with all my being to answer my prayer: help all those that need a home, immigrant and refugee, and all those homeless.

"We must realize that no weapon in the arsenals of the world is so formidable as the will and moral courage of free men and women."

Ronald Reagan

Immigrants come to a country to be free and live and see the moral courage to be free. However, when criminal acts that are treacherous to the people and even to the immigrants involved, sound judgment needs to be taken in swiftly justice; otherwise, we are not helping even the immigrant because we are then fostering crime and injustice and also enabling the immigrant. And in the long run, they are abused and used.

However, when there are devastating abnormalities of human sickness that causes death to a country such as drugs, human trafficking from babies, to human organs, to children, to women, and to men all vulnerable and innocent; we need to question, what shall we do to stop it?

But of the tree of the knowledge of good and evil, you are not to eat; for, the day you eat of that, you are doomed to die.

Gen. 2:17

When humans do evil, eating from the tree of evil death, they become. God is a loving, compassionate God. Let all have sinned ask forgiveness and live in righteousness in, through, and with Jesus Christ, our Lord, and Savior in the Trinity.

We as a people have an "obligation of Law," **servitude (a law or obligation)**; of ζεύγνυμι zeugnumi[ccxcviii] **We are Americans that are with, in, and through God of *nomos*, righteousness to the statutes, and *nomoi* recognize** <u>the rules of Laws of Divine Command of God that have Divine Authority in our land and in the entire Cosmos.</u>[ccxcix]

<u>Otherwise, our country cannot help anyone.</u>
<u>Let us keep America healthy, our virgin nation, with the eternal living waters of God and the Tree of Life to feed all those in need in God's love and truth.</u> **In keeping America free, we need to keep her Safety First.**

And do not say, 'His compassion is great, He will forgive . . . many sins': for with Him are both mercy and retribution, and His anger does not pass from sinners.

Sir. 5:6

*So confess your sins to one another and **pray** for one another to be cured; the heartfelt prayer of someone upright works very powerfully.*

James

5:16

Divine Prayer St Elizabeth Church, Altadena California
March 31, 2018

Entered in the Prayer with Mary,
"America shill is shaky, my daughter!"
I asked Mary,
"What do you mean?"
"Within the spirit of the World, there is work."
"My child, there are satan's angels and God's Angels of light.
The angels of satan know that the people in the light of Christ [the God of Abraham] are growing, more immense, and mighty in Christ. And those here on earth that are in darkness, not knowing God and His light, and are more curious than any time in history; at this time, yet there will be more curiosity and conversions now in the present and present future.

Hence, the angels of satan know this; therefore, the Angels of Light, the Angels of God(God of Abraham). The angels of satan are planning to keep and hold those in darkness by the power and principalities of satan. Hence, the Angels of Light of the God of Abraham are at every corner of America and the world; this is why you were given the song to sing My daughter, [Angels are at every corner of America and the world North, South, East, and West.]

I asked Mary,
"What shall we do, Mary?"

1."Remember, the Israelites were always a small army and overcame evil or paganism and suffering through the faith in (Yahweh) to us in God. [in their obedience to God] and in God's power."

2. "David, the little shepherd boy, overcame the giant. (in God's power.)

My response in prayer with Mary's response:

[ ], ( ) are my response.

"The great Samson's strength of God redeemed God's people because of the obedience of his faith." (Immediate communication with God gave Him His strength. Biblestudy.org Was Samson's strength in his Hair? Obedience, his faith, and this is the communication with God.)

3. "This is what the people of God in America and those believers of the world to have now (the power as David the little shepherd boy and great Samson's strength for the obedience of his faith.).

[Remember, we need to take into consideration all God's humanity. These are His people, all religions, and love them.]

God wants to protect His humanity from the darkness that are deceivers that kill, steal, and destroy.

4. "Hence, the people of God as you were told need to read the book ok f Mark."

5. Also, child the people of God need to [?]... by reading the Word and prayer for the salvation of the people.. that they …. Are by the actions of the love of the people it... will bring them out of the darkness to the light My child.

6. Remember, God is waiting for His people that He created to come to Him.

7. Then Mary told me these things... I was so happy and relieved and in awe. She was covering me with and in her Robe.

Also, Virgin Mary said, "these things America will be healed when all those who are working in the faith of America in the light of Christ. "

8. "Those that are in the darkness. We this ant to heal America, and there will be great beauty and healing and in the " incense of Aroma of God's light of the people because they have the power and love of God."

[There is tenderness, love, patience, though there needs to be a heralding to speak out in truth. I pray I learn more how when I know something is not correct. Help me, Jesus; I should of said this, "what do you want from me."

Today it has taken me hours to find peace to write. And to do my work.]

Yet this needs to be God's truth, not the truth of men. And even in compromising a little bit, there will not be a more excellent fruit.

Yet if we when we have a love of God.. Even in some compromise with repentance and further and full in Christ, we will have a great love of God, and the angels of darkness will be held back by those of God's love with peace and strength, with the Angels of God's light with the people.

9. It is not us who do the miracle; God is the one the Angels of light of God use us and direct us on a mysterious quest of the heaven of light to heal America.

10. Mary, what about the justice messages ... [for us to follow], " My child when one has the heavenly light of Christ in God then life is exchanged from earth to the heavenly and this if on earth is of God's infinite way.. My child, this is the resurrection life, here on earth from heaven giving up the earthly life for God's intended way yet shill living on earth toward God's intended way. On the other hand, my daughter, the darkness, is resurrected to Jesus [in the earth, there is darkness it is resurrected by Jesus Christ love and mystery in the Holy Spirit.] Jesus Christ 's cross (redeems) the darkness of sin and redeems it and transforms it with man and animal and nature and all His creation. Therefore, my child let all the people of God pray unto the Lord, the God of Abraham, and Alpha and Omega. And seek to keep God all the heart and soul. and all of America will be healed, and those in darkness will even come to the light of God. Because remember, child, "the Word became flesh, the Word of god is Christ Humanity."

Book of John

Christ gives life to humanity and power and love and miracle, and in this always now and forever.

So confess your sins to one another and pray for one another to be cured; the heartfelt prayer of someone upright works very powerfully.

James
5:16

Chapter Seven

President Trumps first 2 years in Office 2019[ccc]

Notes and Comments

Now in Jerusalem, there was a man named Simeon. He was an upright and devout man; he looked forward to the restoration of Israel and the Holy Spirit rested on him.

Luke 2:25

Jonathan then took up residence in Jerusalem and began the rebuilding and restoration of the city1Mac. 10:10.As regards the building and restoration of the sanctuary, the expense of the work will be met from the royal exchequer. 1Mac. 10:44

All Americans must review and seek to assess what is our country doing? How is our government? What does God want for our country? These are written aspects of President Trump's work and his team and America, as documented. We know that statistics are not always precisely at the time that they are received. Also, there are times when news and information are correct; however, these documented points are proven in the actions that have been received by witnesses.

My first book, *"Our Need to Give to the World,"* America love in God, Heal America, Best Seller Author.

I wrote this book, promoting all Americans and the world to take care of humanity.

Also, the Divine Messages included the calling of President Trump to be President.

I experienced Divine Commands for America in prayer and supplication. And I sought to promote these Divine Message to tell others everywhere I went and even in the presentation.

Let me tell you, Jesus Christ is the truth and power of the Trinity is the God of Abraham, in Virgin Mary and the Saints is my first love and first direction for them, in them, with them, and through them.

Let me tell you; it is through the Salvation in Christ Jesus that I have lived an understanding through the Holy Scriptures.

I love all humanity though I seek God's purpose in Christ Jesus.

I in loving all humanity.

I it is essential to state this again.

October 31, 2020

Divine Command Vote Trump for the life of our Country

Because I realize there are many tensions and:

" It is time to heal the wounds that divide us, and to k, a new unity based on the common values that unite us."

President Trump.

"Communism is the past. Freedom is the future." America."   President Trump

In fighting for what's good, Trump has taken a strong stance against Communism and Socialism, and the devastating effects were n wherever they've been practiced. His administration is trying to undo the effects these harmful ideologies have had on America.

Part of this effort can be n in the cutting of regulations and taxes that have stymied economic growth.

Trump said in his remarks at the National Prayer Breakfast on February 2, 2017.
"It was the great Thomas Jefferson who said, "The God who gave us life gave us liberty. 'Jefferson asked, " Can the liberties of a nation be secure when we have removed a conviction that these liberties are the gift of God."The Divine Command said, these gifts are from God and have to be directed and used for the Freedom of the people and America. Trump also has made protecting America a key focus of his presidency. He helped prevent a war with North Korea by using diplomatic pressure and

sanctions, combined with a credible military threat. He has focused on rebuilding America's military while simultaneously forging new alliances. Taking a strong stance against China's economic warfare, and has made it clear that the United States will not longer accept China's draining of the U.S. economy, nor its rampant theft of America's intellectual property.

Before President Trump came into office, it is a Divine Command that all the "fighting in (peace) for what's good that President Trump has taken a strong stance."

PRESIDENT TRUMP AND HIS TEAM AND THE AMERICAN PEOPLE HAVE FULFILLED AND ARE FULFILLING THE DIVINE COMMANDS TO TAKE CARE AMERICA FIRST AND RESTORE HER.

1. President Trump and His team have had to fight first TO HELP AMERICA recognizes and s the light of the PAST condition of our country.
2. Then they WORKED AND CONTINUED in strategical **wisdom to List items then use in certain places and Separate Chapter.**

We should ask: What would happen if we do (did) not seek to change and heal America's present landscape in every constituent of life, morally, economically, individual, culturally, and religiously and many other complex political systems?

Divine Command fulfilled

The Seventy ways President Trump Change America for her Protection and Freedom[cccl]

Divine Commands are Continued to being Fulfilled

in President's Trump presidency and America and his team.

Divine Command fulfilled
To Heal America p. 59
Is toward a "Revolution of Love." Love God and the gifts He has given you, use for His intention, and love your neighbor as yourself.,

America love in God and Heal America Now

Our Need to Give to the World, p. 59, -63

they love

Economy

"From sweeping tax reform to support for energy production, President Donald Trump's pro Business policies have boosted the job market, records, in the stock market, and helped individuals and companies to thrive again. The economy hit the Trump Administration 3 percent growth target in the second quarter of 2017 in the second and the third quarters of 2018."

Tax Reform, Stock Market, Record-High Oil Production, GDP growth, Low Gas Prices, Robust Jobs Market, Surge in Manufacturing Activity, Tax Reform benefits, Rise in Middle- Class Income, Opportunity Zones, 2 Million Americans Off Food Stamps, Fixing Workplace Skills Gap

Refer to my book Divine Command fulfilled:

Our Need to Give to the World, America love in God, Heal America p. 73-74,191, 332-339.

Trade

"Trump made waves when he overhauled the 24year old North American Free Trade, (NAFTA) and placed it with the U.S. -Mexico-Canada Agreement (USMCA), which promises production and jobs in the United States. Tariffs on Chinese goods persuaded Chinese leader Xi Jinping to sit-downs with Trump to address Washington's concerns."

NAFTA Replacement: USMCA, Trade War with China, Steel, and Aluminum Tariffs, A New Phase With Europe, Ending TPP,

Refer to my book Divine Command fulfilled:

Our Need to Give to the World, America love in God, Heal America p. 190-191, 333.

Boarder Security

Even though there is a serious threat of heartfelt controversy, there is action to address immigrants and illegal aliens that have never been addressed. "Now today, President Trump, out of all Presidents, is brave to seek to solve the greatest urgency to seek to solve the immigration crisis. Each one involved has to take responsibility for who is interested. I pray the immigrants will not be taken from America.

Refer to my book Divine Command fulfilled:

Our Need to Give to the World, America love in God, Heal America p.316.

"The migrant caravans from Central America have drawn constant media coverage; however, Border Patrol apprehends a caravan's worth of illegal aliens every day. After a sharp decrease in illegal border crossings when Trump took office, the apprehension numbers this fiscal year are on track to completely outstrip last year's 400,000."

"You need to care for the people injustice ethically. Borders, there should be none though protection and safety and justice in an ethical strategy of righteousness."

Our Need to Give to the World, America love in God, Heal America p.23, 316

Deregulation

Cutting Red Tape for Infrastructure Projects

Rolling Back Dodd-Frank

Net Neutrality Rejected

2-for1 Deregulation Plan

"One of Trump's campaign promises was to reduce the over-regulation that hampers American competitiveness and productivity. Highlights include rolling back the 2010 Dodd-Frank Act, thus freeing smaller banks from the higher compliance costs and the act imposed. The Trump administration also repealed the internet regulations known as "net neutrality."

Refer to my book Divine Command fulfilled:

Our Need to Give to the World, America love in God, Heal America p.67-74, 191, 333.

China

"The President successfully brought to the table a relationship of awareness. They were scrutinizing the Chinese investments in the United States, fighting intellectual property theft, challenging unfair trade practices, and adopting.

New National Security Strategy, Scrutinize Chinese Investments, Rewriting Relationship with China, Fighting Intellectual Property Theft, Tariffs to Penalize China, Pressure at the WTO

Refer to my book Divine Command fulfilled:

Our Need to Give to the World, America love in God, Heal America p. 191, 333.

Judiciary

"Trump has nominated more judges to federal courts than any of his five most recent predecessors. Supreme Court Associate Justice Neil Gorsuch was sworn in on April 10, 2017. Associate Justice Brett Kavanaugh was sworn in on Oct. 6, 2018, after an extraordinary battle in a polarized Senate. Trump made 154 appointments as of Jan.3, 2019

Appointments: 154, Confirmation, Rate: 55.2%, Cloture Votes: 48, Roll- Call Vote Rate, Trump- 67.1%

Veterans

"Trump signed multiple bills into law, overhauling the Veterans Affairs Department to increase benefits for veterans and service members. To increase accountability in the troubled agency, the Trump administration has reviewed and demoted, fired, or suspended some 4,300 Veterans. One bill gives veterans the ability to a private doctor if V.A. hospitals are unable to provide the care they need."

Refer to my book Divine Command fulfilled:

Our Need to Give to the World, America love in God, Heal America p.ix, x.

America

"At the center of Trump's presidency has been his moral stance against Communism and his efforts to restore traditional America Values. The Trump administration has also withdrawn the United States from multiple international organizations and pacts because they infringed on U.S. sovereignty."

Taking a Moral Stance Against Communism Socialism, Promote Traditional American Values, Protecting America's Sovereignty.

Fighting the Deep State, Fighting the Leaking, Defending Religious Freedom, Fighting Corruption,

Refer to my book Divine Command fulfilled:

Our Need to Give to the World, America love in God, Heal America p.10, 187-191, 262, 333.

National Security

" One of the key victories under the Trump administration was destroying the ISIS terrorist group's caliphate in October 2017. The President worked to improve national security by upgrading the U.S. nuclear arsenal and establishing a command for military operations in space. The administration has also helped the United States to be ready to defend itself and attack adversaries in cyberspace."

Isis Caliphate Destroyed Establishing Command for Military Operations in Space, Improved Nuclear Arsenal, Allowing the military to fight back in Cyberspace, Ended the Iran Nuclear Deal.

Refer to my book Divine Command fulfilled:

Our Need to Give to the World, America love in God, Heal America p.191, 333.

Foreign Policy

"Negotiations with North Korea defused a tense situation that possibly could have led to war. The President made good on a deceased old U.S. policy by moving the U.S. Embassy in Israel to Jerusalem. The Trump administration also has transformed the U.S. relationship with Saudi Arabia. Pakistan saw hundreds of millions in U.S. aid get cut due to its failure to control terror groups."

Preventing War With North Korea, Suspension of Aid to Pakistan Over Aid to Terror Groups, Transformed relations with Saudi Arabia, Starting Withdrawal of Troops From Syria, Securing Release of American Prisoners Overseas, Moved U.S. Embassy to Jerusalem, Targeting Corruption in Venezuela

Military

"Trump vowed during his campaign to rebuild the U.S. military. In 2018, Trump's defense bill increased $108 billion, or 1 percent, the proposed 2017 budget. The administration's increased military spending has allowed it to acquire large amounts of new defense equipment, including F 35 Joint Strike fighters, ground combat vehicles, and Virginia class submarines."

Troops saw a 2.4 percent pay raise for January 2018, the highest year-over-year increase for service members since 2010.

Increased Funding for Military
Modernizing of Military Equipment
Changing Military Rules of Engagement
Refer to my book Divine Command fulfilled:

Our Need to Give to the World, America love in God, Heal America p. 313.

Law and Order

The battle to eradicate human trafficking has been a focal point of the Trump administration's domestic policy. Trump has signed multiple bills that make it easier to dismantle transnational criminal organizations that traffic and exploit people while also giving victims more power to take legal action.

Great Sheriff's Deputy Luis Flores in Refugio County in Texas on Nov. 10, 2018.

Combating Human Trafficking

Criminal Justice Reform

Taking Down Backpage.com

Our Need to Give to the World, America love in God, Heal America p. 24,339

Environment

Through a bill dubbed the Save Our Seas Act, the Trump administration strengthened efforts to clean debris from the world's oceans. To combat the spread of wildfires like those in California in 2018, the President signed several bills that support preventive measures, such as allowing foresters several bills that support preventive measures.

Signing the Save Our Seas Act
Forest Management to Reduce Wildfires
Our Need to Give to the World, America love in God, Heal America p. 35,313.

Cutting waste

Reducing U.N. Spending
Withdrawing from Universal Postal System
Cutting Costs on New Air Force One
Slashing Use of Government Time on Union Work
Reducing the White House Payroll.

Refer to my book Divine Command fulfilled:

<u>Our Need to Give to the World, America love in God, Heal America p. 333.</u>

Of course, there is tension and severe disagreement.

This is why I have a Demand Command and Messages to write and proclaim.

USE THE FOUR FOUNDATIONAL TRUTHS THEY USED WITHOUT REALIZING IN THAT IS A DIVINE COMMAND THAT WE DO EVERYTHING NOW.

1. PEACE
2. JUSTICE
3. TRANSFORMATIONAL RESTORATION
4. FORWARD BUILDING

The eyes of the Lord watch over those who love him. He is their powerful protection and their strong support, their screen from the desert wind, their shelter from the midday sun, a guard against stumbling, an assurance against a fall.

Sir. 34:16

Fear of the Lord is a paradise of blessing, better protection than the highest reputation.

Sir. 40:27

Chapter Eight

Brief Discussion on America's Production and China's Attempt of Geo-political Position

America and the world, I prepared this document in preparing this book before the Chinese Virus within the world and the passing of the tariff laws in favor of America. I am an American Freedom Warrior that has delivered Divine Messages and Command proven by logic and truth the guided in for American and world issues.[cccii]

But when the kindness and love of God our Saviour for humanity were revealed, ⁵ it was not because of any upright actions we had done ourselves; it was for no reason except his faithful love that He saved us, by means of the cleansing water of rebirth and renewal in the Holy Spirit.

Titus 3:4

We know peace should always be first, last, and always for every simple reason; we know in a peaceful atmosphere a peace with justice, one in which we can be confident can America prosper as we have to know prosperity.

President Eisenhower

"Observe good faith and justice towards all Nations; cultivate peace and harmony with all."

President George Washington

Those who seek peace are looking for honor proposals and genuine progress. America, after World War II, we were the only industrial power that was not damaged in the world. Our Military supremacy was unquestioned. We had harnessed the atom and could unleash its destructive course anywhere in the world. We could have achieved world dominations though that was contrary to the character of our people.

Instead, we wrote a new chapter in the history of humanity. We used our power and wealth to rebuild the world's war-ravaged economy, both East and West, including those nations who have been our enemies. We took the initiative of creating other international institutions, as the United Nations. **We are leaders of goodwill to come together to build bridges of peace and prosperity.** America has no territorial ambitions. We occupy no countries. OUR COMMITMENT OF FREEDOM AND PEACE IS THE SOUL OF AMERICA THAT COMMITMENT IS AS STRONG TODAY AS IT EVER WAS. In each war of the United States, we struggle to defend freedom and democracy. We were never the aggressors. America's strength and, yes, her military power has been a force for peace. **AMERICA'S MILITARY POWER IS FOR PEACE NOT CONQUEST, FOR DEMOCRACY NOT DISPARATISM, FOR FREEDOM NOT TYRANNY,** [ccciii]

Watching the American youth, young people bleed on the battlefield to protect our ideas and protect the rule of law. I have known how important it is to deter conflict. But since I am coming to the Presidency (and since I Lucia giving myself for the calling to be an American and World's Freedom Warrior), the enormity and responsibility of a president's office. We all need to forgive and make a more profound commitment to Godly love. [ccciv]

*The **love** of money is the root of all evils,' and there are some who, pursuing it, have wandered away from the faith and so given their souls any number of fatal wounds.*

1Tim 6:10

Arise to truth blessing that President Trump and the American Freedom Warriors have put Americans first and have diligently and faithfully fulfilled the Divine Messages and Commands and continued to do so.

A great American, Steve Bannon, compares China to 1930s Germany and says the U.S. must confront Beijing Monday, Sep 11, 2017, The Guardian

Steve Bannon, Donald Trump's former consigliere, has compared China to 1930s Germany, warning the country could go down the same dark path if the U.S. fails to challenge its rise. Steve Bannon has said that China's younger generation is 'so patriotic, almost ultra-nationalist.'

"A hundred years from now, this is what they'll remember — what we did to confront China on its rise to world domination," Bannon told the New York Times.

"China right now was Germany in 1930," he said. " It could go one way or the other. The younger generation is so patriotic, almost a global anti-China crusade. The former White House chief strategist has called himself a "street fighter," setting his sights on his next opponent: China. Bannon is convinced the U.S. and China are destined for open conflict and has lambasted the country on everything from trade to intellectual property to North Korea ahead of a speech in Hong Kong on Tuesday.

Steve Bannon, the former White House Chief Strategist, sits down with hedge fund giant Kyle Bass to discuss America's current geopolitical landscape regarding China. Bannon and Bass take a deep dive into Chinese infiltration in U.S. institutions, China's aggressiveness in the South China sea, and the potential for global conflict in the next few years. They were filmed on October 5, 2018, at an undisclosed location.[cccv]

Divine Command and Message fulfilled:

All military forces should be used for the financial protection and safety, and well-being of the people of America and the world. The military build-up is necessary. Mandatory, it has been the Divine Message and Command to have the most strategic and strong military warning.

Sir Harford John Mackinder Birth of GEOPOLITICS[cccvi]

Great Game

1. Control of the Ocean
2. Control of trade routes
3. Colonial Empire
4. The necessity of conserve Empire
5. Geopolitics as a theoretical reflection of Anglo-Saxon Imperialism

Main Geopolitical terms:

Sea Power
Land Power
Rimland
Inner Crescent
Outer Crescent
World Island
Steve Bannon's Warning On China Trade War (w/ Kyle Bass) | Real Vision Classics

Ground for Geopolitics

Sir Harford John Mackinder (1861-1947) found of Geopolitics
The Geographical Pivot of History Article 1904
The opposition between two global Powers: Land Power (Heartland) vs. Sea Power
Sea Power in history: Athens, Carthage, Venice, Dutch, Great Britain
Land Power in History, Sparta, Rome, Austria, Germany, Russia
Sea Power: trade, liberalism, democracy, progress, technology, innovation, oligarchy, science, adventures, entrepreneur's spirit.
Land Power; force, conservatism hierarchy, order, ascetics, aristocracy, religion, ethics, stability.

This dualism served Mackinder to explain the meaning of history. According to Mackinder, the fight or dualism between Land Power and Sea Power is the key to understanding history. We can that this is precisely a kind of explanation or theorization of the Great Game. But this is also Mackinder's generalization because it is not only an explanation of the Great Game. The Great Game – which saw the British Empire trying to control the seas and oceans against the Russian Empire – was a concrete, historical, strategic moment. But Mackinder generalized that the Great Game reflects something deeper, something universal, the basic principles of how human history goes on. This is the basic principle of geopolitics.

MACKINDER'S LAW

Who controls Eastern Europe then controls the Heartland then hypothetically could rule the world?

But let us concentrate on this part of the sentence: "Whoever controls Heartland, rules the world." This is the most crucial point. If Heartland is controlled from outside, the world is ruled by Sea Power. That means the democratic ideal, progress, modernity, and capitalism on a global scale. If Heartland is governed by itself, by Land Power, it is something opposite: eternity, tradition, order, hierarchy, conservatism.

In Mackinder's eyes, Heartland is an object. This object begins with Eastern Europe, as in the Inner Crescent, the coastal line of Eurasia. If the control of this coastal line or zone is strong enough, there is no possibility of direct confrontation between Eurasia, Heartland, and Sea Power. Heartland becomes an object. But of Heartland. But if Heartland begins to be a subject, affirms itself as a geopolitical subject, is awakened or wakes up on its own, then there is a problem for the British Empire's global domination.

This was the main rule of geopolitics from then on. The fight for Eurasia is an application of this principle.

Geo-political Theories
MC KINDERS THEORY OF THE ASIAN LAND MASS
THEORY CUTTING OF THE CHOKE POINTS OF THE OCEANS
SPKMAND THEORY KEEPING YOUR ENEMY OFF OF THE ASIAN LAND MASS

RIMLAND CONCEPT EMPHASIZES THE INNER CRESCENT
 SPYKMAN'S (1893-1943)

Who controls Rimland controls Heartland, who controls Heartland rules the world.

A most geopolitical strategy that we have n
Steve Bannon's Warning on China Trade War

Note: God has control of all things, and I was given in a Divine Message and command years ago to be careful of the China trading. I decided I would support it in theory, not just Divine Revelation. I met a man while doing farming to sell Real Estate; he complained fervently about China and the tariffs that we are putting on China. He happened to know who I was, an Advocate and Consultant for America, and my stance and promotion of the trade urgency to make a fair-business trade. He is an intellectual; maybe he will listen to this factual argument with a geopolitical argument. I think people need to be more aware and educated. Even if you tell them a few sentences to be a catalyst of understanding of the subject, I this would help them realize.

Hegemonic world power China's purpose

CHINA WORLD ORGANIZE
Divine Message 2020
While praying and asking the Lord, "I know what others are thinking about my work." The Spirit of the Lord answered. "Listen to Me, not to men."

I asked, "What about China and what they did?" The Spirit of the Lord stated, "There are a free-will and choice, My child."

I do not have to look at my child for the country, and its people are doing. I have a small itch behind My ear.
They are a part of Me, child. (Then I thought about the body of Christ and the cross.)
"Then the necklace of justice, which as previously stated, Paul extended as far as the feet of this virtue, will seize by a kind of roaring windstorm, and it will begin to stir for the first time."

"Please, do not get excited too soon or alarmed by any prediction or rumors of any letter claiming to come for us, implying that the day of the Lord has already arrived, it cannot happen until the Great Revolt has taken place, the Lost One, (Anti-Christ) has appeared." [cccvii]

Everything God has made has been made in love, humility, and peace. Therefore, we too should be fond of love, we should strive for modesty, and we should keep the peace so that we do not perish with those who have scorned these virtues from the moment of their birth." [cccviii]

The Three forms represent the following virtues: Love is God, who became a human being in humility. From on high, God brought down to our peace, which has to be fought for with difficulty in a changeable world and preserved only with problems. [cccix]

Economic war has been in America, and finally, we have won, since President Trump and the Republican Team has made China accountable to fair-business trading; Mary Virgin Queen spoke to me in a prayer years ago regarding America and how we will become complacent and even ashamed if we do not restore or jobs, manufacturing, and businesses in America. When I was staying in Monrovia years ago, I would pray in front of the grotto at the Maryknoll Sisters; Mary told me many warnings.

These Divine Commands and Messages that I have written some in *Our Need to Give to the world*, and my regular writings, President Trump and the Administration and American Freedom Warriors have answered.

Divine Message October 2,3, 4, 2020 Pasadena
China Stealing information and Technological

All top Universities and Schools and private businesses or areas that produce and share information national of Science and or the extensive and relevant information that can be a danger to humanity needs to be investigated in whether funds and report that was shared with conspicuous or illegal counterparts nationally or internationally.

Divine Message 2019-2020 Protect America from China

This list is not finished. Remember, this is a discussion to be a catalyst for the people to show truth and urgency.

1. Tariffs we need to put on. People cannot become ashamed of not having work and businesses.
2. America needs to bring our businesses back to America.
3. America needs to be self-sufficient, using her resources and natural resources
4. America needs excellent tax incentives for small and larger businesses.
5. All states of America have to go into and where the manufacturing has been lost because of the trade of lower-wage and production costs. American
6. America needs de-regulations with safety nets for all types of manufacturing
7. America needs to be urgently strategic and careful to set up a paradigm to transfer our business to America that could be detrimental to Americans' well-being.
8. Because of the Chinese Virus, there can be an extreme hidden danger with the products that are manufactured in China that Americans use. Because China had a chance to speak up about the Chinese Virus and did not and all the world became in. It makes me deeply sorrowful to say this. However, it is a Divine Message. When I say China in this context, I am referring to the people involved. Another aspect already presented is the war on drugs of heroin that China has used. This point is identified here to show that all substances and businesses related to China need to go through intricately. Also, the loans taken out by governmental business loans by China have used the money to make military tools.

There are lists of great calamities and dangers and corruption, yet we will not speak it

9. Also, to be self-sufficient. If we do not change drastically now, we will not even be able to buy China's products; people will not have the income to purchase them. We know that money has a rolling curb of a current effect that cannot be stopped readily.
10. In reiterating, enter into each state and where we lost manufacturing and rebuild and restore it.
11. We need to make sure that we pass all regulations and safety of the products of all Chinese products and other countries we purchase from.
12. All products that are made for children need to be assessed thoroughly. Foods, clothing, toys, furniture, and even books learning outcomes need to resonate with optimistic values and no hidden damaging meanings.
13. (All baby foods and all products for children, no matter where they are made, need to be thoroughly assessed. Especially immunization medicines.
14. Any foods and pharmaceuticals and clothing dyes and products must be thoroughly assessed and not purchased for the American business. The pharmaceuticals can be a danger to America.
15. In conclusion, America needs to bring back all her business to America.
16. Technological crime stealing information: For reasons discussed above from the safety of the well-being and health of America, also, for America's livelihood, and America has given gifts to be self-sufficient and those bright, educated, and innovative beyond the present understanding, should never be used, abused, defamation, fraudulent utilizing the information of these unique and exotic peoples that understand the present and the future should never be put in a conspiracy. They should be faced and work directly with a team, whether privately, community, or governmental groups. Those who do this to their own peoples also steal products that they should get fair business deals and tariffs.

, arise, to the truth. WE ARE RISING TO GOD'S TRUTH. We ARE OPENING OUR EYES CONTINUALLY to America when we knew we

<u>needed a change to make America great again and protect her freedom. This has been a Divine Command that we voted in President Trump 2016, and NOW AGAIN, WE NEED TO VOTE IN PRESIDENT TRUMP 2020.
NOW WE NEED TO GET ALONG EACH AMERICAN.
GOD IS WAITING, GOD IS YEARNING, AND HIS HEART IS WEEPING, FOR THOSE TO COME TO REPENTANCE NOW. ANY THAT HAS HAD CORRUPTION WITH CHINA OR ANY OTHER INTERNATIONAL OR NATIONAL COUNTRIES TO CEASE WITHOUT ANY FURTHER ADO. MOREOVER, NOW ALL PEOPLES THAT FINANCED THE PROTESTORS TO REPENT</u>

When we open our doors to unfair trade practices and other daily aspects of relationships with other countries, we are then in threat of war from that country. Therefore, we need to be grateful for what strategic plan and action that President Trump and the American Freedom Warriors have made true action to save our country.

Most importantly, God will not allow us to follow the path of injustice, which is the counterparts of the death of freedom.[cccx]

You love uprightness and detest evil. This is why God, your God, has anointed you with the oil of gladness, as none of your rivals. Heb. 1:9

DIVINE MESSAGE 9.4.20 TRUST IN GOD

I what has happened, child.

The Chinese people involved and Conspiracy to make our country America a socialist, communistic country and those who have violently and ignorantly and even those that do not know good from evil caused death and sin to the world. I asked, please forgive them. They do not know what they do, Father. I pleaded with the Spirit of the Lord in pray that many people contracted the Chinese Virus, and the protesting has lost much and their jobs and life well-being. Fathers, Mothers, individual families, all peoples, and children have been abused alike.

The coronavirus has caused a real-world crisis; never in the history of modern times has a sickness stretched across the world.

This is the foreshadowing of China's strategy AND FAILURE to take over the geopolitical power of the world. China's peoples involved.

Also, those of the protesting and the silent Powerful, Socialist, and Communist who have instigated and financed these violent protesting will be judged; the preparation to secretly yet blatantly get Trump removed.

THE SOCIALIST AND POWERFUL AND COMMUNIST THEY HAVE ALSO FAILED.

TRUMP IS IN AND WILL STAY IN. AND WE ALL NEED TO FORGE AHEAD, PUSH AHEAD, AND TRUST IN GOD. God is calling on all the world's people to enter into a relationship with Him to love Him with all their heart and soul.

I will forgive them, though I need to come to Me and enter into forgiveness of themself and turn away from sin.

I will be with you and guide you and help you write. I cannot tell you all things, child.

I have everything in My hand's child. You need to show the truth, child .. show the truth of the facts of President Trump's success and the American Freedom fighters. I saw papers of the charts I made and information to give, whether on the internet or paper.

God Saved us America, Trust in God.

Just as dawn was breaking. This was achieved, thanks to the protection which the Lord granted Judas.

2Mac. 13:17

VIRTUE and integrity be my protection, for my hope, Yahweh, is in you.

Psa. 25:21

Chapter Nine

God's Wisdom

Cal Tech Meeting with Two Scientists

October 5, 2020

The molecules (Electron) are the .. substance of attitudes of organic substance that are life and existence they also have to follow the Commandments that God has created and God's intention at creation otherwise they do not fulfill God's total purpose.

1. The Molecules (and electrons) are controlled in many cases by the hierarchy of other molecules and electrons (All affected by Aristotle's Categories.
2. Also, the Molecules and electrons ... are also controlled by humans that can cause them All affected by the Aristotle's Categories
   1. Not to be God's intention and created that is not what of God.
   2. The intention can be a good one yet does not fulfill what is needed at that time
   3. The intention can be a good one yet is fulfilled at the time.
   4. The molecule's electrons have a particular purpose that God only knows the specific purpose until it is revealed to the people. Molecules and electrons and God's Holy Spirit and all the mystery of the kingdom of God is across the universe. Heaven.. has the answers for the earth.
   5. That prayer Our Father Art in Heaven Hallowed be thy name thy Kingdom Thy will be done on earth as it is in heaven give us this daily bread and forgive us our trespasses as we forgive those who trespass against us.
   6. "on earth and in heaven." There is an exchange .. and a delivering and sharing.. of the purpose from heaven to earth, from earth to heaven. Only in God's purpose. And only for a nurturing. God can only redeem not humans; hence, if the person that needs God's love does not accept His love at the moment of His appointed time that is given from His Father to give to the believer to intercede for the non-believer. There will a relationship with God not received, and even the non-

believer's gift will not be received if God chooses. Remember, though; God never gives up on the non- believer; although, never forget God will not be tested.

3. Molecules and electrons have attitudes .. for example, when you go into a room .. you may feel happiness, saddens seriousness excitement. Even before you do not know what the subject matter is. .. This show proves that molecules and electrons have an attitude in Aristotle Metaphysics. There is the first chapter .. he speaks about attitudes ..

4. Hence, this is essential than to be optimistic and positive. Yet, when there are injustices, there needs to bring relevant reasons and facts. Why is the actions of the molecules and electrons of attitudes that even humans can control to speak loudly?

I. God in the Trinity created the universe.
II. Human Molecules and Electrons to them
III. Molecules and Electrons not connected to them
IV. Synthetic that things made and organic also have control affects with themselves and other molecules and electrons and even control by the person in actual tangible ..and spiritual.
V. When you have a prayerful life of in and through and with God.. works with and through you. To make and live in God's closes intention.
VI. Remember, He who is in me is stronger than he is who of the world.

At this very moment, there is a man that does not want me to write for America. They are Democrats and want a socialized system.

Hence, my molecules and electrons in the power and strength of God's right arm are stronger than the powers and principalities of satan. ...

VII. The Lord tell us that this to shall pass.. Even if you feel there are issues ... then you.. know the molecules and electrons of the thing or person you come in contact with shall pass, and eventually, you are not affected by them because you overpower then in the power of God.. .. because you are in God, He who is in you is more powerful than He who is of the world.

VIII. This is why the Word of God the Holy Scriptures is the voice of God's creation, and the Word of God controls the life of all things. Because again, to reiterate that God is trying to bring all creation back to His heart, He brings His love directly from Himself in the Trinity and Virgin Mary and the Saints to redeem them planting ds. Also, sometimes that all God needs to redeem them. Otherwise, the Trinity needs to bring an actual person and or persons to help those that are not at God's heart.. .. because they need that human communication and they have a psyche that is affected by the communication and actions of God's r to the non-r.

IX. God also has to use the Holy Spirit, Angels, and Saints to help not only the r and the non r.. with an actual person and when an actual person cannot.be accepted.. . because God's purpose is always for making life and making beauty to the utmost.. and there is timing. Because of the .. necessity for God .. to make life in His intention.. sometimes.. God will allow things to happen in treachery so the people... realize He is in control. And also to make them understand He is the Sovereign God .. of all the Universe. That is related the Aristotle Cater

X. Also, the Sacred Heart of Christ Jesus is the living heart in the Trinity of the mystery where the blood of Christ passes through the Sacred Heart passes through that we are apart of His Sacred Heart because He loves us first and then we love Him. There are times when God wants to accomplish in a person something that is timely. Hence, we need to fully dedicate ourself to Him. It is relevant when there is a schedule.. we seek to follow it.. Moreover, some people do not realize that there is a timing.

Chapter Ten

Our Almighty God

Arise in God's Truth America

OUR FAITH IN ALMIGHTY GOOD
PROTECT AND SAVE OUR LEGACY
**These accomplished need to be documented to show that God has His almighty
Hand upon America to Restore her.**
One definition of Peace is working toward receiving Peace from something that needed restitution and was taken or needed to be restored or needed to be reconciled. Hence, President Trump has delivered Peace in the true and evident success that has been delivered in restoring our America.
I would have to say he is also a President to bring Peace to America. He has brought safety and economic recovery to America and her people. Peace is the freedom to be who the individual was created to be.
President Trump is the President of Freedom
President Trump has sought Peace in the protection and restoration of our country.
President Trump is a President of Protection
President Trump is a President of Restoration
President Trump has brought truth to our Country God's truth in following the Divine Commands and Divine Messages
President Trump is the President of God's Truth.
PRESIDENT TRUMP AND THE TEAM THE AMERICAN FREEDOM WARRIORS HAVE FULFILLED THE Divine Commands to RESTORE AMERICA
IN THE book Our _Need to Give to the World, Heal America Love in God_ and OTHER DIVINE MESSAGES BY ME, LISA LUCIA ARDEN that ARE GIVEN TO ME TO RESTORE AMERICA. The reason I mention my name is I want to be identified with God's miracle for the people. It is through, with, and in the people of the love of God that America will continue to be restored.
And under the leadership of President Trump.

President Trump and the Team and WE the American Freedom Warriors have accomplished under the promises, wisdom, strength, righteousness, and truth to bring restoration to America.

WE NEED TO KEEP ON THIS LIFE IN AMERICA OF
AS PRESIDENT TRUMP AS WORK TOWARD
"MAKING AMERICA GREAT AGAIN."

Once the war was over the Revolution continued not on the battlefields but in the legislature.[cccxi] The Revolutionary War, by John Thompson, National Geographic, Society Washington D.C. 2004

NOW FINALLY WE AMERICA UNDER THE PRESIDENCY UNDER PRESIDENT TRUMP

1. RIGHT TO LIFE AND FREEDOM OF RELIGION
2. NOW MILITARY HAS BEEN RESTORED SAFETY. FIRST IT WAS DEPLETED
3. PRODUCTION HAS THE BEST ECONOMY EVER AMERICA HAS HAD

CHINA OVER 25 YEARS HAS MADE 200 BILLION ON TRADE AND USA
550 BILLION
NOW: FOR THE FIRST TIME UNDER PRESIDENT TRUMP, WE TOOK IN BILLIONS FROM CHINA THIS YEAR. THE INK WAS NOT DRYED BEFORE THE CORONA VIRUS WAS KNOW AND CAUSED

4. NATO PARTNERS BEHIND IN DEFENSE PAYMENTS AGREE 130 BILLION MORE WILL PAY MORE WILL ULTIMATELY GO TO 400 BILLION DOLLAR A YEAR.

5. WITHDREW FROM UNFAIR PARIS CLIMATE ACCORD DISADVANTAGE TO AMERICA AND ABSORBING THE TAXES AND COSTS

6. SECURED FOR THE FIRST TIME ENERGY INDEPENDENCE HYDRO BUILDING
7. TAX CUTS IN 3 YEARS STRONGEST ECONOMY
8. ENDED NAPFA NIGHTMARE SIGNED THE MEXICO AND CANADA AGREEMENT INTO LAW
9. GIVING BENEFITS AND TAX DEDUCTIONS FOR AUTO COMPANIES AND OTHER

BUSINESS PUTTING THEIR MANUFACTURING INTO AMERICA AND THE EMPLOYEES AND NOT LEAVING AMERICA FOR OTHER COUNTRIES.
10. WASHINGTON SPECIAL INTEREST TRIED TO STOP THE PRO AMERICAN IMMIGRATION WORKERS THAT PROTECT THE BOARDERS
11. STOPPED ASYLUM FRAUD TOOK DOWN TRAFFICKING OF WOMEN AND CHILDREN
12. ARREST 20,000 GANG MEMBERS AND 500,000 CRIMINAL ALIENS
13. 300 MILES OF BORDER WALL AND WILL BE COMPLETE
14. BORDER CONTROL AGENTS BRAVE PEOPLE COUNTRY LOVES OUR LAW INFORCE AND RESPECT
15. TENNESSE VALLEY AUTHORITY LAID OFF HUNDREDS OF WORKS AND FORCED THEM TO TRADE THEIR LOWER FOREIGN WORKERS REPLACEMENT. AND PROMPTLY REMOVED THE CHAIRMAN OF THE BOARD AND REHIRED THEM BACK NOW GEORGIA, ALABAMA, TENNESSE KENTUCKYM MISSIPPPI, NORTH CAROLINA, AND VIRGINIA
16. LOWER THE COST OF PRESCRIPTION DRUG PRICES THE BEST DEAL 60-70%
17. RIGHT TO TRY
18. VA CHOICE
19. VA ACCOUNTABILITY
20. APPOINTED 300 NEW JUDGES
21. APPOINTED 2 SUPREME COURT JUDGES CRIMINAL JUSTICE REFORM OPPORTUNITY ZONES CRIMINAL JUSTICE REFORM
22. LONG TERM FUNDING BLACK UNIVERSITY AND COLLEGES
23. THE PRESIDENT HAS DONE MORE FOR THE AFRICAN AMERICAN COMMUNITY THAN ANY PRESIDENT THAN ABRAHAM LINCOLN
24. GREATEST JOB NUMBERS FOR THE ASIAN, MEXICANS, AND AFRICAN AMERICA EVER IN HISTORY

25. WHEN PRESIDENT TRUMP TOOK OFFICE MIDDLE EAST WAS IN CHAOS ISIS WAS RAMPAGING IRAN SERIOUS TROUBLE AFGANANSTAN WAR NO END INSIGHT. WITHDREW FROM IRAN NUCLEAR DEAL ONE SIGHTED
26. RECOGNIZE ISRAELS TRUE CAPITAL AND MOVED EMBASSY TO JERUSALEM

WE GOT BUILD NOT PLANNED OF 1 BILLION ... GOT AN EXISTING BUILDING AND OPENED IT LESS THAN 500,000 DOLLARS.

27. ACHIEVE FIRST MIDDLE EAST DEAL IN 25 YEARS
28. OBLITERATED ISIS AND KILLED ITS FOUNDER AND ABU BACAR ALBAGDADI
29. SEPARATED OPERATION ELIMINATE THE MOST TREACHEROUS TERRORIST KASIM SOLAMINI
30. GIVING
31. KEPT AMERICA OUT OF WARS TROOPS ARE COMING HOME
32. SPENT 2.5 TRILLION DOLLARS WAS BADLY DEPLETED
33. THREE SEPARATE PAY RAISE WARRIORS.
34. LAUNCH FIRST NEW BRANCH SINCE THE 7YTHE SPACE FORCE LAST FOUR YEARS OF THE PAST
35. FIX BAD TRADE DEALS JAPAN AND SOUTH KOREA TRADE DEAL THAT TOOK MANY JOBS.
36. BIDEN DID MANY ITEMS OPPOSING COMPLETELY TO BUILD AMERICA'S FREEDOM AND SAFETY. INFLECTED UPON AMERICA

A. VOTED NAPHA DISASTER SINGLE MOST TRADE DEAL ENACTED
B. SUPPORT CHINA'S ENTRY INTO THE WORLD TRAD
AFTER THAT USA LOST ONE IN FOUR MANUFACTURING JOBS
C. LAY OFF OHIO, PENNSYLVANIA, TENNESSE, ALABAMA, MICHIGAN, AND MANY OTHER STATES THEY DID NOT WANT TO HEAR BIDEN THEY WANTED THEIR JOBS BACK

D. AS VICE PRESIDENT, HE SUPPORTED THE TRANSPACIFIC PARTNERSHIP THAT WOULD HAVE BEEN A DEATH SENTENCE TO THE AUTOMOBILE TRADE DEAL
E. HE BACKED THE SOUTH KOREA TRADE DEAL TOOK MANY JOBS FROM OUR COUNTRY, AND PRESIDENT TRUMP REVERSED THIS
F. REPEATED SUPPORT MAS ANMENISTY FOR ILL
G. VOTED IRAQ WAR
H. OPPOSE DID NOT VOTE TO KILL ISIS TERRORIST
I. CHEERED RISE FOR CHINA THAT IS WHY CHINA WANTS HIM IN
J. CHINA ALLOWED THE VIRUS TO COME OUT AND THEY COULD HAVE STOPPED IT.

37. COVID-19

A. WE WILL UNITED AND overcame THE VIRUS
B. WHEN THE CHINA VIRUS HIT, WE LAUNCH THE LARGEST NATIONAL MOBILIZATION EMERGENCY SINCE WORLD WAR II, EVOKING THE DEFENSE INVOKING ACT, WE PRODUCED
C. LARGEST SUPPLY OF VINDALATORS TASK FORCE BY THE VICE PRESIDENT
D. HUNDREDS OF MILLIONS AND MASKS TO OTHER
E. NURSING HOMES EVERYTHING NEED FOR THE VIRUS
F. FIELD HOSPITALS BUILD
G. LOW-RISK AMERICA BE RELEASED TO GO BACK TO SCHOOL AND WORK
H. THEY HAVE TO GET BACK TO WORK
I. SCIENCE GENIUS TO PRODUCE A VACCINE
THREE DIFFERENT VACCINES IN THE FINAL STAGE OF TRIAL RIGHT NOW YEARS AHEAD AS BEFORE. MATTER OF FEW MONTHS 100 AND MILLIONS OF DOSES AND HAVE A SAFE VACCINE THIS YEAR WILL CRUSH THE VIRUS
J. POWERFUL CONVELESCNE SAVE 1000'S OF LIFE
80% SINCE APRIL
K. LOWEST IN THE FATALITY RATE IN ALL NATIONS
L. TESTING SYSTEMS AMERICA HAS THE MOST
M. INACT LARGEST PACKAGE IN HISTORY

38. DEMOCRATIC AGENDA. THERE IS NONE WE KNOW OF 4 TRILLION DOLLAR TAX ON ALL AMERICAN FAMILY ALL THE STOCKS NOW WIIL COLLAPSE

A. CUT TAXES FOR ALL FAMILIES
B. GIVE TAX CREDITS TO BRING JOBS OUT OF CHINA BACK TO AMERICA
C. WE IMPOSE TAXES ON THOSE THAT TRY TO BRING THE JOBS AND COMPANIES TO OVERSEAS
D. JOE BIDEN AGENDA MADE IN CHINA OUR AGENDA IS MADE IN THE USA
E. BIDEN PROMISE TO ABOLISH THE PRODUCTS COAL, SHELL, AND NATURAL GAS, LAYING WASTE, COLORADO, OKLAHOMA, PENNSYLVANIA, OHIO, TEXAS, NEW MEXICO, DESTROYING THOSE STATES, MANY JOBS LOST AND DESTROY AMERICA. HOW IS HE AN ALLIED IN THE LIGHT
F. BIDEN 110 PAGE PLATFORM SUSPENDING ALL REMOVALS OF ILLEGAL ALIENS AND NATIONWIDE TAX RELEASE, AND FREE TAX FUNDED LAWYERS
G. HEALTH CARE DOLLARS FREE,
H. SUPPORTS SANCTUARY CITIES THAT PROTECT CRIMINALS ALIENS
I. PROMISE TO BAND NATION TRAVEL FROM JEHUTI NATIONS
J. PLEDGE INCREASE MISSIONS AND REFUGE BY 700 PERCENT
K. ELIMINATE AMERICAN'S BORDERS IN THE MIDDLE OF A GLOBAL PANDEMIC
L. TAKING THE WALL DOWN
M. NOT SUPPORTING FREE CHOICE OF SCHOOLS (PRESIDENT TRUMP WILL PROVIDE SCHOOL CHOICE AND CHARTER SCHOOL TO EVERY PERSON IN AMERICA.)
N. PRESIDENT WILL ALWAYS SUPPORT TEACHERS
O. DEMOCRATS WILL ALLOW AN ABORTION IN THE 9 MONTHS OF PREGNANCY
P. <u>ALL CHILDREN BORN AND UNBORN HAVE A GOD GIVEN RIGHT TO LIFE</u>
Q. DURING THE DEMOCRAT CONVENTION, THE WORD UNDER GOD WAS REMOVED FROM THE PLEDGE ALLEGIANCE
R. IF THE LEFT GAINS POWER, THEY WILL DEMOLISH THE SUBERTS CONFISCATE YOUR GUNS AND POINT JUSTICES AND WIPE AWAY YOUR SECOND AMENDMENT AND THE OTHER CONSTITUTION FREEDOM BIDEN IS A TROJAN HORSE OF SOCIALISM.
S. DOES NOT HAVE THE STRENGHT TO STAND UP TO MARKISM
T. DANGEROUS BIDEN. REFORM IS ABOLISHING PUBLIC SAFETY.

U.
V. ATTACK ON PUBLIC SAFETY IMMEDIATELY RELEASING 400,000 CRIMINALS ON THE STREET AND INTO YOUR NEIGHBORHOODS
W. BIDEN CUTTING POLICE FUNDS
X. BIDEN ILAN OMAR PROUDLY DISPLAYED HER. ACCEPTED HER.
Y. DETECTIVE FAMILIAR
Z. GIVE LAW ENFORCEMENT OUR POLICE AFRAID TO LOSE JOBS WITH DEMOCRATIC. WE COULD NEVER ALLOW MOB RULE
AA. DEMOCRATIC RUN CITIES VIOLENCE IN THE STREETS CAN BE FIXED IF THEY WANT IT TO. WE MUST ALL HAVE LAW AND ORDER
BB. NOW THE PRESIDENT HAS MADE 10 YEARS IF DESTROY STATUE
CC. BIDEN DONATED TO A FUND OF ANARCHIST, LOOTS, RIOTERS, PROTESTORS
DD. DAVID CAPTAIN HEROIC LEGACY
EE. THE REPUBLICAN PARTY WILL REMAIN THE PATRIOTIC HEROES THAT KEEP AMERICA SAFE AND SALUTE THE AMERICA FLAG
FF. TOP 10 DEMOCRATIC CITIES HAVE HAD THE HIGHEST DEATHS OF AFRICAN AMERICANS 1,000'S AND 1,000'S VICTIMS
GG. LIBERAL IS WILL APPLY THEIR SO-CALLED PEACEFUL DEMONSTRATION IN THE STREETS AND EVERY POWER OF THE OFFICES IN THE GOVERNMENT
HH. DEMOCRATIC POLITICIANS ARE HIRING THE RADICAL PROFESSORS, JUDGES, AND PROSECUTORS
II. WHO IS TRYING TO ABOLISH IMMIGRATION ENFORCEMENT AND ESTABLISH SPEECH CODES DESIGN TO MUSSEL DISSENT?
JJ. SPY ON CAMPAIGN AND THEY GOT CAUGHT
KK. WE MUST RECLAIM FROM THE LEFT AMERICA ARE EXHAUSTED AND WANT TO CANCEL CULTURE. FAR LEFT FORCE YOU TO SAY WHAT YOU KNOW TO BE FALSE AND SCARCE YOU NOT HAVE YOU SAY WHAT YOU KNOW TO BE TRUE.
LL. BIDEN ELIMINATE SCHOOL CHOICE WELL THEY ALLOW THEIR CHILDREN IN THE FINEST SCHOOLS IN THE LAND.
MM. BIDEN TAKES HIS MARCHING ORDERS FROM THE LIBERALS
NN. WANT TO DEFUND POLICE WHILE THEY HAVE ARMED GUARDS
OO. OPEN BOARDERS, THEY WANT WITHOUT

EVERDAY POLICE OFFICERS RISK THEIR LIFE IN THE LIGHT OF DUTY
- PP. SUPPORT 15 MILLION OF AMERICAN JOBS
- QQ. RECOVERING AT A FASTEST RATE THAN
- RR. THE NEXT FOUR YEARS MANUFACTURING SUPERPOWERS OF THE WORLD MEDICAL SUPPLY CHAINS TAKING OUR BUSINESS OUT OF CHINA
- SS. CREATE 10 MILLION JOBS OF THE 10 MONTHS.
- TT. FEDERAL PROSECUTORS IN HIGH CRIME CITIES
- UU. WE WILL BAND SANCTUARY CITIES
- VV. INSURE MEDICAL
- WW. STRIKE DOWN TERRORIST
- XX. KEEP OUT OF WAR
- YY. EQUAL JUSTICE COLOR AND GREED
- ZZ. PROTECT MEDICARE AND SOCIAL SECURITY PLEDGE FROM THE ENTIRE REPUBLICAN PARTY.
- AAA. PROTECT PATIENCE FROM PRE-EXISTING
- BBB. REDUCE MEDICAL BUILDING AND TRANSPARENCY AND REDUCE COST OF DRUGS AND MEDICAL COSTS HEALTH
- CCC. WHEN THE RACE OF THE FIVE G
- DDD. BUILD THE BEST CYBER AND MISSILE DEFENSE ALREADY IN CONSTRUCTION
- EEE. RESTORE PATRIOTISM TO OUR SCHOOLS
- FFF. ALWAYS PROTECT FREE SPEECH ON COLLEGES
- GGG. LAUNCH AMERICAN AMBITION IN SPACE FIRST WOMAN ON THE MOON AND FIRST AMERICA TO LAND ON MARS TO PLACE THE FLAG.
  KEEP AMERICAN ENERGY INDEPEND NUMBER ONE IN THE WORLD
- HHH. OBAMA CARE KNOCKED OUT
- III. RIGHT TO BEAR ARMS WE WILL PROTECT 2ND AMENDMENT
- JJJ. NEXT 4 YEARS WE WILL MAKE THE MANUFACTURING SUPERPOWER OF THE WORLD
- KKK. THUNDERING MESSAGE THEY WILL NEVER FORGET
- LLL. WE ARE HERE, AND THEY ARE NOT THE DEMOCRATS THE HOME IN WASHINGTON D.C.
- MMM. WE WILL BUILD THE CONSTRUCTION OF
- A. COUNTRY NOT A NATION REFUSED TO BE TIGHT DOWN OR REIGNED IN HERE IS NO ONE LIKE AMERICA
- B. DOLLARS TO THE FARMER

1. GIVEN TO THE FARMERS 100 MILLION LUNCHES

2. MANUFACTURING MORE THAN 500,000 JOBS
3. JOBS CREATING 7 MILLION PAYING JOBS
4. MANUFACTURING TO RETURN TO EACH COMPANY THAT DESIRES AND EXCELLENT DE-REGULATIONS BETTER TAX INCENTIVES
5. PROTECTED THE PRE-EXISTING CONDITIONS STRONGLY EVER REPUBLICAN

THERE IS A SAYING WHAT ONE DOES THEY BECOME, NOT UNLESS THEY REPENT TO GOD AND CHANGE AND GO DO RIGHTEOUSNESS.
SOMETIME SOME HAVE TO CARRY THAT CROSS FOR THE PEOPLE.
I HAVE BEEN ARRESTED FOR CONSPIRACY REASON, OPPRESSED, CONSPIRED AGAINST, SUPPRESSED, AND DIED AND CAME BACK TO LIFE, AND ALL SORTS OF INJUSTICES AGAINST ME I CANNOT MENTION.
I ASK GOD WHY HAS THINGS HAPPEN HE SAID, "MY GRACE IS SUFFICIENT FOR YOU."
God's grace is sufficient for America and for each individual to be that American and that person that God has given America the land of great love and freedom poured upon her in every individual's heart even if they do not realize it. Though we have fought in God's strength and promises of righteousness in truth to keep this great love and freedom. And God is always with us, ask God, seekGod, love God with all your heart. God's grace is sufficient for you. God's grace is enough for America.

I am a listener of God's light and wisdom; I am a warrior, I am a messenger of the Divine Messages of the Trinity and the Saints for America and the world for God's glory.

I am a spy of America's lover to seek to prevent her from danger and bring the greatest purpose and in the listening ear and Divine Messages. a spy, finds out what is not good, and expose what is not truth and truth. However, people have to listen to and carry out the Divine Messages. This is what we all need to be. We need to be a spy of on ourselves that nothing seeks to hurt our America and us upon us. And realizing what is happening in all our actions in life. This far and now America and the World, we need to be listeners and spies to protector our

America. Then we need to speak aloud in truth. Things that we do not realize that is and could be treacherous or is impeding us that we do not realize, God will make visible to protect us when we seek righteousness

Yahweh Reigns Forever

The sign of the Covenant Abram's righteousness and Yahweh's granting of the covenant: "I am El Shaddai: follow my ways and be blameless, so that I may grant a covenant between you and me, and multiply you exceedingly. . . . Abram's responsibility to "keep" the that is, to watch over, guard, and maintain it. ^{cccxii}

The conclusion of the Exodus story does not come with the defeat of Pharaoh or with the revelation of the law at Sinai, but with the advent of Yahweh's glory amid the covenant communities. Moses' heroic stature not only from his opposition to Pharaoh and victory over him but also from his role as the leader of Israel. ^{cccxiii}

I call heaven and earth to witness against you this day, that I have set before you life and death, blessing and curse; therefore, choose life, that you and your descendants may live, loving Yahweh your God, obeying His voice, and cleaving to Him; for that means life to you and length of days, that you may dwell in the land which Yahweh swore to your fathers, to Abraham, to Isacc, and to Jacob, to give them.
Deut. 30:19-2

Chapter Eleven

DIVINE MESSAGE 9.26.20

TRINITY PRESENT AT CREATION

SPECIFIC WAY GOD CREATED HUMANS AND ALL THINGS
    GOD CREATION

PLANTS NEED WATER, SUN, NUTRIENTS AND TO BE PLANTED IN SOIL
HUMANS NEED WATER, SUN, NUTRIENTS, AND TO HAVE AN ENVIRONMENT
JUSTICE IS TRUTH JUSTICE IS IN THE MOVEMENT OF TRUTH AND TOWARD THE PUREST TRUTH

SINCE MANY VARIABLES ARE ALWAYS CHANGING IN THE ARISTITOLE CATEGORIES, IT IS IMPORTANT TO HAVE A FOUNDATION THAT IS AGREEABLE FOR JUSTICE LAWS AND REGULATIONS ARE THAT FOUNDATION THAT keeps JUSTICE SAFE. HOWEVER, SINCE THE VARIABLES HAVE BEEN VAST OF THE ARISTOTLE CATEGORIES, FORM CHANGES IN GLOBALIZATION, MULTI-CULTURAL SOCIETIES, JUSTICE HAS CHANGED IMMENSELY. JUSTICE BEGINS FIRST IN THE RESPECT OF HOW ONE TREATS EACH OTHER.

BECAUSE THERE ARE VAST DIFFERENCES OF PRACTICES OF ACCEPTING OR NOT ACCEPTING A CERTAIN COMMUNICATION AND RESPONSIBILITIES OF AN EXCHANGE OF BUSINESS AND EVEN RELATIONSHIPS, THERE MAY NOT BE THE PUREST JUSTICE, AND EVEN AT TIMES JUSTICE MAY NOT BE FULFILLED IN A BALANCE GOOD ENOUGH FOR THE PEOPLE.

THEREFORE, THIS IS WHY VIRTUES ARE ESSENTIAL AND ETHICS FOR THE TRAINING OF ALL EDUCATION AND RESPONSIBILITIES OF BUSINESS EXCHANGE. HENCE THEN WE SHOULD HAVE A MANDATORY UNDERSTANDING OF ETHICS AND VIRTUES TO HAVE BETTER COMMUNICATION. THERE ARE DIFFERENT FORMS OF EDUCATION AND DIFFERENT LEVELS IF THE FOUNDATION OF COMMUNICATION IS NOT WITH RESPECTING ONE ANOTHER. THEN WHEN THERE IS A HUMAN

ACCIDENT, MISS COMMUNICATION, OR ANY PROBLEM OR FAILURE OR ISSUE INTENTIONALLY OR NOT INTENTIONALLY, THERE CAN BE A MORE JUSTICE AND PEACEFUL RESOLUTION WITH LESS OR PERHAPS NO DISAGREEMENTS. I SAY THESE THINGS TO PROVE A POINT HOW PARAMOUNT IT IS TO TEACH ETHICS AND VIRTUES.

LISTEN EVEN THE PROCESS OF THE BODY OF THE BLOOD PASSING THROUGH THE BODY FEEDING ALL THE VEINS AND THE HEART AND ALL THE TISSUES AND ORGANS. THIS IS JUSTICE BECAUSE IT IS LIFE. THE BLOOD HAS A RESPONSIBILITY TO DO THIS, AND IF THE BLOOD AND THE HEART PUMPING DECIDES TO STOP, THERE IS NOT LIFE, AND JUSTICE STOPS. JUSTICE IS A PLAN THAT IS THE DIRECTION ON HOW **TRUTH IS IN LIFE SO LIFE CAN LIVE. JUSTICE IS A PLAN BY THE CREATOR THAT HE HAS CREATED, AND ACTUALLY, GOD WANTS US TO BE APART OF IT; NOW AND THEN WE DO NOT KNOW HOW THINGS SHOULD BE, AND EVEN WE THINK WE KNOW YET IT IS NOT THE BEST WAY FOR THE CREATION OR ACTION WE ARE TRYING TO MAKE OR RESOLVE.**

HOW DO WE CREATE JUSTICE TO BE CLOSEST TO THE PUREST TRUTH? WEseekTHE CREATOR AND THE CREATOR WILL DIRECT US I WHEN I SPEAK OF JUSTICE, I AM NOT SAYING OR JUST REFERRING TO POLITICAL JUSTICE. I AM REFERRING TO ALL THINGS AND SCIENCES AND LIVING OF HUMANITY. JUSTICE POLITICALLY IS DELIVERED WHEN ALL THINGS RELATED TO IT POLITICALLY ARE TOWARD TRUTH AND POLITICALS ARE ALL THINGS RELATED TO HUMANITY; THEREFORE, IT IS SALIENT TO HAVE ALL PARTS OF JUSTICE TOWARD THE PUREST TRUTH, AND THEN YOU WILL HAVE MORE PURE JUSTICE.

IF WE COMPROMISE TO LOW, WITH LESS TRUTH, JUSTICE IN OUR LAND WILL BECOME WHAT GET QUOTE FROM PRESIDENT. SAID IF WE DO NOT HAVE GOD IN OUR COUNTRY, OUR COUNTRY WILL BECOME FULL OF INJUSTICES. WHEN JUSTICE IS EVIDENT, TRUTH HAS TO BE JUSTIFIED. THE CLOSEST TRUTH IS IN GOD. THEREFORE, WE CAN KNOW THE PUREST JUSTICE THAT IS LIFE, AND THEN WE KNOW HOW TO RESTORE OR BRING **JUSTICE BECAUSE GOID** IS THE PUREST JUSTICE AND HE IS THE GREATEST TRUTH. JUSTICE LIFE WHEN LIFE IT IS LIVING AND BEING CONTINUOUSLY TO BRING JUSTICE IS THE RESTORATION OF SOMETHING THAT HAS BEEN

I will teach you everything you need to know, and I will watch you with my eyes.

Jesus Christ said I will send you an advocate, the Holy Spirit, that will guide you and direct you and make you come into understanding of all things.

I shall ask the Father, and H.e will give you another Paraclete to be with you forever.

John 14:16

Chapter Twelve

Revolution of God's Love

God's Love and Ours

Dear friends, let us love one another, for love comes from God. Everyone who loves has been born of God and knows God. [8]

1John 4: 7-8

Lord Jesus Christ, you have taught us to be merciful like the heavenly Father and have told us that
Show us your face, and we will be saved.[cccxiv]

Pope Francis

"The United States is founded on the principle that our right does not come from the government; they come from God. This immortal truth is proclaimed in our Declaration of Independence and enshrined in the First Amendment to our Constitution's Bill of Rights. Our founders understood that no right is more fundamental to a peaceful, prosperous, and virtuous society that the right to follow one's religious convictions."[cccxv]

God in the Divine Command to Give President Trump and the American People

Every revolution was first a thought in one man's mind, and when the same thought occurs
In another man, it is the key to that era.

Ralph Waldo Emerson, "History," Essays, First Series, 1841

America a Country of God for Humanity

God's Love

God's Creation of Man and the Universe
Heal America

Eucharistic Body of rs   God's
love in the People will Heal America

1. Man and Woman and Family
1. Love God with all your heart and your neighbor
Man and Woman and Family
king God's love, reconciliation, transformation,
2. Humanity has dominion over the earth
And continuous healing, protection for family values, and the
3. Life of America is God's intended Goodness
The human d of life.
4. Forgiveness of sin of self and others
5. Tree of Knowledge of Good
5. Tree of life – to overcome the sins of evil
What is all truth and omniscience of God?
    i. Love God with all your Heart and Soul
                  i. How, what, and when do you seek to
ii. Love Your Neighbor as yourself
    God's truth.
6. Virtues – will bring about peace, justice, restoration and forward building in love.
6. Tree of Knowledge of Evil
7. Ethics- Judeo-Christian and universal ethics in agreement.
7. Salvation –
    8. Application and Education of Virtue and Ethics a requirement in
i. Those who .   Business,
public and private schools, universities, and all communities
ii. Those who want salvation.
iii. Even those who are believers and have not
accept God in Jesus Christ.
iv. Repentance
8. Tree of Life in God is first accepting Him and
in all that you do represent Him.
9. America has the "Staff of Authority" when one seeks
Of God's commands, not man's
10. The disciple's study them, (Read the Bible)

God's Relationship with His People

God covenant with His People

Through the might of God, America can be continued to be restored

In His love. He has the Covenant between Yahweh and Abrahamic line.

Today this is all those who accept His Son, Jesus Christ the New Covenant

"*El Shaddia*" means "God of the Mountain." Or "God Almighty."

El Shaddia is "their God." The identity of God can be grasped in relationship to Abram and his descendants.

Abram's <u>righteousness</u> and Yahweh's granting the Covenant: "I am *El Shaddia*: follow my ways and be blameless. . . Abram's responsibility to " keep the Covenant, watch over, guard, and maintain it.[cccxvi]

What is the Covenant between God and His people

The Covenant: is "Love," of loyalty

"*Shema*," of Judaism,(the Hebrew word means "hear"), and the basis of the "great commandment" of Jesus (Matt 22:34-40)

"Hear, O Israel! Our God is Yahweh, Yahweh alone! And love Yahweh your God with all your heart, with all your life, indeed with all your capacity."

Israel was brought out of the land of Egypt, out of the house of bondage, by God.[cccxvii]

We need to live and be and work toward the "Revolution of Love," the "Revolution of God's love,"

so that we will never be bounded into slavery.

George Washington stated regarding the war with Britan:

" He exhorted to his men to remember " that you are Freemen, fighting for the blessings of liberty," and that "slavery will be our portion, and that of your posterity if you do not acquit yourselves like men."[cccxviii]

Today all of us together need to "acquit ourselves like men, " is loving the Lord with all your heart.

Today as Americans, we "Love" God with all our hearts and soul. That is how America is our great

Country, and we are keeping America high.

The Shaping of a Nation.

Americans are heroes that have pledged their sacred honor and their lives to keep America free. [cccxix]

Let us continue to keep the Stars and Stripes rising over America as they first did in

New York Harbor when the British departed in November 1783.[cccxx]

The Age of Enlightenment inspired a revolution: "The ideas of 18th century philosophers Voltaire and Rousseau changed people's opinions.

Early, 17th Century English philosopher John Locke had written that government is a trust, meant to protect the inherent rights of the people, namely

The right to life, liberty, and property.[cccxxi] Today let us

(the First Two Years of America under President Trump).

Let all of us be "merciful as the Father," and reconcile and infuse a Revolution of Love full of justice, peace, restoration, and virtues full of ethics.

Today, now America has an Enlightenment when they voted in President Trump is making America great a have accepted making America first. Restoring America,

1. The Government Trustworthy: Under President Trump and the team and those in congress are to restore and keeping America Great.
2. Protecting the inherent rights of the people
3. Right to life
4. Right to liberty
5. Right to Property

PRESIDENT TRUMP AND THE TEAM AND AMERICANS ARE ENLIGHTENED

WE ARE ALL WORKING TOWARD KEEPING AMERICA GREAT:

We are BLESSED TO HAVE AMERICA GREAT AND KEEPING HER TRUSTWORTHINESS

We are BLESSED TO HAVE AMERICA GREAT AND KEEPING HER PROTECTED

We are BLESSED TO HAVE AMERICA GREAT IN RIGHT TO LIFE

We are BLESSED TO HAVE AMERICA GREAT IN LIBERTY

We are BLESSED TO HAVE AMERICA GREAT TO SUSTAIN OUR PROPERTY

America a Country of God for Humanity

God's Love

God's Personal Relationship with His People

God covenant with His People God's Creation of Man and the Universe AND those who LOVE AMERICA

Bible

We cannot sell American to the opposing forces against her future freedom, protection, economic sustaining power, education, cultural and human rights, and her present and the new d of her legacy.

George Washington stated regarding the war with Britain.

" He exhorted to his men to remember " that you are Freemen, fighting for the blessings of liberty," and that "slavery will be our portion, and that of your posterity if you do not acquit yourselves like men."[cccxxii]

Today all of us together need to "acquit ourselves like men(good humanity, with virtues following Ethics.

Heal America

God's love in the People will Heal America. God can only pour Good over Good.

God can and will redeem when we see Him in forgiveness and reconciliation.

God's intention, Perfect Divine of the Prime Mover,

We are imperfect and incomplete beings (humanity).

United to God that what is an "enjoyment" of the "Perfect Divine," God.

He makes us complete; we never stop growing in Him. Because in Him, we have eternal life.

We need to Reconcile with each other:

TRUTH IN PEACE, TRUTH INJUSTICE, TRUTH IN RESTORATION, TRUTH IN LOVE

THE REVOLUTION OF LOVE FIRST WILL KEEP AMERICA GREAT

LOVE IN:

VIRTUES IN GOD ARE THE ANSWER TO AMERICA'S RESTORATION AND KEEPING HER GREAT.

Listen, peace, justice, and restoration, and love

FOR BELIEVERS IT IS THE PERSONAL RELATIONSHIP FIRST WITH GOD AND SECOND LOVING YOUR NEIGHBOR.

INDIVIDUALLY YET TOGETHER WE WILL KEEP AMERICA GREAT.

We carry America upon our shoulders as God carries us on His.

Americans in everything we do, we seek purity to have the truth.

Globalization: *One of the most serious challenges our countries face is the specter of socialism.*

It's the wrecker of nations and destroyer of societies. "[cccxxiii]

President Trump

VIRTUE and integrity be my protection, for my hope, Yahweh, is in you.

Psa. 25:21

Chapter Thirteen

Pius X

Brief Notes of Contemplation

First Virgin Mary and the Discussion of the Works of Pope Pius X and Aristotle and America 2020

First, Virgin Mary, my deepest friend with Jesus Christ and the Holy Spirit at the table of tutoring in her shimmer effervescent holy robe of blue quintessential love of heaven's power and most incredible Wisdom of God, I seek in prayer, contemplation, listening, waiting and being healed and receiving. And, with Jesus Christ, Pope Pius X has been a man of God I revere; he has been a mentor and guide and protector for me! It is as if he has given me a graduation ceremony robe and hat and tassel. I have sought him in his teachings and prayers when I pray to Jesus Christ and Mary as if I am a student at a table receiving private tutoring covered in his golden-yellow robe and green shawl of wings of wisdom. See I have much to learn and be patient for and to grow in God. And His crown of truth reflects my desire to learn, realizing my ignorance as a human, and only that is good comes for God. And his shoes are enlightened and shimmering with peace.

I was commanded to briefly study these writings and support ideas for men and women that have little faith or need more proof that Jesus Christ in the Trinity of the God of Abraham and Queen Virgin Mary is truly pure.

Pope Pius X speaks of:
Roman Empire. Italy, abandoned by the Emperors of Byzantium, had been left a prey of the still unsettled Lombard. They roamed up and down the whole country, laying waste everywhere with fire and sword and bringing desolation and death in their train. This very city, threatened from without by its enemies, tried from within by the scourges of pestilence, floods, and famine, was reduced to such a miserable plight that it had become a problem how to keep the breath of life in the citizens and the immense multitudes who flocked hither for refuge.[cccxxiv]

The "Lombard" are compared today to some of the protestors that are paid to "bring fire, and sword, and desolation and death in the train." And the "Byzantium Emperors" are compared to the hidden ~~Elite~~, Communist and Socialist and even those have said the "Technologist, and false Media, and corrupt Politicians," that are finance by and the Socialist and Communist Party of the Chinese, that has allowed the spread of the Chinese Virus to try to destroy American and even parts of the world.

Pope Gregory thirteen century himself calls the Church of Rome: "An old ship woefully shattered; for the waters are entering on all sides, and the joints, buffeted by the daily stress of the storm, are growing rotten and herald shipwreck" (*Registrum i., 4 ad Joannem episcop. Constantino.*). **Succeeding not only in making the port despite the raging seas but in saving the vessel from future storms. Gregory himself calls to the Church of Rome:**

The Church of Rome is compared to the America of God that is His land; and His foundation for humanity to live, and be, and have freedom, and to worship Him with all their heart and soul and life bringing justice in the living waters of love of the Spirit of God can redeem all things.

<u>**I am the pilot that takes up the strong hand of God to redeem American.**</u> **Yes, saving the country, America, and the world the vessel of God's heart from the storms of evil, the Socialist, the Communist, and the secret group and technical controls for one world power.**
Let us protect our freedom in America. Let us protect our freedom world.

Pope Gregory, 3. Truly remarkable is the work he was able to effect during his reign of little more than thirteen years. He was the restorer of Christian life in its entirety, stimulating the devotion of the faithful (Joann. Diac., Vita Greg. ii. 51), he preserved and increased the patrimony of the Church, and liberally succored the impoverished people, Christian society, and individual churches, according to the necessities of each. Becoming truly God's Consul (Epitaph), he pushed his productive activity far beyond the walls of Rome, and entirely for the advantage of civilized society. He opposed the unjust claims of the Byzantine Emperors energetically; he checked the audacity and curbed the shameless avarice of the exarchs and the imperial administrators and stood up in public as the defender of social justice. He tamed the ferocity of the Lombards. **Hence, Pope Gregory may justly be called the savior and liberator of Italy - his own land, as he tenderly calls her.**

    Let us be as Pope Gregory to be that "savior and the liberator," of America and the world our land.

    This is the change of the right hand of the Most High, God! And well, may it be said that in the mind of Gregory, the hand of God alone was operative in these great events.^cccxxv The holy Pontiff's profound humility hid from his own sight: instead of using the exalted prestige of the Pontifical dignity, he preferred to call himself the Servant of the Servants of God, a title which he was the first to adopt.^cccxxvi

"Love is the cause of good." ^cccxxvii

> *The grace of our Lord filled me with faith and with the love that is in Christ Jesus.*

1Tim. 1:14

A brief discussion of Aristotle ^cccxxviii

Because Aristotle is one of the most blessed humans in understanding humanity and life in the ancient world, I think it helps discuss a few aspects that relate to our subject.
Also, to serve those who need history to help them be faithful to the restoration of truth in America and the world.

Even in the ancient days of philosophy is was d that there is and now also thought:

" *One-from (God) all other comes to be,"* Aristotle states, God is the Prime Mover.

For those who, we say the Prime Mover is God, the creator. Remember, Aristotle is speaking 300 – 400 before the birth of Jesus Christ. Also, Aristotle states that this "entity, which all other things come to be, is being conserved., God has His hands on the earth and the universe. He is a God of life.

God is a "jealous love" for His humanity. In God not accepting our past mistakes for disrespecting America and putting her in danger in all directions.

God did not give us a spirit of timidity, but the spirit of power and love and self-control.

2Tim. 1:7

God wants us to continue to restore her America the "Sodom and Gamora's" of the areas with all walks of life from the individual, to families, to communities, to business, to government, to leaders, and even to His Church.

God does leave places where there are not His beauty that has completely in His wisdom defined as evil as Sodom and Gamora. Are these the turmoil and treacherous natural disasters we? In saying that, beauty can become evil. This fact shows that evil does exist. There needs to be an awareness and exposure to good and evil.

God of Abraham, He is saving America now at this very moment
"And Hesiod (Look up) says:- "
"First of all things was chaos made, and then
"Broad-breasted earth...
"And love, 'mid all the gods pre-eminent, "
Even in Hesiod's time in love is the most "pre-eminent."[cccxxix]

Genesis 1, The Creation of,
"Broad breast earth," how the earth may we say is all love when in its fullness BECAUSE LOVE IS IS THE MOST "PRE-EMINENT." The universe (earth) is INTENTION TO BE all love with it is be(earth) healed because God conserves it. Hence love will heal all things.

"First of all, things was chaos!" If God can make love out of chaos, look.

He can make our chaos into love.
NOW WE ARE KING TO FIRST WORK IN LOVE
LOVE IS THE MOST PRE-EMINENT.

LOVE IS SPEAKING AND PROCLAIMING IN TRUTH, NOT BRUSHING THINGS TO THE SIDE LIKE YOU DID NOT THEM .. THEY WILL GET WORSE. THIS IS WHAT HAPPEN TO AMERICA.
*"There is **a Mind in nature, just as in animals, and that this is the cause of all order and arrangement....** We know definitely that Anaxagoras adopted this view, but Hermotimus of Calzomenae is credited with having started it earlier. Those thinkers, those who held this view, assumed a principle in things which is the cause of beauty and the sort of caused by the motion which motion is communicated to thing."*[cccxxx]

God is calling us NOW GOD WANTS US TO SPEAK ALOUD OUR VOICE STANDING IN TRUTH. He understands He understands, there has been chaos throughout history.

God has an intention, "Mind of nature. . that this is the cause of all order and arrangement."

The God of Abraham, He has redeemed the world, continually, always never forsaking us; the sun is up high in the morn and moon up high in the evening, and the fields of the harvest are fresh; because the working backs and hands of the field workers have given all their heart and soul; their sweat their hope know their child will be with them in the evening meeting them at their humble home with the fragrance of corn tortilla and Bud Light Beer or even American food of hamburgers and fried chicken and green beans and all the aromas of cooking of the world. Yes, America a family of a Mother of All Nations.

These field workers are Americans. They are the harvest of love giving the food at our tables morning noon and night. The farmers of years of suffering also knowing not how the season will be redeemed. All the workers of every vocation are here. They are Americans, each one of us.

Let us treat those who build America with justice and compassionate laws. Let God's love of all "pre-eminence" of all things be His intention.

God can redeem us and create beauty because we humbled ourselves; We now the people can work together to create jobs, develop finances, create life so that all could live in the wholesomeness of existence with integrity, fullness in life empowered by the workforce.

Chaos can be redeemed by "love pre-eminence" of all things.
Chaos can be redeemed by the conservation of God's love in the people, and in truth, there is love.

, God's love is that redemption of those in power; God's love will preserve those who have sought to create beauty.

God's wisdom in that He gave to humanity at creation was and is perfect. NOW WE ARE RESTORING AMERICA AND REALIZE WE NEED TO BRING

PEACE, JUSTICE, RESTORATION, LOVE

Let us now CONTINUE to LIFT UP AND RESTORE what we have made beauty at the gift from God's hands.

Let us not bring destruction to something that we created and developed America's legacy for generations.

We do not want to be the Hitler of the holocaust of the Jews in the fact of not giving justice to our America and bring violence and death to our legacy and our children's future.
Even now, our America is being RESTORED though we can never forget who helps build it with their hands from farmers, to businessmen, to physicians, to teachers, to police, to politicians, to mothers, to father, to all vocations and all peoples of goodwill.

You, though, have followed my teaching, my way of life, my aims, my faith, my patience and my love, my perseverance

2Tim. 3:10

Yes, all of us have built together America. Mother nature and God Himself will thunder out in voice and heart, "Give My people justice, protect the d of life, protect those in need and empower them with the knowledge to succeed and to be self-sufficient."

Mother nature sending with the Power of the Holy Spirit of the Trinity, will feel the cold spirit and within the cities and communities will be sorrow never forgotten, yet perhaps forgiven. And the Arch Angels of the Arms and Wings of the God of Abraham with hover over the Mountains on High to the truth and protect.

Forgiveness will bring the new life of Seth's d will bloom into the most extraordinary beauty of justice and love.

And mercy from Mother Nature and God Himself will be as a "thief in the night," and take away all evil and compromised beyond recall. In proclaiming that God's roots of His love will breathe life when injustices are redeemed to justice, separating the evil and redeeming evil and useful as a "thief in the night." And taking His people to His heart and those who have repented.

We need to empower humanity in America! As Virgin Mary told me before, America will become ashamed and lazy and not confident and not create if we do not supply jobs, safety, protection of cultural traditions and religious worship, free to develop businesses, fair protection from the government: the government serves the people do respect and work together with the government.

At last, the present government officials and President Trump the light of truth, uplifting America first.

The reason is that this, most of all the senses, makes us know and brings to light many differences between things." 1. Hence, we need to work in negotiable skills to those in power to show whether it is in advocacy and building a community and restoring it, and building each city that needs restoration.

2. We need to allow the people to be stimulated, educated, empowered, trained, free, equipped, and promote justice to be invigorated in the revelation of the senses to invent and create and produce in our God-given country America. And when their friend our neighbor being changed, there will be a change among them that justice will be glowing in their path at every step, and the eyes of their heart will know why needs to be restored and forborne and forgiven and even subsidized, because of those whom the trials have been the most difficult.

4. This is why we need healthy cities to clean up the darkness of injustices.

5. There is an argument that America is not the greatest country anymore because of the statistics shown in comparison to other countries. I refute this because the statistic is incorrectly assessed.

When comparing other countries, their diversity, such as socio-economically, culturally, and all other human conditions, is not equal. The diversity of one country is not the same as the other. The difference causes the statistics to have fluctuation and movement; consequently, when a country has vast diversity, especially with lower socio-economic diversity and lower education development, there will appear to have higher statistics in comparison with other countries that have less diversity.

Arise to God's Truth America has taken in all peoples whether productive or country

1. The liberals air time
2. We have had the highest 7th in Literacy, 27 Math, 22 Science, 49th in life expectancy, 178th in enfant mortality, 3rd in median household income, 4th in labor force, 4th in exports,
   Number incarcerated citizens per capita
   Defense spending.

1. We stood up for what is right
2. We fought for moral reasons
3. We raise wars on poverty, not poor people
4. We Sacrificed we cared about our neighbors
5. We put our money where our mouths were
6. And we never beat our chest
7. We had great technological advances
8. Explored the universe
9. Cured diseases
10. We cultivated the greatest economy
11. I say, " We will work for not to end the world's greatest economy."

Pope Pius X reveals in his Encyclical of Singulari Quadam, **"These are fundamental principles: No matter what the Christian does, even in the realm of temporal goods, he cannot ignore the supernatural good. Rather, according to the dictates of Christian philosophy, he must order all things to the ultimate end, namely, the Highest Good."**[cccxxxi]

We as Americans realize the highest good is to Love God with all your Heart and Soul and then in turn we will love our neighbor as ourselves; hence, loving of the highest good is giving humanity empowerment in God's truth to be that authentic being God created the person for and the will to be.

Why is America the greatest country of God in the world? **Remember even though our statistics are not perfect in production. We have taken on the cross of the burdens of many peoples of all nations to nurture them and give them life. Although the leftist tried to sell America, they lost. America is God's land and the people are at His Sacred Heart in the Trinity. Hence, our heart is the heart of God. Life is not measured by material goods, (even though they are salient to life and a secondary foundation to happiness) life is measured by love the love of God.**

We are the heart of God.
Jesus Christ says,
"I am the vine. You are the branches. If you remain in me and I in you, you will bear much fruit; apart from me, you can do nothing." John 15:5

AMERICA REALIZES WE CANNOT DO NOTHING WITHOUT GOD AND WE HAVE HUMBLED OURSELF REALIZING HE GIVEN ALL WE HAVE.
WE LOVE HIM FIRST WITH ALL OUR HEART, LIFE, AND SOUL AND ENTIRE BEING.

But when the kindness and love of God our Saviour for humanity were revealed, [5] it was not because of any upright actions we had done ourselves; it was for no reason except His own faithful love that He saved us, by means of the cleansing.

Titus 3:4

Though are citizens need to be peace, what a citizen is a "speaking broadly, to secure the independence of life. . . Citizenship does not necessarily depend on the descent." [cccxxxii]

In violence and non-peace, there is no "secure independence of life," which means safety.
Hence, the person is not a good citizen, and perhaps not considered a definition of a citizen, when they do not "secure independence of life," <u>safety.</u>
Furthermore, America is a country of all "descents," a Mother of All Nations, and those are citizens, yet they need to "secure the independence of life." In safety and peace, there is a "secure independence of life."
"Now we say that a good ruler is virtuous and wise and that a citizen taking part in politics must be wise."[cccxxxiii]

Those that are the "master worker," those who know how and why things are done need to act for justice for the entire community of humanity; otherwise, they will treat humans like animals and with the injustice of deformity. Then there will be the death of life.

"Nothing is useful, which is not just."[cccxxxiv]

" A just man never seeks his advantage in another man's disadvantage. But is always on the lookout to{help} others."

"Nothing can be useful that is not virtuous, and nothing can be virtuous if it is not useful."[cccxxxv]

Duties of the Clergy.

Pope Ambrose translated by Euthymius
Book 3 Chapter 1

This is why we in the PAST we have become lower in our production and our country is threatened. Today now we have a SPIRIT OF GOD THAT FLOWS IN THE HEART OF THE PEOPLE, even if it is small we can overcome all things.

To protect America
To educate America
To rebuild America

However, with this new life in the people and let us plead and pray with President Trump, and government:

To "make America great again."
To bring justice to America again.
To take care of the people of America again by empowering them.
To President Trump and the current government are "getting results:"

Letter from President Donald J. Trump, April 2018

1. The economy has created nearly 3 million jobs, the unemployment rate is at a 17-year low, and the stock market continues to soar;
2. Republicans passed massive tax cuts for hardworking Americans and reformed the tax code for the first time in 30years, making it simpler and fairer. We also repealed Obama Care's mandate tax that hit low-and middle-income Americans the hardest;
3. We cut job-killing, Health-care regulations to help American businesses grow and create jobs, eliminating 22 laws for every one new provision; and
4. A record 12 circuit court of appeals judges were confirmed in the first year of my presidency, and I kept my promise to appoint judges who will interpret the law as written, including Associate Jus Neil Gorsuch to the Supreme Court.
5. President Trump on May 16, 2018, has formed a quorum of leaders in California to solve the immigration problem in the safety

and protection of our legacy for California. I pray it is directed toward God's truth and justice.

"We have to recognize, and we here was built is waking up to the fake news. WE are waking up to the lies Liberals have been feeding our country for decades."

Letter from President Donald J. Trump, April 2018

President Trump and the American Government have your back; American strong has the back of God's promises; God is at America on all sides.

"We are still fighting to take back our country, and we will not rest."
Awake, arise see the truth of the Modernist today that want to take our country's justice.
The Catholic Church, and the Church of God, represent justice for humanity. Justice in truth.

Today, in our USA, we have a division; and we cannot let certain communities and states banish and stealthily create conspiracy and hatred to our religious and cultural beliefs and justice and truth to protect the people.

Pope X in the Encyclical of Iamdudum, Long Since, "Government as adopted in that country, there immediately began to be promulgated measures breathing the most implacable hatred of the Catholic religion (justice)? We have seen religious communities evicted from their homes, and most of them driven beyond the Portuguese frontiers We have seen, arising out of an obstinate determination to secularize every civil organization and to leave no trace of religion in the acts of common life, the deletion of the feast days of the Church from the number of public festivals, the abolition of religious oaths, the hasty establishment of the law of divorce and religious instruction banished from the public schools."[cccxxxvi]

Pope Pius X is a Pope to protect God's Church in the treachery of the modernist, here he speaks of Pope Gregory. Today we as a people of America also need to protect our Church and America for God's purpose in our life and freedom of truth.

"He lives eternally in every place by his innumerable good works" (Apud Joann. Diac., Vita Greg. iv. 68) it will surely be given, with the help of Divine grace, to all followers of his wonderful example, to fulfill the duties of their own offices, as far as human weakness permits."[cccxxxvii]

Though as commanded, God only can pour good on America. God accommodates. He will act with force at any time to protect His covenant and intention for justice and life as what it means to be human.

We as a people of America:

"Value of the things that are eternal."

Pope Ambrose

That what is eternal is justice and justice has to permeate.

"Justice is the aim and criterion of all politics."

St. Thomas Aquinas

Yes, this is why God has commanded to enter the Judeo-Christian ethics in the pubic system again now! That is what America was built on the "eternal" truth of God, to pursue justice under all circumstances yet first in peace.

"We have said in the Ethics what the difference is between art and
science and the other kindred faculties; but the point of our present
discussion is this that all men suppose what is called wisdom to
deal with the first causes and the principles of things; so that,
as has been said before, the man of experience is thought to be wiser
than the possessors of any sense-perception whatever the artist wiser
then the men of experience, the master-worker than the mechanic, and
the theoretical kinds of knowledge to be more of the nature of wisdom
Then the productive. Then wisdom is knowledge about certain
principles and causes.

"But the science which investigates causes is also instructive, in a higher degree, for the people who instruct us, are those who tell the causes of each thing. And understanding and knowledge pursued for their own sake are found mostly in the knowledge of that which is most knowable (for he who chooses to know for the sake of knowing will choose most readily that which is most true knowledge, and such is the knowledge of that which is most knowable); and the first principles." Aristotle Metaphysics

"Evidently we have to acquire knowledge of the original causes (for we say we know each thing only when we think we recognize its first cause), and causes are spoken of in four senses. In one of these we mean the substance, i.e., the essence (for the 'why' is reducible finally, to the definition, and the ultimate 'why' is a cause and principle); in another the matter or substratum, in a third the source of the change, and in a fourth the cause opposed to this, the purpose and the good (for this is the end of all generation and change). [cccxxxviii]

Original causes Four Senses:
1. the substance, i.e., the essence
2. the matter or substratum
3. the source of the change
4. the cause opposed to this, the purpose and the good (for this is the end of all generation and change)

"We have stated, then, what is the nature of the science we are searching for, and what is the mark which our search and our whole investigation must reach?"

Notes on Aristotle for the Book 2
Aristotle Metaphysics
I read this after I wrote on in of the command to write of the Divine Messages that

"for there must be some entity-either one or more than one-from which all other
things come to be, it is conserved."

Even in the ancient days of philosophy, it was hypothesized that there was an entity " one-from which all other comes to be," which may we say is God the creator. Remember, Aristotle is speaking in ancient times before Christ. Also, Aristotle states that this "entity, which all other things come to be, is being conserved. , God has His hands on the earth and the universe. He is a God of life.

God does leave places where there is not His beauty completely in His wisdom defined as evil as Sodom and Gamora. He is saving America now at the covenant of the good in Him.

Sodom and Gamora, shows the beauty can become evil. This fact shows that evil exists. There needs to be an awareness and exposure to good and evil.

This is why ethics is the platinum heavenly Christly anchor to bring a free and just country.

"And Hesiod (Look up) says:- "
"First of all things was chaos made, and then
"Broad-breasted earth...
"And love, 'mid all the gods (GOD) pre-eminent, "

Even in Hesiod's time in love is the most "pre-eminent."

Broad breast earth.. how the earth may we say is all love when in its fullness. The world is all love with it is being healed because God conserves it; hence.. love will heal all things.

If God can make love out of chaos, lookup, Genesis. He can cause the chaos that we sought to do better for our world, although we have failed and made it worse.

God is calling out, He understands, He understands, there can be chaos throughout history He has redeemed the world, continually, always never forsaking the sun up high in the morn and moon up high in the evening and the fields of the harvest fresh because the back and hands of the field workers have given all their heart and soul, their sweat their hope know their child will be with them in the evening meeting them at their humble home with the fragrance of corn tortilla and Bud Light Beer or even American food of hamburgers. They are the harvest of love giving the food at our tables morning, noon, and night. The farmers of years of suffering also knowing not how the season will be redeemed. All the workers are here shill they are Americans, Americans, each one of us.

Let us treat those who build America with justice, compassionate laws.

Let God's love of all "pre-eminence" of all things.

We can redeem this chaos of to life and beauty, and when the people work together to create jobs, create finances, create an experience so that all could live in wholesomeness of existence with integrity, fullness in life empowered by the workforce if truth and love.

Chaos can be redeemed by God's "love pre-eminence" of all things.

The conservation of God's love can redeem chaos in the people.

God's love is that redemption of those in power, God's love will preserve those who have sought to create beauty, although chaos was created instead. Let us have a love of "pre-eminence."

.

Let us now CONTINUE to LIFT AND RESTORE what we have made beauty at the gift from God's hands. Let us not bring destruction to something that we created and developed of America's legacy for generations and generations. We do not want to be in America. We do not want to be the Hitler of the holocaust of the Jews in the fact of not giving justice and home and keeping the unity of the immigrant families. Even now, our America is being RESTORED though we can never forget who help build it with their hand, from farmers to businessmen to physicians to teachers to police to politicians to mothers to fathers, to grandmothers to grandfathers. Yes, all of us have built together America. Mother nature and God Himself will thunder out in voice and heart, "Give My people their home and keep them together with the families." Mother nature will feel the spirit that has become cold and within the cities and communities will be sorrow never forgotten yet perhaps forgiven. And mercy from Mother Nature and God Himself will be as a "thief in the night," and take away all evil and compromised beyond recall. And this is before the Second Coming, and otherwise, Mother Nature will weep, and morn and the storms of life will strike the souls in weeping sorrow and not be redeemed until many or all accept the truth.

"A cause which will move things and bring them together. How these
thinkers should be arranged about the priority of discovery let
we are allowed to decide later; but since the contraries of the various
forms of good were also perceived to be present in nature-not only
order and the beautiful, but also disorder and the ugly, and bad
things in more significant number than good, and noble things than
beautiful, therefore another thinker introduced friendship and strife, each
of the two
the cause of one of these two sets of qualities. For if we were to
follow out the view of Empedocles, and interpret it according to its
meaning and not to its lisping expression, we should find that
friendship Is the cause of good things and strife of bad. Therefore, if we said
that Empedocles in a sense both mentions, and is the first to mention," the
bad and the good as principles, we should perhaps be right, since
the cause of all goods is the good itself. the bad and the good as principles, we should possibly be right, since
the reason of all goods is the good itself."

All goods are the good itself; when we seek to correct the immigration policy, there is bad that needs to be revealed. Since there has been dedicated of hidden "bad" upon the immigrants; today, we as a people are forcing hands to be "the cause of all goods is the good itself," to bring truth and transparency to the immigrants.

Furthermore, friendships between immigrants and the country of United States, and the Democrats and the Republicans, there will always be tension and each one considering the definition between "bad" and "good." The question is, what is truth, and justice, and respect to humanity and the country's legal system to citizenship and immigration policy? At present of 2019, finally, the immigration policy has been addressed, many have died without anyone noticed, many have been abused without anyone noticed, many used without anyone noticed. All these evils, of "bad," were kept secret and hidden. Now, good has been redeemed, and "bad" has been exposed.

We as a people need to pray, "Our Lady of Guadalupe, Patroness of America, Pray for us,"

Pray to Mary for Our Nation:

"O God our Creator, from your provident hand we have received our right to life, liberty, and the pursuit of happiness, in this decisive hour in the history of our nation, so that with every trial withstood and every danger overcome------ for the sake of our children, our grandchildren, and all who come after us --- this great land will always be " one nation, under God, indivisible, with liberty and justice for all. **The** Catholic faithful often turns to her to ask for safekeeping as they embark on **their** long migration journey. Pope Pius X declared her as **the** "**Patron** of all Latin **America**," Pope Pius XII called her **the** "Empress of **the Americas**."

Virgin of Guadalupe,
Patroness of unborn children,
we implore your intercession
for every child at risk of abortion.
Help expectant parents to welcome from God
the priceless gift of their child's life.

Console parents who have lost that gift
through abortion,
and lead them to forgiveness and healing
through the Divine Mercy of your Son.

Teach us to cherish
and to care for family and friends
until God calls them home.
Help us never to others as burdens.

Guide our public officials
to defend each and every human life
through just laws.
Inspire us all to bring our faith into public life,
to speak for those who have no voice.

We ask this in the name of your Son,
Jesus Christ, who is Love and Mercy itself.
Amen.

2010 Respect Life Liturgy Guide, **USCCB Secretariat of Pro-Life Activities**

Listen to the baby Jesus; the Jesus of Prague carries the earth in His hands. Jesus's most blessed creation is humans, and He gives us in His Hands; the first purpose for Christ Jesus to come to earth was to redeem us from the first sin Adam and Eve; He Jesus Christ redeemed us already from the cross when we. Jesus' birth was to carry the earth upon His shoulders; a King is born from heaven to earth to give us redemption. The three wise men sought to find Him the One:

"Where is the one who has been born King of the Jews? We saw His star in the east and have come to worship Him." Mat. 2:2

Yes, God is with us. For a son has been born for us, a son has been given to us, and dominion has been laid on his shoulders; and this is the name he has been given, 'Wonder-Counsellor, Mighty-God, Eternal-Father, Prince-of-Peace' [6] *to extend his dominion in boundless peace, over the throne of David and over his kingdom to make it secure and sustain it in fair judgment and integrity. From this time onwards and for ever, the jealous love of Yahweh Sabaoth will do this.* [cccxxxix]

Isaiah 9:5-6

Arise to God's Truth America

Chapter Fourteen

SAFETY FIRST AMERICA

Brief Basic Notes

AMERICA GOD CREATED TO BE SAFETY FIRST
LAWS FOR THE PEOPLE AND SERVE THE PEOPLE
POLICE OFFICERS AND MILITARY RESPECT
CITIZENS RESPECT POLICE AND MILITARY AND COMMUNITY AND CITIZENS

PROTESTORS & SILENT COMMUNISTIC FINANCIERS   AMERICANS
FOR SAFETY FIRST & LIBERTY

SOCIALISTIC FINANCIERS

DONOT RESPECT THE RULE OF LAW
RESPECT THE RULE OF LAW
DONOT RESPECT POLICE AND CITIZENS   RESPECT
POLICE AND CITIZENS
DONOT FUND THE POLICE AND MILITARY   POLICE
FUND AND RESPECT
DONOT RESPECT POLICE AND MILITARY   CITIZENS   RESPECT
POLICE AND MILITARY   DONOT RESPECT CITIZENS COMMUNITY
          CITIZENS RESPECT THE COMMUNITY
VIOLENCE AND CRIMINAL ACTS   CITIZENS   HAVE
PEACEFUL COMMUNICATION
VIOLENCE CAUSES DETORIATION TO   PEACEFUL
COMMUNICATION CAUSES
  OUR AMERICAN LEGACY AND   SOLUTIONS
   FOR PROTECTION OF OUR CHILDREN   OF AMERICA
          LEGACY AND CHILDREN'S FUTURE

VIOLENCE COST BILLIONS OF DOLLARS   PEACEFUL
COMMUNICATION RAISE FUNDS, DESTROYING THE CITIES, BUSINESSES
            PROTECTION AWARENESS, AND RESTORATION
<u>VIOLENCE COST EMOTIONAL SCARRING   PEACEFUL
COMMUNICATION HEALING</u>

ADULTS AND CHILDREN, CREATURES VIOLENCE AND DEFUNDING POLICE CAUSES VULNERABILITY TO OTHER AND SECRET TERRORIST CRIMES VIOLENCE TO OUR NATION AND THREAT FOR ANY OPPOSING DANGER FROM TECHNOLOGY, ANY CRIME, NUCLEAR	ADULTS AND CHILDREN, CREATURES FUNDING POLICE PROTECTS THE COMMUNITIES FROM CRIMES CRIMES, AND SECRET TERRORIST GROUPS SAFETY PROTECT OUR NATION THREAT OF ANY OPPOSING DANGER FROM TECHNOLOGY, ANY CRIME, NUCLEAR

Many Protestors have had EMOTIONAL SCARRING; we need to bring healing and restoration and justice.

Chapter Fifteen

City and State Restoration
Notes of First Development.

LEAD AMBASSADOR

Using the 4 Foundational Truths

Divine Message for the People God's love

For Cities that Need Healing and Restoration and Sustaining

Note each Ambassador has a Data Assistant

Note: There is more than 58,000 individuals in Los Angeles homeless and with mental heal complexities.

Individual Director

Homeless: There can be affordable housing and communities build in the cities and or rural areas across the United States that have a plan and structure to restore, heal, and nurture, and empower these individuals.

Data Assistant

Each one discuss how they will investigate them ..

> Listing each individual and obtaining information
> a. Also, ask questions regarding

Personal: Name, family, children. Country from and culture from.

Age – a. Ask age b. How old do they feel? C. How old were their parents or family members when they died and of what disease. d. Do they have a birth certificate?

Goals: a. What do they want to achieve and have they achieved their goals?

Family: a. Names and ages and vocations of family members and family trees.

Residence: Places of Residences and reasons for leaving, and costs

School: All schools, addresses, and independent study?

Religion: Religion of Parents and family, person religion?

Work: Work independent study to achieve a future goal, all employees.

Income: Where do they get their income?

    a. Ask them where do they get them. b. where do they live all their expenses? C.

Goals in Education: What are the goals they are working on. Also, ask what they wish they could accomplish.

Exercise: What type of activity and what type do they want to achieve? How long have they been exercising?

Diet: What is their diet.

Drug Problems: Are there any family members or themselves that have drug problems. Have they taken drugs? What type of drugs. Have they tried drugs?

Nutritional

Medical a. do they have medical records. b. Do they take pharmacies drugs, and home much do they costs.

What is their health insurance?

Hobbies: What hobbies would they like to do. What hobbies do they do? What hobbies did they do or do?

Finances: What are their regular costs of daily living. Do they have savings? Do they want to learn about the investments?

Other items:

City Utilities Ambassador

    Data Assistant

Recollect this information is Divinely inspired they are Divine message: Water: (Water is the number one natural resource that needs to be maintained. All filters and basins, and piping need to be replaced with the highest and the most sophisticated technological process and

infrastructure. Also, security systems need to be installed in main power centers).

Gas: (Needs to be checked within cities and monitored for any leaks. Gas is the first cause of lung cancer. I think gas should be minimally used in homes; there should be electricity used or solar. All lines and systems need to be checked and monitored. Also, security systems need to be installed in main power centers.)

Electrical the highest technology. All lines and systems need to be checked and monitored. Also, security systems need to be installed in main power centers.)

Gas lines the highest technology. All lines and systems need to be checked and monitored. Also, security systems are mandatory in main power centers.

Sewer lines the highest technology. All lines and systems need to be checked and monitored. Also, security systems are mandatory in main power centers.

Gas lines and of the highest technology. All lines and systems need to be checked and monitored. Also, security systems are mandatory in main power centers.

Rural Areas across the United States

Individuals and volunteer helping Youth and Mental Health issues and City Issues

Note this is just the beginning of ideas to bring a loving hope for the people;

FIND FAMILIES HAVE DRUG PROBLEMS

The retirees and volunteer have lived in great flourishing communities can help those in this deteriorated communities in the more hands-on, way.

Youth

1. Identify volunteer's experiences and what the volunteers feel most comfortable. (Note: presently, many of these homeless live on the street with very little exposure to others. Perhaps there can be a center first built and professionals can help each homeless.)
2. List areas of expertise
3. Have a Volunteer taught a class on ideas of learning?
    1. Daily organization of day
    2. Home care cleaning
    3. Grooming and dressing
    4. Cooking and Meal Preparation
    5. Job and interview preparation
    6. Realizing the contraindications of sexual relationships in High School before life education and life development and marriage responsibilities
    7. Vocational interest
    8. Reading, writing, library reading with books and magazines not online.
    9. Nutrition and shopping
    10. Perhaps home garden even in pots if one lives in apartments, they have community gardens
    11. Communication skills and reconciliation of family and individuals
        a. Poetry day
        b. Speaking day between families
    12. Small business ideas and investment
    13. Art and aesthetics, and training
    14. Music therapy
    15. Survival Training
    16. Vocational Training
    17. Home Education

Drug problems

1. Help children of the family are destroyed by drugs. Drug invested cities they can have be a special friend
2. Retreats to heal
3. Nutritional treatments, de-tox; and training
4. Alternative Medicine, Eastern, and Western De-tox.

Electrotherapy is excellent. Please, refer to the book by
5. Mental Health Hospital
   a. Create a friendly relationship of responsible peoples, as of big brother and big sister programs.
      (This is already in existence. Retirees can do this; however, we know there is some danger present. Therefore, protection is needed.).
   b. Have a Non – Profit that those who can go to a rural place to learn skills and endurance to achieve and follow through.
   c. Innovation of creation

Furthermore, some communities can have a complete restoration with children and adults can be educated and in timely retreats to heal and form their character. Activities to read aloud, to silently read and critically analyze, write, create, develop wholesome reconciliation. Also, all the above aspects are discussed.

Prov. 30:5 *Every word of God is tried:*
He is a shield unto them that take refuge in Him.

God will "shield us when we take refuge in Him" when we seek to help others.

Taking refuge in and protection in the Lord is the King's righteousness, and I am wearing the armor of God, Ephesians chapter 6; God love and justice shield us to then you America are the shield of God to help America.

The Tree of Life of America is shielded in God's love of righteousness in the armor of God. the Tree of life of America is God's Tree that He desires it to be pure, and He is a jealous God.

Jesus as humans need food and water and a good environment to survive and grow, so does the cities and states in unity, and unity in the entire nation, need a healthy plan and intention. When there is great power in the country that controls, the control is mandated in God's natural law to be of God's intentions of His virtues and Word. God will not accept anything less. He accommodates humanity; however, there is a warning when His people are not in His intention, and when His people are treated with injustices.

We as people of America are responsible for taking care of our homeless in Los Angeles in other parts of our nation.

Do not be afraid; God can overcome all things in His love. When we have faith as a mustard seed, we can move mountains.

When Jesus resurrected the child, He said, "little girl arises."

Let the child and the man and woman arise and be protected by the future legacy.

Whether is it is the homeless little girl or boy, woman, or man, whether it is the little girl or boy, woman or man, of great faith as a mustard d to bring life to the homeless, let us be resurrected to and arise to the truth.

Also, the woman and man of the faith of the mustard d can proclaim and work toward encouraging others to restore our system, of mental health and homelessness.

Jesus resurrected Lazarus,

Let the children and the adults be resurrected of the truth that we need to be equipped with to bring a miracle to homelessness across America.

So does a city have a way of building and growing in God's purpose this structuring and outlines will

Father of Jesus Christ will you free all things are in His salvation and those need to be

Freedom: Set your freedom into kindness in having and continue to heal America. Becoming the healing force of America.

For those who in Salvation: Jesus Christ is the Son of God with the power of the Holy Spirit, the trusting One in us, for us to work together.

Ask: would you not want the Creator to show you how to correct the healing of America? You ask how.

He shall guide each leader, [each person] responsibilities to healing the cities.

the city has not always followed the Creator's way of His intention of the way a city is supposed to be. They chose their way, not God's that is why there are problems.

" What do I tell them to those who do not in Your works?"

"Does the birds in the air ask for food? They are taken care of."

the birds generally follow God's will when they are the birds of God's light. Therefore, we are

"Ask and you shall receive knock and the door shall be open see and you shall find."

Tell the leaders to come to Me and ask not of their own plan but My intended plan.

Tell them to follow these and in everything they do as I am their Lord and Savior.

These are God's intended plan for community starts in nature to flow in the garden of the fullness of Creation.

Child many love Me here [and others do not]; I want to take care of them as the Father intended. They are ready to multiply the fish and bread of the heart of God's love, my child; they are ready as I was at the Mount giving the Beatitudes for the people of the community; and states and nations are ready to receive these messages so that My Father's intention of the multiplying of the fish and the bread of a hungry nation that needs healing, and hungry and that is after righteousness, will be fulfilled and their prays answered.

He said, "because the healing America needs redemption of the darkness, to My Light, you will need protection to help you write the commands the Lord God has given you in the solutions to help America let all know that they are a child of God. For those who pray the rosary for those in darkness, there will be miracles. The Holy needs to give the people here of the heart in God Christ Jesus will be a light of the world to multiply the fish and the bread.

They shall be with the protection of God's love, each even under persecution.

[You] upon will show them the way My daughter to help heal America and [all the Church in charge of Jesus Christ. And those whom God chooses rs or not they are all is humanity He loves.]

[We are one body of Christ.]

The Angels of God are with us and protecting us. Even Billy Graham has d in Angels.

Michael Who is like God Gabriel, God's Power Raphael, God's Doctor Archangel,

The Wall
"What shall we do about the.... wall?"

Yet with commands and all of God's purpose. I saw the Robe of Mary's love And she also said, My Lord has given America to the people
 land to place their head on the earth's pillow for freedom and truth and in God's love. This is the Word of God in Jesus Christ, the God of Abraham in the power of the Holy Spirit
America can have a strategy to bring proper citizenship.
Do not take the people from this land; it is theirs. Remember, this also relates to the fact that Socialistic and Communistic ideologies do not want different classes of levels of socio-economic levels of peoples only two classes, the powerful and poor; and; Socialistic and Communistic do not want people to have ownership of anything, especially businesses, and homes, only the powerful.

[Make a strategic and command of good and just laws.]

Remember, they are the ones that are the backbone of America building and loving America. Again to recollect your member as commanded before. Did America put up a wall? When each of the our families came to make life in integrity, hope, and fullness. However, when I asked what we should do about the border, Jesus Christ did say, "Do you lock your doors at night."

People

Look, all life belongs to me; the father's life and the son's life, both alike belong to me. The one who has sinned is the one to die.

Ezekiel 18:

The country is the Peoples

Our government does you have upon your heart in the action of your hands what God has given to you, the oath to be a protector in every way to America?

God's intention the way of His hand upon America:

The government's soul is ordained with an infinite golden flag of the code of arms embroidered with the threads of eternal truth, peace, and justice upon it from heaven to serve the people in God and in trusting God.

God has given each one of us the answers upon our hearts if we would listen, my friend, and go with justice in all we do. Better yet, and to tell you as a father or mother: go in prayer, take a retreat daily to ask God to guide you in all that you do.

"He does not eat at the mountain shrines or lift his eyes to the idols . . . or oppress anyone, or retain a pledge, or commit robbery, but he gives his bread to the hungry and covers the naked with clothing; he keeps his hand from the poor, does not take interest or increase, but executes My ordinances, and walks in My statutes, he will not die for his father's iniquity, he will surely live."

Ezekiel 18: 15-17

Let America live!

America will live when we keep with the jewels that adorn her, your treasures of love. Each one of you has that Tree of Life that is planted in America of who you are, Adorn your Tree of Life with jewels from heavenly omnipotent miracle now, and heavenly omniscient wisdom now all from Today is the most fantastic time in human history of having information upon our fingertips to take upon our hands to heal, sustain, restore, and enlighten America. The people are supposed to serve each other in truth, honesty, justice, and love. That what was given to you

"Justice is the aim and criterion of all politics."

St. Thomas Aquinas

Interviewing Americans:
I asked, small business owner of a Coffee and Tea Restaurant, in La Crescenta, California: What do you think about America? This is his expression, is the most important for us in America.

"Happiness is what you do is the most important to me. My customers, I deliver happiness and return they give me happiness in return and there is unity."

Yes, unity in America is happiness.

I asked, another small business owner Chef for the Hollywood, (Early in the Year 2019)

What do you think about America? " I urgently see the city of Los Angeles and all impoverished areas [throughtout the United States] should have [empowerment for life existence and self-sufficiency and restoration], [yet, organized with an Ambassador] access to help the homeless not just giving a check or handout of food."

Yes, we need to empower the people.

I asked, met a small business owner in Real Estate, California. We need innovative and honest works and a Mentor to teach and direct them.

I asked a Lyft Driver what he thought about America:

He has been in the USA for over 40 years from Armenia, he has raised his family here and loves America; he realizes that the Middle Class needs to come back to the frontline of American business in California and all the states.

"We also need to allow the big companies to come back in California and all states… that have increased their taxes so that the middle class can have jobs. Many companies have moved out of Los Angeles, California because of the high taxes. Therefore, these large companies could not employ the middle class."

I do realize that California was in the greatest debt in history, now that the leaders have gotten her out of debt, we now can help those middle class and lower socio-economical levels with small business and larger business to employ them.

Listen if a few of these major billionaires that have promoted business nationally and internationally were agreeable and negotiable to pay taxes than we could bring an extra and that is a Divine Command to take care of their country and be an as righteous leader; Arise to God leaders, and consequently, living waters of a fresh river of life that will clean up the tragedies and bring living waters as Jesus did at the Wedding Feast, will turn your waters of gifts God gave you to wine that will redeem the United States of America and the world.

Prov. 6:20 My son, keep the commandment of thy father,
 And forsake not the ~~15~~law of thy mother:

Prov. 6:21 Bind them continually upon thy heart;
 Tie them about thy neck.

Prov. 6:22 When thou walkest, it shall lead thee;
 When thou 16sleepest, it shall watch over thee;
 And when thou awakest, it shall talk with thee.
23 For 17the commandment is a lamp, and 18the law is light;
 And reproofs of instruction are the way of life:

Martin Luther King:
All peoples will be all able to join together!

"The rich and the poor, the weak and the strong, the common and the brilliant, the faithless and the faithful, the destitute and the
Will be able to hold hands of their hearts to bring Healing in America, I have a dream today as Martin Luther King has said, to save our American Legacy before it is to late.
Let us continue!

Let us keep on this, path to empower Americans,
Let us keep on this path to create peace
Let us keep on this path to bring justice

Yes
Let us keep on this path to bring healing
Let us keep on this path to keep America forward,
Let us keep on this path to make America great again.
Let us be worthy of the gifts that God has waiting to give us when we act in truth
Let us be worthy of the future that God has planned for us to heal our America when love our neighbor with justice

Let us be worthy of freedom protection of those that will open doors of the inner cities
Pope Ambrose Book 3 Chapter 22 Euthymius
Friends.
"Virtue must never be given up for a sake of a friend."
If one has to bear witness with a friend it must be done with caution
Between a friend's what cantor is when opening the heart."
What freedom
Friendship is the guardian of virtues which not to be found but in like character.
It must be mild in remarking and reverse in its own advantage.
Nothing must be set above virtue
Friendship takes a hirer place for our religion or the love of our fellow citizen in these/
In these matters, true witness is required so the
That truth can prevail.
Friendship should not be used to plot against an innocent one
Friends never should be who desires evil or one who is innocent.
Open thy breast of a friend have a faithful life
My faith in the Constitution is whole and total and I am not going to sit here.

Chapter Sixteen

Human Trafficking

Rice, John Paul, "Important Powerful Message: John Paul Rice, A Child's Voice, The Real Story of the Hidden Network," https://youtu.be/dztir94oaOo

Human, Child Trafficking _oh Jesus I pray that the children and will be redeem and the_
September 2020

John Paul Rice unify together in protecting the people. Abuse of human rights.

"These people that are traffickers own the Politicians."

1. 40,000,000 million people are Trafficked

2. 140 Billion dollar history that is very dark and ugly ties. Goes all the way up to Wall Street and Beyond. Also, the selling of organs of these
3. 5.5 Million trafficking children around the world do not live past 7 or 8 years old
Banking, Hollywood Entertainment, rape and tortured these girls
4. Hidden layer that is We cannot
5. Sacrifice people also
6. The evil Traffickers said this, 'Indeed children human beings are the most useless. "cccxl
7. They harvest organ.
8. In China now there are concentration camps for young Muslims for the amount of 1Million, beating these people, re indoctrinating them and they are raping their wives to start a new.
9. Slave of workers in China.
10. Does not matter whether you are a Democratic and Republican this is
11. Pipeline to Hollywood and all around the world in all different countries.
12. Satanic in the Music industry. They sew it in the consciousness of the Kids to witchcraft. They make it sound fun to attack the children. The singer's diversity and tolerance, taking advantage of people.
13. Slavery of human beings and child abuse issue.
9. Many came from bad homes.

They offer alcohol, drugs, money to lure them in

14. We can have truth art diversity of ideas and truthful information being disclosed. We can have beautiful films. The journey of art is to discover is what in you of the unknown in that you follow to find, and in that discovery, there is the transcendent What did I struggle with and come to confront to with myself and what is right for you. In that honest expression

15. Gatekeepers' knowledge doing their jobs of control. Managers make sure that we do not wake up. It is vital for them. Because they do not want us to have new ideas about things that go outside of the ordinary, orthodoxy of what they want us to know.

16. It preys on children. They want us to think all is ok. The Gate Keepers are the 1 tenth of 1 percent who control everything and have the gull to

tell us we are the problem or white people are the problem or black people are brown people are the problem.

Chapter Seventeen

And now a man came to him and asked, 'Master, what good deed must I do to possess eternal life?' ⁱ⁷ Jesus said to him, 'Why do you ask me about what is good? **There is one alone who is good**. *But if you wish to enter into life, keep the commandments.*

Matt. 19:16

The Decalogue and the natural law

The Ten Commandments belong to God's revelation. At the same time, they teach us the true humanity of man. They bring to light the essential duties, and therefore, indirectly, the fundamental rights inherent corresponding to the human person. The Decalogue contains a privileged expression of the natural law:

From the beginning, God had implanted in the heart of man the precepts of the natural law. Then he was content to remind him of them the Decalogue. [cccxli]

I know for all of us these virtues we all need to work on. I never hear about these in Social Media or the media.

Arise to God's Truth, Restore and Keep our Freedom in America.

After Pope Gregory I released his list of seven deadly sins in 590 AD, the seven virtues became identified as chastity, temperance, charity, diligence, patience, kindness, and humility. Practicing them is saying to protect one against temptation from the seven deadly sins.

Virtue	Latin	Gloss	Sin	Latin
Chastity	Castitas	Purity, abstinence	Lust	Luxuria
Temperance	Temperantia	Humanity, equanimity	Gluttony	Gula

Charity	*Caritas*	Will, benevolence, generosity, sacrifice	Greed	*Avaritia*
Diligence	*Industria*	Persistence, effortfulness, ethics	Sloth	*Acedia*
Patience	*Patientia*	Forgiveness, mercy	Wrath	*Ira*
Kindness	*Humanitas*	Satisfaction, compassion	Envy	*Invidia*
Humility	*Humilitas*	Bravery, modesty, reverence	Pride	*Superbia*

Chapter Eighteen

Conclusion

Is. 9:6 *For to us a child is born,*
to us, a son is given,
and the government will be on His shoulders.

And He will be called
Wonderful Counselor, Mighty God,
Everlasting Father, Prince of Peace.

Is. 9:7 *Of the increase of his government and peace*
there will be no end.

He will reign on David's throne
and over his kingdom,
establishing and upholding it
with justice and righteousness
from that time on and forever.

Jesus Christ it the Light of the World

America Call upon God in Prayer

God is in your heart. He will give you love.
God is at Your Fingertips. He will guide your life.
God is in the path of your feet and legs. He will give you a lighted way.
God is in your life. He will give you peace.
God is in your eyes. He will show you the way.
God is in your work. He will bring the most beautiful creation in you.
God is in your loving. He will give all the love to forgive, live in peace, and love without measure.
God is in your entire being and soul. He will fill you with the Holy Spirit to live a supernatural life.
God is in your arms. He will give you the strength to live and overcome trials and reach happiness.
God is in your mind. He will watch you and is teaching you everything you should know.

God is in your voice. He will give you the song of miracle and voice of power of the life of the tongue.

God is here, now, in the future, and forever. Call upon God in prayer; He is waiting.

God is with you when you pray. He is waiting to give you all the abundant living waters of life.

America Trinity's Intention of Creation is what life is.

We America are God's people. We America are the apple of God's eye. We America have the greatest gift a human can have a love of God and our children and families and friends. We America have been given the greatest <u>gift of Freedom</u>; let us love with all our heart and soul God in that He will live in, with, and through, the life we will continue to restore and flourish and flow in living waters of freedom.

Interview of an American Man of a Heart to Save Freedom and life in the World

An American man, was fervently zealous, telling the problem is in the "technical automation," that will take jobs away, and the people are not educated in the areas to received jobs as needed. I told him we can work in a balance, and we can produce jobs; now that we have small and large business de-regulations, and we are bringing our manufacturing jobs back to the USA under President Trump. Also, we are receiving "fair-business," trades with the Chinese government, and received billions under President Trump 2019 and 2020. Moreover, we can teach the children and adults entrepreneurial skills and trades in education and development that will fulfill the jobs. I told him, " As you stated, some jobs will be lost under automation," though we will balance it in manufacturing in the USA, bringing back small and large businesses giving competitive de-regulations, educating children and adults with entrepreneurial skills and trade skills. And we will have the "billions," from the fair business trade of the tariffs of China. We have to be optimistic. Listen there should also be some constraints on the vast technological powers to control the businesses. Otherwise, if the people cannot create and work in a natural basic development and environment, consequently, the technological powers will not need to be used because they will not have the trading business or tools of substance, and sustenance in the operation of the foundation of the systems and platforms of technological controls. See it is as if the hands and legs and brain and buildings are there in the technological systems, however, if the working projects, goals, mission, ideas, and creations and exchange of businesses and business contracts are not there to fill the automation tool then we have no business. Hence, the balance is mandatory. Remember, all-natural things and God's intentions have a perfect plan, and God can only accommodate so much otherwise there is impeding of life or no life of the action of life, and the subject we are speaking of business and economy and the wellbeing of vocations and life of the people to produce lively hood of the meaning of what it is to be human in the life to exist. I will never forget I did not show up for a hair appointment, and I did not call to cancel. I had severe family issues, and I forgot to appropriately cancel my hair appointment, it was in San Marino, California on Mission and the Salon was called, "The Gates of Spain." The owner said, "this is my *livelihood*, I have to charge you." Although she was also terribly upset with me. I understood. When she said the word, "*livelihood*," it shocked me. Everything, in her job, that she worked for is her *livelihood*," it gave her the sustenance to exist. Therefore, if we do not have the exchange of business and the sustenance of two are more people exchanging business, we will not have our *livelihood*, in America or any place. Therefore, we have the systems and platforms of the automation, though we still need the offer, acceptance, and delivery, of contracts between the people.

DIVINE MESSAGE 9.10.20

Tell the people the Democratic Party they are controlled by the Socialist and Communist and even the infiltration of a robust technological group cause injustices and crimes and control.

The tender Democrat party is no longer those who love their country and want to keep America's FREEDOM because the Democrats are not supported by their leaders that the belief that the government serves the people. There is a hidden power of Communistic and Socialistic and the Technicians of power, and (powerful billionaires) controlling the tender Democratic party, (and USA and the world.) There are proven by the fact that the quiet and visible facts and forces and powerful technicians and heretics as American citizens have conspired against the American people controlling the votes, taking away the American people's justice. Ask yourself what would they do next they were in power? Control the American people their life and even mind. Billionaires of most tremendous monetarily success that most Americans exchange business with have funded many of the violations of the constitutional laws and procedures for the voting; furthermore, billionaires funded the protestors and even the fraudulent machinery, and voting fraudulence. We need to continue to find the fraudulence and bring it to the eyes of the people and take it into the rule of law in that it can be investigated. This is a Divine Command.

The Democrats in America's Freedom need to support the Republicans because they have and will keep the best for the people and put them first. [The silent leaders of the Democrats that are Socialistic and Communistic do not want or do not believe in the classes and ownership and the freedom of the American people that is the meaning of the Communist and also in cases of Socialistic ideologies; let me reiterate that most Democratics did not know the hidden agenda and plan for the Democratic party for 2020 and onward, that has Socialistic, and Communistic ties, proven by the fact of the support of China and family ties to China and other beliefs of **not** putting the American people first (Listed in this book, in fact).

I have given the power now to the Republicans because they are SAVING RESTORING AMERICA
God's will to keep people's Freedom and protection.
I am telling you this Divine Command that My Father has told Me.

Each person has fingerprints. These fingerprints are the written life that God has prepared for each person at creation. Each person has a different fingerprint. Hence, they are individuals; therefore, they have an individual path for their life in God's intended creation. Mary warned us years ago that technology's minds and modern times cannot control technology. God creates each individual for HIS purpose proven in the fact of the fingerprints of each individual; EACH INDIVIDUAL has a particular path that God has intended them to take; therefore, they can direct their life to restore America and the nations of all the world, because their life is planned out for the vessel to be used to be a Light of God for all the nations, to bring the light and love in the salvation of Jesus Christ; in those to whom do not yet seek and live for and in and with the love of God of Abraham in the Trinity toward righteousness in the MYSTERY OF THE OMNIPOTENT Holy Spirit, AND THE REDEEMING CROSS OF CHRIST, God is yearning for their love, He is the Father of all humanity. When a Father is missing His son or daughter, He searches for them with all His heart and soul. Sometimes they find the son or the daughter though they do not accept. Hence, the father keeps on praying. Even if you do not believe in Divine Messages, you need to see the truth and the proven facts for us as Americans to protect our freedom.

The hands of ours in God are His working miracle hands. He said, "Put your hands on those things in life on earth of your hands in faith in Christ Jesus. and you should have miracles in time." Now, we as a nation have to take up our original individual purpose of the fingerprint of God's creation in us. It is directly related and in and through and with God's fingerprints to carry His purpose on earth from heaven. Now, God is calling on all of us to seek this, in that we can restore our lives individually, families, communities, states, and nations.

Since ancient times, the Saints of the Catholic Church have been honored and loved and prayed for God's Salvation. The Spirit of the Lord told me this. Today, we need to realize the Protestant Saints that have passed on heaven and together are true like those of the Catholics Saints and Judaism AND EVEN OTHER religions; we do not know God's decisions. He created all humanity in love. I speak of the Saints because God wants us to go to Him and call upon Him in prayer and give our life to Him in unity with the Trinity so that we can receive His love fully and His Salvation.

The list is endless, here are a few examples having the attributes and work of a Saint, Father Frank PAVONE, Alveda King, Mark Levine, Taylor Marshall, Donald Trump, Patrick Zurek, James Martin, Dinesh D'Sousa, Signey Powell, Fr Leo Patalignhug. We need to find the goodness of God in the people.

Let us keep our eyes fixed on Jesus, who leads us in our faith and brings it to perfection: for the sake of the joy which lay ahead of Him, He endured the cross, disregarding the shame of it, and has taken His seat at the right of God's throne.

Heb. 12:2

He was bearing our sins in His own body on the cross so that we might die to our sins and live for uprightness; through His (crucifixion by His blood) you have been healed and have Salvation.

1Pet. 2:24

I run the way of your commandments, for you have given me the freedom of heart.

Psa. 119:32

But anyone who looks steadily at the perfect law of freedom and keeps to it—not listening and forgetting, but putting it into practice—will be blessed in every undertaking.

James 1:25

Christ was sacrificed once to take away the sins of many people; and He will appear a second time, not to bear sin, but to bring **salvation** *to those who are waiting for Him.*

Heb. 9:28

After this I heard what sounded like the roar of a great multitude in heaven shouting:
"Hallelujah! **Salvation** *and glory and power belong to our God,*

Rev. 19:1

Bibliography

Adam, Klasfeld Prosecution of Child-Sex Traffickers Plummeted Under Trump.https://www.courthousenews.com/prosecution-of-kiddie-traffickers-plummeted-under-trump/.Courthouse New Service. July 16, 2019, p.1. Internet, website.

Altier, Robert Fr. An Examination of Conscience, A Preparation for the Sacrament of Penance. https://www.leafletonline.com/examination-of-conscience. Leaflet Missal Company, 2002.

Euthymius and Phillip Schaff, "Duties of the Clergy translated by Book 3 Chapter 1,(c. 377), (1819-1893), translated by H. De Romestin." https://librivox.org/author/1231. Ambrose, Pope. LibriVox Recordings.Oct 2020.Internet.

America Heritage Foundation, "Declaration of Independence," America Heritage *In Congress, July 4, 1776,* Foundation https://americanheritage.org/bookstore/?gclid=Cj0KCQiAh4j-BRCsARIsAGeV12BwhuXSztvpQj4IvzQwcIBerprbGjJB6lZa4Kml6Tn4c-OqogidPqkaAu6WEALw_wcB
Anderson, Ray S. & Guernsey, Dennis, B. *On Being Family A Social Theology, of the Family*. Grand Rapid, Mich. William B. Eerdmans Publishing Company, 1985.Print.

Antonopoulos, Andreas. *Now in China! "Can't Eat, Can't Travel, Can't Rent. Cashless Society.*, https://www.bitchute.com/video/MKjApAzKlBC7/. Bit Chute. uploaded by Be Inspired, 28, October 2020 Apostolate Family, Consecration, Edits. *Sacred Heart Enthronement.* https://enthronements.com/?gclid=CjwKCAjw2qHsBRAGEiwAMbPoDHTLSCqo6PWji6_6ZfifsA9wlWYe6ixE6as5UcDWpCSI1ITFbG1jJhoCegwQAvD_BwE .Apostolate Family, Consecration. October 31, 2020.Internet

Aquinas, St. Thomas. *Summa Theologica*. Translated by Fathers of the English Dominican Province Digitally produced by Sandra K. Perry. http://www.ccel.org Electronic text from the Christian Classics Ethereal Library, Accordance (Benziger Bros. edition, 1947). Computer Program.

Arden, Lisa, Lucia. *Our Need to Give to the World, America love in God, Heal America*. Pasadena, Lisa Lucia Arden, 2016, 2019.Print.

Aristotle, Aristotle's Categories *Standford. Education. Fri Sep 7, 2007 Tue Nov 5, 2013* https://plato.stanford.edu/entries/aristotle-categories/ ; and https://en.wikipedia.org/wiki/Categories_(Aristotle).Internet.

Aristotle. Translated by W. D. Ross SD. Metaphysics. http://classics.mit.edu//Aristotle/metaphysics.html, Provided by The Internet Classics Archive. 1st Century, B.C. Internet.

Bannon, Steve, "Steve Bannon's Warning On China Trade War (w/ Kyle Bass) | Real Vision Classics" Real Vision Finance, Sep 11, 2017, https://www.youtube.com/watch?v=qH5QzuzD01A&list=PLQXj_KeGx-b7ef-DKTxGaD_5_cmhUx7s_&ab_channel=RealVisionFinance, Internet.

Barron, Bishop. *On Pope Francis and Virtue Ethics*. June 21, 2018, Barron Bishop, https://www.youtube.com/watch?v=G6b1q7l2O_c. Internet.

Bowen, Xiao, *The Epoch Times, Opioid Crisis, As Opioids Ravage Communities, Locals Unite in Response From faith groups to treatment centers, state and local communities are starting to make headway in helping to reduce deaths.* https://reader.epoch.cloud/?token=95cc28b0c05118d932da028fbc2d78b9_5d84ad75_1864061&selDate=20190920, **Epoch Times.** July 16, 2018 p.30. Internet.

Brown, Colin. *New International Dictionary of New Testament Theology*. General Editor
Originally published in German under the title: THEOLOGISCHES BEGRIFFSLEXIKON ZUM NEUEN TESTAMENT Copyright by Theologischer Verlag Rolf Brockhaus, Wuppertal. English language edition OakTree Software ©1967, 1969, 1971.Computer Program.

Brown, by F. S. R. Driver, and C. A. Briggs. B*DB Abridged A Hebrew and English Lexicon of the Old Testament (abridged)*. Oxford: Clarendon Press, Digitized and abridged as a part of the Princeton Theological Seminary Hebrew Lexicon Project under the direction of Dr. J. M.Roberts. OakTree Software, Inc. This electronic adaptation ©2001 OakTree Software, Inc. 1907. Computer Program.

Bultmann, R.*Theology of the New Testament, I, 1952.* The Cambridge History of Later Greek and Early Medieval Philosophy, Volume 1Edited by A. H. Armstrong Cambridge University Press, OakTree Software Accordance Program,1970.Internet Program.

Casey, Maurice. <u>From Jewish Prophet to Gentile God</u>, *The Origins and Development of New Testament Christology*, James Clarke & Co. Ltd, Great Britain, Cambridge, 1991

Catholic Church, *Catholic Catechism (English) The Catechism of the Catholic Church (English) (C. Catechism-E)*. Libreria Editrice Vatican, Vatican City Used by permission of Amministrazione del Patrimonio Della Sede Apostlica, Vatican City Electronic text hypertexted and prepared by OakTree Software, Inc.Version 1.5, 1997.Computer Program.

China, U.S.- News, Epoch, "China Using Fentanyl as Chemical Weapon Against Us," <u>Epoch Times</u> https://www.theepochtimes.com/china-is-deliberately-using-fentanyl-to-destroy-the-us_3058199.html, August 2018. Internet News Paper.

China In Focus (Chinese River Tainted, Turned Blood Red), Epoch Times. https://link.theepochtimes.com/mkt_app/china-in-focus-chinese-river-tainted-turned-blood-red_3465009.html, August 17, 2020. Internet News Paper.

China in Focus, 'YPD Officer's Hidden Ties to the CCP," Epoch Times, https://link.theepochtimes.com/mkt_app/china-in-focus-nypd-officers-hidden-ties-to-the-ccp3510401.html, September 22, 2020. Internet News Paper.

Cohen, David Elliot Text by Peter Robinson, Ronald Reagan, In life Photographs. Created by Foreword by Newt Gingrich and Callista Gingrich, Sterling Publishing, New York, 1976. Print.

Confraternity of Christian Doctrine. NAB Notes New American Bible Notes Scripture marked NAB, are taken from the New American Bible with Revised New Testament, 3211 4th Street, NE, Washington, DC 20017-1194. Accordance Bible Program. All Rights Reserved.
Version 1.7. Copyright © 1986, 1970,1991. Computer Program.

Darton, Longman & Todd, The New Jerusalem Bible (NJB) The New Jerusalem Bible (Doubleday, a division of Bantam Doubleday Dell Publishing Group, Inc. Doubleday, a division of Bantam Doubleday Dell Publishing Group, Inc 1990) **Computer Program.**

Easton, M.G. M.A., D.D., Easton's. Bible Dictionary (Easton) Illustrated Bible Dictionary, Third Edition, published by(Thomas Nelson, 1897.Computer Program.

Environmental Protection Agency, Press Office. *News Releases from Headquarter Water (O.W.) President Trump Signs Executive Order on Modernizing America's Water Resource Management and Water Infrastructure,*
https://www.epa.gov/newsreleases/president-trump-signs-executive-order-modernizing-americas-water-resource-

management the United States Environmental Protection Agency, October 13, 2020.Internet.

Epoch Editors, Medicare for All or 'Medicare for None'? **AMERICAN THOUGHT LEADERS**
Luo, Irene, and Philips, Joshua. *Medicare programs have seen $84.7 billion in total fraud and improper payments last year.* https://www.theepochtimes.com/medicare-for-all-or-medicare-for-none_3068153.html.The Epoch Times, September 5, 2019.Internet

Euthymius and Phillip Schaff, "Duties of the Clergy translated by Book 3 Chapter 1,(c. 377), (1819-1893), translated by H. De Romestin." https://librivox.org/author/1231. Ambrose, Pope. LibriVox Recordings.Oct 2020. Internet.

Fakkert, Jasper Editor-in-Chief Epoch. *President Trump's first two years in Office. Epoch Times Special Edition*, Epoch Times, 2019. Newspaper Print.

Faustina, Kowalska, Maria, Saint. Heaven, *Hell, and Purgatory, According to passages from the Diary of Saint Maria*. Ecclesiastical Approved. http://www.bf.org/bfetexts.htm Marian Press, Stockbridge, Hypertexted and formatted by OakTree Software, Inc. Version 3.4U, 1987. Internet.

Fisher, Ron. *The United States, An Illustrated History.* Published National Geographic Fahey, John M., Jr. President and Chief Executive Officer, New York, 1958, 2007. Print.

Francis Pope. Prayer for Jubilee Year of Mercy. Merciful Like the Father. http://www.vatican.va/content/francesco/en/prayers/documents/papa-francesco_preghiere_20151208_giubileo-straordinariomisericordia.html, Libreria Editrice Vaticana, December 8, 2015- November 20, 2016.Internet.

Gagnon, Louise. MRI Shows Brain Changes From Cannabis use. https://www.auntminnie.com/index.aspx?sec=rca&sub=ismr_2019&pag=dis&ItemID=125536, Aunt Minnie, May 20, 2019, p,1. Internet Website.p.1. Internet.

Garg, Anu. *Wordsmith,* words@wordsmithlorg, USA, May 27, 2011.Email.

Gilbert, George. *America's #1 Futurist Issues Bold Predictions also sees massive shifts taking place.* https://secure.investedbetter.com/internet-reboot/?utm_source=Homepage&utm_medium=Website&utm_campaign=InternetReboot, October 31, 2020.,p.1. Internet.

Harshaw, Tobin. *The Big Iran Threat is Nukes, Not Coronavirus.* https://www.bloomberg.com/opinion/articles/2020-03-08/iran-and-coronavirus-nuclear-weapons-are-the-bigger-threat, Bloomberg Opinion Politics & Policy, March 8, 2020, 8:00 am. Internet.

Hattrup Kathleen N. We're *called to join the army of this "Warrior Queen,"* https://aleteia.org/2018/09E04/were-called-to-join-the-army-of-this-warrior-queen/ Aleteia, September 4, 2018, p.1. Internet.

Hendriksen William. *More than Conquerors, An Interpretation of the Book of Revelation.* Great Britain, Inter-varsity Press, 1962.Print.

Hildegard of Bingen, Edited by Matthew Fox. *Hildegard of Bingen's Book of Divine Works With Letters and Songs.* Bear & Company, Santa Fe, Mexico. 1987. Print.

Imbach, Jeffrey D. *The Recovery of Love, Christian Mysticism and the Addictive Society, Julian of Norwich, John Ruusbroec, Meister Eckhart, Dante Alighieri,* The Crossroad Publishing Company, New York, 1992. Print.

Immigration Act of September 23, 1950, Naturalization Oath of Allegiance to the United States of America, https://www.uscis.gov/citizenship/learn-about-citizenship/the-naturalization-interview-and-test/naturalization-oath-of-allegiance-to-the-united-states-of-america, U.S. Citizens and Immigration Services, Last Update April 23, 2020. Internet.

Job One for Humanity, Editors. Global Warnings: The Job One for Humanity Story and the Latest Global Warming Facts https://www.,.org/about_job_one_for_humanity?gclid=Cj0KCQjw_absBRD1ARIsAO4_D3uuvOPv6SiQXylKhjzgQnb2el4x4sD17KzJ5gzLUA0LsmRkkg9afnIaApaWEALw_wcB Job One For Humanity, October 31, 2020, p.1-10. Internet.

Johnson, Dave. *Armor of God: Gospel of Peace, Life Hope, and Truth.* https://lifehopeandtruth.com/change/christian-conversion/armor-of-god/gospel-of-peace/, Bloomberg Opinion, March 8, 2020. p.1-2. Internet.

Kaster, Carolyn. Photograph: Steve Bannon compares China to 1930s Germany and says the U.S. must confront Beijing. https://www.theguardian.com/us-news/2017/sep/11/steve-bannon-compares-china-to-1930s-germany-and-says-us-must-confront-beijing. The Guardian September 11, 2017. Internet.

Katz, Cheryl. *Yale, Environment 360,* https://e360.yale.edu/features/piling-up-how-chinathe s-ban-on-importing-waste-has- stalled-global-recycling Published at the Yale School of Forestry & Environmental Studies, March 7, 2019, p. 1-4.Internet.

Kiyosaki, Robert. *The Shocking Truth About the Future,* upload, Clarity Coaching- Transforming Lives, July 6, 2019, https://www.youtube.com/watch?v=ftBeTIDv8Vg. Internet.

Keresztry, O. Cist. Roch, Edited by Gregg Andrew C. *Christianity Among Other Religions: Apologetics in a Contemporary Context.* Society of St. Pauls, 2006. Print.

Klasfeld, Adam, "Prosecution of Child-Sex Traffickers Plummeted Under Trump," Courthouse News Service, https://www.courthousenews.com/prosecution-of-kiddie-traffickers-plummeted-under-trump/, July 16, 2019. Print.

Kosloski, Philip. P*lace yourself under the mantle of the Virgin Mary with prayer, Spirituality,* https://aleteia.org/2019/05/04/place-yourself-under-the-mantle-of-the-virgin-mary-with-this-prayer/ Aleteia, May 04, 2019. Internet.

Landes, David S., *The Unbound Prometheus.* Press Syndicate of the University of Cambridge (1969). *Industrial Revolution,* https://en.wikipedia.org/wiki/Industrial_Revolution From Wikipedia, the free encyclopedia, October 31, 2020,. Internet.

Levin, Mark, R. *The Liberty Amendments, Restoring the American Republic, Threshold Editions* New York. A of Simon & Schuster, Inc. 2013.Print.

Levin, Mark R. *Liberty & Tyranny: A Conservative Manifesto.* New York, Threshold Editions, 2009. Marklevinshow.com.Print.

Lightfoot, J.B. Edited and Edited and revised by Holmes, Michael. *The Apostolic Fathers, Second Edition,* Grand Rapids, Michigan Baker Book House, 1994. Print.

Liddell & Scott. (Intermediate) An Intermediate Greek-English Lexicon (Liddell & Scott)

Accordance edition is hypertexted and formatted by OakTree Software, Inc. Version 2.3,1993. Computer Program.

Lloyd-Jones D, Marlyn. *Authority,* Inter-Varsity Fellowship 39 Bedford Square, W.C. I, London, Rocheste144r, Kent, Staples Printers Limited 1967. Print.

Los Angeles Times, Editors. *Homelessness, Human Rights Watch, Environment* www.latimes.com-California https://www.hrw.org/topic/environment?gclid=CjwKCAjw2qHsBR AGEiwAMbPoDDVUhyxdyjd413gRJ-ZbFOcsrls-WqQD4gvxl-1PP2TSxLL9f0pzwRoCKx4QAvD_BwE, Los Angeles Times, October 31, 2020. Internet.

Louw, Johannes P., and Eugene A. Nida. *Louw & Nida Greek-English Lexicon of the New Testament Based on Semantic Domains,* Editors by the United Bible Societies, New York, NY 10023 Second Edition. Used by permission. Landkarten zur Bible, prepared by Karl Elliger, revised by Siegfried Mittmann. Designed by Leonberg. Copyright ©, by Deutsche Bibelgesellschaft, Stuttgart. Software, Inc. Version 4.2, Copyright © 1963, 1978, 1988, 1989 1990. Computer Program.

Mann, Thomas, W. *The Book of the Torah The Narrative Integrity of the Pentateuch,* Atlanta, John Knox Press, 1973. Print.

Mary, Virgin, Queen. *There is an "Economic war," and "Drug War," now.. as Mary Virgin Queen told us in the Divine message: We America have taken heed and put America first.* Uploaded by https://www.youtube.com/watch?v=1jdIshuoRBQ, 2020.Internet.

McClay, Wilfred. M. *Rediscovering the Wisdom in American History* College. Hillsdale College, Imprimis, A Publication Volume 48, Number 7/8 July/August 2019.Print.

Moltmann, Jurgen. *The Church in the Power of the Spirit, A Contribution to Messianic Ecclesiology*, Minneapolis, Fortress Press, 1993.Print.

Morris Edmund. *Theodore Rex Pan. USA, Random House*, September 11, *2001. Print.*

Mounce, William D. D. Bennett edited by Jr. *Mounce Greek Dictionary Mounce Concise Greek-English Dictionary of the New Testament.* Copyright ©http://www.teknia.com/greek-dictionary rights reserved. Accordance edition is hypertexted and formatted by OakTree Software, Inc. Version 3.8. 2011. Computer Program.

Naturalization Oath of Allegiance to the United States of America https://www.uscis.gov/citizenship/learn-about-citizenship/the-naturalization-interview-and-test/naturalization-oath-of-allegiance-to-the-united-states-of-america, U.S. Citizenship, and Immigration Service, July 5, 2020.Internet.

Nave, Orville J., A.M., LL.D. *Nave's Topical Bible Nave's Topical Bible (Nave's).* Public domain. Electronic text downloaded from the Bible Foundation e-Text Library: <http://www.bf.org/bfetexts.htm>Hypertexted and formatted by OakTree Software, Inc. Version 2.9. Computer Program. 1907. Computer Program.

Nyaumon, Chiseigaku Abe, I., "Geopolitical: Theories, Concepts, Schools, and Debates," Tokyo: Kokon Shoin, 1933, Read by Arnold, Jafe, Lecture #2 at the China Institute of Fudan University, Shanghai, China, Eurasianist Archive. December 2018. Geopolitical: Theories, Concepts, Schools, and Debates, https://www.geopolitica.ru/en/article/geopolitics-theories-concepts-schools-and-debates. Internet.

Pantheon Rome, Wikipedia, Editors., https://en.wikipedia.org/wiki/Pantheon,_Rome(1980), 38–39, 38 quoted. Internet.

Paul VI, Pope. *Dogmatic Constitution On the Church, Lumen Gentium Solemnly Promulgated By His Holiness,* Libera Vatican, On November 21, 1964. Internet.

Phillips, Jackson. *Trump Wants to Make America a 'Manufacturing Superpower' Without Reliance on China,* https://link.theepochtimes.com/mkt_app/trump-wants-to-make-america-a-manufacturing-superpower-without-reliance-on-china_3539382.html,Epoch Times, October 14, 2020, p.1. Internet.

Pius X, Pope, "Encyclical of Iucunda Sane On Pope Gregory the Great," To Our Venerable Brethren, the Patriarchs, Primates, Archbishops, Bishops, and other ordinaries in peace and communion with the Apostolic.
(Libreria Editrice Vaticana Given at Rome at St. Peter's on March 12, of the year 1904, on the feast of St. Gregory I. Pope and Doctor of the Church, in the first year of Our Pontificate.) http://www.vatican.va/content/pius-x/en/encyclicals/documents/hf_p-x_enc_12031904_iucunda-sane.html. Internet.

PIUS X Pope, "Encyclical of Singular Quadam of Labor Organizations," To our Beloved Son, George Kopp, Cardinal Priest of the Holy Roman Church, t of Breslau and to the other Archbishops and Bishops of Germany. (Libreria Editrice Vaticana,
Given at Saint Peter's, Rome, on September 24, 1912, the tenth year of Our Pontificate.) http://www.vatican.va/content/pius-x/en/encyclicals/documents/hf_p-x_enc_24091912_singulari-quadam.html.Internet.

Pavone, Frank, Fr. *"Just evil how they treated David !"* Frank, Pavone, https://www.instagram.com/tv/CGA2XeLBFGh/?igshid=6evq06q4qf9q,2020. November 1, 2020 Internet.

Rasmussen, (Arden) Lisa Lucia. *Fuller Theology Seminary Homiletics* PR500 Professor Clayton Schmit, Pasadena, Lisa Lucia Rasmussen, Winter 2002.Print.

Rasmussen, (Arden) Lisa Lucia, *New Testament Exegesis, Phillipians, 3: 7-11*, Philippians NE506, Professor Hansen, February 9, 2000.Print.

Rawls, John, Wikipedia, Wikipedia, the free encyclopedia, November 28, 2020, https://en.wikipedia.org/wiki/John_Rawls., Internet.

Reagan, Ronald President. *"Evil Empire Speech, Greatest Presidential Speeches,"* Apple Music, March 8, 1983. Computer Program.

Reagan, Ronald President. *Speaks at the United Nations General Assembly,* Apple Music Ronald Reagan --- *Greatest Presidential Speeches*, June 17, 1982. Computer Program.

Rice, John, Paul, *Important Powerful Message: John Paul Rice, A Child's Voice,* The Real Story of the Hidden Network, https://www.bitchute.com/video/ULN5oxefGmLE/, Bit Chute, August 15, 2020.Internet.

Ripperger, Father, Our Lady of Sorrows (Latin: Beata Maria Virgo Perdolens), Classic Catholic Audiobooks, November 2020, https://www.youtube.com/watch?v=u8innElHjno. Internet.

Saint Margaret Mary Alacoque. *Sacred Heart Enthronement,* https://enthronements.com/?gclid=CjwKCAjw2qHsBRAGEiwAMbPoDHTLSCqo6PWji6_6ZfifsA9wlWYe6ixE6as5UcDWpCSI1ITFbG1jJhoCegwQAvD_BwE, Sacred Heart, Apostolate, Inc., November 1, 2020.Internet.

Savac, Peter, *"Teen Trapped for Years in Foster Care: There Was No Need to Take Me Away,"* SOCIAL SERVICES, The Epoch Times, September 3, 2019.Newspaper Print.

Sheen Fulton J., Father. *Speaks on The Devil & the Diabolic Venerable.* https://m.youtube.com/watch?v=kpGm9pVHkc0, Catholic World.,November 1, 2020. Internet.

Spinoza, and Elwes, R.H.M., and Cordasco, Francesco Edits, Translated from the Latin With an Introduction. *The Chief Works of Benedict De Spinoza, A Theological-Political Treatise and A Political Treatise.* Dover Publications, Inc. New York, 1951.Print.

Stansberry, Research. *The Battle for America, 2nd Edition Why the 2020 Election Will Cause the Biggest Financial Crisis in U.S. History,* by Stansberry Research Copyright @2019. Print.

Stassen, Glen, H. Just Peacemaking, Transforming Initiatives for Justice and Peace Louisville, Kentucky, Westminister/John Knox Press, 1992. Print.

Staver, Mat. "CA Emergency Hearing Today" Liberty Counsel, Lisa Lucia Arden September 21, 2020, at 1:46:45 PM PDT. Email.

Steenbergen, Van Fernand, and Moonlan, Lawrence Translated. *Epistemology,* from the Fourth French Language Edition. Louvain, Publications New York, Joseph F. Wagner, Inc, 1970. Print.

Storey, William, G., Edits. *Novenas, Prayers of Intercession and Devotion,* Loyola Press, Chicago,2005.Print.

Strong, James, Dr. *Strong's Greek Dictionary of the New Testament.* (Greek Strong's) Public Domain Electronic text downloaded from the Bible Foundation e-Text Library: <http://www.bf.org/bfetexts.htm>
Hypertexted and formatted by Oaktree Software, Inc. Greek text added by OakTree Software, Inc. Version 2.8. 1890. Computer Program.

Strong, James Dr. *Hebrew and Chaldee Dictionary of the Old Testament.* (Hebrew Strong's)Public Domain Electronic text downloaded from the Bible Foundation e-Text Library: http://www.bf.org/bfetexts.htm Hypertexted and formatted by

OakTree Software, Inc. Hebrew text added by OakTree Software, Inc. Version 3.1,1890, Compter Program.

Terrien, Samuel, and Ruth Nanda Anshen Edited. *The Elusive PresenceToward a New Biblical Theology, Religious Perspectives Volume Twenty- Six, Chapter The Prophetic Vision, Founded,* San Francisco, *Planned,* Harper & Row, Publishers 1978. Print.

Thayer, Joseph Henry. *Thayer's Greek-English Lexicon of the New Testament* By Joseph Henry Thayer, D.D. Public Domain Formatted and hypertexted by OakTree Software, Inc. Version 1.7, 1995. Computer Program.

Thompson John M. The Revolutionary War, Washington D.C., National Geographic 2004. Print.

Trump, Donald J. President. *President Trump Unveils His "America First Healthcare Plan."* https://www.youtube.com/watch?v=REy0jyImydA&feature=share. Epoch Times, September 24, 2020. Internet.

Cathey Libby, King Lauren, and Ebbs Stephanie, "Trump, Donald J. President, Republican Convention" (Fort Mc Henry and White House August 24-27, 2020). https://abcnews.go.com/Politics/rnc-2020-day-trump-accept-nomination-white-house/story?id=72577769. August 27, 2020, 9:48 PM. Internet

Trump, Melania. "Be Best. First Lady's, Melania Trump Initiative," (Washington. D.C.,) https://www.whitehouse.gov/people/melania-trump/. October 31, 2020. Internet.

U.S. Department of Homeland Security Edits. Oath of Allegiance for Wikipediahttps://en.wikipedia.org/wiki/Oath_of_Allegiance_(United_States)#cite_note-uscis-9 https://en.wikipedia.org › wiki › Immigration_to_the_United_States June 30, 2010.Internet.

Van Gemeren, Willem A. New International Dictionary of Old Testament Theology & Exegesis General Editor Zondervan, Grand Rapids, Michigan, 49530by Willem A.
Electronic text hypertexted and prepared by OakTree Software, Inc. Version 2.5, Copyright ©1997. Computer Program.

Viète, François. In Artem Analyticien Isagoge (Introduction to the art of analysis) (1591), Analysis and Synthesis in Greek, https://hsm.stackexchange.com/questions/5629/analysis-vs-synthesis-in greek mathematics?utm_medium=organic&utm_source=google_rich_qa&utm_campaign=google_rich_qa. History of Science and Mathematics Beta. January 28, 2017, p. 1. Internet.

Websters, Daniel. Webster's Dictionary Webster's Revised Unabridged Dictionary (Webster) Version published in 1913 by the C. & G. Merriam Co., Springfield, Mass., under the direction of Noah Porter, D.D., LL.D. Electronic text hypertexted and prepared by Oak Tree Software, Inc. Version 1.7, (1913), Computer Program.

Welch, Robert. *The Politician*, Belmont Publishing Company, Massachusetts, 1964. Print.

West, Darrel, and Lansang, Christian. *Global manufacturing Scorecard: How the U.S. Compares to 18 other nations,* https://www.brookings.edu/research/global-manufacturing-scorecard-how-the-us-compares-to-18-other-nations/Brookings, July 10, 2018. Internet.

Pantheon Rome, Wikipedia, Editors., https://en.wikipedia.org/wiki/Pantheon,_Rome(1980), 38–39, 38 quoted. Internet.

Wong, Dorcas and Alexander Chipman, Koty, "The US-China Trade War: A Timeline,"

China Briefing The Briefing, From Dezan Shira & Associates China-briefing.com. https://www.china-briefing.com/news/the-us-china-trade-war-a-timeline/ August 25, 2020. Internet

Yang, Catherine. Jessie Minassian: A Passion for Helping Teen. https://reader.epoch.cloud/?token=58fade886780b498357c0a6 1eaffc92c_5d88b6d0_1864061&selDate=20190923, The Epoch Times, September 9, 2019,.Internet.

Yang, Catherine. Mike Lindell: the Pillow King From drug addict to multi-million-dollar business owner, Lindell is launching a nationwide network to combat drug addiction," The Epoch Times, September 5, 2019. News Paper Print.

[ii] Arden, Lisa Lucia, Our Need to Give to the World, Heal America, Love in God, Pasadena, (California Lisa Lucia Arden 2016, 2019); Goodrick W. Edward, Kohlenberger III R.,John.,and . Swanson A. James, NIV Greek Dictionary Greek to English Dictionary and Index to the NIV New Testament (NIV Greek),(Zondervan NIV Exhaustive Concordance
1999, 1990 by the Zondervan Corporation, Grand Rapids, Michigan 49530, OakTree Software, Inc, Version 1.3, 1407
[i] Louw P. Johannes and Eugene A. Nida, Edits, Louw & Nida Greek-English Lexicon of the New Testament Based on Semantic Domains Second Edition, (The United Bible Societies, New York, NY 10023 1988, 1989 by Landkarten zur Bible, prepared by Karl Elliger, revised by Siegfried Mittmann. Designed by Deutsche Bibelgesellschaft Stuttgart and Kartographisches Institut Helmut Fuchs Leonberg. 1963, 1978, 1990 by Deutsche Bibelgesellschaft, Stuttgart, OakTree Software,

Inc. Version 4.2), **3378**   [3068 & 3069]   יְהוֹה, יהוה, **yhwh, yhwh, n 3446**   [3289**],
3447   [3135]..pr.m.   [root of: 3363 [also used with compound proper names]]. LORD (Yahweh), the proper name of the one true God; knowledge and use of the name implies personal or covenant relationship; the name pictures God as the one who exists and/or causes existence. *(Divine Message enemies that are mine our God's; Go forward daughter, and I will take care of your enemies.)*
[ii] Arden, Lisa Lucia, Our Need to Give to the World, Heal America, Love in God, See Table of Contents.
[iii] Amministrazione del Patrimonio Della Sede Apostlica, The Catechism of the Catholic Church (English) C. Catechism-1997 (Libreria Editrice Vatican, Vatican City) OakTree Software, Inc.Version 1.5,peace. 2305
[iv] Reagan, Ronald President, Greatest Presidential Speeches, Speech to the United Nations General Audience, Apple 7 Music, June 17, 1982

[v] Amministrazione del Patrimonio Della Sede Apostlica,. The Catechism of the Catholic Church (English) C. Catechism-1997,peace.
[vi] Darton, Longman & Todd, The New Jerusalem Bible (NJB) The New Jerusalem Bible (Doubleday, a division of Bantam Doubleday Dell Publishing Group, Inc. Doubleday, a division of Bantam Doubleday Dell Publishing Group, Inc 1990), Isaiah 9:6.

[vii] Strong, James Dr. Hebrew and Chaldee Dictionary of the Old Testament. Hebrew Strong's (Oak Tree Software Version 3.1, 1890), **Peace 8017.** שְׁלֻמִיאֵל **Shlumiy'el.**

שָׁלוֹם shalom, *shaw-lome';* from 7999; safe, i.e. (figuratively) well, happy, friendly; also (abstractly) welfare, i.e. health, prosperity, **peace**:—x do, familiar, x fare, favour, + friend, x great, (good) health, (x perfect, such as be at) peace(-able, -ably), prosper(-ity, -ous), rest, safe(-ty), salute, welfare, (x all is, be) well, x wholly. Hebrew strongs

1. 7999. שָׁלַם shalam, *shaw-lam';* a primitive root; to be safe (in mind, body or estate); figuratively, to be (causatively, make) completed; by implication, to be friendly; by extension, to reciprocate (in various applications):—make amends, (make an) end, finish, full, give again, make good, (re-)pay (again), (make) (to) (be at) peace(-able), that is perfect, perform, (make) prosper(-ous), recompense, render, requite, make restitution, restore, reward, x surely.
2. 8000. שְׁלַם shlam, *shel-am';* (Aramaic) corresponding to 7999; to complete, to restore: —deliver, finish
3. 8001. שְׁלָם shlam, *shel-awm';* (Aramaic) corresponding to 7965; prosperity: —peace.
4. 8002. שֶׁלֶם shelem, *sheh'-lem;* from 7999; properly, requital, i.e. a (voluntary) sacrifice in thanks: —peace offering.
5. 8003. שָׁלֵם shalem, *shaw-lame';* from 7999; complete (literally or figuratively); especially friendly: —full, just, made ready, peaceable, perfect(-ed), quiet, Shalem (by mistake for a name), whole.
6. 8004. שָׁלֵם Shalem, *shaw-lame';* the same as 8003; peaceful; Shalem, an early name of Jerusalem: —Salem.
7. 8005. שִׁלֵּם shillem, *shil-lame';* from 7999; requital: —recompense. (May put this in the terms after use)

[viii] Arden, Lisa, Lucia, Our Need to Give to the World, *America love in God, Heal America*, See Index
[ix] Fakkert, Jasper Editor-in-Chief Epoch, "President Trumps first two years in Office," Epoch Times Special Edition, The Epoch Times, 2019.

[xi] Thompson John M., The Revolutionary War,(National Geographic, Washington D.C., 2004) 81-82.

[xii] Fisher, Ron, United States, An Illustrated History, (Published National Geographic Fahey, John M., Jr. President and Chief Executive Officer 1958, 2007, 84.

[xiii] Fisher, Ron, 82.

[xiv] Aristotle's Categories.

[xv] Wong, Docas, and Koty Chipman, "The US China Trade War: A Timeline," The Briefing, From Dezan Shira & Associates China-briefing.com. (August 25, 2020): 11.

[xvi] Reagan, Ronald President. "Evil Empire Speech, Greatest Presidential Speeches", Apple Music, (March 8, 1983)

[xvii] Strong, James Dr. Hebrew and Chaldee Dictionary of the Old Testament Hebrew Strong's Dictionary*Peace, retribution, security, tranquility → בֶּטַח (safety, H1055); → רָגַע / רָגַע (crust over, come to rest, be quiet, 8088 / H8089; מַרְגּוֹעַ, resting-place, H5273; מַרְגֵּעָה, resting-place, H5276; רָגֵעַ, quiet, resting, H8091; רֶגַע, period, instant, suddenly, every moment, H8092); → שָׁלָה (be quiet, at ease, give false hope, H8922; שְׁלוּ, carefree, at ease, undisturbed, H8929; שָׁלוּ, prosperous, undisturbed, H8930; שַׁלְוָה, secure, heedless, carelessness, H8932; שְׁלִי, quiet, H8952); → שָׁלֵם (have satisfaction, repay, reward, retribute, make peace, H8966; שָׁלוֹם, peace, friendship, happiness, prosperity, health, H8968; שָׁלֵם uninjured, safe, complete, peaceable, H8969; שִׁלֻּמָה, repayment, retribution, H8974); → שָׁקַט (be tranquil, H9200; שֶׁקֶט, tranquillity, H9201); Consent; Rest [quiet, repose]; Safety; Payment; Reconciliation; Salvation; Security; Stillness; Retribution: Theology[xvii]

[xviii] Van Gemeren A. Willem, General Editor, New International Dictionary of Old Testament Theology & Exegesis, (Zondervan, Grand Rapids, Michigan,49530 1997,OakTree Software, Inc. Version 2.5), peace.

[xix] We are all made up of an organic being of the molecules of the Periodic Table of all elements that exist. (And with the breathe of God in us Genesis 2:7.) Human psyche are connected to these organic substances of the technological energy that transposes from and upon the {lines or apparatus } to the point of delievery and desired.

[xx] Trump, Donald J. "President, Republican Convention," Fort Mc Henry and White House August 24-27, 2020.

[xxi] Arden Lisa Lucia, "Our Need to Give to the World," Heal America, Love in God, See Table of Contents.

[xxii] Mounce, William D. and Rick D. Bennett, Jr. Edits, <u>Greek Dictionary Mounce Concise Greek-English Dictionary of the New Testament</u>,(OakTree Inc.,Version 4.3 2011), arising.

[xxiii]Strong, James Dr., <u>Hebrew and Chaldee Dictionary of the Old Testament,</u> שָׁלֹם **shalom,** *shaw-lome′;* from 7999; safe, i.e. (figuratively) well, happy, friendly; also (abstractly) welfare, i.e. health, prosperity, **peace**:—x do, familiar, x fare, favour, + friend, x great, (good) health, (x perfect, such as be at) peace(-able, -ably), prosper(-ity, -ous), rest, safe(-ty), salute, welfare, (x all is, be) well, x wholly. Hebrew strongs7999. שָׁלַם **shalam,** *shaw-lam′;* a primitive root; to be safe (in mind, body or estate); figuratively, to be (causatively, make) completed; by implication, to be friendly; by extension, to reciprocate (in various applications):—make amends, (make an) end, finish, full, give again, make good, (re-)pay (again), (make) (to) (be at) peace(-able), that is perfect, perform, (make) prosper(-ous), recompense, render, requite, make restitution, restore, reward, x surely.8000. שְׁלַם **shlam,** *shel-am′;* (Aramaic) corresponding to 7999; to complete, to restore:—deliver, finish8001. שְׁלָם **shlam,** *shel-awm′;* (Aramaic) corresponding to 7965; prosperity:—peace. 8002. שֶׁלֶם **shelem,** *sheh′-lem;* from 7999; properly, requital, i.e. a (voluntary) sacrifice in thanks:—peace offering. 8003. שָׁלֵם **shalem,** *shaw-lame′;* from 7999; complete (literally or figuratively); especially friendly:—full, just, made ready, peaceable, perfect(-ed), quiet, Shalem (by mistake for a name), whole. 8004. שָׁלֵם **Shalem,** *shaw-lame′;* the same as 8003; peaceful; Shalem, an early name of Jerusalem:—Salem.8005. שִׁלֵּם **shillem,** *shil-lame′;* from 7999; requital:—recompense. (May put this in the terms after use)

[xxiv] Spinoza, Baruch, 85-86.
[xxv] Aquinas, Thomas, St, [I.121].
[xxvi] Strong, James, Dr., <u>Dictionary Strong's Hebrew and Chaldee Dictionary of the Old Testament</u>, peace 8063. שְׂמִיכָה **smiykah,** *sem-ee-kaw′;* from 5564; a run (as sustaining the Oriental sitter):—mantle. 8065. שָׁמַיִן **shamayin,** *shaw-mah′-yin;* (Aramaic) corresponding to 8064:—heaven. 5564. סָמַךְ **çamak,** *saw-mak′;* a primitive root; to prop (literally or figuratively); reflexively, to lean upon or take hold of (in a favorable or unfavorable sense):—bear up, establish, (up-)hold, lay, lean, put, rest self, set self, stand fast, stay (self), sustain. 5094. נָהִיר **nhiyr,** *neh-heere′;* We then will receive the illumination of wisdom of light (Aramaic) or נְהִירוּ **nehiyruw** (Aramaic), *neh-hee-roo*(Aramaic) or נְהִירוּ **nehiyruw** (Aramaic), *neh-hee-roo′;* from the same as 5105; illumination, i.e. (figuratively) **wisdom**:—light.

[xxvii] Kosloski, Philip, "Place yourself under the mantle of the Virgin Mary with prayer," Spirituality, <u>Aleteia</u>, (May 04, 2019),1.

[xxviii] Amministrazione del Patrimonio Della Sede Apostlica,. The Catechism of the Catholic Church (English) C. Catechism-1997, covenant.
[xxix] Amministrazione del Patrimonio Della Sede Apostlica,. The Catechism of the Catholic Church (English) C. Catechism-1997, covenant.
[xxx] Strong, James, Dr., Hebrew Dictionary Strong's Hebrew and Chaldee Dictionary of the Old Testament, **When we have unity for [שָׁלֵם] vb. denom. be in covenant of peace — Qal** *be at peace* (in covt.). **Pu.** *one in covt. of peace* (with י).**Hiph. 1.** *make peace* with, אֶת (עִם); c. אֶל pregn. *submitting unto.* **2.** *cause to be at peace,* אֶת. **Ee+Hoph.** *live in peace with.*

[xxxi] Keresztry, O. Cist. Roch, Edited by Gregg Andrew C, Christianity Among Other Religions: Apologetics in a Contemporary Context, (Society of St. Pauls, 2006), 15-16.
[xxxii] Keresztry, O. Cist. Roch,101.
[xxxiii] Steenberghen, Van Fernand, translated Moonlan, Lawrence, Epistemology Fourth French Language Edition, (Louvain, Publications University Ladeuzeplein, 2, New York, Joseph F. Wagner, Inc, 1970), 192.
[xxxiv] Keresztry, O. Cist. Roch, 15-16, 161.
[xxxv] Amministrazione del Patrimonio Della Sede Apostlica, Catholic Catechism (English) The Catechism of the Catholic Church (English) (C. Catechism-E (Libreria Editrice Vatican, Vatican City 1997, OakTree Software, Inc.Version 1.5), 413-416.
[xxxvi] Amministrazione del Patrimonio Della Sede Apostlica, Vatican II (English) Documents of the II Vatican Council (Libreria Editrice Vatican, Vatican City 1962—1965,OakTree Software, Inc. Version 2.0), Vatican II – E Virtue Dogmatic Constitution on the Church Lumen Gentium CHAPTER II.
[xxxvii] Nave, A.M., D.D Orville J., LL.D. Nave's Topical Bible Nave's Topical Bible, (OakTree Software, Inc. Version 2.9), Virtue.
[xxxviii] Brown, Colin General Editor, New International Dictionary of New Testament Theology German under the title: THEOLOGISCHES BEGRIFFSLEXIKON ZUM NEUEN TESTAMENT
(Theologischer Verlag Rolf Brockhaus, Wuppertal. The Zondervan Corporation, Grand Rapids, Michigan, U.S.A.,The Paternoster Press, Ltd. Exeter, Devon, 1967, 1969, 1971 1975, 1986,
OakTree Software, Inc.Version 3.5), 27 COURAGE.
[xxxix] Amministrazione del Patrimonio Della Sede Apostlica, The Catechism of the Catholic Church (English), PART THREE: LIFE IN CHRIST.
[xl] Amministrazione del Patrimonio Della Sede Apostlica, Catholic Catechism (English) The Catechism of the Catholic Church (English) (C. Catechism-E), **Life in Christ.**

[xli] Amministrazione del Patrimonio Della Sede Apostlica, Catholic Catechism (English) The Catechism of the Catholic Church (English) (C. Catechism-E), **Life in Christ.**

[xlii] Kempis à Thomas, The Imitation of Christ (Harry Planting a of the Christian Classics Ethereal Library Oak Tree Software, Inc. Version 1.5)**,** THE BASIS OF FIRM PEACE OF HEART AND TRUE PROGRESS THE VOICE OF CHRIST.

[xliii] Amministrazione del Patrimonio Della Sede Apostlica, Vatican II (English) Documents of the II Vatican Council (Libreria Editrice Vatican, Vatican City 1962—1965 OakTree Software, Inc. Version 2.0),CHAPTER II, IV 106,156,157.

[xliv] Henry, Matthew Abridged, Matthew Henry's Commentary (Oak Tree Software, Inc. Version 3.2), ON THE PEOPLE OF GOD.

[xlv] Aquinas, Thomas, St., 277.

[xlvi] Amministrazione del Patrimonio Della Sede Apostlica, Vatican II (English) Documents of the II Vatican Council (Libreria Editrice Vatican, Vatican City 1962—1965 Oak Tree Software, Inc. Version 2.0), 78.

[xlvii] Amministrazione del Patrimonio Della Sede Apostlica, Vatican II (English) Documents of the II Vatican Council (Libreria Editrice Vatican, Vatican City 1962—1965 OakTree Software, Inc. Version 2.0),78.

[xlviii] Longman Darton, and Doubleday, Todd, The New Jerusalem Bible , (Bantam Doubleday 1960, Dell Publishing Group, Inc.. Version 2:7), Isaiah 9:6, Note: In this writing, most of the Bible Verses I will use the New Jerusalem Bible.

[xlix] Trunk, Botany, Wikipedia Encyclopedia, https://en.wikipedia.org/wiki/Trunk_(botany)#:~:text=The%20xylem%20also%20stores%20starch,the%20center%20of%20the%20tree. February 17, 2017

[l] Trunk, Botany, **Wikipedia Encyclopedia,** https://en.wikipedia.org/wiki/Trunk_(botany)#:~:text=The%20xylem%20also%20stores%20starch,the%20center%20of%20the%20tree. February 17, 2017.

[li] Webster, Webster's Dictionary,Webster's Revised Unabridged Dictionary, (C. & G. Merriam Co., Springfield, Mass.,1913,Oak Tree Software, Inc. Version 1.5), Retribution.

[lii] Aquinas, Thomas, St, enlightens us of peace, whether peace is the same as a concert (agreement)?

[liii] Aquinas,Thomas, St, Whether peace is a virtue?

[liv] Seven virtues https://en.m.wikipedia.org/wiki/Seven_virtues
[lv] Amministrazione del Patrimonio Della Sede Apostlica, Vatican II (English) Documents of the II Vatican Council (Libreria Editrice Vatican, Vatican City 1962—1965 OakTree Software, Inc. Version 2.0), nuclear.
[lvi] Harshaw, Tobin, "The Big Iran Threat is Nukes, Not Coronavirus", Bloomberg Opinion, Politics & Policy, Bloomberg.com, (March 8, 2020): 8:00am.

[lvii] Van Gemeren A. Willem, General Editor, everything has been immutably foreordained by God; הֶבֶל Eccl. 6:11.
[lviii] Dictionary, "Immutable," Google, https://www.google.com/search?sxsrf=ALeKk03m4lMcQprCLZKJKpwXxpWs5ROG7Q%3A1606435951802&source=hp&ei=b0TAX9HaLsO50PEPuPmIoAQ&q=IMMUTABLE&oq=IMMUTABLE&gs_lcp=CgZwc3ktYWIQA1AAWABg0AJoAHAAeACAAQCIAQCSAQCYAQCgAQdnd3Mtd2l6&sclient=psy-ab&ved=0ahUKEwiRzomiuKHtAhXDHDQIHbg8AkQQ4dUDCAk&uact=5, November 26, 2020.
[lix] Easton, M.A., M.GD.D., Easton's Bible Dictionary Third Edition, (Thomas Nelson, 1897, Oak Tree Software, Inc. Version 3.5), justice.

[lx] Video Advice ,"It will happen on the Election," Control October 20, 2020 https://www.youtube.com/watch?v=cWaiSxr1QkE&ab_channel=VideoAdvice
[lxi] Thayer, Henry Joseph D.D. Thayer's Greek-English Lexicon of the New Testament OakTree Software, Inc. Version 1.7, Holy Spirit.
 31. ἀγγελία; angelia, angelias, hē (angelos), a message, announcement, thing announced; precept declared, 1 John 1:5 (where Rec. has epangelia) (cf. Isa. 28:9); 3:11. (From Homer down.)*
[lxii] Latin Dictionary, (http://www.tidbits.com/matt/LatinDictReadMe.html>. OakTree Software, Inc. Version 1.4), justice **praetor -oris** m. leader, chief; a magistrate, esp. one who helped the consuls by administering **justice**, commanding armies, etc. **praetorianus -a -um** belonging to the imperial Authority, praetorian. **praetorius -a -um** (1) relating to the praetor, pra
etorian. (2) relating to any general or commander; 'praetoria navis', flagship; 'cohors', the general's bodyguard.

[lxiii]Seven virtues, Wikipedia, https://en.m.wikipedia.org/wiki/Seven_virtues, February, 2013.

[lxiv] America Heritage Fountation, "Declaration of Independence," America Heritage In Congress, July 4, 1776 Fountation https://americanheritage.org/bookstore/?gclid=Cj0KCQiAh4j-

BRCsARIsAGeV12BwhuXSztvpQj4IvzQwcIBerprbGjJB6lZa4Kml6Tn4c-OqogidPqkaAu6WEALw_wcB.,

[lxv] Seven Virtues and Deadly Sins

[lxvi] Homelessness, Los Angeles Times, www.latimes.com-california, November 2020.
[lxvii] Reagan, Ronald, "Evil Empire Speech." Greatest Presidential Speeches, Apple Music, March 8, 1983.

[lxviii] Gagnon, Louise, MRI shows brain changes from cannabis use, Aunt Minnie.com contributing writer May 20, 2019, https://www.auntminnie.com/index.aspx?sec=rca&sub=ismr_2019&pag=dis&ItemID=125536, The use of even small amounts of cannabis can cause changes in the brains of adolescents, according to recent studies using MRI. The findings indicate that researchers should pay close attention to increasing cannabis use, especially in vulnerable populations, according to a presentation last week at the Society for Magnetic Resonance Radiographers & Technologists (SMRT) meeting.Studies have shown that adolescents who use marijuana just once or twice experience brain changes that show up on MRI compared with individuals who do not use cannabis. This indicates that cannabis may not be completely harmless, especially for some individuals."The predominant pattern of use is occasional and nonproblematic," said Scott Mackey, PhD, of the department of psychiatry at the University of Vermont in Burlington. "But a considerable portion, about 20% of those who are regular users, will go on to have periods of disordered use at some point in their life."

[lxix] Gagnon, Louise., 1.
[lxx] Gagnon, Louise., 1.
[lxxi] United States Environmental Protection Agency Press Office, Trump J. Donald President ,News Releases from Headquarters ›Water (OW) Signs Executive Order on Modernizing America's Water Resource Management and Water Infrastructure, (https://www.epa.gov/newsreleases/president-trump-signs-executive-order-modernizing-americas-water-resource-management. 10/13/2020 Water https://www.whitehouse.gov/presidential-actions/executive-order-modernizing-americas-water-resource-management-water-infrastructure/
[lxxii] Homelessness, www.latimes.com-california
[lxxiii] Jones, Brad, California 'Laser-Focused ' on Homelessness, Mental Health Reform, Newsom Says. Califronia Gov. Gavin Newsom during an interview in his office at Capitol in Sacramento, California. On Oct. 8,2019, Documented on Epoch, February 20, 2020.

lxxiv The State of Homelessness in America, Counsels of Advisors, September 2019, www.whitehouse.gov

lxxv O'Donnell Norah CBS News' says mostly peaceful protests, caused $1Billion to $2Billion in damage from looting and arson. Foxnews.com, September 17, 2020.

lxxvii Fisher, Ron, 161.

lxxviii Fisher, Ron, 160.

lxxix Morgan, Tom, Saints A Visual Almanac of the Virtuous, Pure, Praiseworthy, and Good, Saint Jerome, (Chronicle Books, San Francisco, 1994), 112.

lxxx Seven virtues and deadly sins.

lxxxi Morgan, Tom,111.

lxxxii Ripperger, Father, Our Lady of Sorrows (Latin: Beata Maria Virgo Perdolens), Classic Catholic Audiobooks, November 2020, Our Lady of Dolores, the Sorrowful Mother or Mother of Sorrows (Latin: Mater Dolorosa), and Our Lady of Piety, Our Lady of the Seven Sorrows or Our Lady of the Seven Dolours are names by which the Virgin Mary is referred to in relation to sorrows in her life. As Mater Dolorosa, it is also a key subject for Marian art +in the Catholic Church. Our Lady of Sorrows: https://www.youtube.com/watch?v=u8innElHjno

lxxxiii Ripperger, Our Lady of Sorrows.

lxxxiv Spinoza, Baruch, The Chief Works of Benedict de Spinoza, Unabridged ,R. H. H. Elwes Translation Theologico-Political Treatise Political Treatise, (Dover Publications, Inc. New York, 1951), 184.

lxxxv Divine Message agreed by Physician in China made the Virus as a Weapon to kill humanity Coronavirus whistleblower speaks out about possible COVID origin on 'Tuc... https://youtu.be/qFlqXPl_hZQ via @YouTube

lxxxvi **China, U.S.- News,** Epoch, China Using Fentanyl as Chemical Weapon Against US, Epoch Times, https://www.theepochtimes.com/china-is-deliberately-using-fentanyl-to-destroy-the-us_3058199.html, August 2018, p. A1

lxxxviiChina in Focus, 'YPD Officer's Hidden Ties to the CCP," Epoch Times, https://link.theepochtimes.com/mkt_app/china-in-focus-nypd-officers-hidden-ties-to-the-ccp3510401.html, September 22, 2020.

lxxxviii Spinoza, Baruch, 183.

lxxxix Arden, Lisa Lucia, Our Need to Give to the World, Love in God, Heal America)

[xc] Arden, Lisa Lucia, Our Need to Give to the World, Heal America Love in God

[xci] Aquinas' Summa, <u>Theologica The Summa Theologica (Summa Theologica)</u>, Translated by Fathers of the English Dominican Province Benziger Bros. edition, 1947, Digitally produced by Sandra K. Perry OakTree Software, Inc. Version 2.6) Summa Theological [II–II.58] OF JUSTICE (TWELVE ARTICLES)
[II–II.58.8]

[xcii] Aquinas, Thomas St, OF JUSTICE (TWELVE ARTICLES) [II–II.58.8],justice.

[xciii] Aquinas, Thomas St, The sacrifice, and justice, justice is more important, justice.

[xciv] **Aquinas, Thomas, St., Second, Justice of Distributive.**

[xcv] Goodrick, Edward W., John R. Kohlenberger III, and James A. Swanson, justice

[xcvi] Arden, Lisa Lucia, *Book Our Need to Give to the World, America love in God, Heal America, See God's intentions.*

[xcvii] Goodrick, Edward W., John R. Kohlenberger III, and James A. Swanson, justice.

[xcviii] Thatcher, Margaret, Margaret Thatcher Autobiography, Harper, Publishers 2013, 99.

[xcix] Levin, Mark, <u>The Liberty Amendments, Restoring the American Republic, Threshold Editions</u>, (A Division of Simon & Schuster, Inc., New York, 2013) 2
https://www.goodreads.com/work/quotes/25004371-the-liberty-amendments-restoring-the-american-republic

[c] Arden, Lisa, Lucia, Our Need to Give to the World. See Table of Contents.

[ci] Feeney, Denis, <u>Literature and Religion at Rome, Cultures, Contexts, an Beliefs</u> (Cambridge University, Press, 1998) 108-109.

[cii] Feeney, Denis, 109-110.

[ciii] Feeney, Denis, 142-143.

[civ] Storey, William G., <u>Novenas, Prayers of Intercession and Devotion</u> (Loyola Press, Chicago) 91.

[cv] Storey, William, G., 212.

[cvi] Strong, James, Dr. *Strong's Greek Dictionary of the New Testament.* (Greek Strong's) Public Domain Electronic text downloaded from the Bible Foundation e-Text Library: <http://www.bf.org/bfetexts.htm>
Hypertexted and formatted by Oaktree Software, Inc. Greek text added by OakTree Software, Inc. Version 2.8. 1890. Computer Program.

[cvii] Storey, p. 163

[cviii] Amministrazione del Patrimonio Della Sede Apostlica, <u>Vatican II (English) Documents of the II Vatican Council</u>,
justice.

[cix] Amministrazione del Patrimonio Della Sede Apostlica, Vatican II (English) Documents of the II Vatican Council, justice.
[cx] Staver, Mat. "CA emergency hearing today" Liberty Counsel, Lisa Lucia Arden September 21, 2020 at 1:46:45 PM PDT
[cxi] Amministrazione del Patrimonio Della Sede Apostlica,. The Catechism of the Catholic Church (English) C. Catechism-1997, **2303**
[cxii] Amministrazione del Patrimonio Della Sede Apostlica,. The Catechism of the Catholic Church (English) C. Catechism-1997,**Nation.**
[cxiii] Amministrazione del Patrimonio Della Sede Apostlica,The Catechism of the Catholic Church (English) C. Catechism-1997 ARTICLE 3: SOCIAL JUSTICE, 1928.
[cxiv] https://www.kingjamesbibleonline.org/Justice.php4
[cxv] Goodrick, Edward, W., Kohlenberger III, John, and Swanson, A. James, justice.
[cxvi] **Aquinas, Thomas, St.**, knowledge of God belongs only to the good.

[cxvii] Amministrazione del Patrimonio Della Sede Apostlica,. The Catechism of the Catholic Church (English) C. Catechism-1997C. 3 Social Justice IV. ECONOMIC ACTIVITY AND SOCIAL JUSTICE.
[cxviii] Amministrazione del Patrimonio Della Sede Apostlica,. The Catechism of the Catholic Church (English) C. Catechism-1997C. Catechis ARTICLE 3: SOCIAL JUSTICE, 1928.
[cxix] Then you will be able to realize that only through His love between you and the Trinity and in the redemption of the Cross of Jesus Christ you will able to live a continued life of forgiveness, of self-sin, forgiveness of others, and most of all the victory over sin and victory over a of a fulfilled life in God even though the
[cxx] Harris, R. Laird Editor; Gleason L. Archer, Jr., Associate Editor; Bruce K. Waltke, Associate Editor
Theological Wordbook of the Old Testament Theological Wordbook of the Old Testament (TWOT)
Copyright © 1980 by The Moody Bible Institute of Chicago Electronic text used by permission. Electronic text hypertexted and prepared by Oak Tree Software, Inc. Version 2.4

[cxxi] Potentiality speak of look it up identify I wrote on this already, find were I wrote about pray as God what to say this is salient of the development of the world at large
[cxxii] LLoyd-Jones D. Marlyn, *Authority* Inter-Varisty Fellowship 39 Bedford Square, W.C. I, London, Staples Printers Limited Rochester, Kent, 1967, p.93

[cxxiii] *John Paul Rice* https://youtu.be/dztir94oaOo, 2020

[cxxiv] Rice, John Paul, "Important Powerful Message: John Paul Rice, A Child's Voice, The Real Story of the Hidden." Network, https://youtu.be/dztir94oaOo ,September 2020.

[cxxv] Pope Pius X, "Encyclical of Singular Quadam of Labor Organizations," To our Beloved Son, George Kopp, Cardinal Priest of the Holy Roman Church, t of Breslau and to the other Archbishops and Bishops of Germany. (Libreria Editrice Vaticana
Given at Saint Peter's, Rome, on September 24, 1912, the tenth year of Our Pontificate.), http://www.vatican.va/content/pius-x/en/encyclicals/documents/hf_p-x_enc_24091912_singulari-quadam.html. p.3.

[cxxvi] Klasfeld, Adam, "Prosecution of Child-Sex Traffickers Plummeted Under Trump," Court house News Service, https://www.courthousenews.com/prosecution-of-kiddie-traffickers-plummeted-under-trump/, July 16, 2019

[cxxvii] Manfredi, Lucas, Fox News, Congress c
https://www.foxnews.com/politics/congressman-calls-out-georgetown-university-over-china-linked-funding, December 9, 2020: 5:30pm

[cxxviii] Cohen, David Ellliot Text by Robinson, Peter, Ronald Reagan, In life Photographs, (Newt Gingrich and Callista Gingrich, Sterling New York ,1976), 668.

[cxxix] Hammer, Josh, "Biden-Harris Would Deal a Huge Blow to Religious Liberty," Epoch Times, https://link.theepochtimes.com/mkt_app/biden-harris-would-deal-a-huge-blow-to-religious-liberty_3532632.html: August 13, 2020.

[cxxx] William, Jordan, "Biden vows to make Equality Act a legislative priority in first 100 days of office," The Hill, https://thehill.com/homenews/campaign/523472-biden-vows-to-make-equality-act-a-legislative-priority-for-first-100-days. October 29, 2020.

[cxxxi] Trump, Donald J. President, "President Trump Unveils His, America First Healthcare Plan," CBNC, https://www.youtube.com/watch?v=REy0jyImydA&feature=share. September 24, 2020.

[cxxxii] Bowen, Ixiao," Opioid Crisis, As Opioids Ravage Communities, Locals Unite in Response From faith groups to treatment centers, state and local communities are starting to make headway in helping to reduce deaths." The Epoch Times, Special Edition.
·https://reader.epoch.cloud/?token=95cc28b0c05118d932da028fbc2d78b9_5d84ad75_1864061&selDate=20190920, 2019.

[cxxxiii] Thatcher Margaret, 103.

[cxxxiv] Note some words are not generally capitalized in the English language; however, I want to get he attention of the reader. Some of these words I want

you to think as a tangible person and in some cases part of God's character. These words capitalized are words that are supported by the Holy Scriptures the Word of God is the characteristic of God Himself. Some of the Words, Freedom, Restoration, Justice, Forward Building in Love, Legacy.

[cxxxv] Thunberg,Greta, The disarming case to act right now on climate change, TEDxStockholm,
I have spoken on the eco-systems in my first book,
https://www.amazon.com/Lisa-Lucia-Arden/e/B079TF9GNQ%3Fref=dbs_a_mng_rwt_scns_share, For years I knocked at doors and emails for the support and awareness of eco-system and poverty issues.
https://www.ted.com/talks/greta_thunberg_the_disarming_case_to_act_right_now_on_climate_change?language=en November 2019.

[cxxxvi] Kowalska, Maria Faustina, Saint, Heaven, Hell and Purgatory, According to passages from the Diary of Saint Maria, (Marian Press, Stockbridge,1987) Ecclesial, Approved.

[cxxxvii] Cohen, David, Elliot, Text by Robinson, Peter, 668.

[cxxxviii] Cohen, David Elliott and Peter Robinson, 668.

[cxxxix] Global, Warming Facts, The Job One for Humanity Story and the Latest Global Warming Facts
https://www.joboneforhumanity.org/about_job_one_for_humanity?gclid=CjOKCQjw_absBRD1ARIsAO4_D3uuvOPv6SiQXylKhjzgQnb2el4x4sD17KzJ5gzLUAOLsmRkkg9afnlaApaWEALw_wcB, Note: Please, see. In this work we have only mentioned the urgencies of global warming and facts and warnings.

[cxl] Garg, Anu,Wordsmith. words@wordsmithlorg, USA, May 27, 2011.

[cxli] Trump, Melania, "Be Best," (White House 2019)
https://www.whitehouse.gov/people/melania-trump/.

[cxlii,cxlii] Arden, Lisa Lucia, Our Need to Give to the Word, Heal America Love in God, See Table Contents.

[cxliii] Brown, Colin, When the end comes the great transformation will come for all. The illustration is used of putting on new clothes (Clothe, art. du/w). This idea may be understood in the context of the initiation rites of the Hel. mystery cults. The inward transformation of the initiate would be symbolized by the laying aside of his old garm ents. New clothes would be put on. The perishable is laid aside; the imperishable, the divine is put on. The initiate was changed into the divine nature, made like the deity (cf. E. Dinkler, "*Die Taufterminologie*," 183 ff., bibliography). Similarly here, the perishable puts on the imperishable; out of what is mortal comes what is immortal (v. 54). Thus "death is swallowed up in victory," which is given "through our Lord Jesus Christ" (vv. 54, 57). Cf. also 2 Cor. 5:1-5, (R. Bultmann *Theology of the New Testament*, I, 1952, 211; Reason, art.).

cxliv Brown, Colin, *G3628 (mimeomai)*, imitate, follow.

cxlv Brown, Colin, *Epistrephoœ*.
cxlvi **Brown, Colin** *Epistrephoœ*.
cxlvii **Sacred Heart Enthronement,**
https://enthronements.com/?gclid=CjwKCAjw2qHsBRAGEiwAMbPoDHTLSCqo6 PWji6_6ZfifsA9wlWYe6ixE6as5UcDWpCSI1ITFbG1jJhoCegwQAvD_BwE
cxlviii Brown, S. R. Driver, and Briggs. C. A., A Hebrew and English Lexicon of the Old Testament (Oxford: Clarendon Press, Princeton Theological Seminary Hebrew Lexicon Project under the direction of Dr. J. M. Roberts. Oak Tree Software, Inc. 1907, 2001 OakTree Software, Inc. Version 3.7) majesty.

cl Brown, Colin, *Epistrephoœ*.
cli Brown, F. S. R. Driver, and C. A. Briggs, A Hebrew and English Lexicon of the Old Testament (abridged), (Oxford: Clarendon Press, 1907) mighty, and strong.

clii Katz, Cheryl, Yale, Environment 360, (Published at the Yale School of Forestry & Environmental Studies, MARCH 7, 2019)
https://e360.yale.edu/features/piling-up-how-chinas-ban-on-importing-waste-has-stalled-global-recycling Cheryl Katz is an independent science writer covering climate change, energy, earth sciences, and environmental health. A former newspaper reporter, she has reported from Iceland to Africa on topics ranging from new geothermal technology to rapidly warming lakes. Her articles have appeared in *Scientific American, National Geographic News* and *Hakai Magazine*, and among other sources.

cliii Kempis à Thomas, Consolation Book Three, The Quest of Divine Help and Confidence in Regaining Grace.
cliv Imbach, Jeffrey D. The Recovery of Love, Christian Mysticism and the Addictive Society, Julian of Norwich, John Ruusbroec, Meister Eckhart, Dante Alighieri, (The Crossroad Publishing Company, New York, 1992), 56
clv Imbach, Jeffrey D., 144.
clvi Imbach, Jeffrey D.,144-145

clvii Brown, by F. S. R. Driver, and C. A. Briggs BDB Abridged A Hebrew and English Lexicon of the Old Testament (Oxford: Clarendon Press, 1907), authority.
[מִשְׁטָר] **n.m. rule, authority**
clviii Strong James Dr., Hebrew Strong's Dictionary Strong's Hebrew and Chaldee Dictionary of the Old Testament Version 3.1, מַטֶּה **matteh**, *mat-teh'*; or (feminine) a **staff**; figuratively, a support of life, e.g. bread

clix Kempis à Thomas, The Fiftieth Chapter: HOW A DESOLATE PERSON OUGHT TO COMMIT HIMSELF INTO THE HANDS OF GOD THE DISCIPLE.
clx Amministrazione del Patrimonio Della Sede Apostlica, Catholic Catechism (English) The Catechism of the Catholic Church (English) (C. Catechism-E) Church., 351.

clxi Brown, Colin, *Epistrephoœ* Bultmann, R. *Theology of the New Testament*, I, 1952, 211; Reason, art. Nouvß.
clxii Brown, Colin, *Epistrephoœ*.
clxiii Amministrazione del Patrimonio Della Sede Apostlica, The Catechism of the Catholic Church (English). 351,854.
clxiv Amministrazione del Patrimonio Della Sede Apostlica, Vatican II (English) Documents of the II Vatican Council 1109.
clxv Amministrazione del Patrimonio Della Sede Apostlica, Vatican II (English) Documents of the II Vatican Council.66 i.
clxvi Amministrazione del Patrimonio Della Sede Apostlica, Vatican II (English) Documents of the II Vatican Council, 1696.

clxvii Amministrazione del Patrimonio Della Sede Apostlica, Vatican II (English) Documents of the II Vatican Council, Part1 CHAPTER III.

clxviii Mounce, William D. and Rick D. Bennett , H6641.
clxix Mounce, William D. and Rick D. Bennett, Jr. Edits, 1 2 Cor 4:7; Col 3:3.; 2 2 Cor 5:1.3 Cf. Mk 2:1-12.
clxx Brown, Colin., Restoration.
clxxi Thayer, Joseph Henry D.D. By Thayer's Greek-English Lexicon of the New Testament Public Domain, Formatted and hypertexted by Oak Tree Software, Inc. Version 1.7, 1411

clxxii Thayer Joseph Henry, D.D. Thayer's Greek-English Lexicon of the New Testament (OakTree Software, Inc. Version 1.7), 1410

clxxiii Strong James, Dr. Greek Strong Greek Strong's Dictionary Strong's Greek Dictionary of the New , 4982
clxxiv Goodrick W. Edward, Kohlenberger III R .,John.,and Swanson A. James , bring safely through διασώζω, **diasǫzō.**
clxxv Amministrazione del Patrimonio Della Sede Apostlica, Catholic Catechism (English) The Catechism of the Catholic Church (English) (C. Catechism-E), Revival REALIZING A REALATIONSHIP WITH GOD.

clxxvi LLoyd-Jones D. Marlyn, Authority, (Inter-Varisty Fellowship 39 Bedford Square, W.C. I, London, Staples Printers Limited Rochester, Kent, 1967),93.

[clxxvii] Van Gemeren A. Willem, General Editor, to stand **Note: *I use the definitions and the study of the words to seek the truth of God purpose and His intentions. I seek to use the information that brings love and also warnings for protection, with Wisdom.*** The word frequently describes God's control over and powerful deeds in the natural realm, including those involving a radical transformation of the natural order. God causes earthquakes to overturn mountains (Job 9:5), unleashes floods that destroy the land (12:15), and controls the day-night cycle, turning the darkness into dawn (Amos 5:10). In the days of Moses he turned the [Vol. 1, p. 1,026] waters of Egypt into blood (Exod 7:17, 20; Ps 78:44; 105:29), drove the locusts into the sea by changing the course of the winds (Exod 10:19), transformed the sea into dry land so that his people might pass through it (Ps 66:6), and turned the rock into a pool so that they might be refreshed (114:8). In the stereotypical and hyperbolic language of judgment, the prophets describe the Lord as dimming the heavenly luminaries (Joel 2:31 [3:4]) and transforming Edom's streams into pitch (Isa 34:9).

[clxxviii] **Van Gebemeren. Esther.**

[clxxix] Spinoza, Baruch, 34, 244.

[clxxx] Spinoza, Baruch, 244.

[clxxxi] Apostolic Fathers. p. 90-91.

[clxxxii] Apostolic Fathers..90-91. "'Potency' having this variety of meanings, so too the 'potent' or 'capable' in one sense will mean that which can begin a movement (or
a change in general, for even that which can bring things to rest is a 'potent' thing) in another thing or in itself qua other; and in one sense that over which something else has such a potency; and in one sense that which has a potency of changing into something, whether for the worse or for the better (for even that which perishes
is thought to be 'capable' of perishing, for it would not have perished if it had not been capable of it; but, as a matter of fact, it has a certain disposition and cause and principle which fits it to suffer this; sometimes it is thought to be of this sort because it has something, sometimes because it is deprived of something; but if privation is
in a sense 'having' or 'habit', everything will be capable by having something, so that things are capable both by having a positive habit and principle, and by having the privation of this, if it is possible to have a privation; and if privation is not in a sense 'habit', 'capable' is used in two distinct senses); and a thing is capable in another
sense because neither any other thing, nor itself qua other, has a potency or principle which can destroy it. Again, all of these are capable either merely because the thing might chance to happen or not to happen, or because it might do so well. This sort of potency is found even in lifeless things, e.g. in instruments; for we say
one lyre can speak, and another cannot speak at all, if it has not a good tone.

"Incapacity is privation of capacity-i.e

[clxxxiv] Strong's Greek Dictionary of the New Testament (Greek Strong's) Public Domain Electronic text downloaded from the Bible Foundation e-Text Library: <http://www.bf.org/bfetexts.htm>Hypertexted and formatted by Oaktree Software, Inc. Greek text added by OakTree Software, Inc.Version 2.8

[clxxxv] Louw P. Johannes and Eugene A. Nida, Love.

[clxxxvi] Wippel John F., The Metaphysical Thought of Thomas Aquinas, From Finite Being to Uncreated Being, (The Catholic University of America Press, Washington D.C. 2000), 326-327.

[clxxxvii] Wippel John F., 326-327.
As for human knowledge of prime matter Thomas holds, as we have in, that we cannot know it in and by itself. This follows from his conviction that it is pure potency and therefore completely undetermined in and of itself. As he explains in q.5,a 3 of his Commentary on the De Triniate.
Prime matter 1) analogy or natural things 2) Actuality and everything is actual when it is a everything is knowable as it is in act not insofar as it is in potency, as it stated in Metaphysics IX. According to this text, therefore, we can know prime matter through the form which actualizes it .. Thomas writes that we can know prime matter by a kind of analogy or proportion: prime matter is related to all forms and privations in the way bronze is related to a statue and to the lack of configuration.

[clxxxviii] Hebrew Strong's Dictionary Strong's Hebrew and Chaldee Dictionary of the Old Testament (Hebrew Strong's) Public Domain Electronic text downloaded from the Bible Foundation e-Text Library: <http://www.bf.org/bfetexts.htm>Hypertexted and formatted by OakTree Software, Inc Hebrew text added by OakTree Software, Inc. Version 3.1, 4392.
מָלֵא **male'**, *maw-lay* she that was with child, fill(-ed, -ed with), full(-ly), multitude, as is worth.[clxxxviii]

[clxxxix] Strong, James, Dr. Strong's Hebrew and Chaldee Dictionary of the Old Testament (Hebrew Strong's), אֵב **'eb,** *abe;* (Aramaic) corresponding to 3:— fruit.

[cxc] PIUS X Pope, "Encyclical of Singular Quadam of Labor Organizations," To our Beloved Son, George Kopp, Cardinal Priest of the Holy Roman Church, t of Breslau and to the other Archbishops and Bishops of Germany. (Libreria Editrice Vaticana,
Given at Saint Peter's, Rome, on September 24, 1912, the tenth year of Our Pontificate.) http://www.vatican.va/content/pius-x/en/encyclicals/documents/hf_p-x_enc_24091912_singulari-quadam.html. p,2

[cxci] Louda and Nida, demons.
[cxcii] Louda and Nida, demons.
[cxciii] Louda and Nida, Reconciliation
[cxciv] Brown, Colin, Reconciliation.
[cxcv] Brown, Colin, **Reconciliation**.
[cxcvi] Liddell and Scott's, **Reconciliation**.
[cxcvii] Kannappan, Raj Libertas, the Publication of Young America's Foundation Winter 2018 Vo. 39. No. 1 pg 26 and 27 Providing the Spirit of Opportunity, By, Director of Young America's Foundations' Center for Entrepreneurship & Free Enterprise pg Editors Jessica Jensen and Raj Kannappan,Reston, Virginia,26 – 27.

[cxcviii] Amministrazione del Patrimonio Della Sede Apostlica, Vatican II (English) Documents of the II Vatican Council 78.
[cxcix] New American Bible Scripture marked NAB, are taken from the New American Bible with Revised New Testament Copyright © 1991, 1986, 1970 by the Confraternity of Christian Doctrine, 3211 4th Street, NE, Washington, DC 20017-1194.
Version 3.3

[cc] Greek-English Lexicon
[cci] Analysis and Synthesis in Greek

https://hsm.stackexchange.com/questions/5629/analysis-vs-synthesis-in greek mathematics?utm_medium=organic&utm_source=google_rich_qa&utm_campaign=google_rich_q

[ccii] Liddell and Scott's, *to be separated and brought* under one name Thuc.= https://en.wikipedia.org/wiki/Thucydides **Thucydides** (/θjuːˈsɪdɪdiːz/; Ancient Greek: Θουκυδίδης, *Thoukydídēs*, [tʰuːkydídɛːs]; c. 460 – c. 400 BC) was an Athenian historian and general. His *History of the Peloponnesian War* recounts the fifth-century BC war between Sparta and Athens until the year 411 BC. Thucydides has been dubbed the father of "scientific history" by those who accept his claims to have applied strict standards of impartiality and evidence-gathering and analysis of cause and effect, without reference to intervention by the deities, as outlined in his introduction to his work.[1][2]

[cciii] Amministrazione del Patrimonio Della Sede Apostlica Documents, of the Vatican II Council 1962—1965 (English), Church.

[ccix] Welch, The Politician, Belmont Publishing Company, Belmont, Massachusetts, 1964, p.205
[ccx] https://www.nps.gov/stli/planyourvisit/basicinfo.htm
[ccxi] Rosenwald Hemann, Hans, Translated, The Saints in Legend and Art, Vol.14 Aurel Bongers Published, Recklinghausen, Germany 8
[ccxii] Rosenwald 8.
[ccxiii] Louw P. Johannes and Eugene A. Nida, Edits, **Sacred**.
[ccxiv] Terrien, Samuel, The elusive Presence, Toward a New Biblical Theology Religious Perspectives, Anshen, Ruth Nanda, Samuel Terrin and By Ruth Nanda Anshen, 1978. FP. 246
[ccxv] Arden, Lisa Lucia, Our Need to Give to the World, America Love in God Heal, Heal America, Published Lisa Lucia Arden, Pasadena California
[ccxvi] Louw P. Johannes and Eugene A. Nida, Sacred.

[ccxvii] **Brown, Colin, Blood.**

[ccxviii] Greek Strong's Dictionary Strong's Greek Dictionary of the New Testament (Greek Strong's Public Domain Electronic text downloaded from the Bible Foundation e-Text Library: http://www.bf.org/bfetexts.htm Hypertexted and formatted by Oaktree Software, Inc.
Greek text added by OakTree Software, Inc. Version 2.8, Blood

[ccxix] Cashless Sociey, https:youtu.be[TVrOLpnal0Q
[ccxx] **Gilbert, George America's #1 Futurist Issues Bold Predictions also s massive shift taking place.** Secure.investedbetter.com

ccxxi Liddell and Scott's, Wisdom.

ccxxii **Hattrup Kathleen N. | We're called to join the army of this "Warrior Queen" Aleteia, Sep 04, 2018** https://aleteia.org/2018/09/04/were-called-to-join-the-army-of-this-warrior-queen/, 1.

ccxxiii Ricoeur, Paul, The Symbolism of Evil, Translated from the French by Emerson Buchanan, Beacon Press, Boston, Ruth Nanda Anshen, 1967. 55

ccxxv Ricoeur, Paul, 55.

ccxxvi Liddell and Scott's, soul.

ccxxvii The Cambridge History of Later Greek and Early Medieval Philosophy, Volume 1

edited by A. H. Armstrong

ccxxviii Liddell and Scott's, soul.

ccxxix Liddell and Scott's, **soul**.

ccxxx Breathe

ccxxxi Cambridge

ccxxxii Louda and Nida, Breath

ccxxxiii Liddell and Scott's, Socio-Religious (11.12–11.54).

ccxxxiv Louw P. Johannes and Eugene A. Nida, 11:9.

ccxxxv NIDOTTE, wisdom

ccxxxvi Ibid, wise

ccxxxvii Liddell and Scott's, wise.

ccxxxviii Liddell and Scott's, wise.

ccxxxix Liddell and Scott's, Wisdom.

ccxl Armstrong, A. H Th 174-175

ccxli Arden, Lisa Lucia, Our Need to Give to the World, prayer 380

ccxlii Armstrong, A. H 176

ccxliii Liddell and Scott, Wisdom

ccxliv Armstrong, A. H. The Cambridge History of Later Greek and Early Medieval Philosophy, Volume 1 edited by p. 177

ccxlv The Cambridge, Ibid, p.177.

ccxlvi Armstrong, p.148
ccxlvii The Summa Theologica, **[I–II.109.4]**
ccxlviii Welch, Robert, 244.
ccxlix Welch, Robert, 240.
ccl Moltmann, Jurgen, The Church in the Power of the Spirit, A Contribution to Messianic Ecclesiology, (Fortress Press, Minneapolis, 1993),42.

ccli Moltmann, Jurgen,. 43.

cclii Aquinas' Thomas, St, Whether man without grace and by his own natural powers can fulfil the commandments of the Law (are peace, justice, restoration, and forward building in life and virtues, [109.4].
ccliii Aquinas' Thomas, St, Whether man without grace and by his own natural powers can fulfil the commandments of the Law? [I–II.109.4].

ccliv Aquinas, Thomas, St, Man by himself can make no wise rise from sin without the help of grace
cclv Aquinas, Thomas, St, [I–II.109.4].
cclvi Wikipedia, "Industrial Revolution," Wikipedia, the free encyclopedia, November 28, 2020, https://en.wikipedia.org/wiki/Industrial_Revolution
cclvii Amministrazione del Patrimonio Della Sede Apostlica, The Catechism of the Catholic Church (English) (C. Catechism-E Wisdom, 301 God upholds and sustains creation.
cclviii Aquinas, Thomas St., [I–II.109.4].
cclix Aquinas, Thomas St., [I–II.109.4].
cclx Spinoza, Baruch 257
cclxi Liddell & Scott , wise.
cclxii Liddell & Scott, wise.
cclxiii Spinoza, Baruch, 245.

cclxiv Spinoza, Baruch, 245.
cclxv Spinoza, Baruch, **247**.
cclxvi Stassen, Glen, H, Just Peacemaking, Transforming Initiatives for Justice and Peace,(Westminster/John Knox Press Louisville, Kentucky, 1992),72.
cclxvii Amministrazione del Patrimonio Della Sede Apostlica, The Catechism of the Catholic Church (English) (C. Catechism-E), Wisdom.

cclxviii Pantheon of Rome all that is Sacred to God
https://en.wikipedia.org/wiki/Pantheon,_Rome

cclxix *Pantheon Rome,* Wikipedia, Editors.,
https://en.wikipedia.org/wiki/Pantheon,Rome(1980), 38–39, 38.

cclxx Pantheon, Rome,
cclxxi Liddell and Scott's, **wise**.
cclxxii Pantheon, Rome.
cclxxiii Casey p. 88
cclxxiv Casey p. 88
cclxxv Anderson, Ray S. & Guernsey Dennis, B., On Being Family A Social Theology, of the Family, William B. Eerdmans Publishing Company, Grand Rapids, Mich. 1985, p. 35
cclxxvi Reagan, Ronald President, Speeches, Ministers. Martin Luther King,
cclxxvii <u>www.ourladyofAmerica.org</u>., **1956**
cclxxviii U.S. Citizenship and Immigration Services., Uscis.gov
cclxxix

November 28, 2020. https://www.uscis.gov/citizenship/learn-about-citizenship/the-naturalization-interview-and-test/naturalization-oath-of-allegiance-to-the-united-states-of-america, Oath of Allegiance.

cclxxx U.S. Citizenship and Immigration Services, **Oath of Allegiance.**
cclxxxi Strong James, Dr., <u>Greek, Dictionary Strong's Greek Dictionary of the New Testament (Greek Strong's).Greek text added by OakTree Software, Inc.Version 2.8</u>, Law.
cclxxxii Strong James, Dr., <u>Greek, Dictionary Strong's Greek Dictionary of the New Testament (Greek Strong's).Greek text added by OakTree Software, Inc.Version 2.8</u>, Law.

cclxxxiii**Brown, Colin**, Law.

cclxxxiv Louw P. Johannes and Eugene A. Nida, **Law.**
cclxxxv Strong James, Dr., <u>Greek, Dictionary Strong's Greek Dictionary of the New Testament (Greek Strong's).Greek text added by OakTree Software, Inc.Version 2.8</u>, Law.

cclxxxvi Websters, Daniel, <u>Webster's Dictionary Webster's Revised Unabridged Dictionary</u> (C. & G. Merriam Co., Springfield, Mass.(1913) OakTree Software, Inc. Version 1.7) Al·le'giance.

cclxxxvii Louw P. Johannes and Eugene A. Nida, Truth.

cclxxxviii Louw P. Johannes and Eugene A. Nida, Truth.

cclxxxix Louw P. Johannes and Eugene A. Nida, **Mental**.

ccxc Louw P. Johannes and Eugene A. Nida, **Mental**.

ccxci **U. S. Citizenship and Immigration Services**, Naturalization Oath of Allegiance to the United States of America https://www.uscis.gov/citizenship/learn-about-citizenship/the-naturalization-interview-and-test/naturalization-oath-of-allegiance-to-the-united-states-of-america., Oath of the Allegiance.

ccxcii VanGemeren A. Willem, immigrant.

ccxciv You must keep the feast of Unleavened Bread because it was on that same day that I brought your armies out of Egypt. You will keep that day, generation after generation; this is a decree for all time. Ex. 12:17 The Israelites also need to keep the feast of the Unleavened Bread.

ccxcv Claire Felter, Danielle Renwick, *and* Amelia Cheatham, "The Immigration Debate," Counsel of Foreign Relations, Immigration to the United States, June 23, 2020. https://www.cfr.org/backgrounder/us-immigration-debate-0?gclid=CjOKCQiAh4j-BRCsARIsAGeV12AsA2BrnzTOc3tNIqq3mIls2Zd-n284K_b8Eq8pmtXCB1YBikIIJikaAkVqEALw_wcB Immigrants comprise almost 14 percent of the U.S. population, or more than 44 million people out of a total of about 327 million, according to the Census Bureau. Together, immigrants and their U.S.-born children make up about 28 percent of U.S. inhabitants. The figure represents a steady rise from 1970, when there were fewer than ten million immigrants in the United States. But there are proportionally fewer immigrants today than in 1890, when foreign-born residents comprised 15 percent of the population. Mexico is the most common country of origin for U.S. immigrants—constituting 25 percent of the immigrant population—but the proportion of immigrants from South and East Asia—who number about 27 percent—is on the rise.

ccxcvi Recovery, Center, "Recovery Centers of America Economic Cost of Substance Abuse in the United StatesRecovery Center" November 28, 2020 . Recoverycentersofamerica.com.

ccxcvii Aristotle, Aristotle's Categories Standford. Education. Fri Sep 7, 2007 Tue Nov 5, 2013https://plato.stanford.edu/entries/aristotle-categories/ ; and https://en.wikipedia.org/wiki/Categories_(Aristotle) A brief explanation (with some alternative translations) is as follows:

1. **Substance** (οὐσία, *ousia*, essence or substance).[6] *Substance* is that which cannot be predicated of anything or be said to be in anything. Hence, *this particular man* or *that particular tree* are Substances. Later in the text, Aristotle calls these particulars "primary substances", to distinguish them from *secondary substances*, which are universals and *can* be predicated. Hence, Socrates is a primary substance, while man is a secondary substance. *Man* is predicated of Socrates, and therefore all that is predicated of man is predicated of Socrates.
2. **Quantity** (ποσόν, *poson*, how much). This is the extension of an object, and may be either discrete or continuous. Further, its parts may or may not have relative positions to each other. All medieval discussions about the nature of the continuum, of the infinite and the infinitely divisible, are a long footnote to this text. It is of great importance in the development of mathematical ideas in the medieval and late Scholastic period. Examples: two cubits long, number, space, (length of) time.
3. **Qualification** or quality (ποιόν, *poion*, of what kind or quality). This determination characterizes the nature of an object. Examples: white, black, grammatical, hot, sweet, curved, straight.
4. **Relative** (πρός τι, *pros ti*, toward something). This is the way one object may be related to another. Examples: double, half, large, master, knowledge.
5. **Where** or place (ποῦ, *pou*, where). Position in relation to the surrounding environment. Examples: in a marketplace, in the Lyceum.
6. **When** or time (πότε, *pote*, when). Position in relation to the course of events. Examples: yesterday, last year.
7. **Being-in-a-position**, posture, attitude (κεῖσθαι, *keisthai*, to lie). The examples Aristotle gives indicate that he meant a condition of rest resulting from an action: *'Lying', 'sitting', 'standing'*. Thus *position* may be taken as the end point for the corresponding action. The term is, however, frequently taken to mean the relative position of the parts of an object (usually a living object), given that the position of the parts is inseparable from the state of rest implied.
8. **Having** or state, condition (ἔχειν, *echein*, to have or be). The examples Aristotle gives indicate that he meant a condition of rest resulting from an affection (i.e. being acted on): *'shod', 'armed'*. The term is, however, frequently taken to mean the determination arising from the physical accoutrements of an object: one's shoes, one's arms, etc. Traditionally, this category is also called a *habitus* (from Latin *habere*, to have).

9. **Doing** or action (ποιεῖν, *poiein*, to make or do). The production of change in some other object (or in the agent itself *qua* other).
10. **Being affected** or affection (πάσχειν, *paschein*, to suffer or undergo). The reception of change from some other object (or from the affected object itself *qua* other). Aristotle's name *paschein* for this category has traditionally been translated into English as "affection" and "passion" (also "passivity"), easily misinterpreted to refer only or mainly to affection as an emotion or to emotional passion. For action he gave the example, *'to lance', 'to cauterize';* for affection, *'to be lanced', 'to be cauterized.'* His examples make clear that action is to affection as the active voice is to the passive voice — as *acting* is to *being acted on*.

ccxcviii Louw P. Johannes and Eugene A. Nida, **Law.**
ccxcix Louw P. Johannes and Eugene A. Nida, **Law.**
ccc Fakkerrt Jasper Editor-in-Chief President, "Trumps first 2 years in Office," Epoch,Times Special Edition, 3-29.

ccci Fakkerrt Jasper Editor-in-Chief .
cccii Arden, Lisa, Lucia, Our Need to Give to the World, *America love in God, Heal America*, Publisher Lisa Lucia Arden, Pasadena California, 2016, 2019

ccciii **President Ronald Reagan, "Speaks at the United Nations General Assembly," Ronald Reagan Greatest Presidential Speeches, June 17, 1982.**
ccciv **President Ronald Reagan Speaks at the United Nations General Assembly.**
cccv Bannon, Steve, "Steve Bannon's Warning On China Trade War (w/ Kyle Bass) | Real Vision Classics" Real Vision Finance, https://www.youtube.com/watch?v=qH5QzuzD01A&list=PLQXj_KeGx-b7ef-DKTxGaD_5_cmhUx7s_&ab_channel=RealVisionFinance. Sep 11, 2017.

cccvi **Nyaumon, Chiseigaku Abe, I., "Geopolitical: Theories, Concepts, Schools, and Debates," Tokyo: Kokon Shoin, 1933, Read by Arnold, Jafe, Lecture #2 at the China Institute of Fudan University, Shanghai, China, Eurasianist Archive. December 2018.** Geopolitical: Theories, Concepts, Schools, and Debates, https://www.geopolitica.ru/en/article/geopolitics-theories-concepts-schools-and-debates
cccvii **Hildegard of Bingen, Edited by Matthew Fox.** *Hildegard of Bingen's Book of Divine Works With Letters and Songs.* Bear & Company, Santa Fe, Mexico. 1987), 208.

cccviii **Hildegard of Bingen, 208.**

cccix Hildegard, Saint, 208.

cccx Religious belief in the Judeo-Christian understanding injustices that are against them. These people of light are targeted by the secret groups of masonites and other evil counterparts evil of demons with the minds of the individuals and society where the live.

cccxi Thompson, John, 167.

cccxii Mann, W. Thomas, 38.
cccxiii Mann, W. Thomas ,78-79.
cccxiv Pope Francis Prayer for Jubilee Year of Mercy. Merciful Like he Father, December 8, 2015- November 20th 2016.
cccxv cccxv Gregory, Stephen, "President Trump on Globalism, Socialism, and Religious Freedom." Epoch Times, Nation September 26-October 2, 2019, A3

cccxvi Mann, Thomas, W., "The Book of the Torah, The Narrative Integrity of he Pentateuch"
(John Knox Press, Atllanta, 1973), 38.
cccxvii Mann, John, W. 150.
cccxviii Thompson, John, 59.
cccxix Thompson, John, 15.
cccxx Thompson, John, 187.
cccxxi Thompson, John, 24.
cccxxii Thompson, p.59
cccxxiii Gregory, Stephen, "President Trump on Globalism, Socialism, and Religious Freedom." Epoch Times, Nation September 26-October 2, 2019, A3.
cccxxiv Pius X, Pope, "Encyclical of Iucunda Sane On Pope Gregory the Great," To Our Venerable Brethren, the Patriarchs, Primates, Archbishops, Bishops, and other ordinaries in peace and communion with the Apostolic.
(Libreria Editrice Vaticana Given at Rome at St. Peter's on March 12, of the year 1904, on the feast of St. Gregory I. Pope and Doctor of the Church, in the first year of Our Pontificate.) http://www.vatican.va/content/pius-x/en/encyclicals/documents/hf_p-x_enc_12031904_iucunda-sane.html. Roman Empire. Italy, abandoned by the Emperors of Byzantium, had been left a prey of the still unsettled Lombard.

cccxxv Pope Pius, "Encyclical of Iucunda Sane On Pope Gregory the Great," X, 3.
cccxxvi Pope Pius, "Encyclical of Iucunda Sane On Pope Gregory the Great." X, 1-5.
cccxxvii Aristotle, Metaphysics, 27.
cccxxviii Aristotle, Metaphysics, 27.

cccxxix Aristotle Copy right Available online at http://classics.mit.edu//Aristotle/metaphysics.html **Metaphysics** (Greek: τὰ μετὰ τὰ φυσικά; Latin: *Metaphysica*[1]) is one of the principal works of Aristotle and the first major work of the branch of philosophy with the same name. The principal subject is "being qua being," or being insofar as it is being. It examines what can be asserted about any being insofar as it is and not because of any special qualities it has. Also covered are different kinds ()of causation, form and matter, the existence of mathematical objects, and a prime-mover God. https://en.wikipedia.org/wiki/Metaphysics

cccxxx Aristotle, Metaphysics, 25.
cccxxxi Pope, Pius X, "Encyclical of Singular Quadam of Labor Organizations," To our Beloved Son, George Kopp, Cardinal Priest of the Holy Roman Church, t of Breslau and to the other Archbishops and Bishops of Germany. (Libreria Editrice Vaticana,
Given at Saint Peter's, Rome, on September 24, 1912, the tenth year of Our Pontificate.) http://www.vatican.va/content/pius-x/en/encyclicals/documents/hf_p-x_enc_24091912_singulari-quadam.html p.3.

cccxxxii Aristotle, Politics, III. II.1-3,185-187.
cccxxxiii Aristotle, Politics, III. II. 395, 189.
cccxxxiv Ambrose, Pope. Duties of the Clergy translated by Euthymius Book 3 Chapter 1,(c. 377), and Phillip Schaff (1819-1893). translated by H. De Romestin." https://librivox.org/author/1231. LibriVox Recordings,Oct 2020. Book 3 Chapter 1.

cccxxxv Ambrose, Pope, Book 3 Chapter 1.

cccxxxvi Pius X, Pope, "Encyclical of Iucunda Sane On Pope Gregory the Great," To Our Venerable Brethren, the Patriarchs, Primates, Archbishops, Bishops, and other ordinaries in peace and communion with the Apostolic.
(Libreria Editrice Vaticana Given at Rome at St. Peter's on March 12, of the year 1904, on the feast of St. Gregory I. Pope and Doctor of the Church, in the first year of Our Pontificate.) http://www.vatican.va/content/pius-x/en/encyclicals/documents/hf_p-x_enc_12031904_iucunda-sane.html 1-5.
cccxxxvii **Pope Pius X,** "Encyclical of Iucunda Sane On Pope Gregory the Great," **1-5.**

cccxxxviii Aristotle. Translated by W. D. Ross SD. Metaphysics. http://classics.mit.edu//Aristotle/metaphysics.html, Provided by The Internet Classics Archive. 1st Century, B.C. Internet. Part 1 and 2.

Part 1

cccxxxix The New Jerusalem Bible (NJB) The New Jerusalem Bible. Copyright © 1990 by Darton, Longman & Todd Limited and Doubleday, a division of Bantam Doubleday Dell Publishing Group, Inc. All rights reserved. Published by arrangement with Doubleday, a division of Bantam Doubleday Dell Publishing Group, Inc. Isaiah 9:6

cccxl Rice, John Paul, Important Powerful Message: John Paul Rice, A Child's Voice, The Real Story of the Hidden Network, https://youtu.be/dztir94oaOo, September 2020.
cccxli Amministrazione del Patrimonio Della Sede Apostlica, Catholic Catechism (English) The Catechism of the Catholic Church (English) (C. Catechism-E), 2070.

www.ingramcontent.com/pod-product-compliance
Lightning Source LLC
Chambersburg PA
CBHW050300010526
44108CB00040B/1901